Sources of

THE MAKING OF THE WEST

PEOPLES AND CULTURES

Sixth Edition

Volume II: Since 1500

KATHARINE J. LUALDI
Southern Maine Community College

 bedford/st.martin's
Macmillan Learning
Boston | New York

For Bedford/St. Martin's

Vice President, Editorial, Macmillan Learning Humanities: Edwin Hill
Senior Program Director for History: Michael Rosenberg
Senior Program Manager for History: William J. Lombardo
History Marketing Manager: Melissa Rodriguez
Director of Content Development, Humanities: Jane Knetzger
Developmental Editor: Evelyn Denham
Content Project Manager: Lidia MacDonald-Carr
Senior Workflow Project Manager: Jennifer Wetzel
Production Coordinator: Brianna Lester
Senior Media Project Manager: Michelle Camisa
Media Editor: Tess Fletcher
Manager of Publishing Services: Andrea Cava
Project Management: Lumina Datamatics, Inc.
Composition: Lumina Datamatics, Inc.
Photo Permissions Manager: Jennifer MacMillan
Photo Researcher: Bruce Carson
Text Permissions Researcher: Arthur Johnson, Lumina Datamatics, Inc.
Text Permissions Manager: Kalina Ingham
Director of Design, Content Management: Diana Blume
Cover Design: William Boardman
Cover Art: *River Lock*, 1957 (oil on canvas), Greenham, Robert Duckworth (1906–76) /
    Private Collection / Milne & Moller, London / Bridgeman Images
Printing and Binding: LSC Communications

Manufactured in the United States of America.

1 2 3 4 5 6 7   23 22 21 20 19 18

For information, write: Bedford/St. Martin's, 75 Arlington Street, Boston, MA 02116

ISBN 978-1-319-15452-3

Acknowledgments
Text acknowledgments and copyrights appear at the back of the book on pages A-1–A-5, which constitute an extension of the copyright page. Art acknowledgments and copyrights appear on the same page as the art selections they cover.

Sources of
THE MAKING OF THE WEST

PEOPLES AND CULTURES

Volume II: Since 1500

Preface

D esigned to accompany *The Making of the West* and *The Making of the West, Value Edition, Sources of The Making of the West* is intended to help instructors bring the history of Western civilization to life for their students. This thoroughly revised collection parallels the major topics and themes covered in each chapter of *The Making of the West* and offers instructors many opportunities to promote classroom discussion of primary documents and to help students develop essential historical thinking skills. By engaging with primary sources, students will come to see that the study of history is not fixed but is an ongoing process of evaluation and interpretation.

Guided by the textbook's integrated narrative that weaves together social, cultural, political, and economic history, each chapter brings together a variety of source types illuminating historical experience from many perspectives. This edition has been revised to include visual sources as well as a new comparative source feature in every chapter, "Sources in Conversation." I have included more than thirty new sources that both broaden and deepen coverage. With new documents covering perspectives from Eastern Europe and the Middle East, a new emphasis on geographic and quantitative sources, and new selections by essential authors from Cicero and Dante to Wollstonecraft and Fanon, this edition provides sources for instructors to consider the history of the West from within and without.

To assist students with their journey into the past, each chapter opens with a summary that situates the sources within the broader historical context and addresses their relationship to one another and to the main themes in the corresponding chapter of *The Making of the West*, Sixth Edition. An explanatory headnote accompanies each source to provide fundamental context on the author or creator and the source while highlighting its historical significance. Revised and expanded discussion questions guide students through evaluating the sources, considering questions of context and audience, and engaging with scholarly arguments. Each chapter concludes with a set of comparative questions intended to encourage students both to see how sources can inform and challenge each other and to prompt them to make historical connections. These editorial features intentionally strengthen the coherence of each chapter as a unit while allowing instructors to choose sources and questions that best suit their specific goals and methods. Within each chapter, the documents also were selected based on their accessibility, depth in content, and appeal to students. For this reason, when necessary, I have carefully edited documents to speak to specific themes without impairing the documents' overall sense and tone. I have also included documents of varying lengths to increase their utility for both short class exercises and outside writing assignments.

Of course, asking the right questions and finding the right answers is at the heart of "doing" history. For this reason, *Sources of The Making of the West*, Sixth Edition, begins with an introduction on how to interpret written and visual primary sources that leads students step-by-step through the process of historical analysis. A brief overview of what this process entails is followed by an extended discussion of the process at work in the analysis of two sources drawn specifically from this collection. I adopted this approach for the Introduction to help students move easily from abstract concepts to concrete examples. As a result, the Introduction does not rely on telling students what to do but rather on showing them how to do it for themselves based on the raw data of history.

New to This Edition

In response to instructors' comments and recommendations, as well as new scholarship, I have made several changes for the sixth edition. This edition contains over thirty new written and visual sources that complement the thematic and chronological framework of the textbook and highlight the intellectual, emotional, and visual landscapes of many different peoples and places. These sources have been selected to reflect an expanded understanding of the West that allows us to consider key cultural, social, political, economic, and intellectual developments in a new light and within broader contexts. To that end, each chapter contains both visual sources and a "Sources in Conversation" comparative source set. These paired sources deepen the interpretive possibilities of the individual sources while providing students more opportunities to develop their historical thinking skills. The digital version of this collection, available in LaunchPad, goes even further with assignable auto-graded multiple-choice questions to accompany each source.

In this edition, I have incorporated a wider variety of source types, including more quantitative and visual sources, while focusing on themes that carry across historical time periods. Students will examine historical responses to inequality by analyzing records of an ancient Greek auction of confiscated slaves, excerpts from the city of Norwich Poor Rolls of 1570, and graphs that capture the current distribution of global wealth. They will engage with different conceptions of world geography, ranging from the thirteenth-century Hereford map to the nineteenth-century Imperial Federation map of the British Empire. I ask students to consider how communities define themselves through new sources, including a Greek Janiform flask, a Levantine Torah niche, and a popular eighteenth-century ceramic motif, as well as excerpts from Cicero's *In Defense of Archias*, Hume's *Of National Characters*, and Fanon's *The Wretched of the Earth*. Other new sources ground history in the lives of everyday people, including a Roman household shrine, a medieval Labors of the Month sculpture, a portrait of a family at tea, and a firsthand account of Soviet collectivization. Finally, I invite students to reflect on how we remember and memorialize history with Picasso's *Guernica*, photographer Nick Ut's memory of capturing a famous Vietnam photo, and Bosnian artist Aida Sehovic's interactive memorial to the Serebrenica genocide.

Acknowledgments

Many people deserve thanks for helping to bring this sixth edition to fruition. First among them are the authors of *The Making of the West*: Lynn Hunt, Thomas R. Martin, Barbara H. Rosenwein, and Bonnie G. Smith. Many thanks as well to reviewers of the previous edition who provided valuable insights and suggestions: Jean Berger, University of Wisconsin, Fox Valley; Edwin Bezzina, Grenfell Campus Memorial University; Dorothea Browder, Western Kentucky University; Eric Cimino, Molloy College; Courtney Doucette, Rutgers University; Valeria L. Garver, Northern Illinois University; Michael McGregor, Northern Virginia Community College; Jennifer M. Morris, College of Mount St. Joseph; Jason E. St. Pierre, University of Massachusetts, Lowell; Sarah L. Sullivan, McHenry County College; Paul Teverow, Missouri Southern State University; Leigh Ann Whaley, Acadia University; David K. White, McHenry County College; and, Corinne Wieben, University of Northern Colorado.

I would also like to thank Anne Thayer, Jeannine Uzzi, Nancy Artz, and Helen Evans for their expertise and editorial assistance with sources as well as the team at Bedford/ St. Martin's: Michael Rosenberg, Bill Lombardo, Leah Strauss, Evelyn Denham, Belinda Huang, Emily Brower, and Lidia MacDonald-Carr.

Contents

Introduction: Working with Historical Sources

The long history of Western civilization encompasses a broad range of places and cultures. Textbooks provide an essential chronological and thematic framework for understanding the formation of the West as a cultural and geographical entity. Yet the process of historical inquiry extends beyond textbook narratives into the thoughts, words, images, and experiences of people living at the time. Primary sources expose this world so that you can observe, analyze, and interpret the past as it unfolds before you. History is thus not a static collection of facts and dates. Rather, it is an ongoing attempt to make sense of the past and its relationship to the present through the lens of both written and visual primary sources.

Sources of The Making of the West, Sixth Edition, provides this lens for you, with a wide range of engaging sources — from Egyptian tomb art to an engraving of a London coffee-house to firsthand accounts of student revolts. When combined, the sources reflect historians' growing appreciation of the need to examine Western civilization from different conceptual angles — political, social, cultural, and economic — and geographic viewpoints. The composite picture that emerges reveals a variety of historical experiences shaping each era from both within and outside Europe's borders. Furthermore, the documents here demonstrate that the most historically significant of these experiences are not always those of people in formal positions of power. Men and women from all walks of life have also influenced the course of Western history.

The sources in this reader were selected with an eye toward their ability not only to capture the multifaceted dimensions of the past but also to ignite your intellectual curiosity. Each written and visual source is a unique product of human endeavor and as such is often colored by the personal concerns, biases, and objectives of the author or creator. Among the most exciting challenges facing you is to sift through these nuances to discover what they reveal about the source and its broader historical context.

Interpreting Written Sources

Understanding a written document and its connection to larger historical issues depends on knowing which questions to ask and how to find the answers. The following six questions will guide you through this process of discovery. Like a detective, you will begin by piecing together basic facts and then move on to more complex levels of analysis, which usually requires reading any given source more than once. You should keep these questions in mind every time you read a document, no matter how long or how short, to help you uncover its meaning and significance. As you practice actively reading these texts and thinking critically about them, you will improve your ability to read and think like a historian. Soon enough, you will be asking your own questions and conducting your own historical analysis.

1. Who wrote this document, when, and where?

The "doing" of history depends on historical records, the existence of which in turn depends on the individuals who composed them in a particular time and place and with specific goals in mind. Therefore, before you can begin to understand a document and its significance, you need to determine who wrote it and when and where it was written. Ultimately, this information will shape your interpretation because the language of documents often reflects the author's social and/or political status as well as the norms of the society in which the author lived.

2. What type of document is this?

Because all genres have their own defining characteristics, identifying the type of document at hand is vital to elucidating its purpose and meaning. For example, in content and organization, an account of a saint's life looks very different from an imperial edict, which in turn looks very different from a trial record. Each document type follows certain rules of composition that shape what authors say and how they say it.

3. Who is the intended audience of the document?

The type of source often goes hand in hand with the intended audience. For example, popular songs in the vernacular are designed to reach people across the socioeconomic spectrum, whereas papal bulls written in Latin are directed to a tiny, educated, and predominantly male elite. Moreover, an author often crafts the style and content of a document to appeal to a particular audience and to enhance the effectiveness of his or her message.

4. What are the main points of this document?

All primary sources contain stories, whether in numbers, words, and/or images. Before you can begin to analyze their meanings, you need to have a good command of a document's main points. For this reason, while reading, you should mark words, phrases, and passages that strike you as particularly important to create visual and mental markers that will help you navigate the document. Don't worry about mastering all of the details; you can work through them later once you have sketched out the basic content.

5. Why was this document written?

The simplicity of this question masks the complexity of the possible answers. Historical records are never created in a vacuum; they were produced for a reason, whether public or private, pragmatic or fanciful. Some sources will state outright why they were created, whereas others will not. Yet, with or without direct cues, you should look for less obvious signs of the author's intent and rhetorical strategies as reflected in word choice, for example, or the way in which a point is communicated.

6. What does this document reveal about the particular society and period in question?

This question strikes at the heart of historical analysis and interpretation. In its use of language, its structure, and its biases and assumptions, every source opens a window into its author and time period. Teasing out its deeper significance will allow you to assess the value of a source and to articulate what it adds to our understanding of the historical context in which it is embedded. Thus, as you begin to analyze a source fully, your own interpretive voice will assume center stage.

As you work through each of these questions, you will progress from identifying the basic content of a document to inferring its broader meanings. At its very heart, the study of primary sources centers on the interplay between "facts" and interpretation. To help you engage in this interplay, let us take a concrete example of a historical document. Read it carefully, guided by the questions outlined above. In this way, you will gain insight into this particular text while training yourself in interpreting written primary sources in general.

1. Legislating Tolerance

Henry IV, *Edict of Nantes* (1598)

The promulgation of the Edict of Nantes in 1598 by King Henry IV (r. 1589–1610) marked the end of the French Wars of Religion by recognizing French Protestants as a legally protected religious minority. Drawing largely on earlier edicts of pacification, the Edict of Nantes was composed of ninety-two general articles, fifty-six secret articles, and two royal warrants. The two series of articles represented the edict proper and were registered by the highest courts of law in the realm (parlements). The following excerpts from the general articles reveal the triumph of political concerns over religious conformity on the one hand and the limitations of religious tolerance in early modern France on the other.

Henry, by the grace of God, King of France, and Navarre, to all present, and to come, greeting. Among the infinite mercies that it has pleased God to bestow upon us, that most signal and remarkable is, his having given us power and strength not to yield to the dreadful troubles, confusions, and disorders, which were found at our coming to this kingdom, divided into so many parties and factions, that the most legitimate was almost the least, enabling us with constancy in such manner to oppose the storm, as in the end to surmount it, now reaching a part of safety and repose for this state. . . . For the general difference among our

---

Modernized English text adapted from Edmund Everard, *The Great Pressures and Grievances of the Protestants in France* (London, 1681), 1–5, 10, 14, 16.

good subjects, and the particular evils of the soundest parts of the state, we judged might be easily cured, after the principal cause (the continuation of civil war) was taken away. In which having, by the blessing of God, well and happily succeeded, all hostility and wars through the kingdom being now ceased, we hope that we will succeed equally well in other matters remaining to be settled, and that by this means we shall arrive at the establishment of a good peace, with tranquility and rest. . . . Among our said affairs . . . one of the principal has been the complaints we have received from many of our Catholic provinces and cities, that the exercise of the Catholic religion was not universally re-established, as is provided by edicts or statutes heretofore made for the pacification of the troubles arising from religion; as well as the supplications and remonstrances which have been made to us by our subjects of the Reformed religion, regarding both the non-fulfillment of what has been granted by the said former laws, and that which they desired to be added for the exercise of their religion, the liberty of their consciences and the security of their persons and fortunes; presuming to have just reasons for desiring some enlargement of articles, as not being without great apprehensions, because their ruin has been the principal pretext and original foundation of the late wars, troubles, and commotions. Now not to burden us with too much business at once, as also that the fury of war was not compatible with the establishment of laws, however good they might be, we have hitherto deferred from time to time giving remedy herein. But now that it has pleased God to give us a beginning of enjoying some rest, we think we cannot employ ourself better than to apply to that which may tend to the glory and service of His holy name, and to provide that He may be adored and prayed unto by all our subjects: and if it has not yet pleased Him to permit it to be in one and the same form of religion, that it may at the least be with one and the same intention, and with such rules that may prevent among them all troubles and tumults. . . . For this cause, we have upon the whole judged it necessary to give to all our said subjects one general law, clear, pure, and absolute, by which they shall be regulated in all differences which have heretofore risen among them, or may hereafter rise, wherewith the one and other may be contented, being framed according as the time requires: and having had no other regard in this deliberation than solely the zeal we have to the service of God, praying that He would from this time forward render to all our subjects a durable and established peace. . . . We have by this edict or statute perpetual and irrevocable said, declared, and ordained, saying, declaring, and ordaining;

That the memory of all things passed on the one part and the other, since the beginning of the month of March 1585 until our coming to the crown, and also during the other preceding troubles, and the occasion of the same, shall remain extinguished and suppressed, as things that had never been. . . .

We prohibit to all our subjects of whatever state and condition they be, to renew the memory thereof, to attack, resent, injure, or provoke one another by reproaches for what is past, under any pretext or cause whatsoever, by disputing, contesting, quarrelling, reviling, or offending by factious words; but to contain themselves, and live peaceably together as brethren, friends, and fellow-citizens, upon penalty for acting to the contrary, to be punished for breakers of peace, and disturbers of the public quiet.

We ordain, that the Catholic religion shall be restored and re-established in all places, and quarters of this kingdom and country under our obedience, and where the exercise of the same has been interrupted, to be there again, peaceably and freely exercised without any trouble or impediment. . . .

And not to leave any occasion of trouble and difference among our subjects, we have permitted and do permit to those of the Reformed religion, to live and dwell in all the cities and places of this our kingdom and countries under our obedience, without being inquired after, vexed, molested, or compelled to do any thing in religion, contrary to their conscience. . . .

We permit also to those of the said religion to hold, and continue the exercise of the same in all the cities and places under our obedience, where it was by them established and made public at several different times, in the year 1586, and in 1597.

In like manner the said exercise may be established, and re-established in all the cities and places where it has been established or ought to be by the Statute of Pacification, made in the year 1577. . . .

We prohibit most expressly to all those of the said religion, to hold any exercise of it . . . except in places permitted and granted in the present edict. As also not to exercise the said religion in our court, nor in our territories and countries beyond the mountains, nor in our city of Paris, nor within five leagues of the said city. . . .

We prohibit all preachers, readers, and others who speak in public, to use any words, discourse, or propositions tending to excite the people to sedition; and we enjoin them to contain and comport themselves modestly, and to say nothing which shall not be for the instruction and edification of the listeners, and maintaining the peace and tranquility established by us in our said kingdom. . . .

They [French Protestants] shall also be obliged to keep and observe the festivals of the Catholic Church, and shall not on the same days work, sell, or keep open shop, nor likewise the artisans shall not work out of their shops, in their chambers or houses privately on the said festivals, and other days forbidden, of any trade, the noise whereof may be heard outside by those that pass by, or by the neighbors. . . .

We ordain, that there shall not be made any difference or distinction upon the account of the said religion, in receiving scholars to be instructed in the universities, colleges, or schools, nor of the sick or poor into hospitals, sick houses or public almshouses. . . .

We will and ordain, that all those of the Reformed religion, and others who have followed their party, of whatever state, quality or condition they be, shall be obliged and constrained by all due and reasonable ways, and under the penalties contained in the said edict or statute relating thereunto, to pay tithes to the curates, and other ecclesiastics, and to all others to whom they shall appertain. . . .

To the end to re-unite so much the better the minds and good will of our subjects, as is our intention, and to take away all complaints for the future; we declare all those who make or shall make profession of the said Reformed religion, to be capable of holding and exercising all estates, dignities, offices, and public charges whatsoever. . . .

We declare all sentences, judgments, procedures, seizures, sales, and decrees made and given against those of the Reformed religion, as well living as dead, from the death of the deceased King Henry the Second our most honored Lord and father in law, upon the occasion of the said religion, tumults and troubles since happening, as also the execution of the same judgments and decrees, from henceforward canceled, revoked, and annulled. . . .

Those also of the said religion shall depart and desist henceforward from all practices, negotiations, and intelligences, as well within or without our kingdom; and the said assemblies and councils established within the provinces, shall readily separate, and also all the leagues and associations made or to be made under any pretext, to the prejudice of our present edict, shall be cancelled and annulled, . . . prohibiting most expressly to all our subjects to make henceforth any assessments or levies of money, fortifications, enrollments of men, congregations and assemblies of other than such as are permitted by our present edict, and without arms. . . .

We give in command to the people of our said courts of parlement, chambers of our courts, and courts of our aids, bailiffs, chief-justices, provosts and other of our justices and officers to whom it appertains, and to their lieutenants, that they cause to be read, published, and registered this present edict and ordinance in their courts and jurisdictions, and the same keep punctually, and the contents of the same to cause to be enjoined and used fully and peaceably to all those to whom it shall belong, ceasing and making to cease all troubles and obstructions to the contrary, for such is our pleasure: and in witness hereof we have signed these presents with our own hand; and to the end to make it a thing firm and stable for ever, we have caused to put and endorse our seal to the same. Given at *Nantes* in the month of April in the year of Grace 1598, and of our reign the ninth.

Signed

HENRY

1. Who wrote this document, when, and where?

Many documents will not answer these questions directly; therefore, you will have to look elsewhere for clues. In this case, however, the internal evidence is clear. The author is Henry IV, king of France and Navarre, who issued the document in the French town of Nantes in 1598. Aside from the appearance of his name in the edict, there are other, less explicit markers of his identity. He uses the first-person plural ("we") when referring to himself, a grammatical choice that both signals and accentuates his royal stature.

2. What type of document is this?

In this source, you do not have to look far for an answer to this question. Henry IV describes the document as an "edict," "statute," or "law." These words reveal the public and official nature of the document, echoing their use in our own society today. Even if you do not know exactly what an edict, statute, or law meant in late sixteenth-century terms, the document itself points the way: "we [Henry IV] have upon the whole, judged it necessary to give to all our subjects one general law, clear, pure, and absolute. . . ." Now you know that the document is a body of law issued by King Henry IV in 1598, which helps to explain its formality as well as the predominance of legal language.

3. Who is the intended audience of the document?

The formal and legalistic language of the edict suggests that Henry IV's immediate audience is not the general public but rather some form of political and/or legal body.

The final paragraph supports this conclusion. Here Henry IV commands the "people of our said courts of parlement, chambers of our courts, and courts of our aids, bailiffs, chief-justices, provosts, and other of our justices and officers . . ." to read and publish the edict. Reading between the lines, you can detect a mixture of power and dependency in Henry IV's tone. Look carefully at his verb choices throughout the edict: *prohibit, ordain, will, declare, command.* Each of these verbs casts Henry IV as the leader and the audience as his followers. This strategy was essential because the edict would be nothing but empty words without the courts' compliance. Imagine for a moment that Henry IV was not the king of France but rather a soldier writing a letter to his wife or a merchant preparing a contract. In either case, the language chosen would have changed to suit the genre and audience. Thus, identifying the relationship between author and audience can help you to understand what the document both does and does not say.

4. What are the main points of this document?

To answer this question, you should start with the preamble, for it explains why the edict was issued in the first place: to replace the "frightful troubles, confusions, and disorders" in France with "one general law . . . by which they [our subjects] might be regulated in all differences which have heretofore risen among them, or may hereafter rise. . . ." But what differences specifically? Even with no knowledge of the circumstances surrounding the formulation of the edict, you should notice the numerous references to "the Catholic religion" and "the Reformed religion." With this in mind, read the preamble again. Here we learn that Henry IV had received complaints from Catholic provinces and cities and from Protestants ("our subjects of the Reformed religion") regarding the exercise of their respective religions. Furthermore, as the text continues, since "it has pleased God to give us a beginning of enjoying some rest, we think we cannot employ ourself better than to apply to that which may tend to the glory and service of His holy name, and to provide that He may be adored and prayed unto by all our said subjects, and if it has not yet pleased Him to permit it to be in one and the same form of religion, that it may be at the least with one and the same intention, and with such rules that may prevent among them all troubles and tumults. . . ." Now the details of the document fall into place. Each of the articles addresses specific "rules" governing the legal rights and obligations of French Catholics and Protestants, ranging from where they can worship to where they can work.

5. Why was this document written?

As we have already seen, Henry IV relied on the written word to convey information and, at the same time, to express his "power" and "strength." The legalistic and formal nature of the edict aided him in this effort. Yet, as Henry IV knew all too well, the gap between law and action could be large indeed. Thus, Henry IV compiled the edict not simply to tell people what to do but to persuade them to do it by delineating the terms of religious coexistence point by point and presenting them as the best safeguard against the return of confusion and disorder. He thereby hoped to restore peace to a country that had been divided by civil war for the previous thirty-six years.

6. What does this document reveal about the particular society and period in question?

Historians have mined the Edict of Nantes for insight into various facets of Henry IV's reign and Protestant–Catholic relations at the time. Do not be daunted by such complexity; you should focus instead on what you see as particularly predominant and revealing themes. One of the most striking in the Edict of Nantes is the central place of religion in late sixteenth-century society. Our contemporary notion of the separation of church and state had no place in the world of Henry IV and his subjects. As he proclaims in the opening lines, he was king "by the Grace of God" who had given him "virtue" and "strength." Furthermore, you might stop to consider why religious differences were the subject of royal legislation in the first place. Note Henry IV's statement that "if it has not yet pleased Him [God] to permit [Christian worship in France] to be in one and the same form of religion, that it may at the least be with one and the same intention. . . ." What does this suggest about sixteenth-century attitudes toward religious difference and tolerance? You cannot answer this question simply by reading the document in black-and-white terms; you need to look beyond the words and between the lines to draw out the document's broader meanings.

Interpreting Visual Sources

Historians do not rely on written records alone to reconstruct the past; they also turn to nonwritten sources, which are equally varied and rich. Nonwritten sources range from archaeological and material sources to sculpture, paintings, and photographs. This book includes a range of visual representations to enliven your view of history while enhancing your interpretive skills. Interpreting a visual document is very much like interpreting a nonvisual one — you begin with six questions similar to the ones you have already applied to a written source and move from ascertaining the "facts" of the document to a more complex analysis of the visual document's historical meanings and value.

1. Who created this image, when, and where?

Just as with written sources, identifying the artist or creator of an image and when and where it was produced will provide a foundation for your interpretation. Some visual sources, such as a painting or political cartoon signed by the artist, are more forthcoming in this regard. But if the artist is not known (and even if he or she is), there are other paths of inquiry to pursue. Did someone commission the production of the image? What was the historical context in which the image was produced? Piecing together what you know on these two fronts will allow you to draw some basic conclusions about the image.

2. What type of image is this?

The nature of a visual source shapes its form and content because every visual genre has its own conventions. Take a map as an example. At the most basic level, maps are composites of images created to convey topographical and geographical information about a particular place, whether a town, a region, or a continent. Think about how you use maps in your own life. Sometimes they can be fanciful in their designs, but typically they have a practical function — to enable the viewer to get from one place to another or at the very least to get a sense of an area's spatial characteristics. A formal portrait, by contrast, would conform to a different set of conventions and, of equal significance, a different set of viewer expectations and uses.

3. Who are the intended viewers of the image?

As with written sources, identifying the relationship between the image's creator and audience is essential to illuminate fully what the artist is trying to convey. Was the image intended for the general public, such as a photograph published in a newspaper? Or was the intended audience more private? Whether public, private, or somewhere in between, the creator's target audience shapes his or her choice of subject matter, format, and style, which in turn should shape your interpretation of its meaning and significance.

4. What is the central message of the image?

Images convey messages just as powerfully as the written word. The challenge is to learn how to "read" pictorial representations accurately. Since artists use images, color, and space to communicate with their audiences, you must train your eyes to look for visual rather than verbal cues. A good place to start is to note the image's main features, followed by a closer examination of its specific details and their interrelationship.

5. Why was this image produced?

Images are produced for a range of reasons — to convey information, to entertain, or to persuade, to name just a few. Understanding the motivations underlying an image's creation is key to unraveling its meaning (or at least what it was supposed to mean) to people at the time. For example, the impressionist painters of the nineteenth century did not paint simply to paint — their style and subject matter intentionally challenged contemporary artistic norms and conventions. Without knowing this, you cannot appreciate the broader context and impact of impressionist art.

6. What does this image reveal about the society and time period in which it was created?

Answering the first five questions will guide your answer here. Identifying the artist, the type of image, and when, where, and for whom it was produced allows you to step beyond a literal reading of the image into the historical setting in which it was produced. Although the meaning of an image can transcend its historical context, its point of origin and intended audience cannot. Therein rests an image's broader value as a window onto the past, for it is a product of human activity in a specific time and place, just like written documents.

Guided by these six questions, you can evaluate visual sources on their own terms and analyze the ways in which they speak to the broader historical context. Once again, let's take an example.

2. Illustrating an Indigenous Perspective

Lienzo de Tlaxcala (c. 1560)

Like Bernal Díaz del Castillo, the peoples of central Mexico had a stake in recording the momentous events unfolding around them, for they had long believed that remembering the past was essential to their cultural survival. Traditionally, local peoples used pictoriographic representations to record legends, myths, and historical events. After the Spaniards' arrival, indigenous artists borrowed from this tradition to produce their own accounts of the conquest, including the image below. It is one of a series contained in the Lienzo de Tlaxcala, *painted on cloth in the mid-sixteenth century. Apparently, the* Lienzo *was created for the Spanish viceroy to commemorate the alliance of the Tlaxcalans with the Spaniards. The Tlaxcalans were enemies of the Aztecs and after initial resistance to the Spanish invasion decided to join their forces. This particular image depicts two related events. The first is the meeting between the Aztec leader Moctezuma and Hernán Cortés in Tenochtitlán in August 1519. Cortés is accompanied by Doña Marina, his translator and cultural mediator; Moctezuma appears with warriors at his side. Rather than showing Moctezuma in his traditional garb, the artist dressed him in the manner of the Tlaxcalans. Both sit in European-style chairs, a nod to European artistic influence, and a Tlaxcalan headdress is suspended in*

the air between them. Game and fowl offered to the Spaniards are portrayed at the bottom. Within a week of this meeting, Cortés imprisoned Moctezuma in his own palaces with the Tlaxcalans' help. Moctezuma the prisoner appears in the upper right of the image as an old, weak ruler whose sun has set.

1. Who created this image, when, and where?

In this case, you will have to rely on the headnote to answer these questions. The image was created by an unknown Tlaxcalan artist in the mid-sixteenth century as part of a pictorial series, the *Lienzo de Tlaxcala*, depicting the Spanish conquest of Aztec Mexico. Although the image commemorates events that took place in 1519, it was produced decades later, when Spanish imperial control was firmly entrenched. Thus, the image represents a visual point of contact between Spanish and indigenous traditions in the age of European global expansion. Although knowing the identity of the artist would be ideal, the fact that he was Tlaxcalan is of greater value. The Tlaxcalans had allied themselves with the Spanish and considered the *Lienzo* a way of highlighting their role in the Aztecs' defeat.

2. What type of image is this?

On the one hand, this image fits into a long pictorial tradition among the peoples of central Mexico. Before the conquest, they had no alphabetic script. Instead, they drew on a rich repertoire of images and symbols to preserve legends, myths, and historical events. These images and symbols, which included the stylized warriors shown here, were typically painted into books made of deerskin or a plant-based paper. On the other hand, the image also reveals clear European influences, most noticeably in the type of chair in which both Cortés and Moctezuma sit. Looking at the image again with these dual influences in mind, think about how the pictorial markers allowed both indigenous and Spanish viewers to see something recognizable in an event that marked the destruction of one world and the creation of another.

3. Who are the intended viewers of the image?

As the headnote reveals, the image's creator had a specific audience in mind, a Spanish colonial administrator. You should take this fact into account as you think about the image's meaning and significance. Just because a Tlaxcalan artist created the image does not necessarily mean that it represents an unadulterated native point of view. And just because the image documents two historical events does not necessarily mean that the "facts" are objectively presented.

4. What is the central message of the image?

There are many visual components of this image, each of which you should consider individually and then as part of the picture as a whole. As you already know, the artist combined indigenous and European representational traditions. What does this suggest about the image's message? The merging of these two traditions represents the alliance the Tlaxcalans forged with the Spanish. Looking closer, think about how the two leaders, Cortés and Moctezuma, are represented. Cortés is accompanied by his translator, Doña Marina, a Nahua woman. Originally a slave, she had been given to Cortés after his defeat of the Maya at Potonchan. She became a crucial interpreter and cultural mediator for Cortés in the world of the Mexica. Language appears here as a source of his power as well as his alliance with the Tlaxcalans. Although the Spanish contingent was relatively small, thousands of Tlaxcalan and other native warriors entered Tenochtitlán with them, a show of force not lost on local residents. The artist captures this fact by clothing Moctezuma in Tlaxcalan dress — he had once ruled over them, but now he was to be ruled. Soon after this meeting, Moctezuma was imprisoned in his own palaces. The artist captures this event in the upper right, where Moctezuma is shown as a prisoner.

5. Why was this image produced?

Examining this image reveals the complexity of this question, regardless of the nature of the source. At first glance, the answer is easy: the image was created to commemorate specific events. Yet given what you know about the setting in which the image was produced, the "why" takes on a deeper meaning. The image does not simply record events; it sets a scene in which multiple meanings are embedded — the chairs, Doña Marina, the warriors — that suggest how the Spanish conquest transformed native culture. The image thus served a dual function — to inform the Spanish of the Tlaxcalans' role in the conquest while affirming Spanish dominance over them.

6. What does this image reveal about the society and time period in which it was created?

Answering this question requires you to step beyond a literal meaning of the image into the historical setting in which it was produced. Here you will uncover multiple layers of the image's broader significance. Consider the artist, for example, and his audience. What does the fact that a native artist created the image for a Spanish audience suggest about the nature of Spanish colonization? Clearly, the Spaniards did not make their presence felt as a colonial power simply by seizing land and treasure; they also reshaped indigenous people's understanding of themselves in both the past and the present. That the Tlaxcalans expressed this understanding visually in a historical document lent an air of permanence and legitimacy to Spanish colonization and, equally important, to the Tlaxcalans' contributions to it.

Conclusion

Through your analysis of historical sources, you will not only learn details about the world in which the sources were created but also become an active contributor to our understanding of these details' broader significance. Written documents and visual and material sources don't just "tell" historians what happened; they require historians to step into their own imaginations as they strive to understand the past. In this regard, historians' approach to primary sources is exactly that which is described here. They determine the basics of the source — who created it, when, and where — as a springboard for increasingly complex levels of analysis. Each level builds upon the other, just like rungs on a ladder. If you take the time to climb each rung in sequence, you will be able to master the content of a source and to use it to make your own historical arguments. The written and visual primary sources included in *Sources of The Making of the West*, Sixth Edition, will allow you to participate firsthand in the process of historical inquiry by exploring the people, places, and sights of the past and how they shaped their own world and continue to shape ours today.

Global Encounters and the Shock of the Reformation
1492–1560

I n the late fifteenth century, Europe stood on the threshold of profound transformations both within its borders and beyond. Portuguese fleets had opened up new trade
routes extending along the West African coast to Calicut, India, the hub of the spice trade.
Their success whet Europeans' appetite for maritime exploration, with Spain ultimately
taking the lead. The Spaniards' colonization of the Caribbean was in full gear by 1500,
and from there they moved westward into Mexico. The first two documents illuminate
aspects of the Spanish conquest of Mexico from both Spanish and indigenous perspectives. As they suggest, European colonization permanently changed the lives of indigenous peoples of the Americas, often with devastating results. The third document reveals
that some Europeans openly criticized colonization while at the same time embracing
the opportunities it provided to spread Catholic Christianity. Catholicism had long been
a unifying force in the West. In the early sixteenth century, however, the religious landscape shifted dramatically. Problems within the Catholic Church combined with the
spirit and methods of the Renaissance to usher in the Protestant Reformation, a time
of questioning, reform, and revolt. Documents 4 and 5 allow us to see the Reformation
through the eyes of two of its leaders, Martin Luther and John Calvin, as well as its impact
on everyday life. Together, their ideas helped to shatter the religious unity of Europe. As
the final document attests, despite the many challenges it faced, Catholicism underwent
its own process of change and renewal.

1. Worlds Collide
Bernal Díaz del Castillo,
The True History of the Conquest of New Spain (c. 1567)

*By the mid-sixteenth century, Spain had built an empire in the Americas that extended
from Mexico to Chile. The Spanish crown especially prized Mexico, then called "New Spain,"
because of the precious metals (gold and silver) found there. Numerous Spanish accounts of*

the conquest of Mexico have survived, perhaps none more vivid than that of Bernal Díaz del Castillo (1495–1583). Díaz had been in the thick of colonization from an early age, having joined a Spanish expedition to Panama in 1514 and two more to Mexico before meeting up with Hernán Cortés (1485–1547) in Cuba. In 1519, Cortés led a group of conquistadors, including Díaz, to the Mexican heartland, which they ultimately brought under Spanish control. By the mid-1550s, Díaz had begun to record his version of events, which he called The True History of the Conquest of New Spain, *to counter what he considered to be "false" histories by people who had not participated in the conquest. Díaz was also sensitive to critics of the colonists' treatment of indigenous peoples. Completed around 1567, the book languished in obscurity until its publication in 1632. In the excerpt that follows, Díaz recounts a key moment in the conquest: the Spaniards' arrival in Tenochtitlán, the Aztec capital, on November 8, 1519. Here Cortés and his men were greeted by the Aztec leader, Moctezuma, with great hospitality. In its close attention to detail, Díaz's description reveals a blend of wonder and disdain underlying Spanish attitudes toward Aztec civilization.*

When Cortés was told that the Great Montezuma was approaching, and he saw him coming, he dismounted from his horse, and when he was near Montezuma, they simultaneously paid great reverence to one another. Montezuma bade him welcome and our Cortés replied through Doña Marina[1] wishing him very good health. And it seems to me that Cortés, through Doña Marina, offered him his right hand, and Montezuma did not wish to take it, but he did give his hand to Cortés and then Cortés brought out a necklace which he had ready at hand, made of glass stones, which I have already said are called Margaritas, which have within them many patterns of diverse colors, these were strung on a cord of gold and with musk so that it should have a sweet scent, and he placed it round the neck of the Great Montezuma and when he had so placed it he was going to embrace him, and those great Princes who accompanied Montezuma held back Cortés by the arm so that he should not embrace him, for they considered it an indignity.

Then Cortés through the mouth of Doña Marina told him that now his heart rejoiced at having seen such a great Prince, and that he took it as a great honor that he had come in person to meet him and had frequently shown him such favor.

Then Montezuma spoke other words of politeness to him, and told two of his nephews who supported his arms, the Lord of Texcoco and the Lord of Coyoacan, to go with us and show us to our quarters, and Montezuma with his other two relations, the Lord of Cuitlahuac and the Lord of Tacuba who accompanied him, returned to the

From Bernal Díaz del Castillo, *The True History of the Conquest of New Spain*, vol. 2, trans. Alfred Percival Maudslay (London: The Hakluyt Society, 1910), 41–44, 55–59.

[1]A Nahua slave of a Maya cacique, she was given to Cortés by the Maya after their defeat at Potonchan. Speaking both Nahuatl and Yucatec Maya, she (and the ex-Maya captive Gerónimo de Aguilar) became crucial interpreters for Cortés as he entered the world of the Mexica. She was also the mother of Cortés's illegitimate son, Martín. See Stuart B. Schwartz, ed., *Victors and Vanquished: Spanish and Nahua Views of the Conquest of Mexico* (Boston: Bedford/St. Martin's, 2000), 251. [Schwartz's note.]

city, and all those grand companies of Caciques[2] and chieftains who had come with him returned in his train. . . . Thus space was made for us to enter the streets of Mexico, without being so much crowded. But who could now count the multitude of men and women and boys who were in the streets and on the azoteas, and in canoes on the canals, who had come out to see us. It was indeed wonderful, and, now that I am writing about it, it all comes before my eyes as though it had happened but yesterday. Coming to think it over it seems to be a great mercy that our Lord Jesus Christ was pleased to give us grace and courage to dare to enter into such a city; and for the many times He has saved me from danger of death, as will be seen later on, I give Him sincere thanks, and in that He has preserved me to write about it, although I cannot do it as fully as is fitting or the subject needs. Let us make no words about it, for deeds are the best witnesses to what I say here and elsewhere.

Let us return to our entry to Mexico. They took us to lodge in some large houses, where there were apartments for all of us, for they had belonged to the father of the Great Montezuma, who was named Axayaca, and at that time Montezuma kept there the great oratories for his idols, and a secret chamber where he kept bars and jewels of gold, which was the treasure that he had inherited from his father Axayaca, and he never disturbed it. They took us to lodge in that house, because they called us Teules, and took us for such, so that we should be with the Idols or Teules which were kept there. However, for one reason or another, it was there they took us, where there were great halls and chambers canopied with the cloth of the country for our Captain, and for every one of us beds of matting with canopies above, and no better bed is given, however great the chief may be, for they are not used. And all these palaces were [coated] with shining cement and swept and garlanded.

As soon as we arrived and entered into the great court, the Great Montezuma took our Captain by the hand, for he was there awaiting him, and led him to the apartment and saloon where he was to lodge, which was very richly adorned according to their usage, and he had at hand a very rich necklace made of golden crabs, a marvelous piece of work, and Montezuma himself placed it round the neck of our Captain Cortés, and greatly astonished his [own] Captains by the great honor that he was bestowing on him. When the necklace had been fastened, Cortés thanked Montezuma through our interpreters, and Montezuma replied—"Malinche, you and your brethren are in your own house, rest awhile," and then he went to his palaces which were not far away, and we divided our lodgings by companies, and placed the artillery pointing in a convenient direction, and the order which we had to keep was clearly explained to us, and that we were to be much on the alert, both the cavalry and all of us soldiers. A sumptuous dinner was provided for us according to their use and custom, and we ate it at once. So this was our lucky and daring entry into the great city of Tenochtitlan, Mexico. . . .

Thanks to our Lord Jesus Christ for it all. . . .

---

[2] A Taino word meaning ruler, brought from the Indies to Mexico by the Spanish and used to refer to native rulers in Mexico and Latin America in general. See Schwartz, *Victors and Vanquished*, 254. [Schwartz's note.]

Let us leave this talk and go back to our story of what else happened to us, which I will go on to relate. . . .

The next day Cortés decided to go to Montezuma's palace, and he first sent to find out what he intended doing and to let him know that we were coming. . . .

When Montezuma knew of our coming he advanced to the middle of the hall to receive us, accompanied by many of his nephews, for no other chiefs were permitted to enter or hold communication with Montezuma where he then was, unless it were on important business. Cortés and he paid the greatest reverence to each other and then they took one another by the hand and Montezuma made him sit down on his couch on his right hand, and he also bade all of us to be seated on seats which he ordered to be brought.

Then Cortés began to make an explanation through our interpreters Doña Marina and Aguilar, and said that he and all of us were rested, and that in coming to see and converse with such a great Prince as he was, we had completed the journey and fulfilled the command which our great King and Prince had laid on us. But what he chiefly came to say on behalf of our Lord God had already been brought to his [Montezuma's] knowledge through his ambassadors, Tendile, Pitalpitoque and Quintalbor, at the time when he did us the favor to send the golden sun and moon to the sand dunes; for we told them then that we were Christians and worshipped one true and only God, named Jesus Christ, who suffered death and passion to save us, and we told them that a cross (when they asked us why we worshipped it) was a sign of the other Cross on which our Lord God was crucified for our salvation, and that the death and passion which He suffered was for the salvation of the whole human race, which was lost, and that this our God rose on the third day and is now in heaven, and it is He who made the heavens and the earth, the sea and the sands, and created all the things there are in the world, and He sends the rain and the dew, and nothing happens in the world without His holy will. That we believe in Him and worship Him, but that those whom they look upon as gods are not so, but are devils, which are evil things, and if their looks are bad their deeds are worse, and they could see that they were evil and of little worth, for where we had set up crosses such as those his ambassadors had seen, they dared not appear before them, through fear of them, and that as time went on they would notice this.

The favor he now begged of him was his attention to the words that he now wished to tell him; then he explained to him very clearly about the creation of the world, and how we are all brothers, sons of one father, and one mother who were called Adam and Eve, and how such a brother as our great Emperor, grieving for the perdition of so many souls, such as those which their idols were leading to Hell, where they burn in living flames, had sent us, so that after what he [Montezuma] had now heard he would put a stop to it and they would no longer adore these Idols or sacrifice Indian men and women to them, for we were all brethren, nor should they commit sodomy or thefts. He also told them that, in course of time, our Lord and King would send some men who among us lead very holy lives, much better than we do, who will explain to them all about it, for at present we merely came to give them due warning, and so he prayed him to do what he was asked and carry it into effect.

As Montezuma appeared to wish to reply, Cortés broke off his argument, and to all of us who were with him he said: "with this we have done our duty considering it is the first attempt."

Montezuma replied—"Señor Malinche, I have understood your words and arguments very well before now, from what you said to my servants at the sand dunes, this about three Gods and the Cross, and all those things that you have preached in the towns through which you have come. We have not made any answer to it because here throughout all time we have worshipped our own gods, and thought they were good, as no doubt yours are, so do not trouble to speak to us any more about them at present. Regarding the creation of the world, we have held the same belief for ages past, and for this reason we take it for certain that you are those whom our ancestors predicted would come from the direction of the sunrise." . . .

. . . Then Cortés and all of us answered that we thanked him sincerely for such signal good will, and Montezuma said, laughing, for he was very merry in his princely way of speaking: "Malinche, I know very well that these people of Tlaxcala with whom you are such good friends have told you that I am a sort of God or Teul, and that everything in my houses is made of gold and silver and precious stones, I know well enough that you are wise and did not believe it but took it as a joke. Behold now, Señor Malinche, my body is of flesh and bone like yours, my houses and palaces of stone and wood and lime; that I am a great king and inherit the riches of my ancestors is true, but not all the nonsense and lies that they have told you about me, although of course you treated it as a joke, as I did your thunder and lightning."

Cortés answered him, also laughing, and said that opponents and enemies always say evil things, without truth in them, of those whom they hate, and that he well knew that he could not hope to find another Prince more magnificent in these countries, and, that not without reason had he been so vaunted to our Emperor.

While this conversation was going on, Montezuma secretly sent a great Cacique, one of his nephews who was in his company, to order his stewards to bring certain pieces of gold, which it seems must have been put apart to give to Cortés, and ten loads of fine cloth, which he apportioned, the gold and mantles between Cortés and the four captains, and to each of us soldiers he gave two golden necklaces, each necklace being worth ten pesos, and two loads of mantles. The gold that he then gave us was worth in all more than a thousand pesos and he gave it all cheerfully and with the air of a great and valiant prince.

DISCUSSION QUESTIONS

1. How does Díaz describe Tenochtitlán and the Aztec leader Moctezuma? What impressed him in particular? What does he seem to criticize, and why?

2. How does Díaz portray Cortés and his interactions with Moctezuma? What was the role of Doña Marina in their exchanges?

3. In what ways is Díaz's account colored by his own preconceptions and beliefs as a European in a foreign land?

4. Based on this account, what motivated Díaz and other conquistadors? What did the New World have to offer them?

2. Illustrating an Indigenous Perspective
Lienzo de Tlaxcala (c. 1560)

Like Bernal Díaz del Castillo, the peoples of central Mexico had a stake in recording the momentous events unfolding around them, for they had long believed that remembering the past was essential to their cultural survival. Traditionally, local peoples used pictoriographic representations to record legends, myths, and historical events. After the Spaniards' arrival, indigenous artists borrowed from this tradition to produce their own accounts of the conquest, including the image below. It is one of a series contained in the Lienzo de Tlaxcala, *painted on cloth in the mid-sixteenth century. Apparently, the* Lienzo *was created for the Spanish viceroy to commemorate the alliance of the Tlaxcalans with the Spaniards. The Tlaxcalans were enemies of the Aztecs and, after initial resistance to the Spanish invasion, decided to join their forces. This particular image depicts two related events. The first is the meeting between the Aztec leader Moctezuma and Hernán Cortés in Tenochtitlán in August 1519. Cortés is accompanied by Doña Marina, his translator and cultural mediator; Moctezuma appears with warriors at his side. Rather than showing Moctezuma in his traditional garb, the artist dressed him in the manner of the Tlaxcalans. Both sit in European-style chairs, a nod to European artistic influence, and a Tlaxcalan headdress is suspended in the air between them. Game and fowl offered to the Spaniards are*

The British Library, London, UK / Bridgeman Images

portrayed at the bottom. Within a week of this meeting, Cortés imprisoned Moctezuma in his own palaces with the Tlaxcalans' help. Moctezuma the prisoner appears in the upper right of the image as an old, weak ruler whose sun has set.

DISCUSSION QUESTIONS

1. In what ways do the artist's depictions of Cortés and Moctezuma differ? What do the depictions share?

2. Why do you think the artist chose to depict Moctezuma in Tlaxcalan dress? How was this choice related to the artist's audience and the message he sought to convey?

3. What are the possible strengths of a visual source like this for historians? What are the possible weaknesses?

3. Defending Indigenous Humanity

Bartolomé de Las Casas, *In Defense of the Indians* (c. 1548–1550)

Indigenous peoples in the Americas suffered heavily under Spanish colonization. Millions died as the result of war and disease, and many who survived were used as forced labor. The fate of indigenous Americans did not go unnoticed in Europe, where the ethical and legal basis of their harsh treatment became the subject of significant debate. Charles V, king of Spain and the Holy Roman Emperor, added fuel to the fire. In 1550, he ordered a panel of lawyers and theologians at the University of Valladolid to evaluate the positions of two prominent opposing voices on the issue, Juan Ginés de Sepúlveda (1490–1573) and Bartolomé de Las Casas (1474–1566). Drawing heavily on Aristotle's notion that hierarchy was natural, Sepúlveda argued that the Spanish had the right to enslave indigenous Americans because they were an inferior and less civilized people. Las Casas, whose response is excerpted below, rejected Sepúlveda's position, based in part on his own experience living in Spanish America. Here he witnessed firsthand the devastating human impact of colonization and was ultimately swayed by the local Dominican monks' campaign against the mistreatment of Indians. He joined the Dominican order and thereafter was a vocal advocate for indigenous Americans until his death in 1566. Although the Valladolid panel did not declare a winner, in practice Las Casas's views were drowned out by Sepúlveda and other advocates of slavery and conquest.

As a result of the points we have proved and made clear, the distinction the Philosopher [Aristotle] makes between the two above-mentioned kinds of barbarian is evident. For those he deals with in the first book of the *Politics*, and whom we have just discussed, are barbarians without qualification, in the proper and strict sense of the word, that is, dull witted and lacking in the reasoning powers necessary for self-government. They are without laws, without king, etc. For this reason they are by nature unfitted for rule.

However, he admits, and proves, that the barbarians he deals with in the third book of the same work have a lawful, just, and natural government. Even though they lack the

From *In Defense of the Indians*, trans. Stafford Poole (DeKalb: Northern Illinois University Press, 1974), 41–46.

art and use of writing, they are not wanting in the capacity and skill to rule and govern themselves, both publicly and privately. Thus they have kingdoms, communities, and cities that they govern wisely according to their laws and customs. Thus their government is legitimate and natural, even though it has some resemblance to tyranny. From these statements we have no choice but to conclude that the rulers of such nations enjoy the use of reason and that their people and the inhabitants of their provinces do not lack peace and justice. Otherwise they could not be established or preserved as political entities for long. This is made clear by the Philosopher and Augustine. Therefore not all barbarians are irrational or natural slaves or unfit for government. Some barbarians, then, in accord with justice and nature, have kingdoms, royal dignities, jurisdiction, and good laws, and there is among them lawful government.

Now if we shall have shown that among our Indians of the western and southern shores (granting that we call them barbarians and that they are barbarians) there are important kingdoms, large numbers of people who live settled lives in a society, great cities, kings, judges and laws, persons who engage in commerce, buying, selling, lending, and the other contracts of the law of nations, will it not stand proved that the Reverend Doctor Sepúlveda has spoken wrongly and viciously against peoples like these, either out of malice or ignorance of Aristotle's teaching, and, therefore, has falsely and perhaps irreparably slandered them before the entire world? From the fact that the Indians are barbarians it does not necessarily follow that they are incapable of government and have to be ruled by others, except to be taught about the Catholic faith and to be admitted to the holy sacraments. They are not ignorant, inhuman, or bestial. Rather, long before they had heard the word Spaniard they had properly organized states, wisely ordered by excellent laws, religion, and custom. They cultivated friendship and, bound together in common fellowship, lived in populous cities in which they wisely administered the affairs of both peace and war justly and equitably, truly governed by laws that at very many points surpass ours, and could have won the admiration of the sages of Athens. . . .

Now if they are to be subjugated by war because they are ignorant of polished literature, let Sepúlveda hear Trogus Pompey:

> Nor could the Spaniards submit to the yoke of a conquered province until Caesar Augustus, after he had conquered the world, turned his victorious armies against them and organized that barbaric and wild people as a province, once he had led them by law to a more civilized way of life.

Now see how he called the Spanish people barbaric and wild. I would like to hear Sepúlveda, in his cleverness, answer this question: Does he think that the war of the Romans against the Spanish was justified in order to free them from barbarism? And this question also: Did the Spanish wage an unjust war when they vigorously defended themselves against them?

Next, I call the Spaniards who plunder that unhappy people torturers. Do you think that the Romans, once they had subjugated the wild and barbaric peoples of Spain, could with secure right divide all of you among themselves, handing over so many head of both males and females as allotments to individuals? And do you then conclude that the Romans could have stripped your rulers of their authority and consigned all of you, after you had been deprived of your liberty, to wretched labors, especially in searching for gold and silver lodes and mining and refining the metals? And if the Romans finally did that, . . . [would you not judge] that you also have the right to defend your freedom, indeed your very life, by war? Sepúlveda, would you have permitted Saint James to evangelize your own people of Córdoba in that way? For God's sake and man's faith in him, is this the way to impose the yoke of Christ on Christian men? Is this the way to remove wild barbarism from the minds of barbarians? Is it not, rather, to act like thieves, cutthroats, and cruel plunderers and to drive the gentlest of people headlong into despair? The Indian race is not that barbaric, nor are they dull witted or stupid, but they are easy to teach and very talented in learning all the liberal arts, and very ready to accept, honor, and observe the Christian religion and correct their sins (as experience has taught) once priests have introduced them to the sacred mysteries and taught them the word of God. They have been endowed with excellent conduct, and before the coming of the Spaniards, as we have said, they had political states that were well founded on beneficial laws.

Now if Sepúlveda had wanted, as a serious man should, to know the full truth before he sat down to write with his mind corrupted by the lies of tyrants, he should have consulted the honest religious who have lived among those peoples for many years and know their endowments of character and industry, as well as the progress they have made in religion and morality. . . .

From this it is clear that the basis for Sepúlveda's teaching that these people are uncivilized and ignorant is worse than false. Yet even if we were to grant that this race has no keenness of mind or artistic ability, certainly they are not, in consequence, obliged to submit themselves to those who are more intelligent and to adopt their ways, so that, if they refuse, they may be subdued by having war waged against them and be enslaved, as happens today. For men are obliged by the natural law to do many things they cannot be forced to do against their will. We are bound by the natural law to embrace virtue and imitate the uprightness of good men. No one, however, is punished for being bad unless he is guilty of rebellion. Where the Catholic faith has been preached in a Christian manner and as it ought to be, all men are bound by the natural law to accept it, yet no one is forced to accept the faith of Christ. No one is punished because he is sunk in vice, unless he is rebellious or harms the property and persons of others. No one is forced to embrace virtue and show himself as a good man. . . .

. . . Therefore, not even a truly wise man may force an ignorant barbarian to submit to him, especially by yielding his liberty, without doing him an injustice. This the poor Indians suffer, with extreme injustice, against all the laws of God and of men and against the law of nature itself.

DISCUSSION QUESTIONS

1. Why does Las Casas reject Sepúlveda's argument? What is the basis of his reasoning?

2. How does Las Casas depict indigenous American civilization? What attributes does he highlight, and why?

3. Why does Las Casas cite the example of Rome's conquest of Spain under Caesar Augustus to support his point?

4. Despite Las Casas's vigorous defense of the Indians, what prejudices and assumptions of his own did he bring to bear in this work?

4. Scripture and Salvation

Martin Luther, *Freedom of a Christian* (1520)

German monk Martin Luther's attempt to reform the Catholic Church from within developed into a new branch of Christianity known as Protestantism. After his excommunication by Pope Leo X in 1520, Luther published several treatises that attacked church authority, clerical celibacy, and the sacraments while illuminating his evangelical theology. He set forth the guiding principles of his beliefs with particular clarity in Freedom of a Christian. *Although originally written in Latin and addressed to the pope, the tract was soon translated into German and widely circulated among Luther's ever-growing number of followers. In the excerpt that follows, Luther defined what became a central tenet of the reform movement: faith in Christ and his promise of salvation is all that a Christian needs to be saved from sin.*

Many people have considered Christian faith an easy thing, and not a few have given it a place among the virtues. They do this because they have not experienced it and have never tasted the great strength there is in faith. It is impossible to write well about it or to understand what has been written about it unless one has at one time or another experienced the courage which faith gives a man when trials oppress him. But he who has had even a faint taste of it can never write, speak, meditate, or hear enough concerning it. It is a living "spring of water welling up to eternal life," as Christ calls it in John 4 [:14].

As for me, although I have no wealth of faith to boast of and know how scant my supply is, I nevertheless hope that I have attained to a little faith, even though I have been assailed by great and various temptations; and I hope that I can discuss it, if not more elegantly, certainly more to the point, than those literalists and subtle disputants have previously done, who have not even understood what they have written. . . .

First, let us consider the inner man to see how a righteous, free, and pious Christian, that is, a spiritual, new, and inner man, becomes what he is. It is evident that no external thing has any influence in producing Christian righteousness or freedom. . . . It does not help the soul if the body is adorned with the sacred robes of priests or dwells in sacred places or is occupied with sacred duties or prays, fasts, abstains from certain kinds of food, or does any work that can be done by the body and in the body. . . .

One thing, and only one thing, is necessary for Christian life, righteousness, and freedom. That one thing is the most holy Word of God, the gospel of Christ, as Christ says, John 11 [:25], "I am the resurrection and the life; he who believes in me, though he die, yet shall he live"; and John 8 [:36], "So if the Son makes you free, you will be free indeed"; and Matt. 4 [:4], "Man shall not live by bread alone, but by every word that proceeds from the mouth of God." Let us then consider it certain and firmly established that the soul can do without anything except the Word of God and that where the Word of God is missing there is no help at all for the soul. If it has the Word of God it is rich and

From Martin Luther, *Christian Liberty*, ed. Harold J. Grimm (Philadelphia: Fortress Press, 1957), 6–10.

lacks nothing since it is the Word of life, truth, light, peace, righteousness, salvation, joy, liberty, wisdom, power, grace, glory, and of every incalculable blessing. . . .

You may ask, "What then is the Word of God, and how shall it be used, since there are so many words of God?" I answer: The Apostle explains this in Romans 1. The Word is the gospel of God concerning his Son, who was made flesh, suffered, rose from the dead, and was glorified through the Spirit who sanctifies. To preach Christ means to feed the soul, make it righteous, set it free, and save it, provided it believes the preaching. Faith alone is the saving and efficacious use of the Word of God. . . . Therefore it is clear that, as the soul needs only the Word of God for its life and righteousness, so it is justified by faith alone and not any works. . . .

When you have learned this you will know that you need Christ, who suffered and rose again for you so that, if you believe in him, you may through this faith become a new man in so far as your sins are forgiven and you are justified by the merits of another, namely, of Christ alone. . . .

DISCUSSION QUESTIONS

1. According to Luther, what is faith, and where does it come from?

2. How can an individual Christian become a "new man" through such faith?

3. By defining faith alone as essential to salvation, in what ways does Luther undermine basic Catholic teachings?

4. What authority does Luther draw on to defend his point of view? What does this reveal about the basis of his theology?

5. Reforming Christianity

SOURCES IN CONVERSATION | John Calvin, *Ordinances for the Regulation of Churches* (1547) and *Registers of Consistory of Geneva* (1542–1543)

In 1533–1534, while studying in Paris at the same time as Ignatius of Loyola (1491–1556), Frenchman John Calvin (1509–1564) became a convert to the reform movement. Fleeing the dangers of Paris, Calvin settled in Geneva, where he remained for the majority of his life, intent upon transforming it into his vision of a godly city. Geneva soon became a haven for reformers and a training ground for preachers. Theologically, Calvin embraced Luther's

John Calvin, *Ordinances for the Regulation of Churches* (1547), in Merry Wiesner-Hanks, ed., *Religious Transformations in the Early Modern World* (Boston: Bedford/St.Martins, 2009), 77–78, and *From Registers of the Consistory of Geneva in the Time of Calvin*, Volume 1, 1542–1544, ed. Robert M. Kingdon, trans. M. Wallace McDonald (Grand Rapids, MI: William B. Eerdmans, 2002), 13, 155, 161–62, 252.

doctrine that people cannot earn their salvation, and he then took it further. He argued that God had ordained every person to salvation or damnation before the beginning of time (predestination); only God's chosen "elect" would be saved. For Calvin, a righteous life might be a sign that the person had been chosen for salvation. With this goal in mind, in Geneva Calvin and his officials set up a strict system of moral and religious discipline, issuing ordinances such as the ones excerpted below to regulate public and family life. A group of pastors and laymen, known as the consistory, was established to investigate and discipline improper conduct and belief. People from all walks of life were called before consistorial officials to account for alleged infractions. Written notes were taken at such sessions in real time and were then later revised into official minutes — these minutes have survived in abundance. While one step removed from the encounters they describe, the selections here provide a view of how Calvin's vision played out in the lives of ordinary people.

Ordinances for the Regulation of Churches (1547)

Blasphemy

Whoever shall have blasphemed, swearing by the body or by the blood of our Lord, or in similar manner, he shall be made to kiss the earth for the first offence; for the second to pay 5 sous,[1] and for the third 6 sous, and for the last offence be put in the pillory for one hour.

Drunkenness

1. That no one shall invite another to drink under penalty of 3 sous.
2. That taverns shall be closed during the sermon, under penalty that the tavern-keeper shall pay 3 sous, and whoever may be found therein shall pay the same amount.
3. If any one be found intoxicated he shall pay for the first offence 3 sous and shall be remanded to the consistory; for the second offence he shall be held to pay the same sum of 6 sous, and for the third 10 sous and be put in orison.

Songs and Dances

If any one sing immoral, dissolute or outrageous songs, or dance the *virollet* or other dance, he shall be put in prison for three days and then sent to the consistory.

Usury

That no one shall take upon interest or profit more than five percent, upon penalty of confiscation of the principal and of being condemned to make restitution as the case may demand.

---

[1]**sou:** A small coin.

Games

That no one shall play at any dissolute game or at any game whatsoever it may be, neither for gold nor silver nor for any excessive stake, upon penalty of 5 sous and forfeiture of stake played for. . . .

Concerning the Celebration of the Marriage

That the parties at the time when they are to be married shall go modestly to the church, without drummers and minstrels, preserving an order and gravity becoming to Christians; and this before the last stroke of the bell, in order that the marriage blessing may be given before the sermon. If they are negligent and come too late they shall be sent away.

Registers of Constitory of Geneva (1542–1543)

Thursday, March 2, 1542

Pernete, wife of Master Robert the pack-saddler.

Asked about the discipline and fashion of living in her household according to the Word of God, about songs, sermons and her faith and her servants and maids. And she gave a sound explanation of her faith and creed. The consistory gave her proper remonstrances to buy a Bible to put before her people to read instead of game boards, cards, songs, and to eschew all dice.

Tevenete, wife of Master Jaques Emyn, pack-saddler.

She was sufficiently admonished, First given proper admonitions concerning attendance at sermons, her faith, the manner of living in religion and her foreign guests. And she could not say her creed, at least the confession. She was admonished that within a month she should learn to render a better account of her creed and that she buy a Bible to show to the guests in her house. Also that she have good servants and maids and that God not be blasphemed or offended in her house.

Thursday, December 14, 1542

Mychie, daughter of Gallatin, from Peney.

Answers that she does not want her promised husband because he has nothing and it is better that she be with her father than elsewhere in difficulty. And that she swore faith to him and does not want him to be her husband for the reason above, and that she has not been debauched.

Jehan Jallio, promised husband of the said Mychie, on the said marriage. Answers no, because the girl does not want it. And if it pleases the Council he is ready to marry her if she wants it, and it is not his fault, and he has done nothing to make her refuse him.

The said Michie recalled. Answers when she swore faith to him he had plenty of goods, and no one tried to prevent her from doing this. Says that if she gives him her goods he will waste them, and she would not know what to do with him. Remanded to respond whether she wants it or not on leaving here, and if not that she be kept in this city until tomorrow. Asked for a term to respond and have counsel from her mother and her friends, since it pleases the Seigneurie, and to marry him next Tuesday, and they agreed to this.

Thursday, December 21, 1542

Françoys Comparet.

Because of games. Answers that he goes to the sermon when he can and sometimes with friends to drink, and yesterday they drank a pot of wine together with good company. And answers nine sous for three, and he was not there, and he lost three sous per man. And that he was at the sermon Sunday and . . .[2] preached. Said the prayer and the confession. Remonstrances just as to the other, and let him abstain from the next Communion.

François Comparet the younger, brother of the aforesaid François, in the bakery. Goes to the sermon on Sundays when he can, and they bake every day at seven o'clock in their shop and go to the market to supply the shop. And said the prayer in Latin. And it is only about six months ago that he came to this city. Wat at the vespers sermon Sunday.

Camparet's widow,[3] mother of the two named above, because she does not discipline her children, who are badly taught in all good morals. Answers that other young boys lead them astray and ruin them, and they are good children and obedient, and they were not at the scandal that was made thus, and she does not know what it is. And goes willingly to the sermons when she can, and above all on Sundays. The younger son does not come to Communion. The consistory advises that she watch out from now on, that she teach her children and frequent the sermons and the catechism on Sundays; otherwise the Council will see to her. And that the children frequent the sermons.

Thursday, May 10, 1543

Donne Aymaz Charletaz, daughter of D[omaine] d'Arloz.

Because of usury, and that she is a rebel against the Seigneurie. Begged mercy of God and the Seigneurie. Answers that she was ill and did not lend at interest and gave her money to the merchants to use and they give her what they choose, because she has nothing to live on otherwise and has no other lands or goods. And that no one asks her anything or complains of her, and she has been a widow 40 years, and then she had 300 écus and now does not have 300 florins. And she submits herself to prison if she has ever spoken against the Gospel, and she left the neighborhood of Faucigny to come here to the Gospel.

DISCUSSION QUESTIONS

1. What type of behaviors do the Ordinances prohibit? What do these prohibitions reveal about Calvin's vision for an ideal Christian society?

---

[2]Name omitted.
[3]Jaquema, widow of Claude Comparet.

2. What evidence do the consistory records offer on how Calvin's vision was translated into practice in Geneva? What specific offenses did the consistory focus on, and why?

3. What forms of discipline did the consistory impose for these offenses? What functions do you think their admonitions and instructions served in the community as a whole?

6. Responding to Reformation
St. Ignatius of Loyola, *A New Kind of Catholicism*
(1546, 1549, 1553)

The interests of Ignatius of Loyola (1491–1556), born of a Spanish noble family, centered more on chivalry than religion before his serious injury at the Battle of Pamplona in 1520. While recovering, he experienced a conversion when he began reading the only books available to him, The Golden Legend *(about saints' lives) and the* Life of Christ. *After begging and spending time at the monastery of Montserrat, he began work on* The Spiritual Exercises, *a manual of discernment for the pilgrim journeying to God. After studying at the University of Paris, Ignatius, Francis Xavier (1506–1552), and other friends made vows of chastity and poverty, determining to travel to Jerusalem. When this became impossible, they went to Italy. The Society of Jesus (the Jesuits), founded by Ignatius and his early companions, was officially recognized by Pope Paul III in 1540 as a new order directly under the papacy. Its spirituality would be expressed most prominently through teaching and missionary work. The following letters of Ignatius reveal a new form of Catholic spiritual expression that was active and apostolic in its orientation. It was less a "response" to Protestantism than a model for Catholic life and work. Along with the works of other early Jesuits, it embodied a new spirit that so many had sought but not found in the late medieval church.*

Conduct at Trent: On Helping Others, 1546

Our main aim [to God's greater glory] during this undertaking at Trent is to put into practice (as a group that lives together in one appropriate place) preaching, confessions and readings, teaching children, giving good example, visiting the poor in the hospitals, exhorting those around us, each of us according to the different talents he may happen to have, urging on as many as possible to greater piety and prayer. . . .

In their preaching they should not refer to points of conflict between Protestants and Catholics, but simply exhort all to upright conduct and to ecclesiastical practice, urging everyone to full self-knowledge and to greater knowledge and love of their Creator and Lord, with frequent allusions to the Council. At the end of each session, they should (as has been mentioned) lead prayers for the Council.

From Joseph A. Munitiz and Philip Endean, eds. and trans., *Saint Ignatius of Loyola, Personal Writings: Reminiscences, Spiritual Diary, Select Letters, Including the Text of The Spiritual Exercises* (New York: Penguin Books, 1996), 165, 166, 230, 233–34, 257, 259, 262–63.

They should do the same with readings as with sermons, trying their best to influence people with greater love of their Creator and Lord as they explain the meaning of what is read; similarly, they should lead their hearers to pray for the Council. . . .

They should spend some time, as convenient, in the elementary teaching of youngsters, depending on the means and disposition of all involved, and with more or less explanation according to the capacity of the pupils. . . . Let them visit the almshouses once or twice a day, at times that are convenient for the patients' health, hearing confessions and consoling the poor, if possible taking them something, and urging them to the sort of prayers mentioned above for confession. If there are three of ours in Trent, each should visit the poor at least once every four days.

When they are urging people in their dealings with them to go to confession and communion, to say mass frequently, to undertake the Spiritual Exercises and other good works, they should also be urging them to pray for the Council.

It was said that there are advantages in being slow to speak and measured in one's statements when doctrinal definitions are involved. The opposite is true when one is urging people to look to their spiritual progress. Then one should be eloquent and ready to talk, full of sympathy and affection.

Spreading God's Word in a German University, 1549

The aim that they should have above all before their eyes is that intended by the Supreme Pontiff who has sent them: to help the University of Ingolstadt, and as far as is possible the whole of Germany, in all that concerns purity of faith, obedience to the Church, and firmness and soundness of doctrine and upright living. . . .

They must be very competent in them, and teach solid doctrine without many technical terms (which are unpopular), especially if these are hard to understand. The lectures should be learned yet clear, sustained in argument yet not long-winded, and delivered with attention to style. . . . Besides these academic lectures, it seems opportune on feast days to hold sermons on Bible readings, more calculated to move hearts and form consciences than to produce learned minds. . . . They should make efforts to attract their students into a friendship of spiritual quality, and if possible towards confession and making the Spiritual Exercises, even in the full form, if they seem suitable to join the Society. . . .

On occasion they should give time to works of mercy of a more visible character, such as in hospitals and prisons and helping other kinds of poor; such works arouse a "sweet fragrance" in the Lord. Opportunity may also arise to act as peacemakers in quarrels and to teach basic Christian doctrine to the uneducated. Taking account of local conditions and the persons concerned, prudence will dictate whether they should act themselves or through others.

They should make efforts to make friends with the leaders of their opponents, as also with those who are most influential among the heretics or those who are suspected of it yet seem not absolutely immovable. They must try to bring them back from their error by sensitive skill and signs of love. . . . All must try to have at their finger-tips the main points concerning dogmas of faith that are subjects of controversy with heretics, especially at the time and place when they are present, and with those persons with whom they are dealing. Thus they will be able, whenever opportunity arises, to put forward and defend the Catholic truth, to refute errors and to strengthen the doubtful and wavering, whether by lectures and sermons or in the confessional and in conversations. . . .

It will be helpful to lead people, as far as possible, to open themselves to God's grace, exhorting them to a desire for salvation, to prayer, to alms, and to everything that conduces to receiving grace or increasing it. . . .

Let [the duke] understand also what glory it will mean for him if he is the first to introduce into Germany seminaries in the form of such colleges, to foster sound doctrine and religion.

The Final Word on Obedience, 1553, to the Brothers in Portugal

To form an idea of the exceptional intrinsic value of this obedience in the eyes of God Our Lord, one should weigh both the worth of the noble sacrifice offered, involving the highest human power, and the completeness of the self-offering undertaken, as one strips oneself of self, becoming a "living victim" pleasing to the Divine Majesty. Another indication is the intensity of the difficulty experienced as one conquers self for love of God, opposing the natural human inclination felt by us all to follow our own opinions. . . .

Let us be unpretentious and let us be gentle! God Our Lord will grant the grace to enable you, gently and lovingly, to maintain constantly the offering you have made to Him. . . .

All that has been said does not exclude your bringing before your superiors a contrary opinion that may have occurred to you, once you have prayed about the matter and you feel that it would be proper and in accord with your respect for God to do so. . . . Such is the model on which divine Providence "gently disposes all things," so that the lower via the middle, and the middle via the higher, are led to their final ends. . . . The same can be seen upon the earth with respect to all secular constitutions that are duly established, and with respect to the ecclesiastical hierarchy, which is subordinated to you in virtue of holy obedience to select among the many routes open to you that which will bring you back to Portugal as soon and as safely as possible. So I order you in the name of Christ Our Lord to do this, even if it will be so as to return soon to India. . . . Firstly, you are well aware how important for the upkeep and advancement of Christianity in those lands, as also in Guinea and Brazil, is the good order that the King of Portugal can grant from his kingdom. When a prince of such Christian desires and holy intentions as is the King of Portugal receives information from someone of your experience about the state of affairs in those parts, you can imagine what influence this will have on him to do much more in the service of God Our Lord and for the good of those countries that you will describe to him. . . .

You are also aware how important it is for the good of the Indies that the persons sent there should be suitable for the aim that one is pursuing in those and in other lands. . . . Quite apart from all these reasons, which apply to furthering the good of India, it seems to me that you would fire the King's enthusiasm for the Ethiopian project, which has been planned for so many years without anything effective having been seen. Similarly, with regard to the Congo and Brazil, you could give no small help from Portugal, which you cannot do from India as there are not the same commercial relations. If people in India consider that your presence is important given your post, you can continue to act as superior no less from Portugal than from Japan or China, and probably much better. Just as you have gone away on other occasions for longer periods, do the same now.

DISCUSSION QUESTIONS

1. What does the Catholic life mean to Ignatius?

2. What advice does Ignatius offer about dealing with the problem of heresy?

3. What role will Jesuits play throughout Europe and the rest of the world according to Ignatius's instructions?

4. How does Ignatius think political leaders can be enlisted to support the aims of the Catholic reform movement?

COMPARATIVE QUESTIONS

1. How do Bernal Díaz del Castillo, the *Lienzo de Tlaxcala*, and Bartolomé de Las Casas portray indigenous peoples? Can you trust these portraits? What do they reveal about the ways in which Europeans and indigenous peoples viewed themselves?

2. According to Las Casas, indigenous Americans were not "barbarians" because they had many marks of "civilization," including cities and self-sustaining governments. What evidence can you find in Díaz to support this view?

3. What similarities do you see among Luther's, Calvin's, and Ignatius's models of Christian life? Where do they diverge?

4. How do you think Las Casas might have responded to Ignatius's advice to Jesuit missionaries in Portugal? What does this suggest about the role of Catholic Christianity in European colonization?

Wars of Religion and Clash of Worldviews
1560–1648

For kings, nobles, and ordinary folk alike, the late sixteenth through mid-seventeenth centuries were a time of turmoil and change, as the following documents illustrate. Religious wars galvanized much of Europe during this period, fueled by both ecclesiastical and lay leaders' attempts to maintain the commonly held idea that political and social stability depended on religious conformity. With the escalation of violence, however, some people came to question — and in some cases openly criticize — conventional views about the basic order of governance. They argued successfully that peace would come only if state interests took precedence over religious ones (Documents 1 to 3). Some governments attempted to harness these changes to better understand and help their struggling populations (Document 4). Europeans' views of the earth and the heavens also expanded in response to the rise of new scientific methods and discoveries (Document 5), while, at the same time, the lure of traditional beliefs remained strong within communities struggling to make sense of the upheavals occurring around them (Document 6).

1. Legislating Tolerance
Henry IV, *Edict of Nantes* (1598)

The promulgation of the Edict of Nantes in 1598 by King Henry IV (r. 1589–1610) marked the end of the French Wars of Religion by recognizing French Protestants as a legally protected religious minority. Drawing largely on earlier edicts of pacification, the Edict of Nantes was composed of ninety-two general articles, fifty-six secret articles, and two royal warrants. The two series of articles represented the edict proper and were registered by the highest courts of law in the realm (parlements). The following excerpts from the general

Modernized English text adapted from Edmund Everard, *The Great Pressures and Grievances of the Protestants in France* (London, 1681), 1–5, 10, 14, 16.

*articles reveal the triumph of political concerns over religious conformity on the one hand
and the limitations of religious tolerance in early modern France on the other.*

Henry, by the grace of God, King of France, and Navarre, to all present, and to come,
greeting. Among the infinite mercies that it has pleased God to bestow upon us, that
most signal and remarkable is, his having given us power and strength not to yield to
the dreadful troubles, confusions, and disorders, which were found at our coming to this
kingdom, divided into so many parties and factions, that the most legitimate was almost
the least, enabling us with constancy in such manner to oppose the storm, as in the end
to surmount it, now reaching a part of safety and repose for this state. . . . For the general difference among our good subjects, and the particular evils of the soundest parts
of the state, we judged might be easily cured, after the principal cause (the continuation
of civil war) was taken away. In which having, by the blessing of God, well and happily
succeeded, all hostility and wars through the kingdom being now ceased, we hope that
we will succeed equally well in other matters remaining to be settled, and that by this
means we shall arrive at the establishment of a good peace, with tranquility and rest. . . .
Among our said affairs . . . one of the principal has been the complaints we have received
from many of our Catholic provinces and cities, that the exercise of the Catholic religion
was not universally re-established, as is provided by edicts or statutes heretofore made
for the pacification of the troubles arising from religion; as well as the supplications and
remonstrances which have been made to us by our subjects of the Reformed religion,
regarding both the non-fulfillment of what has been granted by the said former laws,
and that which they desired to be added for the exercise of their religion, the liberty of
their consciences and the security of their persons and fortunes; presuming to have just
reasons for desiring some enlargement of articles, as not being without great apprehensions, because their ruin has been the principal pretext and original foundation of the late
wars, troubles, and commotions. Now not to burden us with too much business at once,
as also that the fury of war was not compatible with the establishment of laws, however
good they might be, we have hitherto deferred from time to time giving remedy herein.
But now that it has pleased God to give us a beginning of enjoying some rest, we think
we cannot employ ourself better than to apply to that which may tend to the glory and
service of His holy name, and to provide that He may be adored and prayed unto by all
our subjects: and if it has not yet pleased Him to permit it to be in one and the same form
of religion, that it may at the least be with one and the same intention, and with such
rules that may prevent among them all troubles and tumults. . . . For this cause, we have
upon the whole judged it necessary to give to all our said subjects one general law, clear,
pure, and absolute, by which they shall be regulated in all differences which have heretofore risen among them, or may hereafter rise, wherewith the one and other may be contented, being framed according as the time requires: and having had no other regard in
this deliberation than solely the zeal we have to the service of God, praying that He would
from this time forward render to all our subjects a durable and established peace. . . .
We have by this edict or statute perpetual and irrevocable said, declared, and ordained,
saying, declaring, and ordaining;

That the memory of all things passed on the one part and the other, since the beginning of the month of March 1585 until our coming to the crown, and also during the

other preceding troubles, and the occasion of the same, shall remain extinguished and suppressed, as things that had never been. . . .

We prohibit to all our subjects of whatever state and condition they be, to renew the memory thereof, to attack, resent, injure, or provoke one another by reproaches for what is past, under any pretext or cause whatsoever, by disputing, contesting, quarrelling, reviling, or offending by factious words; but to contain themselves, and live peaceably together as brethren, friends, and fellow-citizens, upon penalty for acting to the contrary, to be punished for breakers of peace, and disturbers of the public quiet.

We ordain, that the Catholic religion shall be restored and re-established in all places, and quarters of this kingdom and country under our obedience, and where the exercise of the same has been interrupted, to be there again, peaceably and freely exercised without any trouble or impediment. . . .

And not to leave any occasion of trouble and difference among our subjects, we have permitted and do permit to those of the Reformed religion, to live and dwell in all the cities and places of this our kingdom and countries under our obedience, without being inquired after, vexed, molested, or compelled to do any thing in religion, contrary to their conscience. . . .

We permit also to those of the said religion to hold, and continue the exercise of the same in all the cities and places under our obedience, where it was by them established and made public at several different times, in the year 1586, and in 1597.

In like manner the said exercise may be established, and re-established in all the cities and places where it has been established or ought to be by the Statute of Pacification, made in the year 1577 . . .

We prohibit most expressly to all those of the said religion, to hold any exercise of it . . . except in places permitted and granted in the present edict. As also not to exercise the said religion in our court, nor in our territories and countries beyond the mountains, nor in our city of Paris, nor within five leagues of the said city. . . .

We prohibit all preachers, readers, and others who speak in public, to use any words, discourse, or propositions tending to excite the people to sedition; and we enjoin them to contain and comport themselves modestly, and to say nothing which shall not be for the instruction and edification of the listeners, and maintaining the peace and tranquility established by us in our said kingdom. . . .

They [French Protestants] shall also be obliged to keep and observe the festivals of the Catholic Church, and shall not on the same days work, sell, or keep open shop, nor likewise the artisans shall not work out of their shops, in their chambers or houses privately on the said festivals, and other days forbidden, of any trade, the noise whereof may be heard outside by those that pass by, or by the neighbors. . . .

We ordain, that there shall not be made any difference or distinction upon the account of the said religion, in receiving scholars to be instructed in the universities, colleges, or schools, nor of the sick or poor into hospitals, sick houses or public almshouses. . . .

We will and ordain, that all those of the Reformed religion, and others who have followed their party, of whatever state, quality or condition they be, shall be obliged and constrained by all due and reasonable ways, and under the penalties contained in the said edict or statute relating thereunto, to pay tithes to the curates, and other ecclesiastics, and to all others to whom they shall appertain. . . .

To the end to re-unite so much the better the minds and good will of our subjects, as is our intention, and to take away all complaints for the future; we declare all those who make or shall make profession of the said Reformed religion, to be capable of holding and exercising all estates, dignities, offices, and public charges whatsoever. . . .

We declare all sentences, judgments, procedures, seizures, sales, and decrees made and given against those of the Reformed religion, as well living as dead, from the death of the deceased King Henry the Second our most honored Lord and father in law, upon the occasion of the said religion, tumults and troubles since happening, as also the execution of the same judgments and decrees, from henceforward canceled, revoked, and annulled. . . .

Those also of the said religion shall depart and desist henceforward from all practices, negotiations, and intelligences, as well within or without our kingdom; and the said assemblies and councils established within the provinces, shall readily separate, and also all the leagues and associations made or to be made under any pretext, to the prejudice of our present edict, shall be cancelled and annulled, . . . prohibiting most expressly to all our subjects to make henceforth any assessments or levies of money, fortifications, enrollments of men, congregations and assemblies of other than such as are permitted by our present edict, and without arms. . . .

We give in command to the people of our said courts of parlement, chambers of our courts, and courts of our aids, bailiffs, chief-justices, provosts and other of our justices and officers to whom it appertains, and to their lieutenants, that they cause to be read, published, and registered this present edict and ordinance in their courts and jurisdictions, and the same keep punctually, and the contents of the same to cause to be enjoined and used fully and peaceably to all those to whom it shall belong, ceasing and making to cease all troubles and obstructions to the contrary, for such is our pleasure: and in witness hereof we have signed these presents with our own hand; and to the end to make it a thing firm and stable for ever, we have caused to put and endorse our seal to the same. Given at *Nantes* in the month of April in the year of Grace 1598, and of our reign the ninth.

Signed

HENRY

DISCUSSION QUESTIONS

1. What are the edict's principal objectives?
2. In what ways does the edict balance the demands of both French Catholics and Protestants?
3. What limits does the edict place on Protestants' religious rights?
4. Did Henry IV regard this edict as a permanent solution to the religious divisions in the realm? Why or why not?

2. Barbarians All

Michel de Montaigne, *Of Cannibals* (1580s)

The Edict of Nantes was a victory not only for Henry IV but also for the politiques, moderate French Catholics and Calvinists who advocated putting the viability of the state ahead of religious uniformity. Their support of religious toleration emerged in direct response to the violence and futility of civil war. French nobleman Michel de Montaigne (1533–1592) was among the most influential voices of moderation and open-mindedness in war-torn France. Alongside his public life as a lawyer and government official, Montaigne was a prolific writer who invented a new genre in European literature, the essay, as a concise form of expression. An excerpt from one of his best-known essays, "Of Cannibals," follows. Here Montaigne casts his gaze in two directions: at newly colonized peoples in the Americas and at his fellow citizens consumed by religious hatred. In the process, he questions the basis of Europeans' supposed moral and cultural superiority over the "barbarians" of the New World.

I long had a man in my house that lived ten or twelve years in the New World, discovered in these latter days, and in that part of it where Villegaignon landed, which he called Antarctic France.[1] This discovery of so vast a country seems to be of very great consideration. I cannot be sure, that hereafter there may not be another, so many wiser men than we having been deceived in this. I am afraid our eyes are bigger than our bellies, and that we have more curiosity than capacity; for we grasp at all, but catch nothing but wind. . . .

This man that I had was a plain ignorant fellow, and therefore the more likely to tell truth: for your better-bred sort of men are much more curious in their observation, 'tis true, and discover a great deal more; but then they gloss upon it, and to give the greater weight to what they deliver, and allure your belief, they cannot forbear a little to alter the story; they never represent things to you simply as they are, but rather as they appeared to them, or as they would have them appear to you, and to gain the reputation of men of judgment, and the better to induce your faith, are willing to help out the business with something more than is really true, of their own invention. Now in this case, we should either have a man of irreproachable veracity, or so simple that he has not wherewithal to contrive, and to give a colour of truth to false relations, and who can have no ends in forging an untruth. Such a one was mine; and besides, he has at diverse times brought to me several seamen and merchants whom he had known on this same voyage. I shall therefore content myself with his information, without inquiring what the cosmographers say to the business. . . .

Now, to return to my subject, I find that there is nothing barbarous and savage in this nation, by anything that I can gather, excepting, that everyone gives the title of barbarism to everything that is not in use in his own country. As, indeed, we have no other level of truth and reason than the example and idea of the opinions and customs of the place wherein we live: there is always the perfect religion, there the perfect government, there

---

Modernized English text adapted from Michel de Montaigne, *Essays of Montaigne*, trans. Charles Cotton, ed. William Carew Hazlitt (London: Reeves and Turner, 1877), 249, 252, 253, 255, 258, 259, 260.
[1]Brazil, where he arrived in 1557. [Ed.]

the most exact and accomplished usage of all things. They are savages at the same rate that we say fruits are wild, which nature produces of herself and by her own ordinary progress; whereas, in truth, we ought rather to call those wild whose natures we have changed by our artifice and diverted from the common order. In those, the genuine, most useful, and natural virtues and properties are vigorous and sprightly, which we have helped to degenerate in these, by accommodating them to the pleasure of our own corrupted palate. And yet for all this, our taste confesses a flavour and delicacy excellent even to emulation of the best of ours, in several fruits wherein those countries abound without art or culture. . . .

These nations then seem to me to be so far barbarous, as having received but very little form and fashion from art and human invention, and consequently to be not much remote from their original simplicity. The laws of nature, however, govern them still, not as yet much vitiated with any mixture of ours: . . .

There is no manner of traffic, no knowledge of letters, no science of numbers, no name of magistrate or political superiority; no use of service, riches or poverty, no contracts, no successions, no dividends, no properties, no employments, but those of leisure, no respect of kindred, but common, no clothing, no agriculture, no metal, no use of corn or wine; the very words that signify lying, treachery, dissimulation, avarice, envy, detraction, pardon, never heard of. . . .

They have continual war with the nations that live further within the mainland, beyond their mountains, to which they go naked, and without other arms than their bows and wooden swords, fashioned at one end like the head of our javelins. The obstinacy of their battles is wonderful, and they never end without great effusion of blood: for as to running away, they know not what it is. Everyone for a trophy brings home the head of an enemy he has killed, which he fixes over the door of his house. After having a long time treated their prisoners very well, and given them all the regales they can think of, he to whom the prisoner belongs, invites a great assembly of his friends. He ties a rope to one of the arms of the prisoner, of which, at a distance, out of his reach, he holds the one end himself, and gives to the friend he loves best the other arm to hold after the same manner; and they two, in the presence of all the assembly, dispatch him with their swords. After that, they roast him, eat him amongst them, and send some chops to their absent friends. They do not do this, as some think, for nourishment . . . but as a representation of an extreme revenge; as will appear by this: that having observed the Portuguese, who were in league with their enemies, to inflict another sort of death upon any of them they took prisoners, which was to bury them in the earth up to the waist, to shoot at the remaining part till it was stuck full of arrows, and then to hang them, they thought those people of the other world (as being men who had sown the knowledge of a great many vices amongst their neighbours, and who were much greater masters in all sorts of mischief than they) did not exercise this sort of revenge without a meaning, and that it must needs be more painful than theirs, they began to leave their old way, and to follow this. I am not sorry that we should here take notice of the barbarous horror of so cruel an action, but that, seeing so clearly into their faults, we should be so blind to our own. I conceive there is more barbarity in eating a man alive, than when he is dead; in tearing a body limb from limb by racks and torments, that is yet in perfect sense; in roasting it by degrees; in causing it to be bitten and worried by dogs and swine (as we have not only read, but lately seen, not amongst inveterate and mortal enemies, but among neighbours and fellow-citizens, and, which is worse, under colour of piety and religion), than to roast and eat him after he is dead. . . .

We may then call these people barbarous, in respect to the rules of reason: but not in respect to ourselves, who in all sorts of barbarity exceed them. Their wars are throughout noble and generous, and carry as much excuse and fair pretense, as that human malady is capable of; having with them no other foundation than the sole jealousy of valour. Their disputes are not for the conquest of new lands, for these they already possess are so fruitful by nature, as to supply them without labour or concern, with all things necessary, in such abundance that they have no need to enlarge their borders. And they are, moreover, happy in this, that they only covet so much as their natural necessities require: all beyond that is superfluous to them.

DISCUSSION QUESTIONS

1. How does Montaigne describe the indigenous Americans?

2. How does indigenous American culture compare to that of Europeans' according to Montaigne? Who is more barbaric, and why? Why does Montaigne make such a comparison?

3. What does this essay suggest about the ways in which the colonization of the New World affected European identity and self-understanding?

3. Defending Religious Liberty

Apology of the Bohemian Estates (May 25, 1618)

Even as Henry IV worked to bring peace between French Catholics and Calvinists, an even bloodier chapter in European religious wars lay ahead. By the early 1600s, Calvinists had grown in numbers and political clout in the Holy Roman Empire, but unlike their French counterparts, they did not enjoy full legal recognition. The kingdom of Bohemia was a hotbed of Calvinist discontent within the empire. Bolstered by a long tradition of defending their religious liberty, in 1609 the nobles, knights, and city dwellers who met in the local Bohemian legislature (estates) gained a series of concessions, much to the outrage of the king-elect, Ferdinand II. Working in tandem with regents ruling in the name of the current king and Holy Roman Emperor Matthias, Ferdinand II moved to suppress both Protestantism and the local Bohemian estates and bring them more fully under imperial rule. The Protestant leaders reacted angrily, hurling two representatives of the king and their secretary out a window during a meeting to protest Ferdinand's demands. This event, the so-called defenestration of Prague, marked the first salvo in the Thirty Years' War. The document below is an extract from the Protestant rebels' Apology defending their actions in Prague. To garner support for their cause, they had the Apology published across Europe. Thus, from its very onset, the war would be waged both in battle and in the court of public opinion.

From *The Thirty Years War: A Documentary History*, ed. and trans. Tryntje Helfferich (Indianapolis: Hackett Publishing Company, 2009), 20–23, 29–30.

Apology, or Letter of Excuse, Concerning the Inevitable Causes That Forced All Three Estates of the Commendable Kingdom of Bohemia Who Receive the Body and Blood of the Lord Christ in Both Kinds[1] to Act in Their Own Defense

We, the representatives of the lords, knights, and cities of Prague, Kuttenberg, and other places: all three estates of this kingdom of Bohemia who receive the body and blood of our Lord Jesus Christ in both kinds, who confess to the Bohemian Confession,[2] and who are now assembled at the castle of Prague, unanimously make it known, both in the name of those present and also on behalf of all those absent, that:

In previous years, all three estates and inhabitants of the kingdom have faced, suffered, and endured many and various kinds of terrible hardships and tribulations in both political and ecclesiastical affairs. These were instigated and provoked by evil and turbulent people, both clergy and laymen, but especially by members of the Jesuit sect, whose impetuses, writings, and endeavors have always been aimed primarily toward fraudulently subjugating not only His Majesty,[3] but also all Protestant residents and estates of this entire kingdom under the lordship of the Roman See,[4] a foreign authority. Hereafter, however, in the years 1609 and [16]10 a perfect peace was erected. The Letter of Majesty[5] of His Imperial Majesty of blessed memory, Emperor Rudolph [II],[6] as well as an accommodation[7] made by both sides (Catholics and Protestants) and a general diet,[8] all forcefully confirmed and approved that no side would molest the other; but rather, according to the accommodation that they had made and erected between them, both Catholics and Protestants might and ought freely and peacefully to serve the Lord God everywhere, in any place, and without any interruption by either ecclesiastic or temporal authority. And all of this and more was contained and indicated by the said Letter of Majesty, the accommodation, and the general diet.

---

[1]Inspired by the message of Jan Hus (see Chapter 13, Document 4), Christians in Bohemia had gained the right to receive Communion in both kinds in the mid-fifteenth century. They later became the core of the Protestant movement in the region. [Ed.]

[2]The Bohemian Confession was a statement of faith made at the 1575 Diet of Prague. It was generally based on the Lutheran Augsburg Confession (1530), but was vague enough eventually to represent a basic point of agreement for all non-Catholics in Bohemia, including the Brethren, Lutherans, and Calvinists.

[3]The king of Bohemia King Matthias was both Holy Roman Emperor and king of Bohemia. [Ed.]

[4]The papacy.

[5]The Letter of Majesty was signed by Emperor Rudolph II on July 9, 1609. It affirmed the Bohemian Confession, guaranteed religious freedom in the kingdom, established a unified Protestant consistory for church government, gave control of the University of Prague to the Protestants, allowed the estates to appoint twenty-four religious Defenders, and allowed the estates to keep their existing churches and build new ones on crown lands.

[6]Emperor Rudolph II (1552–1612) was king of Bohemia from 1575 to 1611. . . .

[7]The accommodation, also referred to elsewhere as the union, was an agreement made between the Protestant and Catholic estates over certain points of contention not covered by the Letter of Majesty.

[8]A general diet was a meeting of the full Bohemian parliament. In addition to serving as the principal political and legislative body, the Bohemian diet also claimed the right to elect the king.

At the assumption of his reign in this kingdom and following the customs of this land, His Imperial Majesty, now our most gracious king and lord, also admirably and powerfully approved and confirmed this — not only generally, but also specifically.

Yet nevertheless, the above-mentioned enemies of the king, land, and general peace spared no effort to find a way to negate the concord (which had been both desired and confirmed) and to carry out their evil, extremely dangerous, and pernicious intentions toward this kingdom and our successors. Thus even at the time when the above-mentioned peace and accommodation were being made and ratified, they advanced other persons who were, like them, Catholics; and they refused to subscribe to the Letter of Majesty and the erected accommodation, or to the amnesty.[9] . . . Instead they strove to abolish completely all of this, truly proving their malicious disposition and intentions toward quite a few members of the estates. . . .

[The authors accuse these men, whom they call traitors, of attempting to block the proper line of royal succession in order to undermine Bohemian Protestantism.]

Then, using the Jesuits and other tools of theirs, [these enemies] once again began to issue a variety of abuse, slander, and denunciations against Protestants, giving people to understand, both in public writings and by word of mouth, that we were heretics, with whom (according to their teaching) one was not bound to keep any faith, either promised or proscribed, no matter its importance. They also dishonored us with all kinds of ignominious names and demonstrated great contempt for our teachings and the Protestant religion, and in their libelous publications also proclaimed that Protestants and all of those who were not Roman Catholic had rejected a life of honor: thereby animating the secular authorities to use fire and sword to eradicate Protestantism. And so that they could all the more easily deceive the people and provoke and bring about mistrust among the Protestant members of the estates, the enemies of this territory and of the common peace also tried to sow division among the Defenders[10] (who, with the gracious approval and ratification of His Majesty, had for very good reasons been decreed by us to be protectors of our religion — something that the oft-mentioned Letter of Majesty had granted and approved), and thereby to abolish completely the Protestant consistory.[11] . . .

Furthermore, it is more than sufficiently known and evident that, desiring to place honorable people under suspicion and cause them trouble, they [our enemies] brought everything to bear against them — even if it ran contrary to all right, equitableness, and every good order — and used both unusual and usual means to take numerous people's belongings and subject them to great hardships. Especially when it came to Evangelicals, they withheld, at the very least, their rights and justice, and tried to make black seem white, white black, loyal and obedient subjects of His Imperial Majesty disloyal, and, on the contrary, the disloyal loyal. Meanwhile they honored and elevated frivolous and evil people while helping to belittle and bring into contempt those who were well behaved. At the same time, they badly plagued, on account of religion, not only their own subjects but also those of the entire land, including without distinction both those under His Imperial Majesty's control and those who

---

[9]The amnesty was proclaimed by Rudolph II in order to protect both Catholics and non-Catholics from punishment for their actions prior to the issuance of the Letter of Majesty.

[10]The Defenders were a group of twenty-four men appointed by the estates, whose job it was to protect the religious liberties and rights of non-Catholics in the kingdom.

[11]The consistory was the instrument of church government. . . .

belonged to the ecclesiastical properties; and they used unheard-of atrocities to force people to convert to the Catholic religion against their will and against the clear language of the Letter of Majesty. Indeed, the royal judges' threats against the royal free cities brought several of these cities to the point at which they were forced to agree no longer to stand with the estates [of Bohemia], nor to be counted among their number. [The enemies] planned to do even more evil things, and when we asked them if their advice [to the emperor] had not caused the above-mentioned letter and our denunciation, they neither could, nor did, deny it.

For these above-enumerated reasons, we proceeded against two of their members — namely, Wilhelm Slawata von Chlum und Kosumberg and Jaroslav Borsita von Martinitz, otherwise known as Smeczensky[12] — as destroyers of the law and the common peace, and also because they did not keep in mind the offices and positions in which they found themselves, but instead evilly misused them toward the belittlement of the authority of His Imperial Majesty, our king and lord, as well as toward the abolishment of the common peace in this kingdom of Bohemia. And after determining from their past publications that they were indeed such as they appeared to be, in accordance with the old custom we threw both of them, along with a secretary (their sycophant who had, among other things, caused great disruptions in the towns of Prague), out the window.[13] And we shall proceed further against them (for they are still living) and their goods, as well as against all those whom they represent and defend, those who wish to persecute us or anyone else by whatever ways or means, and equally all who are destroyers of the Letter of Majesty and union, or who would perpetrate similar crimes. . . .

To which end, we, at this, our assembly at the castle of Prague, have established a kingdomwide system of defense for the good of His Imperial Majesty and this kingdom (our dear fatherland), and for the protection of our wives and children from all kinds of danger. And through this action we do not intend to do anything against His Imperial Majesty, our most gracious king and lord, nor desire to cause any inopportuneness for peaceable people or our dear Catholic friends (as long as they themselves desire to live in peace). For it is commonly recognized and known that by this action no further layperson or clergyman shall be harmed, nor any tumult result, but rather good peace shall be maintained everywhere — both in the cities of Prague and in the entire kingdom — except only for the above-listed unavoidable reasons, and then only when we neither should nor can do otherwise or any less.

DISCUSSION QUESTIONS

1. Whom do the estates target as their enemies, and why? How do they use the *Apology* as a means of justifying their actions against imperial authority?

2. Why do you think the estates chose not to target the king and Holy Roman Emperor, Matthias, for criticism? In what ways do you think this may have reflected their strategy to win support for their cause?

3. What does this document suggest about the religious causes of the Thirty Years' War? How did politics come into play?

---

[12]Two of the regents assembled to hear the estates' grievances. [Ed.]
[13]This act, the Defenestration of Prague, occurred on May 23, 1618.

4. Codifying Poverty

City of Norwich, *Poor Rolls* (1570)

During this time of religious warfare and social strife, a combination of population growth and monetary inflation further added to the sufferings of everyday people. In the second half of the sixteenth century, England's population alone grew by 70 percent. Coupled with rising food prices and a weak economy, the number of impoverished people skyrocketed. King Henry VIII's break from the Catholic Church and establishment of the Church of England meant the end of traditional sources of Catholic charity. During the reign of Elizabeth I (r. 1558–1603), both Parliament and local communities stepped in to fill the void, working to codify and centralize poor relief in new ways. With a population of approximately ten thousand, the city of Norwich was a pioneer on this front. In 1570, city leaders conducted a detailed census of the poor in order to determine the scope of poverty in the city as well as who was receiving relief at the time. The resulting document included hundreds of entries, encompassing close to three thousand local men, women, and children. The excerpts below are typical of the document as a whole. Census takers categorized the poor based on their place of residence, age, gender, and ability and/or willingness to work. As part of a broader trend of codifying the poor, the census divides the poor into three distinct groups: people worthy of alms because they were unable to work due to age or infirmity, people who allegedly could work but chose not to do so ("indifferent"), and the working poor. Although the results of the census prompted the city to double the number of people receiving aid, many were left to fend for themselves, a struggle that captures the difficulties faced by everyday people during a time of great change.

These be the names of the poor within the said City [of Norwich in the parish of St. Peter's of Southgate] as they were viewed in the year of our Lord God 1570.

Richard Rich of the age of 35 years, a husbandman who works with Mrs. Cantrell and does not stay with his wife (except at times) and helps her little. And Margaret his wife of the age of 40 years she spins white warp [wool yarn] and Joan her daughter, of the age of 12 years, that also spins the same. And Simon her son of the age of 8 years who goes to school. And Alice and Faith the eldest of the age of 8 years and the other of the age of 3 years, and have dwelt here 2 years since Whitsuntide. . . .

No alms and very poor. Able to work. To go away.

Peter Browne (porter) a cobbler of the age of 50 years and has little work. And Agnes his wife of the age of 52 years that does not work, but has been sick since Christmas but when in good health she spins white warp having three daughters, the one of the age of 18 years, and the other of the age of 14 years, and the other of the age of 13 years, who all spin when they can get it, but now they are without work: they have dwelt here these 20 years, and they have one daughter Elizabeth who is idle and sent from service with William Naught of Thorp, where she dwelt three quarters of a year.

4 pennies a week and very poor. Able to work.

Modernized English text adapted from E. M. Leonard, *The Early History of English Poor Relief* (Cambridge: Cambridge University Press, 1900), 308–10.

Rafe Claxton, boot wright, is abroad at work, and comfort his wife to his power, and is of the age of 43 years, and Anne his wife that is of the age of 27 years, and two sons; the eldest of the age of 4 years; she [the wife] spins white warp and he has dwelt here ever and now she is pregnant. . . .	4 pennies a week. Indifferent.
Thomas Matheu laborer, who is gone from his wife being of the age of 40 years, from whom she has no help, and Margaret his wife of the age of 32 years, and has no children, she spins white warp, and has dwelt here (ever) and knows not where her husband is.	No alms. Very poor.
William Brydges of the age of 40 years (a laborer) and Joan his wife, of the age of 23 years, she spins white warp, having one son and one daughter: the eldest of the age of 8 years, and they keep together and have dwelt here eight years.	No alms. Very poor. Able to work.
Also there is Thomas Gared and his wife but they live by their labor.	Indifferent.
Thomas Wylson, of the age of 30 years a basket maker, and Katherine his wife of the age of 25 years who makes buttons having two daughters the eldest of the age of 5 years, they have dwelt here ever.	Indifferent. No alms.
Myhell Coke, of the age of 40 years a laborer and his wife, of the age of 50 years, they live together, and have dwelt here about three years.	Indifferent. No alms.
Nycholas Fyld of the age of 30 years sometimes a painter, and Rose his wife of the age of 30 years who spins white warp having two sons, the eldest of the age of 6 years, and have dwelt there ever.	Very poor. No alms.

DISCUSSION QUESTIONS

1. What details do each of these entries have in common? What does this suggest about broader efforts to codify poor relief at the time?

2. Based on these excerpts, what factors do you think contributed to rising poverty rates in England?

3. What kind of work did the people included in the census do, and what does this reveal about the English economy in the late sixteenth century?

4. What does the census suggest about the family structure among the poor at the time?

5. The Scientific Challenge

Galileo, *Letter to the Grand Duchess Christina* (1615)

Italian born and educated, Galileo Galilei (1564–1642) was among the most illustrious proponents of the new science in the seventeenth century. Early in his studies, he embraced the theory held by Nicolaus Copernicus (1473–1543) that the sun, not the Earth, was at the center of the universe. Having improved on the newly invented telescope in 1609, Galileo was able to substantiate the heliocentric view that the earth revolved around the sun through

From *Discoveries and Opinions of Galileo*, trans. Stillman Drake (New York: Doubleday, 1957), 175–86.

his observations of the moon and planets. Because Galileo's work challenged both traditional scientific and religious views, it sparked considerable controversy. In the letter excerpted here, written in 1615 to Grand Duchess Christina of Tuscany, an important Catholic patron of learning, Galileo defends the validity of his findings while striving to separate matters of religious faith from the study of natural phenomena.

Galileo Galilei to The Most Serene Grand Duchess Mother

Some years ago, as Your Serene Highness well knows, I discovered in the heavens many things that had not been seen before our own age. The novelty of these things, as well as some consequences which followed from them in contradiction to the physical notions commonly held among academic philosophers, stirred up against me no small number of professors — as if I had placed these things in the sky with my own hands in order to upset nature and overturn the sciences. . . .

Well, the passage of time has revealed to everyone the truths that I previously set forth. . . . But some, besides allegiance to their original error, possess I know not what fanciful interest in remaining hostile not so much toward the things in question as toward their discoverer. No longer being able to deny them, these men now take refuge in obstinate silence, but being more than ever exasperated by that which has pacified and quieted other men, they divert their thoughts to other fancies and seek new ways to damage me. . . .

Persisting in their original resolve to destroy me and everything mine by any means they can think of, these men are aware of my views in astronomy and philosophy. They know that as to the arrangement of the parts of the universe, I hold the sun to be situated motionless in the center of the revolution of the celestial orbs while the earth rotates on its axis and revolves about the sun. . . .

Now as to the false aspersions which they so unjustly seek to cast upon me, I have thought it necessary to justify myself in the eyes of all men, whose judgment in matters of religion and of reputation I must hold in great esteem. I shall therefore discourse of the particulars which these men produce to make this opinion detested and to have it condemned not merely as false but as heretical. To this end they make a shield of their hypocritical zeal for religion. They go about invoking the Bible, which they would have minister to their deceitful purposes. Contrary to the sense of the Bible and the intention of the holy Fathers, if I am not mistaken, they would extend such authorities until even in purely physical matters — where faith is not involved — they would have us altogether abandon reason and the evidence of our senses in favor of some biblical passage, though under the surface meaning of its words this passage may contain a different sense. . . .

The reason produced for condemning the opinion that the earth moves and the sun stands still is that in many places in the Bible one may read that the sun moves and the earth stands still. Since the Bible cannot err, it follows as a necessary consequence that anyone takes an erroneous and heretical position who maintains that the sun is inherently motionless and the earth movable.

With regard to this argument, I think in the first place that it is very pious to say and prudent to affirm that the holy Bible can never speak untruth — whenever its true meaning is understood. But I believe nobody will deny that it is often very abstruse, and may say things which are quite different from what its bare words signify. Hence in expounding the Bible if one were always to confine oneself to the unadorned grammatical meaning, one might fall into error. Not only contradictions and propositions far from true might thus be made to appear in the Bible, but even grave heresies and follies. Thus it would be necessary to assign to God feet, hands, and eyes, as well as corporeal and human affections, such as anger, repentance, hatred, and sometimes even the forgetting of things past and ignorance of those to come. These propositions uttered by the Holy Ghost were set down in that manner by the sacred scribes in order to accommodate them to the capacities of the common people, who are rude and unlearned. For the sake of those who deserve to be separated from the herd, it is necessary that wise expositors should produce the true senses of such passages, together with the special reasons for which they were set down in these words. This doctrine is so widespread and so definite with all theologians that it would be superfluous to adduce evidence for it.

Hence I think that I may reasonably conclude that whenever the Bible has occasion to speak of any physical conclusion (especially those which are very abstruse and hard to understand), the rule has been observed of avoiding confusion in the minds of the common people which would render them contumacious toward the higher mysteries. Now the Bible, merely to condescend to popular capacity, has not hesitated to obscure some very important pronouncements, attributing to God himself some qualities extremely remote from (and even contrary to) His essence. Who, then, would positively declare that this principle has been set aside, and the Bible has confined itself rigorously to the bare and restricted sense of its words, when speaking but casually of the earth, of water, of the sun, or of any other created thing? Especially in view of the fact that these things in no way concern the primary purpose of the sacred writings, which is the service of God and the salvation of souls — matters infinitely beyond the comprehension of the common people.

This being granted, I think that in discussions of physical problems we ought to begin not from the authority of scriptural passages, but from sense-experiences and necessary demonstrations; for the holy Bible and the phenomena of nature proceed alike from the divine Word, the former as the dictate of the Holy Ghost and the latter as the observant executrix of God's commands. It is necessary for the Bible, in order to be accommodated to the understanding of every man, to speak many things which appear to differ from the absolute truth so far as the bare meaning of the words is concerned. But Nature, on the other hand, is inexorable and immutable; she never transgresses the laws imposed upon her, or cares a whit whether her abstruse reasons and methods of operations are understandable to men. For that reason it appears that nothing physical which sense-experience sets before our eyes, or which necessary demonstrations prove to us, ought to be called in question (much less condemned) upon the testimony of biblical passages which may have some different meaning beneath their words. For the Bible is not chained in every expression to conditions as strict as those which govern all physical effects; nor is God any less excellently revealed in Nature's actions than in the sacred statements of the Bible. . . .

From this I do not mean to infer that we need not have an extraordinary esteem for the passages of holy Scripture. On the contrary, having arrived at any certainties in physics, we ought to utilize these as the most appropriate aids in the true exposition of the

Bible and in the investigation of those meanings which are necessarily contained therein, for these must be concordant with demonstrated truths. I should judge that the authority of the Bible was designed to persuade men of those articles and propositions which, surpassing all human reasoning, could not be made credible by science, or by any other means than through the very mouth of the Holy Spirit.

Yet even in those propositions which are not matters of faith, this authority ought to be preferred over that of all human writings which are supported only by bare assertions or probable arguments, and not set forth in a demonstrative way. This I hold to be necessary and proper to the same extent that divine wisdom surpasses all human judgment and conjecture.

But I do not feel obliged to believe that that same God who has endowed us with senses, reason, and intellect has intended to forego their use and by some other means to give us knowledge which we can attain by them. He would not require us to deny sense and reason in physical matters which are set before our eyes and minds by direct experience or necessary demonstrations. This must be especially true in those sciences of which but the faintest trace (and that consisting of conclusions) is to be found in the Bible. Of astronomy, for instance, so little is found that none of the planets except Venus are so much as mentioned, and this only once or twice under the name of "Lucifer." If the sacred scribes had had any intention of teaching people certain arrangements and motions of the heavenly bodies, or had they wished us to derive such knowledge from the Bible, then in my opinion they would not have spoken of these matters so sparingly in comparison with the infinite number of admirable conclusions which are demonstrated in that science. . . .

From these things it follows as a necessary consequence that, since the Holy Ghost did not intend to teach us whether heaven moves or stands still, whether its shape is spherical or like a discus or extended in a plane, nor whether the earth is located at its center or off to one side, then so much the less was it intended to settle for us any other conclusion of the same kind. And the motion or rest of the earth and the sun is so closely linked with the things just named, that without a determination of the one, neither side can be taken in the other matters. Now if the Holy Spirit has purposely neglected to teach us propositions of this sort as irrelevant to the highest goal (that is, to our salvation), how can anyone affirm that it is obligatory to take sides on them, and that one belief is required by faith, while the other side is erroneous? Can an opinion be heretical and yet have no concern with the salvation of souls? Can the Holy Ghost be asserted not to have intended teaching us something that does concern our salvation? I would say here something that was heard from an ecclesiastic of the most eminent degree: "That the intention of the Holy Ghost is to teach us how one goes to heaven, not how heaven goes." . . .

From this it is seen that the interpretation which we impose upon passages of Scripture would be false whenever it disagreed with demonstrated truths. And therefore we should seek the incontrovertible sense of the Bible with the assistance of demonstrated truth, and not in any way try to force the hand of Nature or deny experiences and rigorous proofs in accordance with the mere sound of words that may appeal to our frailty. . . .

To that end they would forbid him the use of reason, divine gift of Providence, and would abuse the just authority of holy Scripture — which, in the general opinion of theologians, can never oppose manifest experiences and necessary demonstrations when rightly understood and applied. If I am correct, it will stand them in no stead to go running to the Bible to cover up their inability to understand (let alone resolve) their opponents' arguments.

DISCUSSION QUESTIONS

1. What do you think was Galileo's goal in writing this letter to the grand duchess?
2. What is the basis of the attacks against Galileo by his critics?
3. According to Galileo, what role should the Bible play in scientific inquiry?
4. How does this document lend support to historians who have credited Galileo for helping to popularize the principles and methods of the new science?

6. The Persecution of Witches

SOURCES IN CONVERSATION | *The Witch of Newbury* (1643) and *The Trial of Suzanne Gaudry* (1652)

Even as the new science gained support, most Europeans continued to believe in the super-natural. This belief found violent expression in a wave of witchcraft persecutions across Europe between 1560 and 1640. Older, poorer women often living on the margins of society were typical targets, and they were subjected to both formal trials and summary executions as these documents attest. The first is the cover page of a pamphlet published in England in 1643 about an event that became notorious at the time. With the English civil war in full swing, a group of parliamentary forces passing through the town of Newbury spotted a woman walking in a river with a plank. From their vantage point, she appeared to be danc-ing on the water's surface with no aid, a sure sign she was under the devil's influence, sym-bolized here by the two ravens hovering above. After she came to shore, the soldiers brought her to their commanders. When they asked her who she was and she refused to answer, they decided to execute her on the spot. The selections from the trial records of Suzanne Gaudry included below likewise attest to the predominant notion that the witches were not only agents of the devil but also most likely to be women. Although both sources originated at a time when the number of witch hunts and persecutions were in decline, they highlight the persistence of a deeply felt fear among many people regarding the presence of diabolical forces in everyday life.

From Alan C. Kors and Edward Peters, eds., *Witchcraft in Europe, 1100–1700: A Documentary History* (Philadelphia: University of Pennsylvania Press, 1972), 266–75.

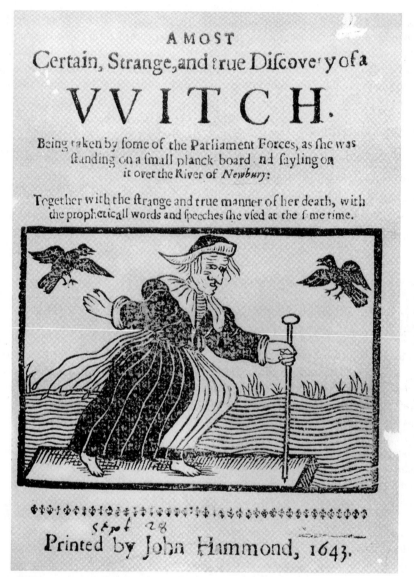

A MOST
Certain, Strange, and true Difcove·y of a
VVITCH.

Being taken by fome of the Parliament Forces, as fhe was
ftanding on a fmall planck-board, and fayling on
it over the River of *Newbury*:

Together with the ftrange and true manner of her death, with
the propheticall words and fpeeches fhe vfed at the fame time.

Printed by John Hammond, 1643.

Private Collection / Bridgeman Images

At Ronchain, 28 May, 1652. . . . Interrogation of Suzanne Gaudry, prisoner at the court of Rieux. Questioned about her age, her place of origin, her mother and father.

— Said that she is named Suzanne Gaudry, daughter of Jean Gaudry and Marguerite Gerné, both natives of Rieux, but that she is from Esgavans, near Odenarde, where her family had taken refuge because of the wars, that she was born the day that they made bonfires for the Peace between France and Spain, without being able otherwise to say her age.

Asked why she has been taken here.

— Answers that it is for the salvation of her soul.

— Says that she was frightened of being taken prisoner for the crime of witchcraft.

Asked for how long she has been in the service of the devil.

— Says that about twenty-five or twenty-six years ago she was his lover, that he called himself Petit-Grignon, that he would wear black breeches, that he gave her the name Magin, that she gave him a pin with which he gave her his mark on the left shoulder, that he had a little flat hat; said also that he had his way with her two or three times only.

Asked how many times she has been at the nocturnal dance.

— Answers that she has been there about a dozen times, having first of all renounced God, Lent, and baptism; that the site of the dance was at the little marsh of Rieux, understanding that there were diverse dances. The first time, she did not recognize anyone there, because she was half blind. The other times, she saw and recognized there Noelle and Pasquette Gerné, Noelle the wife of Nochin Quinchou and the other of Paul Doris, the widow Marie Nourette, not having recognized others because the young people went with the young people and the old people with the old. [. . .]

Interrogated on how and in what way they danced.

— Says that they dance in an ordinary way, that there was a guitarist and some whistlers who appeared to be men she did not know; which lasted about an hour, and then everyone collapsed from exhaustion.

Inquired what happened after the dance.

— Says that they formed a circle, that there was a king with a long black beard dressed in black, with a red hat, who made everyone do his bidding, and that after the dance he made a . . . [the word is missing in the text], and then everyone disappeared. . . .

Questioned if she has abused the Holy Communion.

— Says no, never, and that she has always swallowed it. Then says that her lover asked her for it several times, but that she did not want to give it to him.

After several admonitions were sent to her, she has signed this

Mark

X

Suzanne Gaudry

Second Interrogation, May 29, 1652, in the Presence of the Afore-Mentioned

This prisoner, being brought back into the chamber, was informed about the facts and the charges and asked if what she declared and confessed yesterday is true.

— Answers that if it is in order to put her in prison it is not true; then after having remained silent said that it is true.

Asked what is her lover's name and what name has he given himself.

— Said that his name is Grinniou and that he calls himself Magnin.

Asked where he found her the first time and what he did to her.

— Answers that it was in her lodgings, that he had a hide, little black breeches, and a little flat hat; that he asked her for a pin, which she gave to him, with which he made his mark on her left shoulder. Said also that at the time she took him oil in a bottle and that she had thoughts of love.

Asked how long she has been in subjugation to the devil.

— Says that it has been about twenty-five or twenty-six years, that her lover also then made her renounce God, Lent, and baptism, that he has known her carnally three or four times, and that he has given her satisfaction. And on the subject of his having asked her if she wasn't afraid of having a baby, says that she did not have that thought.

Asked how many times she found herself at the nocturnal dance and carol and who she recognized there.

— Answers that she was there eleven or twelve times, that she went there on foot with her lover, where the third time she saw and recognized Pasquette and Noelle Gerné, and Marie Homitte, to whom she never spoke, for the reason that they did not speak to each other. And that the sabbat took place at the little meadow. . . .

Asked what occurred at the dance and afterwards.

— Says that right after the dance they put themselves in order and approached the chief figure, who had a long black beard, dressed also in black, with a red hat, at which point they were given some powder, to do with it what they wanted; but that she did not want to take any.

Charged with having taken some and with having used it evilly.

— Says, after having insisted that she did not want to take any, that she took some, and that her lover advised her to do evil with it; but that she did not want to do it.

Asked if, not obeying his orders, she was beaten or threatened by him, and what did she do with this powder.

— Answers that never was she beaten; she invoked the name of the Virgin [and answered] that she threw away the powder that she had, not having wanted to do any evil with it.

Pressed to say what she did with this powder. Did she not fear her lover too much to have thrown it away?

— Says, after having been pressed on this question, that she made the herbs in her garden die at the end of the summer, five to six years ago, by means of the powder, which she threw there because she did not know what to do with it. [. . .]

Charged once more with having performed some malefice with this powder, pressed to tell the truth.

— Answers that she never made any person or beast die; then later said that she made Philippe Cornié's red horse die, about two or three years ago, by means of the powder, which she placed where he had to pass, in the street close to her home.

Asked why she did that and if she had had any difficulty with him.

— Says that she had had some difficulty with his wife, because her cow had eaten the leeks. [. . .]

After having been admonished to think of her conscience, was returned to prison after having signed this

Mark

X

Suzanne Gaudry

Deliberation of the Court of Mons — June 3, 1652

The under-signed advocates of the Court of Mons have seen these interrogations and answers. They say that the aforementioned Suzanne Gaudry confesses that she is a witch, that she has given herself to the devil, that she has renounced God, Lent, and baptism, that she has been marked on the shoulder, that she has cohabited with him and that she has been to the dances, confessing only to have cast a spell upon and caused to die a beast of Philippe Cornié; but there is no evidence for this, excepting a prior statement. For this reason, before going further, it will be necessary to become acquainted with, to examine and to probe the mark, and to hear Philippe Cornié on the death of the horse and on when and in what way he died. . . .

Deliberation of the Court of Mons — June 13, 1652

[The Court] has reviewed the current criminal trial of Suzanne Gaudry, and with it the trial of Antoinette Lescouffre, also a prisoner of the same office.

It appeared [to the Court] that the office should have the places probed where the prisoners say that they have received the mark of the devil, and after that, they must be interrogated and examined seriously on their confessions and denials, this having to be done, in order to regulate all this definitively. . . .

Deliberation of the Court of Mons — June 22, 1652

The trials of Antoinette Lescouffre and Suzanne Gaudry having been described to the undersigned, advocates of the Court of Mons, and [the Court] having been told orally that the peasants taking them to prison had persuaded them to confess in order to avoid imprisonment, and that they would be let go, by virtue of which it could appear that the confessions were not so spontaneous:

They are of the opinion that the office, in its duty, would do well, following the two preceding resolutions, to have the places of the marks that they have taught us about probed, and if it is found that these are ordinary marks of the devil, one can proceed to their examination; then next to the first confessions, and if they deny [these], one can proceed to the torture, given that they issue from bewitched relatives, that at all times they have been suspect, that they fled to avoid the crime [that is to say, prosecution for the crime of witchcraft], and that by their confessions they have confirmed [their guilt], notwithstanding that they have wanted to revoke [their confessions] and vacillate. . . .

Third Interrogation, June 27, in the Presence of the Afore-Mentioned

This prisoner being led into the chamber, she was examined to know if things were not as she had said and confessed at the beginning of her imprisonment.

— Answers no, and that what she has said was done so by force.

Asked if she did not say to Jean Gradé that she would tell his uncle, the mayor, that he had better be careful . . . and that he was a Frank.

— Said that that is not true.

Pressed to say the truth, that otherwise she would be subjected to torture, having pointed out to her that her aunt was burned for this same subject.

— Answers that she is not a witch.

Interrogated as to how long she has been in subjection to the devil, and pressed that she was to renounce the devil and the one who misled her.

— Says that she is not a witch, that she has nothing to do with the devil thus that she did not want to renounce the devil, saying that he has not misled her, and upon inquisition of having confessed to being present at the carol, she insisted that although she had said that, it is not true, and that she is not a witch.

Charged with having confessed to having made a horse die by means of a powder that the devil had given her.

— Answers that she said it, but because she found herself during the inquisition pressed to say that she must have done some evil deed; and after several admonitions to tell the truth:

She was placed in the hands of the officer of the *haultes oeuvres* [the officer in charge of torture], throwing herself on her knees, struggling to cry, uttering several exclamations, without being able, nevertheless, she shed a tear. Saying at every moment that she is not a witch.

The Torture

On this same day, being at the place of torture.

This prisoner, before being strapped down, was admonished to maintain herself in her first confessions and to renounce her lover.

— Said that she denies everything she has said, and that she has no lover. Feeling herself being strapped down, says that she is not a witch, while struggling to cry.

Asked why she fled outside the village of Rieux.

— Says that she cannot say it, that God and the Virgin Mary forbid her to; that she is not a witch. And upon being asked why she confessed to being one, said that she was forced to say it.

Told that she was not forced, that on the contrary she declared herself to be a witch without any threat.

— Says that she confessed it and that she is not a witch, and being a little stretched [on the rack] screams ceaselessly that she is not a witch, invoking the name of Jesus and of Our Lady of Grace, not wanting to say any other thing.

Asked if she did not confess that she had been a witch for twenty-six years.

— Says that she said it, that she retracts it, crying Jésus-Maria, that she is not a witch.

Asked if she did not make Philippe Cornié's horse die, as she confessed.

— Answers no, crying Jésus-Maria, that she is not a witch.

The mark having been probed by the officer, in the presence of Doctor Bouchain, it was adjudged by the aforesaid doctor and officer truly to be the mark of the devil.

Being more tightly stretched upon the torture-rack, urged to maintain her confessions.

— Said that it was true that she is a witch and that she would maintain what she had said.

Asked how long she has been in subjugation to the devil.

— Answers that it was twenty years ago that the devil appeared to her, being in her lodgings in the form of a man dressed in a little cow-hide and black breeches.

Interrogated as to what her lover was called.

— Says that she said Petit-Grignon, then, being taken down [from the rack] says upon interrogation that she is not a witch and that she can say nothing.

Asked if her lover has had carnal copulation with her, and how many times.

— To that she did not answer anything; then, making believe that she was ill, not another word could be drawn from her.

As soon as she began to confess, she asked who was alongside of her, touching her, yet none of those present could see anyone there. And it was noticed that as soon as that was said, she no longer wanted to confess anything.

Which is why she was returned to prison.

Verdict

July 9, 1652   In the light of the interrogations, answers and investigations made into the charge against Suzanne Gaudry, coupled with her confessions, from which it would appear that she has always been ill-reputed for being stained with the crime of witchcraft, and seeing that she took flight and sought refuge in this city of Valenciennes, out of fear of being apprehended by the law for this matter; seeing how her close family were also stained with the same crime, and the perpetrators executed; seeing by her own confessions that she is said to have made a pact with the devil, received the mark from him, which in the report of *sieur* Michel de Roux was judged by the medical doctor of Ronchain and the officer of *haultes oeuvres* of Cambrai, after having proved it, to be not a natural mark but a mark of the devil, to which they have sworn with an oath; and that following this, she had renounced God, Lent, and baptism and had let herself be known carnally by him, in which she received satisfaction. Also, seeing that she is said to have been a part of nocturnal carols and dances. Which are crimes of divine lèse-majesty:

For expiation of which the advice of the under-signed is that the office of Rieux can legitimately condemn the aforesaid Suzanne Gaudry to death, tying her to a gallows, and strangling her to death, then burning her body and burying it there in the environs of the woods.

At Valenciennes, the 9th of July, 1652. To each [member of the Court] 4 *livres*, 16 *sous*. . . . And for the trip of the aforementioned Roux, including an escort of one soldier, 30 *livres*.

DISCUSSION QUESTIONS

1. According to the trial record, why was Suzanne Gaudry targeted for persecution? What does this reveal about contemporary beliefs in witches and their powers?
2. How would you characterize the legal procedures used in this trial? How might the procedures help to explain the widespread consistency in the content of confessions throughout the period of witchcraft persecutions?

3. How would you describe the physical appearance of the Newbury witch? Do you think it was based on a real likeness? Why or why not? What does this indicate about contemporary notions of witchcraft and their persistence over time?

4. What do these two documents suggest about the religious anxieties of the seventeenth century?

COMPARATIVE QUESTIONS

1. How do the Edict of Nantes, "Of Cannibals," and Galileo's letter support scholars who argue that amidst the conflicts of this period, many European leaders and thinkers increasingly gave precedence to secular concerns over religious ones?

2. Despite the gradual trend in Europe toward secularization during the seventeenth century, what do the *Apology*, Galileo's letter, Suzanne Gaudry's trial records, and the Newbury witch image reveal about the continued importance of religion in shaping Europeans' self-understanding?

3. What do "Of Cannibals" and the witchcraft documents suggest about the role of violence in European society and culture?

4. In what ways is Galileo's emphasis on the value of observation and personal experience reflected in the Gaudry trial? What does this suggest about the impact of the new science on traditional beliefs?

5. What do the trial of Suzanne Gaudry, the Newbury witch image, and the Norwich poor rolls tell us about how European society treated those on the margins?

Absolutism, Constitutionalism, and the Search for Order
1640–1715

The wars of religion not only left bitter memories in late seventeenth-century Europe but also ruined economies and weakened governments. In response, many people sought to impose order on the turbulent world in a variety of ways. All of the documents in this chapter reveal that, politically, the quest for stability fueled the development of two rival systems of state building — absolutism and constitutionalism. Despite their differences, rulers within both systems centralized power and expanded bureaucracies, casting an increasingly wide net over their subjects' lives. The first document casts a critical eye on how this process played out in France in the court of Louis XIV. Not everyone submitted willingly to the expansion of state power, however. On the one hand, such resistance could have permanent repercussions, as it did during the English civil war and the ensuing debate over the nature of authority (Documents 2 to 4). On the other hand, challenges to increased state control elsewhere in Europe ultimately were no match for established governments, as the fifth document illustrates. Outside the political realm, European elites worked to set themselves apart from lower-class culture in new ways, including through their artistic tastes (Document 6).

1. The Sun King
Louis de Rouvroy, Duke of Saint-Simon, *Memoirs* (1694–1723)

A nobleman and godson of Louis XIV, Louis de Rouvroy, Duke of Saint-Simon (1675–1755), was raised at the royal palace of Versailles. He began recording his life and impressions of the court at the age of nineteen and continued for almost three decades. The result was his

Bayle St. John, trans., *The Memoirs of the Duke of Saint Simon*, vol. 2 (Philadelphia: Gebbie and Co., 1890), 363–69.

multivolume Memoirs, *which paint an intimate portrait of the Sun King and the workings of the absolutist state. Saint-Simon was not an entirely objective observer, however. Having never achieved great success within the court, he often viewed it through the lens of his own resentment. This excerpt provides insight into both the reasons behind Louis XIV's move to Versailles and his method of rule there.*

Let me touch now upon some other incidents in his career, and upon some points in his character.

He early showed a disinclination for Paris. The troubles that had taken place there during the minority made him regard the place as dangerous; he wished, too, to render himself venerable by hiding himself from the eyes of the multitude; all these considerations fixed him at St. Germains soon after the death of the Queen, his mother. It was to that place he began to attract the world by fêtes and gallantries, and by making it felt that he wished to be often seen.

His love for Madame de la Vallière, which was at first kept secret, occasioned frequent excursions to Versailles, then a little card castle, which had been built by Louis XIII. — annoyed, and his suite still more so, at being frequently obliged to sleep in a wretched inn there, after he had been out hunting in the forest of Saint Leger. That monarch rarely slept at Versailles more than one night, and then from necessity; the King, his son, slept there, so that he might be more in private with his mistress; pleasures unknown to the hero and just man, worthy son of Saint Louis, who built the little château.

These excursions of Louis XIV. by degrees gave birth to those immense buildings he erected at Versailles; and their convenience for a numerous court, so different from the apartments at St. Germains, led him to take up his abode there entirely shortly after the death of the Queen. He built an infinite number of apartments, which were asked for by those who wished to pay their court to him; whereas at St. Germains nearly everybody was obliged to lodge in the town, and the few who found accommodation at the château were strangely inconvenienced.

The frequent fêtes, the private promenades at Versailles, the journeys, were means on which the King seized in order to distinguish or mortify the courtiers, and thus render them more assiduous in pleasing him. He felt that of real favours he had not enough to bestow; in order to keep up the spirit of devotion, he therefore unceasingly invented all sorts of ideal ones, little preferences and petty distinctions, which answered his purpose as well.

He was exceedingly jealous of the attention paid him. Not only did he notice the presence of the most distinguished courtiers, but those of inferior degree also. He looked to the right and to the left, not only upon rising but upon going to bed, at his meals, in passing through his apartments, or his gardens of Versailles, where alone the courtiers were allowed to follow him; he saw and noticed everybody; not one escaped him, not even those who hoped to remain unnoticed. He marked well all absentees from the court, found out the reason of their absence, and never lost an opportunity of acting towards them as the occasion might seem to justify. With some of the courtiers (the most distinguished), it was a demerit not to make the court their ordinary abode; with others 'twas a fault to come but rarely; for those who never or scarcely ever came it was certain disgrace. When their names were in any way mentioned, "I do not know them," the King would reply haughtily. Those who presented themselves but seldom were thus characterised: "They are people I never see;" these decrees were irrevocable. He could not bear people who liked Paris.

Louis XIV. took great pains to be well informed of all that passed everywhere; in the public places, in the private houses, in society and familiar intercourse. His spies and tell-tales were infinite. He had them of all species; many who were ignorant that their information reached him; others who knew it; others who wrote to him direct, sending their letters through channels he indicated; and all these letters were seen by him alone, and always before everything else; others who sometimes spoke to him secretly in his cabinet, entering by the back stairs. These unknown means ruined an infinite number of people of all classes who never could discover the cause; often ruined them very unjustly; for the King, once prejudiced, never altered his opinion, or so rarely, that nothing was more rare. He had, too, another fault, very dangerous for others and often for himself, since it deprived him of good subjects. He had an excellent memory; in this way, that if he saw a man who, twenty years before, perhaps, had in some manner offended him, he did not forget the man, though he might forget the offence. This was enough, however, to exclude the person from all favour. The representations of a minister, of a general, of his confessor even, could not move the King. He would not yield.

The most cruel means by which the King was informed of what was passing — for many years before anybody knew it — was that of opening letters. The promptitude and dexterity with which they were opened passes understanding. He saw extracts from all the letters in which there were passages that the chiefs of the post-office and then the minister who governed it, thought ought to go before him; entire letters, too, were sent to him, when their contents seemed to justify the sending. Thus the chiefs of the post, nay, the principal clerks were in a position to suppose what they pleased and against whom they pleased. A word of contempt against the King or the government, a joke, a detached phrase, was enough. It is incredible how many people, justly or unjustly, were more or less ruined, always without resource, without trial, and without knowing why. The secret was impenetrable; for nothing ever cost the King less than profound silence and dissimulation. . . .

He liked splendour, magnificence, and profusion in everything: you pleased him if you shone through the brilliancy of your houses, your clothes, your table, your equipages. Thus a taste for extravagance and luxury was disseminated through all classes of society; causing infinite harm, and leading to general confusion of rank and to ruin.

DISCUSSION QUESTIONS

1. How did Louis XIV use court etiquette as a form of power?

2. Why did nobles reside at Versailles? What benefits did they gain?

3. What is Saint-Simon's attitude toward Louis XIV's style of governing?

4. In what ways did court life embody the principles of absolutism?

2. Regime Change

SOURCES IN CONVERSATION | *The Trial of Charles I* and *The Confession of Richard Brandon the Hangman* (1649)

The seventeenth century was particularly turbulent in England, where Protestants, Catholics, royalists, and parliamentary supporters vied for power. The English king Charles I (r. 1625–1649) had long chafed under Parliament's demands for participation in government. Adamant in his belief in his divine right to rule, Charles worked to strengthen his grip over Parliament, setting the stage for war. As the conflict spilled from the halls of government onto the battlefield in 1642, each side accused the other of undermining the ancient legal rights of the people and the legal balance between the king and the two houses of Parliament enshrined in the English constitution. Parliamentary forces ultimately defeated the king's army, and Charles surrendered in 1646. Three years later, he was brought before a parliamentary high court for trial on the charge of treason. Below are extracts from the first three days of the proceedings when the king and his opponents each laid the foundations of their case. The proceedings culminated in Charles's condemnation and a death sentence. He was beheaded on January 30, 1649, as a huge crowed looked on. Richard Brandon claimed to have been Charles's executioner and published a short tract the same year lamenting his role in the king's death. Although Brandon was the Common Hangman of London at the time, whether he beheaded Charles I is questionable; his identity would have been concealed on the scaffold, and his confession was published after his death. Even so, the woodcut print included on the tract's title page offers an important contemporary view of the scene. When set against the backdrop of the civil war, the trial and execution raised a host of enduring questions regarding the nature of political authority.

Having again placed himself in his Chair, with his face towards the Court, silence being again ordered, the Lord President stood up, and said,

LORD PRESIDENT: Charles Stuart, king of England, the Commons of England assembled in Parliament being deeply sensible of the calamities that have been brought upon this nation, which is fixed upon you as the principal author of it, have resolved to make inquisition for blood; and according to that debt and duty they owe to justice, to God, the kingdom, and themselves, and according to the fundamental power that rests in themselves, they have resolved to bring you to Trial and Judgment; and for that purpose have constituted this High Court of Justice, before which they are brought.

This said, Mr. Cook, Solicitor for the Commonwealth standing within a bar on the right hand of the Prisoner, offered to speak; but the king having a staff in his hand, held it up, and laid it on the said Mr. Cook's shoulder two or three times, bidding him hold. Nevertheless, the Lord President ordering him to go on, he said,

MR. COOK: My lord, I am commanded to charge Charles Stuart King of England, in the name of the Commons of England, with Treason and High Misdemeanors; I desire the said Charge may be read.

From *State Trials: Political and Social*, vol. I, ed. H. L. Stephen (London: Duckworth and Co., 1899), 78–87, 89, 91–94.

The said Charge being delivered to the Clerk of the Court, the Lord President ordered it should be read; but the king bid him hold. Nevertheless, being commanded by the Lord President to read it, the Clerk begun, and the Prisoner sat down again in his chair, looking sometimes on the High Court, sometimes up to the Galleries; and having risen again, and turned about to behold the guards and spectators, sat down, looking very sternly, and with a countenance not at all moved, till these words, viz.: — "Charles Stuart to be a Tyrant and Traitor," etc. were read; at which he laughed, as he sat, in the face of the Court.

The Charge being read, the Lord President replied;

LORD PRESIDENT: Sir, You have now heard your Charge, containing such matter as appears in it; you find, that in the close of it, it is prayed to the Court, in the behalf of the commons of England, that you answer to your Charge. The Court expects your Answer.

KING: . . . Remember I am your king, your lawful king, and what sins you bring upon your heads, and the judgment of God upon this land; think well upon it, I say, think well upon it, before you go further from one sin to a greater; therefore let me know by what lawful authority I am seated here, and I shall not be unwilling to answer. In the mean time, I shall not betray my trust; I have a trust committed to me by God, by old and lawful descent; I will not betray it, to answer to a new unlawful authority; therefore resolve me that and you shall hear more of me.

LORD PRESIDENT: If you had been pleased to have observed what was hinted to you by the Court, at your first coming hither, you would have known by what authority; which authority requires you, in the name of the people of England, of which you are elected king, to answer them.

KING: No. Sir, I deny that.

LORD PRESIDENT: If you acknowledge not the authority of the Court, they must proceed.

KING: I do tell them so; England was never an elective kingdom, but an hereditary kingdom, for near these thousand years; therefore let me know by what authority I am called hither. I do stand more for the Liberty of my people, than any here that come to be my pretended Judges; and therefore let me know by what lawful authority I am seated here, and I will answer it; otherwise I will not answer it. . . .

LORD PRESIDENT: The Court expects you should give them a final Answer; their purpose is to adjourn to Monday next; if you do not satisfy yourself, though we do tell you our authority, we are satisfied with our authority, and it is upon God's authority and the kingdom's; and that peace you speak of will be kept in the doing of justice, and that is our present work. . . .

At the High Court of Justice sitting in Westminster Hall, Monday, January 22, 1649. . . .

LORD PRESIDENT: Sir, You may remember at the last Court you were told the occasion of your being brought hither, and you heard a Charge read against you, containing a Charge of High Treason and other high crimes against this realm of England: you heard likewise, that it was prayed in the behalf of the People, that you should give an Answer to that Charge, that thereupon such proceedings might be had, as should be agreeable to justice. You were then pleased to make some scruples concerning the authority of this Court, and knew not by what authority you were brought hither; you did divers times propound your questions, and were as often answered. That it was by authority of the Commons of England assembled in parliament, that did think fit to call you to account for those high and capital Misdemeanours wherewith you were then charged. Since that the Court hath taken into consideration what you then said; they are fully satisfied with their own authority, and they hold it fit you should stand satisfied with it too; and they do require it, that you do give a positive and particular Answer to this Charge that is exhibited against you; they do expect you should either confess or deny it; if you deny, it is offered in the behalf of the kingdom to be made good against you; their authority they do avow to the whole world, that the whole kingdom are to rest satisfied in, and you are to rest satisfied with it. And therefore you are to lose no more time, but to give a positive Answer thereunto.

KING: When I was here last, it is very true, I made that question; truly if it were only my own particular case, I would have satisfied myself with the protestation I made the last time I was here against the Legality of this Court, and that a king cannot be tried by any superior jurisdiction on earth; but it is not my case alone, it is the Freedom and the Liberty of the people of England; and do you pretend what you will, I stand more for their Liberties. For if power without law may make laws, may alter the fundamental laws of the kingdom, I do not know what subject he is in England, that can be sure of his life, or any thing that he calls his own: therefore when that I came here, I did expect particular reasons to know by what law, what authority you did proceed against me here. And therefore I am a little to seek what to say to you in this particular, because the affirmative is to be proved, the negative often is very hard to do: but since I cannot persuade you to do it, I shall tell you my reasons as short as I can — My Reasons why in conscience and the duty I owe to God first, and my people next, for the preservation of their lives, liberties, and estates I conceive I cannot answer this, till I be satisfied of the legality of it. All proceedings against any man whatsoever —

LORD PRESIDENT: Sir, I must interrupt you, which I would not do, but that what you do is not agreeable to the proceedings of any court of justice: You are about to enter into argument, and dispute concerning the Authority of this Court, before whom you appear as a Prisoner, and are charged as an high Delinquent: if you take upon you to dispute the Authority of the Court, we may not do it, nor will any court give way unto it: you are to submit unto it, you are to give a punctual and direct Answer, whether you will answer your charge or no, and what your Answer is.

KING: Sir, By your favour, I do not know the forms of law: I do know law and reason, though I am no lawyer professed; but I know as much law as any gentleman in England; and therefore (under favour) I do plead for the Liberties of the People of England more than you do: and therefore if I should impose a belief upon any man, without reasons given for it, it were unreasonable: but I must tell you, that that reason that I have, as thus informed, I cannot yield unto it.

LORD PRESIDENT: Sir, I must interrupt you, you may not be permitted; you speak of law and reason; it is fit there should be law and reason, and there is both against you. Sir, the Vote of the Commons of England assembled in parliament, it is the reason of the kingdom, and they are these that have given to that law, according to which you should have ruled and reigned. Sir, you are not to dispute our Authority, you are told it again by the Court. Sir, it will be taken notice of, that you stand in contempt of the Court, and your contempt will be recorded accordingly. . . .

At the High Court of Justice sitting in Westminster Hall, Tuesday, January 23, 1649. . . .

LORD PRESIDENT: Sir, you have heard what is moved by the Counsel on the behalf of the kingdom against you. . . . You were told, over and over again, That the Court did affirm their own jurisdiction; that it was not for you, nor any other man, to dispute the jurisdiction of the supreme and highest Authority of England, from which there is no appeal, and touching which there must be no dispute; yet you did persist in such carriage, as you gave no manner of obedience, nor did you acknowledge any authority in them, nor the High Court that constituted this Court of Justice. Sir, I must let you know from the Court, that they are very sensible of these delays of yours, and that they ought not, being thus authorised by the supreme Court of England, to be thus trifled withal; and that they might in justice, if they pleased, and according to the rules of justice, take advantage of these delays and proceed to pronounce judgment against you; yet nevertheless they are pleased to give direction, and on their behalfs I do require you, that you make a positive Answer unto this Charge that is against you, Sir, in plain terms, for Justice knows no respect of persons; you are to give your positive and final Answer in plain English, whether you be Guilty or Not Guilty of these Treasons laid to your charge.

The King, after a little pause, said,

KING: When I was here yesterday, I did desire to speak for the Liberties of the people of England; I was interrupted; I desire to know yet whether I may speak freely or not.

LORD PRESIDENT: Sir, you have had the Resolution of the Court upon the like question the last day, and you were told that having such a Charge of so high a nature against you, and your work was, that you ought to acknowledge the jurisdiction of the Court, and to answer to your Charge. Sir, if you answer to your Charge, which the Court gives you leave now to do, though they might have taken the advantage of your contempt; yet if you be able to answer to your Charge, when you have once answered, you shall be heard at large, make the best defence you can. . . .

KING: For the Charge, I value it not a rush; it is the Liberty of the People of England that I stand for. For me to acknowledge a new Court that I never heard of before, I that am your King, that should be an example to all the people of England for to uphold justice, to maintain the old laws: indeed I do not know how to do it. You spoke very well the first day that I came here (on Saturday) of the obligations that I had laid upon me by God, to the maintenance of the Liberties of my people; the same obligation you spake of, I do acknowledge to God that I owe to him, and to my people, to defend as much as in me lies the ancient laws of the kingdom: therefore, until that I may know that this is not against the fundamental Laws of the kingdom, by your favour I can put in no particular Charge. If you will give me time, I will shew you my Reasons why I cannot do it, and this —

Here, being interrupted, he said,

By your favor, you ought not to interrupt me: How I came here, I know not; there's no law for it to make your king your prisoner. . . .

Here the Lord President said, Sir, you must know the pleasure of the Court.

KING: By your favour, sir.

LORD PRESIDENT: Nay, sir, by your favour, you may not be permitted to fall into those discourses; you appear as a Delinquent, you have not acknowledged the authority of the Court, the Court craves it not of you; but once more they command you to give your positive Answer. — Clerk, do your duty.

KING: Duty, Sir!

The Clerk reads.

"Charles Stuart, king of England, you are accused in behalf of the commons of England of divers Crimes and Treasons, which Charge hath been read unto you: the Court now requires you to give your positive and final Answer, by way of confession or denial of the Charge."

KING: Sir, I say again to you, so that I might give satisfaction to the people of England of the clearness of my proceeding, not by way of Answer, not in this way, but to satisfy them that I have done nothing against that trust that has been committed to me, I would do it; but to acknowledge a new Court, against their Privileges, to alter the fundamental laws of the kingdom — sir, you must excuse me.

LORD PRESIDENT: Sir, this is the third time that you have publicly disowned this Court, and put an affront upon it. How far you have preserved the privileges of the people, your actions have spoke it; but truly, Sir, men's intentions ought to be known by their actions; you have written your meaning in bloody characters throughout the whole kingdom. But, Sir, you understand the pleasure of the Court. — Clerk, Record the Default. — And, Gentlemen, you that took charge of the Prisoner, take him back again.

Universal History Archive / Universal Images Group / REX / Shutterstock

DISCUSSION QUESTIONS

1. According to the prosecution, why did Parliament have both a duty and a right to bring charges against the king?

2. What does the high court's argument suggest about its understanding of the role of Parliament in governance and its relationship to the monarchy?

3. In what way does the woodcut's depiction of the public nature of Charles's execution visually reinforce this understanding?

4. In his defense, why does the king refuse to acknowledge the court's authority to bring charges against him? In doing so, what did he reveal about his views on the basis of royal authority?

3. Civil War and Social Contract

Thomas Hobbes, *Leviathan* (1651)

Thomas Hobbes (1588–1679), an English philosopher with close aristocratic and royalist ties, viewed England's troubles as an indictment of traditional political thinking. According to Hobbes, in their natural state humans were violent and prone to war. Absolute authority was the only way to counter this threat to social order. Whether this authority rested in a king or a parliament was immaterial to Hobbes; what mattered was that it gained its power from a social contract, or "covenant," between ruler and ruled. Individuals agreed to relinquish their right to govern themselves to an absolute ruler in exchange for collective peace and defense. Hobbes published his views in 1651 in his book Leviathan, *most of which he wrote during the final stage of the English civil war while living in exile in France, where he was the tutor of the future king Charles II. The excerpt that follows speaks not only to Hobbes's understanding of human nature, absolute authority, and the social contract but also to the relationship among them.*

Of the Natural Condition of Mankind as Concerning Their Felicity and Misery

Nature hath made men so equal in the faculties of body and mind as that, though there be found one man sometimes manifestly stronger in body or of quicker mind than another, yet when all is reckoned together the difference between man and man is not so considerable as that one man can thereupon claim to himself any benefit to which another may not pretend as well as he.

From this equality of ability ariseth equality of hope in the attaining of our ends. And therefore if any two men desire the same thing, which nevertheless they cannot both enjoy, they become enemies; and in the way to their end (which is principally their own

---

From Thomas Hobbes, *Leviathan*, Renascence Editions, at www.luminarium.org/renascence-editions/hobbes/leviathan.html.

conservation, and sometimes their delectation only) endeavor to destroy or subdue one another. And from hence it comes to pass that where an invader hath no more to fear than another man's single power, if one plant, sow, build, or possess a convenient seat, others may probably be expected to come prepared with forces united to dispossess and deprive him, not only of the fruit of his labor, but also of his life or liberty. And the invader again is in the like danger of another. . . .

   . . . [M]en have no pleasure (but on the contrary a great deal of grief) in keeping company where there is no power able to overawe them all. For every man looketh that his companion should value him at the same rate he sets upon himself, and upon all signs of contempt or undervaluing naturally endeavors, as far as he dares (which amongst them that have no common power to keep them in quiet is far enough to make them destroy each other), to extort a greater value from his contemners, by damage; and from others, by the example. So that in the nature of man, we find three principal causes of quarrel. First, competition; secondly, diffidence; thirdly, glory. The first maketh men invade for gain; the second, for safety; and the third, for reputation. The first use violence, to make themselves masters of other men's persons, wives, children, and cattle; the second, to defend them; the third, for trifles, as a word, a smile, a different opinion, and any other sign of undervalue, either direct in their persons or by reflection in their kindred, their friends, their nation, their profession, or their name. Hereby it is manifest that during the time men live without a common power to keep them all in awe, they are in that condition which is called war; and such a war as is of every man against every man. For war consisteth not in battle only, or the act of fighting, but in a tract of time, wherein the will to contend by battle is sufficiently known: and therefore the notion of time is to be considered in the nature of war, as it is in the nature of weather. For as the nature of foul weather lieth not in a shower or two of rain, but in an inclination thereto of many days together: so the nature of war consisteth not in actual fighting, but in the known disposition thereto during all the time there is no assurance to the contrary. All other time is peace.

   Whatsoever therefore is consequent to a time of war, where every man is enemy to every man, the same consequent to the time wherein men live without other security than what their own strength and their own invention shall furnish them withal. In such condition there is no place for industry, because the fruit thereof is uncertain: and consequently no culture of the earth; no navigation, nor use of the commodities that may be imported by sea; no commodious building; no instruments of moving and removing such things as require much force; no knowledge of the face of the earth; no account of time; no arts; no letters; no society; and which is worst of all, continual fear, and danger of violent death; and the life of man, solitary, poor, nasty, brutish, and short. . . .

Of the Causes, Generation, and Definition of a Commonwealth

The final cause, end, or design of men (who naturally love liberty, and dominion over others) in the introduction of that restraint upon themselves, in which we see them live in Commonwealths, is the foresight of their own preservation, and of a more contented life thereby; that is to say, of getting themselves out from that miserable condition of war which is necessarily consequent, as hath been shown, to the natural passions of men when there is no visible power to keep them in awe, and tie them by fear of punishment to the performance of their covenants. . . .

The only way to erect such a common power, as may be able to defend them from the invasion of foreigners, and the injuries of one another, and thereby to secure them in such sort as that by their own industry and by the fruits of the earth they may nourish themselves and live contentedly, is to confer all their power and strength upon one man, or upon one assembly of men, that may reduce all their wills, by plurality of voices, unto one will: which is as much as to say, to appoint one man, or assembly of men, to bear their person; and every one to own and acknowledge himself to be author of whatsoever he that so beareth their person shall act, or cause to be acted, in those things which concern the common peace and safety; and therein to submit their wills, every one to his will, and their judgments to his judgment. This is more than consent, or concord; it is a real unity of them all in one and the same person, made by covenant of every man with every man, in such manner as if every man should say to every man: I authorize and give up my right of governing myself to this man, or to this assembly of men, on this condition; that thou give up, thy right to him, and authorize all his actions in like manner. This done, the multitude so united in one person is called a COMMONWEALTH; in Latin, CIVITAS. This is the generation of that great LEVIATHAN, or rather, to speak more reverently, of that mortal god to which we owe, under the immortal God, our peace and defense. For by this authority, given him by every particular man in the Commonwealth, he hath the use of so much power and strength conferred on him that, by terror thereof, he is enabled to form the wills of them all, to peace at home, and mutual aid against their enemies abroad. And in him consisteth the essence of the Commonwealth; which, to define it, is: one person, of whose acts a great multitude, by mutual covenants one with another, have made themselves every one the author, to the end he may use the strength and means of them all as he shall think expedient for their peace and common defense. . . .

Of the Rights of Sovereigns by Institution

A Commonwealth is said to be instituted when a multitude of men do agree, and covenant, every one with every one, that to whatsoever man, or assembly of men, shall be given by the major part the right to present the person of them all, that is to say, to be their representative; every one, as well he that voted for it as he that voted against it, shall authorize all the actions and judgments of that man, or assembly of men, in the same manner as if they were his own, to the end to live peaceably amongst themselves, and be protected against other men.

From this institution of a Commonwealth are derived all the rights and faculties of him, or them, on whom the sovereign power is conferred by the consent of the people assembled.

First, because they covenant, it is to be understood they are not obliged by former covenant to anything repugnant hereunto. And consequently they that have already instituted a Commonwealth, being thereby bound by covenant to own the actions and judgments of one, cannot lawfully make a new covenant amongst themselves to be obedient to any other, in anything whatsoever, without his permission. And therefore, they that are subjects to a monarch cannot without his leave cast off monarchy and return to the confusion of a disunited multitude; nor transfer their person from him that beareth it to another man, other assembly of men: for they are bound, every man to every man, to own and be reputed author of all that already is their sovereign shall do and judge fit to be done; so that any one man dissenting, all the rest should break their covenant made to that man, which is injustice: and they have also every man given the sovereignty to him that beareth their person; and therefore if they depose him, they take from him that which is his own, and so again it is injustice. Besides, if he that attempteth to depose his sovereign be killed or punished by him for such attempt, he is author of his own punishment, as being, by the institution, author of all his sovereign shall do; and because it is injustice for a man to do anything for which he may be punished by his own authority, he is also upon that title unjust. And whereas some men have pretended for their disobedience to their sovereign a new covenant, made, not with men but with God, this also is unjust: for there is no covenant with God but by mediation of somebody that representeth God's person, which none doth but God's lieutenant who hath the sovereignty under God. But this pretence of covenant with God is so evident a lie, even in the pretenders' own consciences, that it is not only an act of an unjust, but also of a vile and unmanly disposition.

Secondly, because the right of bearing the person of them all is given to him they make sovereign, by covenant only of one to another, and not of him to any of them, there can happen no breach of covenant on the part of the sovereign; and consequently none of his subjects, by any pretence of forfeiture, can be freed from his subjection. That he which is made sovereign maketh no covenant with his subjects before hand is manifest; because either he must make it with the whole multitude, as one party to the covenant, or he must make a several covenant with every man. With the whole, as one party, it is impossible, because as they are not one person: and if he make so many several covenants as there be men, those covenants after he hath the sovereignty are void; because what act soever can be pretended by any one of them for breach thereof is the act both of himself, and of all the rest, because done in the person, and by the right of every one of them in particular. Besides, if any one or more of them pretend a breach of the covenant made by the sovereign at his institution, and others or one other of his subjects, or himself alone, pretend there was no such breach, there is in this case no judge to decide the controversy: it returns therefore to the sword again; and every man recovereth the right of protecting himself by his own strength, contrary to the design they had in the institution. It is therefore in vain to grant sovereignty by way of precedent covenant. The opinion that any monarch receiveth his power by covenant, that is to say, on condition, proceedeth from want of understanding this easy truth: that covenants being but words, and breath, have no force to oblige, contain, constrain, or protect any man, but what it has from the public sword; that is, from the untied hands of that man, or assembly of men, that hath the sovereignty, and whose actions are avouched by them all, and performed by the strength of them all, in him united. But when an assembly of men is made sovereign, then no man imagineth any such covenant to have passed in the institution: for no man is so dull as to say, for example, the people of Rome made a covenant with the Romans to hold the sovereignty on such or such conditions; which not performed, the Romans might lawfully depose the Roman people. That men see not the reason to be alike in a monarchy and in a popular government proceedeth from the ambition of some that are kinder to the government of an assembly, whereof they may hope to participate, than of monarchy, which they despair to enjoy.

Thirdly, because the major part hath by consenting voices declared a sovereign, he that dissented must now consent with the rest; that is, be contented to avow all the actions he shall do, or else justly be destroyed by the rest. For if he voluntarily entered into the congregation of them that were assembled, he sufficiently declared thereby his will, and therefore tacitly covenanted, to stand to what the major part should ordain: and therefore if he refuse to stand thereto, or make protestation against any of their decrees, he does contrary to his covenant, and therefore unjustly. And whether he be of the congregation or not, and whether his consent be asked or not, he must either submit to their decrees or be left in the condition of war he was in before; wherein he might without injustice be destroyed by any man whatsoever.

Fourthly, because every subject is by this institution author of all the actions and judgments of the sovereign instituted, it follows that whatsoever he doth, can be no injury to any of his subjects; nor ought he to be by any of them accused of injustice. For he that doth anything by authority from another doth therein no injury to him by whose authority he acteth: but by this institution of a Commonwealth every particular man is author of all the sovereign doth; and consequently he that complaineth of injury from his sovereign complaineth of that whereof he himself is author, and therefore ought not to accuse any man but himself; no, nor himself of injury, because to do injury to oneself is impossible. It is true that they that have sovereign power may commit iniquity, but not injustice or injury in the proper signification.

Fifthly, and consequently to that which was said last, no man that hath sovereign power can justly be put to death, or otherwise in any manner by his subjects punished. For seeing every subject is author of the actions of his sovereign, he punisheth another for the actions committed by himself.

DISCUSSION QUESTIONS

1. How does Hobbes describe human nature? How might the events of the English civil war have shaped his views?

2. What is Hobbes's definition of the "Leviathan"? How is his definition linked to his understanding of the basis and role of absolute authority?

3. What does Hobbes mean by the "covenant" between sovereign and subject? How did this differ from the traditional understanding of absolute authority based on divine right?

4. According to Hobbes, did subjects bound by this covenant have the right to challenge sovereign power? Why or why not?

4. The Consent of the Governed

John Locke, *The Second Treatise of Government* (1690)

Hobbes's fellow Englishman John Locke (1632–1704) likewise viewed the tumults of his day with a critical eye. Although the English civil war ended with the restoration of Charles II to the throne, new troubles loomed. Charles openly sympathized with Catholics, as did his brother and heir, James II. Fearful of the ties between Catholicism and French absolutism, in 1678 Parliament denied the right of a Catholic to inherit the crown. Charles resisted this move, sparking a succession crisis. Locke fled to the Dutch Republic in 1683 with his patron, the Earl of Shaftesbury, who opposed a Catholic monarch. While abroad, Locke worked on his Two Treatises of Government, *which he published upon his return to England after the Glorious Revolution of 1688. A selection from the* Second Treatise *follows. As it reveals, although Locke shared Hobbes's interest in the origins of civil society, his anti-absolutist stance stood in sharp contrast to Hobbes's position. For Locke, ultimate authority rests in the will of the majority of propertied men who, in exchange for protection, endow the state with the authority to rule over them. Yet this power is not limitless. Just as the majority grants the state its power, so too can it justifiably resist it if it fails to fulfill its part of the social contract.*

Of the Beginning of Political Societies

Men being, as has been said, by nature, all free, equal, and independent, no one can be put out of this estate, and subjected to the political power of another, without his own consent. The only way whereby any one divests himself of his natural liberty, and puts on the bonds of civil society, is by agreeing with other men to join and unite into a community for their comfortable, safe, and peaceable living one amongst another, in a secure enjoyment of their properties, and a greater security against any, that are not of it. This any number of men may do, because it injures not the freedom of the rest; they are left as they were in the liberty of the state of nature. When any number of men have so consented to make one community or government, they are thereby presently incorporated, and make one body politic, wherein the majority have a right to act and conclude the rest. . . .

And thus every man, by consenting with others to make one body politic under one government, puts himself under an obligation, to every one of that society, to submit to the determination of the majority, and to be concluded by it; or else this original compact, whereby he with others incorporates into one society, would signify nothing, and be no compact, if he be left free, and under no other ties than he was in before in the state of nature. For what appearance would there be of any compact? what new engagement if he were no farther tied by any decrees of the society, than he himself thought fit, and did actually consent to? This would be still as great a liberty, as he himself had before his compact, or any one else in the state of nature hath, who may submit himself, and consent to any acts of it if he thinks fit. . . .

Whosoever therefore out of a state of nature unite into a community, must be understood to give up all the power, necessary to the ends for which they unite into society, to the majority of the community, unless they expressly agreed in any number greater than the majority. And this is done by barely agreeing to unite into one political society, which is all the compact that is, or needs be, between the individuals, that enter into, or make up a commonwealth. And thus that, which begins and actually constitutes any political

---

From John Locke, *Second Treatise on Government*, at www.ilt.columbia.edu/aca-demic/digitexts/locke/second/locke2nd.txt.

society, is nothing but the consent of any number of freemen capable of a majority to unite and incorporate into such a society. And this is that, and that only, which did, or could give beginning to any lawful government in the world.

Of the Ends of Political Society and Government

If man in the state of nature be so free, as has been said; if he be absolute lord of his own person and possessions, equal to the greatest, and subject to nobody, why will he part with his freedom? why will he give up this empire, and subject himself to the dominion and control of any other power? To which it is obvious to answer, that though in the state of nature he hath such a right, yet the enjoyment of it is very uncertain, and constantly exposed to the invasion of others: for all being kings as much as he, every man his equal, and the greater part no strict observers of equity and justice, the enjoyment of the property he has in this state is very unsafe, very unsecure. This makes him willing to quit a condition, which, however free, is full of fears and continual dangers: and it is not without reason, that he seeks out, and is willing to join in society with others, who are already united, or have a mind to unite, for the mutual preservation of their lives, liberties and estates, which I call by the general name, property.

The great and chief end, therefore, of men's uniting into commonwealths, and putting themselves under government, is the preservation of their property. To which in the state of nature there are many things wanting.

First, there wants an established, settled, known law, received and allowed by common consent to be the standard of right and wrong, and the common measure to decide all controversies between them: for though the law of nature be plain and intelligible to all rational creatures; yet men being biased by their interest, as well as ignorant for want of study of it, are not apt to allow of it as a law binding to them in the application of it to their particular cases.

Secondly, In the state of nature there wants a known and indifferent judge, with authority to determine all differences according to the established law: for every one in that state being both judge and executioner of the law of nature, men being partial to themselves, passion and revenge is very apt to carry them too far, and with too much heat, in their own cases; as well as negligence, and unconcernedness, to make them too remiss in other men's.

Thirdly, In the state of nature there often wants power to back and support the sentence when right, and to give it due execution. They who by any injustice offended, will seldom fail, where they are able, by force to make good their injustice; such resistance many times makes the punishment dangerous, and frequently destructive, to those who attempt it.

Thus mankind, notwithstanding all the privileges of the state of nature, being but in an ill condition, while they remain in it, are quickly driven into society. Hence it comes to pass, that we seldom find any number of men live any time together in this state. The inconveniences that they are therein exposed to, by the irregular and uncertain exercise of the power every man has of punishing the transgressions of others, make them take sanctuary under the established laws of government, and therein seek the preservation of their property. It is this makes them so willingly give up every one his single power of punishing, to be exercised by such alone, as shall be appointed to it amongst them; and by such rules as the community, or those authorized by them to that purpose, shall agree on. And in this we have the original right and rise of both the legislative and executive power, as well as of the governments and societies themselves.

For in the state of nature, to omit the liberty he has of innocent delights, a man has two powers.

The first is to do whatsoever he thinks fit for the preservation of himself, and others within the permission of the law of nature: by which law, common to them all, he and all the rest of mankind are one community, make up one society, distinct from all other creatures. And were it not for the corruption and viciousness of degenerate men, there would be no need of any other; no necessity that men should separate from this great and natural community, and by positive agreements combine into smaller and divided associations.

The other power a man has in the state of nature, is the power to punish the crimes committed against that law. Both these he gives up, when he joins in a private, if I may so call it, or particular politic society, and incorporates into any commonwealth, separate from the rest of mankind.

The first power, viz. of doing whatsoever he thought for the preservation of himself, and the rest of mankind, he gives up to be regulated by laws made by the society, so far forth as the preservation of himself, and the rest of that society shall require; which laws of the society in many things confine the liberty he had by the law of nature.

Secondly, The power of punishing he wholly gives up, and engages his natural force, (which he might before employ in the execution of the law of nature, by his own single authority, as he thought fit) to assist the executive power of the society, as the law thereof shall require: for being now in a new state, wherein he is to enjoy many conveniences, from the labor, assistance, and society of others in the same community, as well as protection from its whole strength; he is to part also with as much of his natural liberty, in providing for himself, as the good, prosperity, and safety of the society shall require; which is not only necessary, but just, since the other members of the society do the like.

But though men, when they enter into society, give up the equality, liberty, and executive power they had in the state of nature, into the hands of the society, to be so far disposed of by the legislative, as the good of the society shall require; yet it being only with an intention in every one the better to preserve himself, his liberty, and property; (for no rational creature can be supposed to change his condition with an intention to be worse) the power of the society, or legislative constituted by them, can never be supposed to extend farther, than the common good; but is obliged to secure every one's property, by providing against those three defects above mentioned, that made the state of nature so unsafe and uneasy. And so whoever has the legislative or supreme power of any commonwealth, is bound to govern by established standing laws, promulgated and known to the people, and not by extemporary decrees; by indifferent and upright judges, who are to decide controversies by those laws; and to employ the force of the community at home, only in the execution of such laws, or abroad to prevent or redress foreign injuries, and secure the community from inroads and invasion. And all this to be directed to no other end, but the peace, safety, and public good of the people.

DISCUSSION QUESTIONS

1. According to Locke, what is man's natural state? What are its chief characteristics?

2. Why would men relinquish the natural state to form a government? What advantages does government offer?

3. How does Locke describe the relationship between a government and its subjects? What are its terms and conditions?

4. How does Locke's proposed system guard against absolute or arbitrary power?

5. Opposing Serfdom

Ludwig Fabritius, *The Revolt of Stenka Razin* (1670)

Despite its geographic and cultural isolation from the rest of Europe, Russia watched its neighbors carefully and crafted its own brand of absolutism. In the process, Tsar Alexei (r. 1645–1676) legally combined millions of slaves and free peasants into a single serf class bound to the land and their aristocratic masters. Not everyone passively accepted this fate, however. In 1667, a Cossack named Stenka Razin (c. 1630–1671) led a revolt against serfdom that gained considerable support among people whose social and economic status was threatened by the tsar's policies, including soldiers from peasant stock. Razin's ultimate defeat at the hands of the tsar explains the close ties between the Russian government's enhanced power and the enforcement of serfdom. Ludwig Fabritius (1648–1729), a Dutch soldier who lived in Russia from 1660 to 1677 while employed as a military expert in the Russian army, wrote the following account of one stage of the revolt.

Then Stenka with his company started off upstream, rowing as far as Tsaritsyn, whence it took him only one day's journey to Panshin, a small town situated on the Don. Here he began straightaway quietly gathering the common people around him, giving them money, and promises of great riches if they would be loyal to him and help to exterminate the treacherous boyars.[1]

This lasted the whole winter, until by about spring he had assembled 4,000 to 5,000 men. With these he came to Tsaritsyn and demanded the immediate surrender of the fortress; the rabble soon achieved their purpose, and although the governor tried to take refuge in a tower, he soon had to give himself up as he was deserted by one and all. Stenka immediately had the wretched governor hanged; and all the goods they found belonging to the Tsar and his officers as well as to the merchants were confiscated and distributed among the rabble.

Stenka now began once more to make preparations. Since the plains are not cultivated, the people have to bring their corn from Nizhniy-Novgorod and Kazan down the

---

From Anthony Glenn Cross, ed., *Russia under Western Eyes, 1517–1825* (Boston: St. Martin's Press, 1971), 120–23.

[1]This term refers to a class of noblemen.

Volga in big boats known as *nasady*, and everything destined for Astrakhan has first to pass Tsaritsyn. Stenka Razin duly noted this, and occupied the whole of the Volga, so that nothing could get through to Astrakhan. Here he captured a few hundred merchants with their valuable goods, taking possession of all kinds of fine linen, silks, striped silk material, sables, soft leather, ducats, talers, and many thousands of rubles in Russian money and merchandise of every description. . . .

In the meantime four regiments of *streltsy* [musketeers] were dispatched from Moscow to subdue these brigands. They arrived with their big boats and as they were not used to the water, were easily beaten. Here Stenka Razin gained possession of a large amount of ammunition and artillery-pieces and everything else he required. While the above-mentioned [musketeers] were sent from Moscow, about 5,000 men were ordered up from Astrakhan by water and by land to capture Stenka Razin. As soon as he had finished with the former, he took up a good position, and, being in possession of reliable information regarding our forces, he left Tsaritsyn and came to meet us half way at Chernyy Yar, confronting us before we had suspected his presence or received any information about him. We stopped at Chernyy Yar for a few days and sent out scouts by water and by land, but were unable to obtain any definite information. On 10 July [sic: June] a council of war was held at which it was decided to advance and seek out Stenka. The next morning, at 8 o'clock, our look-outs on the water came hurriedly and raised the alarm as the Cossacks were following at their heels. We got out of our boats and took up battle positions. General Knyaz Semen Ivanovich Lvov went through the ranks and reminded all the men to do their duty and to remember the oath they had taken to His Majesty the Tsar, to fight like honest soldiers against these irresponsible rebels, whereupon they all unanimously shouted: "Yes, we will give our lives for His Majesty the Tsar, and will fight to the last drop of our blood."

In the meantime Stenka prepared for battle and deployed on a wide front; to all those who had no rifle he gave a long pole, burnt a little at one end, and with a rag or small hook attached. They presented a strange sight on the plain from afar, and the common soldiers imagined that, since there were so many flags and standards, there must be a host of people. They [the common soldiers] held a consultation and at once decided that this was the chance for which they had been waiting so long, and with all their flags and drums they ran over to the enemy. They began kissing and embracing one another and swore with life and limb to stand together and to exterminate the treacherous boyars, to throw off the yoke of slavery, and to become free men.

The general looked at the officers and the officers at the general, and no one knew what to do; one said this, and another that, until finally it was decided that they and the general should get into the boats and withdraw to Astrakhan. But the rascally [musketeers] of Chernyy Yar stood on the walls and towers, turning their weapons on us and opened fire; some of them ran out of the fortress and cut us off from the boats, so that we had no means of escape. In the meantime those curs of ours who had gone over to the Cossacks came up from behind. We numbered about eighty men, officers, noblemen, and clerks. Murder at once began. Then, however, Stenka Razin ordered that no more officers were to be killed, saying that there must be a few good men among them who should be pardoned, whilst those others who had not lived in amity with their men should be condemned to well-deserved punishment by the Ataman and his *Krug*. A *Krug* is a meeting convened by the order of the Ataman, at which the Cossacks stand in a circle with the standard in the center; the Ataman then takes his place beside his best officers, to whom he divulges his wishes, ordering them to make these known to the common brothers and to hear their opinion on the matter. . . .

A *Krug* was accordingly called and Stenka asked through his chiefs how the general and his officers had treated the soldiers under their command. Thereupon the unscrupulous curs, [musketeers] as well as soldiers, unanimously called out that there was not one of them who deserved to remain alive, and they all asked that their father Stepan Timofeyevich Razin should order them to be cut down. This was granted with the exception of General Knyaz Semen Ivanovich Lvov, whose life was specially spared by Stenka himself. The officers were now brought in order of rank out of the tower, into which they had been thrown bound hand and foot the previous day, their ropes were cut and they were led outside the gate. When all the bloodthirsty curs had lined up, each was eager to deal his former superior the first blow, one with the sword, another with the lance, another with the scimitar, and others again with martels, so that as soon as an officer was pushed into the ring, the curs immediately killed him with their many wounds; indeed, some were cut to pieces and straightaway thrown into the Volga. My stepfather, Paul Rudolf Beem, and Lt. Col. Wundrum and many other officers, senior and junior, were cut down before my eyes.

My own time had not yet come: this I could tell by the wonderful way in which God rescued me, for as I — half-dead — now awaited the final blow, my [former] orderly, a young soldier, came and took me by my bound arms and tried to take me down the hill. As I was already half-dead, I did not move and did not know what to do, but he came back and took me by the arms and led me, bound as I was, through the throng of curs, down the hill into the boat and immediately cut my arms free, saying that I should rest in peace here and that he would be responsible for me and do his best to save my life. . . . Then my guardian angel told me not to leave the boat, and left me. He returned in the evening and brought me a piece of bread which I enjoyed since I had had nothing to eat for two days.

The following day all our possessions were looted and gathered together under the main flag, so that both our bloodthirsty curs and the Cossacks got their share.

DISCUSSION QUESTIONS

1. What do you think motivated Razin and his followers to take action?
2. Why were Razin and his forces able to defeat the tsar's soldiers?
3. With whom do you think Fabritius's sympathies lay, and why?

6. Genre Painting

Pieter Bruegel the Younger, *A Village Kermis* (1628)

The search for order characteristic of the seventeenth century reached far beyond politics. Protestant and Catholic reformers bemoaned what they regarded to be uncivilized and ungodly practices among the general population, particularly peasants. Peasants were by far the largest segment of European society, and popular forms of entertainment, such as village fairs and festivals, were a staple of peasant life. Even as they became targets of disdain, peasant revelries feature prominently in Dutch and Flemish genre scene painting from the mid-sixteenth through the seventeenth centuries. Pieter Bruegel the Elder (c. 1525–1569) is credited with inventing the tradition, and many other artists followed suit, including his son Pieter Bruegel the Younger (c. 1564–1638). His painting reproduced here depicts a type of outdoor festival common at the time known as a kermis. The term combines the Dutch words for "church" and "mass" in reference to the mass said in honor of the local parish's patron saint. Yet the party afterward is what captured Bruegel's imagination. The entire village has come out to celebrate; they drink, jest, and dance around a maypole. Social elites were the principal buyers of this type of painting for reasons scholars continue to debate. On the one hand, they suggest, the painting itself serves as a piece of entertainment as the viewer watches the merriment and boisterous behavior unfold. On the other, the genre's implicit moral message likely appealed to the upper classes as they sought to set themselves apart from the masses.

A Village Kermesse and Peasants Dancing Round a Maypole, by Pieter Brueghel the Younger (c. 1564–1638) / Private Collection / Photo © Christie's Images / Bridgeman Images

DISCUSSION QUESTIONS

1. Describe the scene depicted in the painting. Do you think it was intended to be a realistic re-creation of everyday life?

2. What kinds of peasant activities does Bruegel depict, and how does he portray the individual villagers themselves?

3. In what ways do you think this painting may have appealed to elite buyers looking to distinguish their way of life from that of the lower classes?

COMPARATIVE QUESTIONS

1. What do these documents suggest about the basis of authority in constitutional and absolutist states? What features differentiated them as systems of government? What features did they share?

2. What similarities and differences do you see between Locke's and Hobbes's views of human nature and government? In what ways were both of them responding to the debate over political authority encapsulated by Charles I's trial?

3. In what ways does Bruegel's representation of peasant life in the Netherlands differ from that provided by Fabritius's account of the revolt against serfdom in Russia? What factors should you consider in evaluating these differences?

4. Based on Charles I's trial and the account of Stenka Razin's revolt, what factors set the English and Russian states apart? How might this help to explain why Charles I's autocratic rule failed in England while the tsar's flourished in Russia?

17

The Atlantic System and Its Consequences
1700–1750

The growth of European domestic economies and overseas colonization during the eighteenth century infused Europe with money, new products, and a new sense of optimism about the future. Yet, as Document 1 illustrates, the good times came at a horrible price for millions of African slaves who formed the economic backbone of the Atlantic system by toiling on plantations in New World colonies. Meanwhile, Europeans enjoyed slave-produced goods. New forms of social interaction emerged hand in hand with new consumption patterns, most notably at coffeehouses. Document 2 gives us a flavor of early coffeehouse culture in London, where these establishments had spread from the Ottoman Empire along trading routes. As we see in Document 3, while men ruled the public sphere of the coffeehouse, women ruled the domestic sphere through the new social custom of tea drinking in the home. Changes were also under way on the political front with the stabilization of the European state system. Consequently, states such as Russia shone more brightly over the political landscape while others lost their luster. Document 4 illuminates Tsar Peter I's diverse strategies for transforming Russia into a great power closely modeled on its western European counterparts. Documents 5 and 6 reveal that intellectual circles were also ablaze with change as scholars and writers cast political, social, and religious issues in a new critical and secular light.

1. Captivity and Enslavement

Olaudah Equiano, *The Interesting Narrative of the Life of Olaudah Equiano Written by Himself* (1789)

The autobiography of Olaudah Equiano (c. 1745–1797) puts a human face on the eighteenth-century Atlantic slave trade and its consequences. As he describes, he was born in what is now Nigeria and was captured by local raiders and sold into slavery in his early teens. He gained his freedom in 1766 and soon thereafter became a vocal supporter of the English abolitionist movement. He published his autobiography in 1789, a best seller in its day, with numerous editions published in Britain and America. In the following excerpt, Equiano recounts his journey on the slave ship that took him away from his homeland, his freedom, and his very identity. Millions of others shared this same fate. Scholars have discovered new evidence that suggests Equiano was born an enslaved person in South Carolina, so it is likely that early parts of his autobiography melded the oral history of other enslaved people with Equiano's personal experiences and emotional responses. Regardless of where Equiano was in fact born, his book is invaluable as a first-person account of slavery and one of few texts written in English during the eighteenth century by a person of African descent.

The first object which saluted my eyes when I arrived on the coast was the sea, and a slave ship which was then riding at anchor, and waiting for its cargo. These filled me with astonishment, which was soon converted into terror . . . when I was carried on board. I was immediately handled, and tossed up to see if I were sound, by some of the crew; and I was now persuaded that I had got into a world of bad spirits, and that they were going to kill me. Their complexions too differing so much from ours, their long hair, and the language they spoke (which was very different from any I had ever heard)? united to confirm me in this belief. Indeed such were the horrors of my views and fears at the moment that, if ten thousand worlds had been my own, I would have freely parted with them all to have exchanged my condition with that of the meanest slave in my own country. When I looked round the ship too and saw a large furnace or copper, boiling, and a multitude of black people, of every description, chained together, every one of their countenances expressing dejection and sorrow, I no longer doubted of my fate; and, quite overpowered with horror and anguish, I fell motionless on the deck, and fainted. When I recovered a little, I found some black people about me, who I believed were some of those who had brought me on board, and had been receiving their pay; they talked to me in order to cheer me, but all in vain. I asked them if we were not to be eaten by those white men with horrible looks, red faces, and long hair. They told me I was not: and one of the crew brought me a small portion of spirituous liquor in a wine glass; but being afraid of him I would not take it out of his hand. One of the blacks therefore took it from him and gave it to me, and I took a little down my palate, which instead of reviving me, as they thought it would, threw me into the greatest consternation at the strange feeling it produced, having never tasted such any liquor before. Soon after this the blacks who brought me on board went off, and left me abandoned to despair.

I now saw myself deprived of all chance of returning to my native country or even the least glimpse of gaining the shore, which I now considered as friendly; and I even wished for my former slavery, in preference to my present situation, which was filled with horrors of every kind, still heightened by my ignorance of what I was to undergo. I was not long suffered to indulge my grief; I was soon put down under the decks, and there I received such a salutation in my nostrils as I had never experienced in my life: so that, with the loathsomeness of the stench, and crying together, I became so sick and low that I was not able to eat, nor had I the least desire to taste anything.

From *The interesting narrative of the life of Olaudah Equiano, Written by Himself* (Penryn, England: W. Cock, 1815), 50, 51, 52, 53, 55, 56, 58, 60. https://catalog.hathitrust.org/Record/101686769.

I now wished for the last friend, death, to relieve me; but soon, to my grief, two of the white men offered me eatables; and on my refusing to eat, one of them held me fast by the hands, and laid me across, I think, the windlass, and tied my feet, while the other flogged me severely. I had never experienced anything of this kind before; and although not being used to the water, I naturally feared that element the first time I saw it, yet, nevertheless could I have got over the nettings, I would have jumped over the side, but I could not; and, besides, the crew used to watch us very closely who were not chained down to the decks, least we should leap into the water; and I have seen some of these poor African prisoners most severely cut for attempting to do so, and hourly whipped for not eating. This indeed was often the case with myself. In a little time after, amongst the poor chained men I found some of my own nation, which in a small degree gave ease to my mind; I inquired of these what was to be done with us? They gave me to understand we were to be carried to these white people's country to work for them. I then was a little revived, and thought if it were no worse than working, my situation was not so desperate: but still I feared I should be put to death, the white people looked and acted, as I thought, in so savage a manner; for I had never seen among my people such instances of brutal cruelty; and this not only shewn towards us blacks but also to some of the whites them-selves. One white man in particular I saw, when we were permitted to be on deck, flogged so unmercifully with a large rope near the foremast that he died in consequence of it; and they tossed him over the side as they would have done a brute. This made me fear these people the more; and I expected nothing less than to be treated in the same manner. . . .

At last, when the ship we were in had got in all her cargo, they made ready with many fearful noises, and we were all put under deck so that we could not see how they managed the vessel. But this disappointment was the last of my sorrow. The stench of the hold, while we were on the coast, was so intolerably loathsome, that it was dangerous to remain there for any time, and some of us had been permitted to stay on the deck for the fresh air; but now that the whole ship's cargo were confined together, it became absolutely pesti-lential. The closeness of the place, and the heat of the climate, added to the number in the ship, which was so crowded, that each had scarcely room to turn himself, almost suffo-cated us. This produced copious perspirations, so that the air soon became unfit for respi-ration, from a variety of loathsome smells, and brought on a sickness among the slaves, of which many died, thus falling victims to the improvident avarice, as I may call it, of their purchasers. This deplorable situation was again aggravated by the galling of the chains, now become insupportable; and the filth of the necessary tubs, into which the children often fell, and were almost suffocated. The shrieks of the women, and the groans of the dying, rendered the whole a scene of horror almost inconceivable. Happily, perhaps, for myself, I was soon reduced so low here that it was thought necessary to keep me almost always on deck; and from my extreme youth, I was not put in fetters. In this situation I expected every hour to share the fate of my companions, some of whom were almost daily brought upon deck at the point of death, which I began to hope would soon put an end to my miseries. . . .

At last we came in sight of the island of Barbados, at which the whites on board gave a great shout, and made many signs of joy to us. We did not know what to think of this; but as the vessel drew nearer, we plainly saw the harbor and other ships of different kinds and sizes; and we soon anchored amongst them off Bridgetown. Many merchants and planters now came on board, though it was in the evening. They put us in separate parcels, and examined us attentively. They also made us jump, and pointed to the land, signifying we were to go there. . . . We were not many days in the merchant's custody before we were sold after their usual manner, which is this: On a signal given, (as the beat of a drum) the buyers rush at once into the yard where the slaves are confined, and make choice of that parcel they like best. The noise and clamor with which this is attended and the eagerness visible in the countenances of the buyers, serve not a little to increase the apprehensions of the terrified Africans, who may well be supposed to consider them as the ministers of that destruction to which they think themselves devoted. In this manner, without scruple, are relations and friends separated, most of them never to see each other again. I remember in the vessel in which I was brought over, in the men's apartment, there were several brothers, who, in the sale, were sold in different lots; and it was very moving on this occasion to see and hear their cries at parting. O, ye nominal Christians! might not an African ask you, learned you this from your God who says unto you, Do unto all men as you would men should do unto you?

DISCUSSION QUESTIONS

1. What are Equiano's impressions of the white men on the ship and their treatment of the slaves? How does this treatment reflect the slave traders' primary concerns?

2. What message do you think Equiano sought to convey to his readers? Based on this message, to whom do you think his book especially appealed?

3. What do the last lines of this excerpt suggest about the connection between Equiano and the abolitionists' use of Christianity in their arguments against slavery?

2. A "Sober and Wholesome Drink"

SOURCES IN CONVERSATION | *A Brief Description of the Excellent Vertues of That Sober and Wholesome Drink, Called Coffee* (1674) and *The Coffee House Mob* (1710)

The expansion of the slave trade in the late seventeenth and eighteenth centuries was directly linked to Europeans' appetite for the commodities the labor of enslaved people produced, including coffee. With the drink came the rise of a new type of gathering place, the coffeehouse. In 1652, a Greek merchant who had learned to make coffee while working in a Turkish trading port opened the first coffeehouse in western Europe in London. Long a tradition in the Islamic world, the number of coffeehouses in London — and eventually all over Europe — exploded when western European trading nations moved into the business of coffee production. Coffeehouses became places for men to meet for company and conversation, often with a political bent. The broadsheet transcribed here illuminates the origins of European coffeehouse culture as merchants sought to entice customers to partake in the

Transcription of original, as reproduced in Markman Ellis, ed., *Eighteenth-Century Coffee-House Culture*, vol. 1, *Restoration Satire* (London: Pickering & Chatto, 2006), 129.

sociability of the coffeehouse. Composed of two poems, the broadsheet was printed in 1674, most likely as an advertisement for coffee, coffeehouses, and the retail coffee business of Paul Greenwood situated in the heart of London's textile district. The first poem contrasts the detrimental effects of alcohol with the "sober and merry" effects of coffee. The second describes the rules of behavior coffeehouse patrons were expected to follow. Scholars have suggested that, despite its slightly satirical tone, the poem is an accurate portrayal of the regulations governing coffeehouses. However, the engraving "The Coffee House Mob" indicates that these regulations may not always have been followed. It shows men in a coffeehouse drinking coffee, reading newspapers, and violently arguing — one patron even splashes his coffee into the face of another! For opponents of coffeehouse culture, including Edward Ward, the author of the book in which the engraving appeared, the coffeehouse fostered uncivil and even seditious behavior, not reasoned discussion.

A Brief Description of the Excellent Vertues of that Sober and Wholesome Drink, called Coffee, and its incomparable effects in preventing or curing most diseases incident to humane bodies (London, printed for Paul Greenwood ... who selleth the best Arabian Coffee-Powder and Chocolate, made in Cake or in Roll, after the Spanish Fashion, &c., 1674).[1]

When the sweet Poison of the Treacherous Grape,
Had Acted on the world a General Rape;
Drowning our very Reason and our Souls
In such deep Seas of large o'reflowing Bowls,
That New Philosophers Swore they could feel
The Earth to Stagger, as her Sons did Reel:
When Foggy Ale, leavying up mighty Trains
Of muddy Vapors, had besieg'd our Brains;
And Drink, Rebellion, and Religion too,
Made Men so Mad, they knew not what to do;
Then Heaven in Pity, to Effect our Cure,
And stop the Ragings of that Calenture,
First sent amongst us this All-*healing-Berry*,
At once to make us both *Sober* and *Merry*.
        Arabian coffee, a Rich Cordial
To Purse and Person Beneficial,
Which of so many Vertues doth partake
Its Country's called *Felix* for its sake.[2]
From the Rich Chambers of the Rising Sun,

---

[1]**Chocolate, made in Cake or in Roll, after the Spanish Fashion:** chocolate is made from the fermented, roasted, and ground beans of the cocoa tree (*Theobroma cacao*). Imported from Spanish America, chocolate was sold as a bitter paste made up into small cylindrical cakes or rolls, which were used in the preparation of hot drinks with the addition of water, sugar, and sometimes eggs. Only in the nineteenth century was eating chocolate developed.

[2]**Country's called Felix:** Arabia Felix (Arabia the happy), the name of one of three zones of the Arabian peninsula in classical geography, roughly corresponding to modern Yemen.

. . .

COFFEE arrives, that Grave and wholesome Liquor,
That heals the Stomack, makes the Genius quicker,
Relieves the Memory, Revives the Sad,
And cheers the Spirits, without making Mad;

. . .

Its constant Use the sullenest Griefs will Rout,
Remove the Dropsie, gives ease to the Gout,[3]

. . .

A Friendly Entercourse[4] it doth Maintain
Between the Heart, the Liver, and the Brain,

. . .

Nor have the LADIES reason to Complain,
As fumbling Doe-littles[5] are apt to Faign;
COFFEE's no Foe to their obliging Trade,
By it Men rather are more active made;
'Tis stronger Drink, and base adulterate Wine;
Enfeebles Vigor, and makes Nature Pine;
Loaden with which, th' Impotent Sott is Led
Like a Sowe'd Hogshead to a Misses Bed;[6]
But this Rare Settle-Brain prevents those Harms,[7]
Conquers Old Sherry, and brisk Claret Charms.
Sack, I defie thee with an open Throat,
Whilst Truly COFFEE is my Antedote

. . .

The RULES and ORDERS of the COFFEE-HOUSE.[8]
Enter Sirs Freely, But first if you please,

---

[3]**Dropsie . . . Gout**: dropsy, a morbid condition characterized by the accumulation of watery fluid in the serous cavities; gout, a disease characterized by the painful inflammation of the smaller joints (*Oxford English Dictionary*).
[4]**Entercourse**: intercourse, communication between something, here the heart, liver, and brain.
[5]**fumbling Doe-littles**: one who does little, a lazy person (*OED*).
[6]**th' Impotent . . . to a Misses Bed**: a complicated disparagement: a sot is one who dulls or stupefies himself with drink, here to the state of impotence, who must be induced to visit a young woman's bed, like a pickled or soused pig's head (an unwieldy and unrewarding dish).
[7]**Settle-Brain**: something that calms the brain (*OED*).
[8]**The RULES . . . COFFEE-HOUSE**: an ironic title for a satire on coffee-house sociability. "Rules and Orders" is a commonplace phrase in legal discourse, signifying the administrative regulations of certain judicial institutions, especially courts of law, or the body of rules followed by an assembly.

Peruse our Civil-Orders,[9] which are these.
First, Gentry, Tradesmen, all are welcome hither,
And may without Affront sit down Together:
Pre-eminence of Place, none here should Mind,[10]
But take the next fit Seat that he can find:
Nor need any, if Finer Persons come,
Rise up for to assigne to them his Room;
To limit Mens Expense, we think not fair,
But let him forfeit Twelve-pence that shall Swear:
He that shall any Quarrel begin,
Shall give each Man a Dish t' Atone the Sin;
And so shall He, whose Complements extend
So far to drink in COFFEE to his Friend;
Let Noise of loud Disputes be quite forborn,
No Maudlin Lovers[11] here in Corners Mourn,
But all be Brisk, and Talk, but not too much
On Sacred things, Let none presume to touch,
Nor Profane Scripture, or sawcily wrong
Affairs of State[12] with an Irreverent Tongue:
Let Mirth be Innocent, an each Man see,
That all his Jests without Reflection be;
To keep the House more Quiet, and from Blame,
We Banish hence Cards, Dice, and every Game:
Nor can allow of Wagers, that Exceed
Five shillings, which oft-times much Trouble Breed;
Let all that's lost, or forfeited be spent
In such Good Liquor as the House doth Vent,
And Customers endeavor to their Powers,
For to observe still seasonable Howers.
Lastly, let each Man what he calls for Pay,
And so you're welcome to come every Day.

---

[9]**Civil-Orders**: the civil laws. A term in legal debate current in the period.

[10]**Pre-eminence of Place, none here should Mind**: seats around the table in the coffee room were not organized hierarchically, referring to the custom in coffee-houses, that each man should take the next free seat around the table.

[11]**Maudlin Lovers**: men who discuss their illicit gallantries and amors in a mawkish or sentimental manner, one of the ordeals of the coffee-house.

[12]**Affairs of State**: transactions concerning the state or nation, politics. The coffee-houses had come to be emblematic locations for debate on public affairs by those outside the court and ministry, where it was still assumed that ordinary people did not need to know about the state and its affairs.

Engraving by Edward Ward, from "Vulgus Britannicus," 1710 / Private Collection / Bridgeman Images

DISCUSSION QUESTIONS

1. What does the imprint of the broadsheet, which lists where and by whom the poem was printed, suggest about changing consumption patterns at the time and their links to Europe's growing worldwide economic connections?

2. According to the first poem, what were the medicinal effects of coffee? How might these effects have contributed to coffeehouses' growing popularity?

3. Based on the "Rules and Orders," what type of people frequented early coffeehouses? How would you describe their social interactions there?

4. Describe the scene in the engraving *The Coffee House Mob*. Based on this scene, why do you think coffeehouse rules legislated against swearing, disputes, and noise in coffeehouses?

3. A Domestic Drink

Richard Collins, *A Family at Tea* (c. 1726)

Rowdy or not, coffeehouses became a permanent fixture in seventeenth-century masculine public life. By contrast, tea, originally an exclusive import from China and later a product of British East India Company trade and of the plantation economy, was integrated into

Painting by Richard Collins, c. 1727 / Victoria and Albert Museum, London, UK / DEA Picture Library / AGE Fotostock

women's private domestic domains. Not only was tea a luxury item during this time, but the way of serving and drinking it also came to be seen as a hallmark of female refinement. The conversation piece, a type of portrait painting that became fashionable in the 1720s and early 1730s in England, illuminates the link between women, femininity, and tea forged during this time. Rather than portraying its subjects in formal or idealized settings, conversation pieces shifted attention to men, women, and children engaged in simple pleasures inside the home, including the drinking of tea. The subject matter of A Family at Tea *by Richard Collins is typical of the genre. It depicts a well-off family seated around a tea table and prominently displays their expensive silver and porcelain tea equipage: a sugar dish, a tea canister, sugar tongs, a hot-water jug, a spoon boat with teaspoons, a slop bowl, and a teapot. The composition of the painting highlights the manner in which the family consumes their tea, with the woman placed prominently alongside the tea table to showcase her role as beacon of civility, high social standing, and domestic calm.*

DISCUSSION QUESTIONS

1. Note the variation in the positions of the three figures, including the direction of their gazes. In what ways do these differences visually emphasize the woman's place of importance within the tableaux?

2. While in practice children were excluded from tea parties, they were frequently included in conversation piece paintings such as Rollins's. What role might the child play in the composition of the painting and the message the artist sought to convey?

3. Based on this painting, what type of life did tea and tea drinking embody during this period?

4. Westernizing Russian Culture

Peter I, *Decrees and Statutes* (1701–1723)

During the eighteenth century, European states turned much of their attention to the political and military scene burgeoning within Europe, vying to keep one step ahead of their rivals. Russian tsar Peter I (r. 1689–1725) was especially successful at this game, transforming Russia into a formidable European power with all the trappings of an absolutist state, including a strong army and centralized bureaucracy. After spending time abroad, notably in England and the Dutch Republic, Peter came to admire western European technology, commerce, and customs and worked relentlessly to refashion Russia accordingly. For him, Westernization was more than an act of admiration; it provided him with powerful tools for enhancing Russia's status on the European stage. Below are several decrees and a statute he issued seeking to reform various aspects of Russian life and society, all with the aim of bringing them more in line with western European models.

From *A Source Book for Russian History from Early Times to 1917,* vol. 2, ed. George Vernadsky (New Haven, CT: Yale University Press, 1972), 347, 357–58, and Eugene Schuyler, *Peter the Great: Emperor of Russia* (New York: Charles Scribner's Sons, 1884), 140–41.

The Decree on "German" Dress, 1701

Western ["German"] dress shall be worn by all the boyars, okol'nichie,[1] members of our councils and of our court . . . gentry of Moscow, secretaries . . . provincial gentry, deti boiarskie,[2] gosti,[3] government officials, strel'tsy,[4] members of the guilds purveying for our household, citizens of Moscow of all ranks, and residents of provincial cities . . . excepting the clergy (priests, deacons, and church attendants) and peasant tillers of the soil. The upper dress shall be of French or Saxon cut, and the lower dress and underwear — [including] waistcoat, trousers, boots, shoes, and hats — shall be of the German type. They shall also ride German saddles. [Likewise] the womenfolk of all ranks, including the priests', deacons', and church attendants' wives, the wives of the dragoons, the soldiers, and the strel'tsy, and their children, shall wear Western ["German"] dresses, hats, jackets, and underwear — undervests and petticoats — and shoes. From now on no one [of the above-mentioned] is to wear Russian dress or Circassian coats, sheepskin coats, or Russian peasant coats, trousers, boots, and shoes. It is also forbidden to ride Russian saddles, and the craftsmen shall not manufacture them or sell them at the marketplaces. [Note: For a breach of this decree a fine was to be collected at the town gates: forty copecks from a pedestrian and two rubles from a mounted person.]

The Decree on the Shaving of Beards and Moustaches, January 16, 1705

A decree to be published in Moscow and in all the provincial cities: Henceforth, in accordance with this, His Majesty's decree, all court attendants . . . provincial service men, government officials of all ranks, military men, all the gosti, members of the wholesale merchants' guild, and members of the guilds purveying for our household must shave their beards and moustaches. But, if it happens that some of them do not wish to shave their beards and moustaches, let a yearly tax be collected from such persons: from court attendants . . . provincial service men, military men, and government officials of all ranks — 60 rubles per person; from the gosti and members of the wholesale merchants' guild of the first class — 100 rubles per person; from members of the wholesale merchants' guild of the middle and the lower class [and] . . . from [other] merchants and townsfolk — 60 rubles per person; . . . from townsfolk [of the lower rank], boyars' servants, stagecoachmen, waggoners, church attendants (with the exception of priests and deacons), and from Moscow residents of all ranks — 30 rubles per person. Special badges shall be issued to them from the Prikaz of Land Affairs [of Public Order] . . . which they must wear. . . . As for the peasants, let a toll of two half-copecks per beard be collected at the town gates each time they enter or leave a town; and do not let the peasants pass the town gates, into or out of town, without paying this toll.

---

[1]**boyars, okol'nichie**: Nobles of the highest and second-highest rank, respectively. [Ed.]
[2]**boiarskie**: Sons of boyars. [Ed.]
[3]**gosti**: Merchants who often served the tsar in some capacity. [Ed.]
[4]**strel'tsy**: Members of the imperial guard stationed in Moscow. [Ed.]

Decree on the Invitation to Foreigners, April 17, 1702

It is sufficiently known in all the lands which the Almighty has placed under our rule, that since our accession to the throne all our efforts and intentions have tended to govern this realm in such a way that all of our subjects should, through our care for the general good, become more and more prosperous. For this end, we have always tried to maintain internal order, to defend the State against invasion, and in every possible way to improve and to extend trade. With this purpose we have been compelled to make some necessary and salutary changes in the administration, in order that our subjects might more easily gain a knowledge of matters of which they were before ignorant, and become more skilful in their commercial relations. We have therefore given orders, made dispositions, and founded institutions indispensable for increasing our trade with foreigners, and shall do the same in future. Nevertheless we fear that matters are not in such a good condition as we desire, and that our subjects cannot in perfect quietness enjoy the fruits of our labours, and we have therefore considered still other means to protect our frontier from the invasion of the enemy, and to preserve the rights and privileges of our State, and the general peace of all Christians, as is incumbent on a Christian monarch to do. To attain these worthy aims, we have endeavoured to improve our military forces, which are the protection of our State, so that our troops may consist of well-drilled men, maintained in perfect order and discipline. In order to obtain greater improvement in this respect, and to encourage foreigners, who are able to assist us in this way, as well as artists and artisans profitable to the State, to come in numbers to our country, we have issued this manifesto, and have ordered printed copies of it to be sent throughout Europe.

And as in our residence of Moscow, the free exercise of religion of all other sects, although not agreeing with our church, is already allowed, so shall this be hereby confirmed anew in such wise that we, by the power granted to us by the Almighty, shall exercise no compulsion over the consciences of men, and shall gladly allow every Christian to care for his own salvation at his own risk.

The Statute of the College of Manufactures, December 3, 1723

His Imperial Majesty is diligently striving to establish and develop in the Russian Empire such manufacturing plants and factories as are found in other states, for the general welfare and prosperity of his subjects. He [therefore] most graciously charges the College of Manufactures to exert itself in devising the means to introduce, with the least expense, and to spread in the Russian Empire these and other ingenious arts, and especially those for which materials can be found within the empire; [the College of Manufactures] must also consider the privileges that should be granted to those who might wish to found manufacturing plants and factories.

His Imperial Majesty gives permission to everyone, without distinction of rank or condition, to open factories wherever he may find suitable. This provision must be made public everywhere. . . .

In granting a privilege to establish a factory, the college must take care not to debar others who might later wish to establish similar factories. For competition between manufacturers may not only help industrial growth but also ameliorate the quality of goods and keep prices at a reasonable level, thereby benefiting all His Majesty's subjects. At the same time, in cases where existing factories are sufficient for the general needs, the college must see to it that the creation of new ones does not lead to a deterioration of original manufactures, especially through the production of inferior goods, even though they may sell at a low price. . . .

Factory owners must be closely supervised, in order that they have at their plants good and experienced [foreign] master craftsmen, who are able to train Russians in such a way that these, in turn, may themselves become masters, so that their produce may bring glory to the Russian manufactures. . . .

The factories and plants that have been built or will be built at His Majesty's expense should be turned over to private individuals as soon as they are put into good condition; let the college exert itself to this end. . . .

By the former decrees of His Majesty commercial people were forbidden to buy villages [i.e., to own serfs], the reason being that they were not engaged in any other activity beneficial for the state save commerce; but since it is now clear to all that many of them have started to found manufacturing establishments and build plants, both in companies and individually, which tend to increase the welfare of the state — and many of them have already started production; therefore permission is granted both to the gentry and to men of commerce to acquire villages for these factories without hindrance, [but] with the permission of the College of Manufactures, on the condition, however, that such villages remain permanently attached to the said factories. . . .

In order to stimulate voluntary immigration of various craftsmen from other countries into the Russian Empire, and to encourage them to establish factories and manufacturing plants freely and at their own expense, the College of Manufactures must send appropriate announcements to the Russian envoys accredited at foreign courts. The envoys should then, in an appropriate way, bring these announcements to the attention of men of various professions, urge them to come to settle in Russia, and help them to move.

DISCUSSION QUESTIONS

1. Why do you think Peter I targeted the appearance of Russians as part of his Westernization policy? What benefits do you think he hoped to gain?

2. Why did Peter I want to encourage foreigners to move to Russia? What did he offer them as incentives?

3. What do the decree on foreigners and the statute of the College of Manufactures suggest about Peter I's understanding of the role of commerce in building the power of the Russian state? In what ways was this understanding in line with broader changes in the European economy at the time?

5. Early Enlightenment

Voltaire, *Letters concerning the English Nation* (1733)

As Europe's economy expanded and its state system stabilized, many people were optimistic about human nature and its potential for improvement. This sentiment found expression in an intellectual movement known as the Enlightenment, the term used to describe a group of writers and scholars who brought a new critical, scientific, and secular approach to the study of society and its problems. François-Marie Arouet (1694–1778), known by his pen name, Voltaire, was the most prominent early Enlightenment writer. After one of several clashes with church and state officials in his native France, Voltaire left the country, ultimately finding himself in 1726 in England, where he lived for several years. While there, Voltaire learned English and became an admiring observer of English political institutions and customs, using comparison with them to criticize religious intolerance and Catholic censorship in France. All the while, Voltaire wrote letters to his friends intended to amuse them with his observations while rallying them around the principles of the Enlightenment. In this selection from a letter on John Locke, Voltaire develops the argument that religion should be considered a matter of faith and conscience and be separated from arguments concerning philosophy.

Such a multitude of reasoners having written the romance of the soul, a sage at last arose who gave, with an air of the greatest modesty, the history of it. Mr. Locke has displayed the human soul in the same manner as an excellent anatomist explains the springs of the human body. He everywhere takes the light of physics for his Guide. He sometimes presumes to speak affirmatively, but then he presumes also to doubt. Instead of concluding at once what we know not, he examines gradually what we would know. He takes an infant at the instant of his Birth; he traces, step by step, the progress of his understanding; examines what things he has in common with beasts, and what he possesses above them. Above all he consults himself; the being conscious that he himself thinks.

I shall leave, says he, to those who know more of this matter than myself, the examining whether the soul exists before or after the organization of our bodies. But I confess that it is my lot to be animated with one of those heavy souls which do not think always; and I am even so unhappy as not to conceive that it is more necessary the soul should think perpetually than that bodies should be forever in motion.

With regard to myself, I shall boast that I have the honour to be as stupid in this particular as Mr. Locke. No one shall ever make me believe that I think always; and I am as little inclined as he could be to fancy that some weeks after I was conceived I was a very learned soul, knowing at that time a thousand things which I forgot at my birth, and possessing when in the womb (though to no manner of purpose) knowledge which I lost the instant I had occasion for it, and which I have never since been able to recover perfectly.

Mr. Locke, after having destroyed innate ideas; after having fully renounced the vanity of believing that we think always; after having laid down, from the most solid principles, that ideas enter the mind through the senses; having examined our simple and complex ideas; having traced the human mind through its several operations; having showed that all the languages in the world are imperfect, and the great abuse that is made of words every moment; he at last comes to consider the extent or rather the narrow limits of human knowledge. It was in this chapter he presumed to advance, but very modestly, the following words: "We shall, perhaps, never be capable of knowing, whether a Being, purely material, thinks or not." This sage assertion was, by more divines than one, looked upon as a scandalous declaration that the soul is material and mortal. Some Englishmen, devout after their way, sounded an alarm. The superstitious are the same in society as cowards in

From *The Enlightenment: A Comprehensive Anthology*, ed. Peter Gay (New York: Simon and Schuster, 1973), 162–66.

an army; they themselves are seized with a panic fear, and communicate it to others. It was loudly exclaimed that Mr. Locke intended to destroy religion; nevertheless, religion had nothing to do in the affair, it being a question purely philosophical, altogether independent of faith and revelation. Mr. Locke's opponents needed but to examine, calmly and impartially, whether the declaring that matter can think implies a contradiction, and whether God is able to communicate thought to matter. But divines are too apt to begin their declarations with saying that God is offended when people differ from them in opinion. . . . If I might presume to give my opinion on so delicate a subject after Mr. Locke, I would say that men have long disputed on the nature and the immortality of the soul. With regard to its immortality, it is impossible to give a demonstration of it, since its nature is still the subject of controversy; which, however, must be thoroughly understood before a person can be able to determine whether it be immortal or not. Human reason is so little able, merely by its own strength, to demonstrate the immortality of the soul, that it was absolutely necessary religion should reveal it to us. It is of advantage to society in general that mankind should believe the soul to be immortal; faith commands us to do this; nothing more is required, and the matter is cleared up at once. But it is otherwise with respect to its nature; it is of little importance to religion, which only requires the soul to be virtuous, what substance it may be made of. It is a clock which is given us to regulate, but the artist has not told us of what materials the spring of this clock is composed.

I am a body and, I think, that's all I know of the matter. Shall I ascribe to an unknown cause what I can so easily impute to the only second cause I am acquainted with? Here all the School philosophers interrupt me with their arguments and declare that there is only extension and solidity in bodies, and that there they can have nothing but motion and figure. Now, motion, figure, extension and solidity cannot form a thought, and consequently the soul cannot be matter. All this, so often repeated, mighty series of reasoning, amounts to no more than this: I am absolutely ignorant what matter is; I guess but imperfectly some properties of it; now, I absolutely cannot tell whether these properties may be joined to thought. As I therefore know nothing, I maintain positively that matter cannot think. In this manner do the Schools reason.

Mr. Locke addressed these gentlemen in the candid, sincere manner following: At least confess yourselves to be as ignorant as I. Neither your imaginations nor mine are able to comprehend in what manner a body is susceptible of ideas; and do you conceive better in what manner a substance, of what kind so ever, is susceptible of them? As you cannot comprehend either matter or spirit, why will you presume to assert anything?

The superstitious man comes afterwards, and declares that all those must be burnt for the good of their souls who so much as suspect that it is possible for the body to think without any foreign assistance. But what would these people say should they themselves be proved irreligious? And, indeed, what man can presume to assert, without being guilty at the same time of the greatest impiety, that it is impossible for the Creator to form matter with thought and sensation? Consider only, I beg you, what a dilemma you bring yourselves into, you who confine in this manner the power of the Creator. Beasts have the same organs, the same sensations, the same perceptions as we; they have memory, and combine certain ideas. In case it was not in the power of God to animate matter and inform it with sensation, the consequence would be either that beasts are mere machines or that they have a spiritual soul.

Methinks it is clearly evident that beasts cannot be mere machines, which I prove thus: God has given them the very same organs of sensation as to us: If therefore they have no sensation, God has created a useless thing; now, according to your own confession, God does nothing in vain; he therefore did not create so many organs of sensation merely for them to be uninformed with this faculty; consequently beasts are not mere machines. Beasts, according to your assertion, cannot be animated with a spiritual soul; you will therefore, in spite of yourself, be reduced to this only assertion, *viz.* that God has endued the organs of beasts, who are mere matter, with the faculties of sensation and perception, which you call instinct in them. But why may not God, if he pleases, communicate to our more delicate organs that faculty of feeling, perceiving and thinking which we call human reason? To whatever side you turn, you are forced to acknowledge your own ignorance and the boundless power of the Creator. Exclaim therefore no more against the sage, the modest philosophy of Mr. Locke, which, so far from interfering with religion, would be of use to demonstrate the truth of it, in case Religion wanted any such support. For what philosophy can be of a more religious nature than that which, affirming nothing but what it conceives clearly, and conscious of its own weakness, declares that we must always have recourse to God in our examining of the first principles.

Besides, we must not be apprehensive that any philosophical opinion will ever prejudice the religion of a country. Though our demonstrations clash directly with our mysteries, that's nothing to the purpose, for the latter are not less revered upon that account by our Christian philosophers, who know very well that the objects of reason and those of faith are of a very different nature. Philosophers will never form a religious sect, the reason of which is, their writings are not calculated for the vulgar, and they themselves are free from enthusiasm. If we divide mankind into twenty parts, it will be found that nineteen of these consist of persons employed in manual labour, who will never know that such a man as Mr. Locke existed. In the remaining twentieth part how few are readers? And among such as are so, twenty amuse themselves with romances to one who studies philosophy. The thinking part of mankind are confined to a very small number, and these will never disturb the peace and tranquillity of the world.

Neither Montaigne, Locke, Bayle, Spinoza, Hobbes, Lord Shaftesbury, Collins nor Toland lighted up the firebrand of discord in their countries; this has generally been the work of divines, who, being at first puffed up with the ambition of becoming chiefs of a sect, soon grew very desirous of being at the head of a party. But what do I say? All the works of the modern philosophers put together will never make so much noise as even the dispute which arose among the Franciscans merely about the fashion of their sleeves and of their cowls.

DISCUSSION QUESTIONS

1. How does Voltaire describe Locke's approach to human understanding and knowledge?

2. Why do you think Voltaire admired this approach? In what ways did it reflect his own thinking as an Enlightenment writer?

3. Notice Voltaire's frequent use of contrast between faith and reason, religion and philosophy, faith and nature. Why are such contrasts important to Voltaire's argument? And why did some people object to making them in the first place?

6. Questioning Women's Submission

Mary Astell, *Reflections upon Marriage* (1706)

Like Voltaire, English author Mary Astell (1666–1731) helped to shape the course of the Enlightenment by surveying society with a critical eye. First published anonymously in 1700, Reflections upon Marriage, *one of her best-known books, highlights Astell's keen interest in the institution of marriage, education, and relations between the sexes. As she writes in the preface, she purposely did not reveal her name so as not to distract her readers from the book's content. However, by the third edition (published in 1706), Astell felt compelled to share a key feature of her identity. Contrary to rumors that a man may have written the original manuscript, she proclaims that the author is "happily of the feminine Gender." In the excerpt below, Astell begins by summarizing her approach and intentions and then turns to the topic at hand: women's inequality in general and their submissive role in marriage in particular. Alternatively referring to herself as "she" and "Reflector," she argues that just as one should abhor the use of arbitrary power within the state, so, too, should one within the family. Among the book's principal goals was to present spinsterhood as a viable alternative to marriage. Perhaps not surprisingly, Astell herself never married.*

Far be it from her to stir up Sedition of any sort, none can abhor it more; and she heartily wishes that our Masters would pay their Civil and Ecclesiastical Governors the same Submission, which they themselves extract from their Domestic Subjects. Nor can she imagine how she any way undermines the Masculine Empire, or blows the Trumpet of Rebellion to the Moiety of Mankind. Is it by exhorting Women, not to expect to have their own Will in any thing, but to be entirely Submissive, when once they have made choice of a Lord and Master, though he happen not to be so Wise, so Kind, or even so Just a Governor as was expected? She did not indeed advise them to think his Folly Wisdom, nor his Brutality that Love and Worship he promised in his Matrimonial Oath, for this required a Flight of Wit and Sense much above her poor Ability, and proper only to Masculine Understandings. However she did not in any manner prompt them to Resist, or to Abdicate the Perjured Spouse, though the Laws of GOD and the Land make special Provision for it, in a case wherein, as is to be feared, few Men can truly plead Not Guilty.

'Tis true, through Want of Learning, and of that Superior Genius which Men as Men lay claim to, she was ignorant of the *Natural Inferiority* of our Sex, which our Masters lay down as a Self-Evident and Fundamental Truth.[1] She saw nothing in the Reason of Things, to make this either a Principle or a Conclusion, but much to the contrary; it being Sedition at least, if not Treason to assert it in this Reign. For if by the Natural Superiority of their Sex, they mean that every Man is by Nature superior to every Woman, which is

---

From Bridget Hill, ed., *The First English Feminist: Reflections upon Marriage and Other Writings by Mary Astell* (New York, St. Martin's Press, 1986), 162–66.

[1]Possibly a reference to William Nichols, D.D., *The Duty of Inferiours Towards Their Superiours in Five Practical Discourses* (1701), in which he argued that man possesses "a higher state of natural perfection and dignity, and thereupon puts in a just claim of superiority, which everything which is of more worth has a right to, over that which has less" (pp. 87–88).

the obvious meaning, and that which must be stuck to if they would speak Sense, it would be a Sin in *any* Woman to have Dominion over *any* Man, and the greatest Queen ought not to command but to obey her Footman, because no Municipal Laws can supersede or change the Law of Nature; so that if the dominion of the Men be such, the *Salique Law*, as unjust as *English Men* have ever thought it, ought to take place over all the Earth, and the most glorious Reigns in the *English, Danish, Castilian*, and other Annals, were wicked Violations of the Law of Nature!

If they mean that *some* Men are superior to *some* Women, this is no great Discovery; had they turned the Tables they might have seen that *some* Women are Superior to *some* Men. Or had they been pleased to remember their Oaths of Allegiance and Supremacy, they might have known that *One* Woman is superior to *All* the Men in these Nations, or else they have sworn to very little purpose. And it must not be supposed, that their Reason and Religion would suffer them to take Oaths, contrary to the Law of Nature and Reason of things.

By all which it appears, that our Reflector's Ignorance is very pitiable, it may be her Misfortune but not her Crime, especially since she is willing to be better informed, and hopes she shall never be so obstinate as to shut her Eyes against the Light of Truth, which is not to be charged with Novelty, how late soever we may be blessed with the Discovery. Nor can Error, be it as Ancient as it may, ever plead Prescription against Truth. And since the only way to remove all Doubts, to answer all Objections, and to give the Mind entire Satisfaction, is not by *Affirming*, but by *Proving*, so that every one may see with their *own* Eyes, and Judge according to the best of their *own* Understandings, She hopes it is no Presumption to insist on this Natural Right of Judging for her self, and the rather, because by quitting it, we give up all the Means of Rational Conviction. Allow us then as many Glasses as you please to help our Sight, and as many good Arguments as you can afford to Convince our Understandings: But don't exact of us we beseech you, to affirm that we see such things as are only the Discovery of Men who have quicker Senses; or that we understand and Know what we have by Hearsay only, for to be so excessively Complaisant, is neither to see nor to understand.

That the Custom of the World has put Women, generally speaking, into a State of Subjection, is not denied; but the Right can no more be proved from the Fact, than the Predominancy of Vice can justify it. A certain great Man has endeavored to prove by Reasons not contemptible, that in the Original State of things the Woman was the Superior, and that her Subjection to the Man is an Effect of the Fall, and the Punishment of her Sin. And that Ingenious Theorist Mr. *Whiston*[2] asserts, That before the Fall there was a greater equality between the two Sexes. However this be 'tis certainly no Arrogance in a Woman to conclude, that she was made for the Service of GOD, and that this is her End. Because GOD made all Things for Himself, and a Rational Mind is too noble a Being to be Made for the Sake and Service of any Creature. The Service she at any time becomes obliged to pay to a Man, is only a Business by the Bye. Just as it may be any Man's Business

---

[2]William Whiston (1667–1752), divine, mathematician, and Newtonian. Author of many works including *A New Theory of the Earth* (1696). He succeeded Newton as the Lucasian Professor and did much to popularize Newton's ideas. In 1710 he was deprived of his chair for casting doubt on the doctrine of the Trinity.

and Duty to keep Hogs; he was not Made for this, but if he hires himself out to such an Employment, he ought conscientiously to perform it. Nor can anything be concluded to the contrary from St. *Paul's* Argument, *I Cor. II.* For he argues only for Decency and Order, according to the present Custom and State of things. Taking his Words strictly and literally, they prove too much, in that *Praying and Prophecying in the Church* are allowed the Women, provided they do it with their Head Covered, as well as the Men; and no inequality can be inferred from hence, their Reverence to the Sacred Oracles who engage them in such Disputes. And therefore the blame be theirs, who have unnecessarily introduced them in the present Subject, and who by saying that the *Reflections* were not agreeable to Scripture, oblige the Reflector to shew that those who affirm it must either mistake her Meaning, or the Sense of Holy Scripture, or both, if they think what they say, and do not find fault merely because they resolve to do so. For had she ever writ any thing contrary to those sacred Truths, she would be the first in pronouncing its Condemnation.

But what says the Holy Scripture? It speaks of Women as in a State of Subjection, and so it does of the *Jews* and *Christians* when under the Dominion of the *Chaldeans* and *Romans*, requiring of the one as well as of the other a quiet submission to them under whose Power they lived. But will any one say that these had a *Natural Superiority* and Right to Dominion? that they had a superior Understanding, or any Pre-eminence, except what their greater Strength acquired? Or that the other were subjected to their Adversaries for any other Reason but the Punishment of their sins, and in order to their Reformation? Or for the Exercise of their Vertue, and because the Order of the World and the Good of Society required it?

If Mankind had never sinned, Reason would always have been obeyed, there would have been no struggle for Dominion, and Brutal Power would not have prevailed. But in the lapsed State of Mankind, and now that Men will not be guided by their Reason but by their Appetites, and do not what they *ought* but what they *can*, the Reason, or that which stands for it, the Will and Pleasure of the Governor is to be the Reason of those who will not be guided by their own, and must take place for Order's sake, although it should not be conformable to right Reason. Nor can there be any Society great or little, from Empires down to private Families, with a last Resort, to determine the Affairs of that Society by an irresistible Sentence. Now unless this Supremacy be fixed somewhere, there will be a perpetual Contention about it, such is the love of Dominion, and let the Reason of things be what it may, those who have least Force, or Cunning to supply it, will have the Disadvantage. So that since Women are acknowledged to have least Bodily strength, their being commanded to obey is in pure kindness to them and for their Quiet and Security, as well as for the Exercise of their Vertue. But does it follow that Domestic Governors have more Sense than their Subjects, any more than that other Governors have? We do not find that any Man thinks the worse of his own Understanding because another has superior Power; or concludes himself less capable of a Post of Honor and Authority, because he is not Preferred to it. How much time would lie on Men's hands, how empty would the Places of Concourse be, and how silent most Companies, did Men forbear to Censure their Governors, that is in effect to think themselves Wiser. Indeed Government would be much more desirable than it is, did it invest the Possessor with a superior Understanding as well as Power. And if mere Power gives a Right to Rule, there can be no such thing as Usurpation; but a Highway-Man so long as he has strength to force, has also a Right to require our Obedience.

Again, if Absolute Sovereignty be not necessary in a State, how comes it to be so in a family? or if in a Family why not in a State; since no Reason can be alledged for the one that will not hold more strongly for the other? If the Authority of the Husband so far as it extends, is sacred and inalienable, why not of the Prince? The Domestic Sovereign is without Dispute Elected, and the Stipulations and Contract are mutual, is it not then partial in Men to the last degree, to contend for, and practice that Arbitrary Dominion in their Families, which they abhor and exclaim against in the State? For if Arbitrary Power is evil in itself, and an improper Method of Governing Rational and Free Agents, it ought not to be Practiced any where; Nor is it less, but rather more mischievous in Families than in Kingdoms, by how much 100000 Tyrants are worse than one. What though a Husband can't deprive a Wife of Life without being responsible to the Law, he may however do what is much more grievous to a generous Mind, render Life miserable, for which she has no Redress, scarce Pity which is afforded to every other Complainant. It being thought a Wife's Duty to suffer everything without Complaint. *If all Men are born free*, how is it that all Women are born slaves? as they must be if the being subjected to the *inconstant, uncertain, unknown, arbitrary Will* of Men, be the *perfect Condition of Slavery*? and if the Essence of Freedom consists, as our Masters say it does, in having a *standing Rule to live by*? And why is Slavery so much condemned and strove against in one Case, and so highly applauded, and held so necessary and so sacred in another?

DISCUSSION QUESTIONS

1. According to Mary Astell, what is women's customary status in society, and why? What evidence does Astell present to challenge this status?

2. What does the language Astell uses reveal about her style of thinking and basic intellectual beliefs?

3. Why do you think scholars characterize *Reflections upon Marriage* as a "feminist" work?

COMPARATIVE QUESTIONS

1. What do the first three documents reveal about late seventeenth- and eighteenth-century Europeans and their customs? In what ways were these customs a direct product of the European expansion of trade and the colonial plantation economy?

2. Some scholars argue that, through their leading role in new domestic patterns of tea drinking as depicted in Collins's painting, women gained some measure of self-agency and authority in eighteenth-century England. What do you think Mary Astell would have made of this claim, and why?

3. How did both Voltaire and Peter I challenge the status quo with the hope of transforming society and politics? What do you think they would have thought of each other's tactics, and why?

4. Voltaire was a deep admirer of English society. What do you think he would have made of Astell's criticisms? What does this suggest about the limitations of Enlightenment ideals?

5. In what ways do Equiano, Voltaire, and Astell challenge conventional Christian authority and beliefs? What does this suggest about the place of Christianity in European society and culture at the time?

The Promise of Enlightenment
1750–1789

The following documents represent some of the many voices of the Enlightenment, an intellectual and cultural movement during the eighteenth century that captured the minds of middle- and upper-class people across Europe and in British and French North America. As self-proclaimed "philosophes," writers of the Enlightenment were united by their belief that reason was the key to humanity's advancement as the basis of truth, liberty, and justice. Thus, for them, ideas were not abstract concepts confined to the printed page; rather, they were powerful tools for exposing society's ills and offering solutions. Philosophes cultivated and disseminated their ideals through letters, published works, and personal exchanges, often coming into conflict with church and state authorities in the process (Documents 1, 3, and 4). Yet by mid-century, people as diverse as the king of Prussia (Document 5) and a French artisan (Document 2) began to echo the Enlightenment principle that progress depended on destroying all barriers to reason, including religious intolerance and outmoded economic and judicial practices. At the same time, however, the final document demonstrates that the promise of the Enlightenment was not without contradictions.

1. Rethinking Modern Civilization

Jean-Jacques Rousseau, *Discourse on the Origin and Foundations of Inequality among Men* (1753)

Since its beginnings as an intellectual movement against absolutism, the Enlightenment had become a formidable force of change by the mid-eighteenth century. Today, Jean-Jacques Rousseau (1712–1778) is considered one of the most influential and original of the

From Jean-Jacques Rousseau, *Discourse on the Origin and Foundations of Inequality among Men*, trans. and ed. Helena Rosenblatt (Boston: Bedford/St. Martin's, 2011), 42–43, 83–85, 87–91, 93–95.

Enlightenment writers due to his broad range of interests and talents. Yet in his lifetime, the public's reception of his ideas was less certain, varying from widespread disdain to adulation. While embracing Enlightenment principles, Rousseau did not accept them at face value; instead, he subjected them to rigorous examination and critique. The document here reveals Rousseau as a man who was simultaneously of and ahead of his times. He wrote it in 1753 as part of an essay competition in which writers were invited to respond to the question, "What is the origin of inequality among men, and is it authorized by natural law?" Since the seventeenth century, political thinkers like Locke and Hobbes had argued that the origins of governments stemmed from a contract formed between "naturally" free and equal individuals. For Rousseau, the assumption that free individuals would willingly give up their freedom was based on faulty logic and, as such, needed to be exposed to the light of reason. This is precisely what he set out to do in his essay. Only by tearing down the falsehoods on which contemporary society was based could people establish the right kind of political order.

Precisely what, then, is at issue in this discourse? To mark, in the progress of things, the moment when, right replacing violence, nature was subjected to law; to explain by what marvelous chain of events the strong could resolve to serve the weak, and the people to buy an imaginary peace at the price of real felicity.

The philosophers who have examined the foundations of society have all felt it necessary to return as far back as the state of nature, but none of them has reached it. Some have not hesitated to ascribe to man in that state the notion of the just and the unjust, without bothering to show that he must have had that notion, or even that it would have been useful to him. Others have spoken of the natural right that each person has to preserve what belongs to him, without explaining what they meant by belonging. Still others, first giving the stronger authority over the weaker, had government arise immediately, without thinking of the time that must have elapsed before the words *authority* and *government* could have meaning among men. Finally, all of them, speaking continually of need, avarice, oppression, desires, and pride, transported to the state of nature ideas they acquired in society: They spoke of savage man and they described civil man. . . .

Let us therefore begin by setting aside all the facts, for they do not affect the question. The research that can be pursued on this subject should not be taken for historical truths, but only for hypothetical and conditional reasonings better suited to clarify the nature of things than to show their real origin, like those our physicists make every day concerning the formation of the world. Religion commands us to believe that since God himself drew men out of the state of nature immediately after the creation, they are unequal because he wanted them to be, but it does not forbid us to form conjectures, drawn solely from the nature of man and the beings surrounding him, about what humankind could have become if it had remained abandoned to itself. That is what I am being asked, and what I propose to examine in this discourse. . . .

Second Part

Nascent government did not have a constant and regular form. The lack of philosophy and experience allowed only present inconveniences to be perceived, and one thought of remedying others only as they presented themselves. Despite all the labors of the wisest legislators, the political state remained forever imperfect because it was almost the work of chance, and because, as having begun badly, time revealed its defects and suggested remedies but could never repair the vices of the constitution.... At first, society consisted only of some general conventions, which all individuals pledged to observe, and by which the community became the guarantor for each individual. Experience had to show how weak such a constitution was, and how easy it was for lawbreakers to avoid conviction or punishment for faults of which the public alone was to be witness and judge; the law had to be evaded in a thousand ways; inconveniences and disorders had to keep multiplying before men finally thought of confiding to private individuals the dangerous trust of public authority, and committed to magistrates the care of enforcing observance of the deliberations of the people. For to say that leaders were chosen before the confederation was created and that the ministers of laws existed before the laws themselves is a supposition that does not permit of serious debate.

It would be no more reasonable to believe that at first peoples threw themselves into the arms of an absolute master without conditions and for all time, and that the first means of providing for the common security imagined by proud and unconquered men was to rush into slavery. In fact, why did they give themselves superiors if not to defend themselves against oppression, and to protect their goods, their liberties, and their lives, which are, so to speak, the constituent elements of their being? ... It is therefore incontestable, and it is the fundamental maxim of all political right, that peoples have given themselves leaders to defend their liberty and not to enslave themselves....

Our politicians propound the same sophisms about the love of liberty that our philosophers made about the state of nature; on the basis of the things they see, they judge of very different things which they have not seen, and they attribute to men a natural inclination to servitude because of the patience with which the men who are before their eyes bear their servitude, not realizing that it is as true of liberty as it is of innocence and virtue, that their value is felt only as long as one enjoys them oneself, and the taste for them is lost as soon as they are lost....

As an untamed steed bristles its mane, stamps the ground with its hoof, and breaks away impetuously at the mere approach of the bit, while a trained horse patiently endures the whip and the spur, so barbarous man does not bend his head for the yoke that civilized man wears without a murmur, and he prefers the most turbulent freedom to tranquil subjection. Therefore it is not by the degradation of enslaved peoples that man's natural dispositions for or against servitude must be judged, but by the marvels done by all free peoples to guard themselves from oppression. I know that the former do nothing but boast incessantly of the peace and quiet they enjoy in their chains.... But when I see the others sacrifice pleasures, rest, wealth, power, and life itself for the preservation of this sole good which is so disdained by those who have lost it; when I see animals born free and abhorring captivity break their heads against the bars of their prison; when I see multitudes of entirely naked savages scorn European voluptuousness and brave hunger, fire, the sword, and death to preserve only their independence, I sense that it is not for slaves to reason about liberty....

Without entering at present into the research yet to be undertaken on the nature of the fundamental compact of all government, I here limit myself, in following common opinion, to consider the establishment of the body politic as a true contract between the people and the leaders it chooses for itself: a contract by which the two parties obligate themselves to observe laws that are stipulated in it and that form the bonds of their union. The people having, in regard to social relations, united all their wills into a single one, all the articles on which this will expresses itself become so many fundamental laws obligating all members of the state without exception, and one of these laws regulates the choice and power of magistrates charged with watching over the execution of the others. This power extends to everything that can maintain the constitution, without going so far as to change it. To it are joined honors that render the laws and their ministers respectable and, for the latter personally, prerogatives that compensate them for the difficult labors that good administration requires. The magistrate, for his part, obligates himself to use the power confided in him only according to the intention of the constituents, to maintain each one in the peaceable enjoyment of what belongs to him, and to prefer on all occasions the public utility to his own interest.

Before experience had shown or knowledge of the human heart had made men foresee the inevitable abuses of such a constitution, it must have appeared all the better because those who were charged with watching over its preservation were themselves the most interested in it. For the magistracy and its rights being established only upon the fundamental laws, should they be destroyed the magistrates would immediately cease to be legitimate, the people would no longer be bound to obey them; and since it would have been the law and not the magistrate that constituted the essence of the state, everyone would return by right to his natural liberty.

If one only paused to reflect on it attentively, this would be confirmed by new reasons, and it would be evident from the nature of the contract that it could not be irrevocable: For if there were no superior power which could guarantee the fidelity of the contracting parties or force them to fulfill their reciprocal engagements, the parties would remain sole judges in their own case, and each would always have the right to renounce the contract as soon as he found either that the other had violated its terms, or that the conditions ceased to suit him. It is on this principle that the right to abdicate can, it seems, be based. Now to consider, as we are doing, only what is of human institution, if the magistrate, who has all the power in his hands and who appropriates for himself all the advantages of the contract, nevertheless had the right to renounce his authority, then there is all the more reason that the people, who pay for all the faults of the leaders, should have the right to renounce their dependence. . . .

The different forms of governments owe their origin to the greater or lesser differences that were found among individuals at the moment of institution. If one man was eminent in power, virtue, wealth, or credit, he alone was elected magistrate, and the state became monarchical. If several men approximately equal among themselves prevailed over all others, they were elected jointly and there was an aristocracy. Those whose fortune or talents were less disproportionate, and who were the least removed from the state of nature, kept the supreme administration in common and formed a democracy. Time confirmed which of these forms was the most advantageous for men. Some remained solely subject to laws, others were soon obeying masters. Citizens wanted only to keep their freedom; subjects thought only of depriving their neighbors of theirs, since they could not bear that others should enjoy a good which they no longer enjoyed themselves. In a word, on one side were wealth and conquests, and on the other happiness and virtue. . . .

Political distinctions necessarily bring about civil distinctions. Growing inequality between the people and its leaders soon makes itself felt among private individuals, where it is modified in a thousand ways according to passions, talents, and circumstances. The magistrate cannot usurp illegitimate power without creating clients to whom he is forced to yield some part of it. Besides, citizens let themselves be oppressed only insofar as they are carried away by blind ambition; and looking more below than above them, domination becomes dearer to them than independence, and they consent to wear chains in order to give them to others in turn. It is very difficult to reduce to obedience someone who does not seek to command; and the most adroit politician would never succeed in subjecting men who wanted only to be free. But inequality spreads without difficulty among ambitious and cowardly souls, always ready to run the risks of fortune, and to dominate or serve almost indifferently, according to whether it proves favorable or adverse to them. . . .

In discovering and following thus the forgotten and lost routes that must have led man from the natural state to the civil state; in reestablishing, along with the intermediary positions I have just noted, those that the pressure of time has made me suppress or that imagination has not suggested to me, every attentive reader cannot fail to be struck by the immense space that separates these two states. It is in this slow succession of things that he will see the solution to an infinite number of problems of morals and politics which the philosophers cannot resolve. He will sense that, the humankind of one age not being the humankind of another. . . . In a word, he will explain how the soul and human passions, altering imperceptibly, change their nature so to speak; why our needs and our pleasures change their objects in the long run; why, original man vanishing by degrees, society no longer offers to the eyes of the wise man anything except an assemblage of artificial men and factitious passions which are the work of all these new relations and have no true foundation in nature. What reflection teaches us on this subject, observation confirms perfectly; savage man and civilized man differ so much in the bottom of their hearts and inclinations that what constitutes the supreme happiness of one would reduce the other to despair. The former breathes only tranquility and liberty; he wants only to live and remain idle; and even the perfect quietude of the stoic does not approach his profound indifference for all other objects. On the contrary, the citizen, always active, sweats, agitates himself, torments himself incessantly in order to seek still more laborious occupations; he works to death, he even rushes to it in order to get in condition to live, or renounces life in order to acquire immortality. He pays court to the great whom he hates, and to the rich whom he scorns. He spares nothing in order to obtain the honor of serving them; he proudly boasts of his baseness and their protection; and proud of his slavery, he speaks with disdain of those who do not have the honor of sharing it. . . . Such is, in fact, the true cause of all these differences; the savage lives within himself; the sociable man, always outside of himself, knows how to live only in the opinion of others; and it is, so to speak, from their judgment alone that he draws the sentiment of his own existence. . . .

I have tried to set forth the origin and progress of inequality, the establishment and abuse of political societies insofar as these things can be deduced from the nature of man by the light of reason alone, and independently of the sacred dogmas which give to sovereign authority the sanction of divine right. It follows from this exposition that inequality, being almost nonexistent in the state of nature, draws its force and growth from the development of our faculties and the progress of the human mind, and finally becomes stable and legitimate by the establishment of property and laws. It follows, further, that moral inequality, authorized by positive right alone, is contrary to natural right whenever it is not combined in the same proportion with physical inequality: a distinction which sufficiently determines what one ought to think in this regard of the sort of inequality that reigns among all civilized people; since it is manifestly against the law of nature, in whatever manner it is defined, that a child command an old man, an imbecile lead a wise man, and a handful of men be glutted with superfluities while the starving multitude lacks necessities.

DISCUSSION QUESTIONS

1. How does Rousseau describe the state of nature? In what ways does he think it contrasts to civil society as it developed over time?

2. Why does he think this contrast is important to understanding the foundations of government and its role in the origin of inequality among people?

3. Rousseau proposes that rather than being based on inequalities, governments should be established "as a true contract between the people and the leaders." What does he mean by "a true contract"? In what ways does he present it as a solution to contemporary society's ills?

2. An Enlightened Worker

Jacques-Louis Ménétra, *Journal of My Life* (1764–1802)

Even if the philosophes directed their message to the educated elite, Journal of My Life *by Jacques-Louis Ménétra (b. 1738) suggests that at least some people from the lower classes heard it too. Born in Paris, Ménétra learned to read and write in local parish schools. Following his father's example, he became a master glazier. He began his journal in 1764 and organized it principally around his recollections of his journeyman's "tour de France" from 1757 to 1764. He eventually returned to Paris, where he set up his own business. Coincidentally, while completing a job at a local boardinghouse in 1770, he and Rousseau crossed paths, and they struck up a casual friendship. The excerpt that follows dates from years before their encounter, but it provides insight into why the two men got along so well. It reveals not only Ménétra's quick wit and sense of adventure but also his affinity for the intellectual spirit of criticism that characterized the Enlightenment. Alongside the tales of his amusements, he commented on many of the fundamental issues of the day, including the question of religious tolerance. The document is printed as originally written, without punctuation.*

From Jacques-Louis Ménétra, *Journal of My Life*, intro. Daniel Roche, trans. Arthur Goldhammer (New York: Columbia University Press, 1986), 129–30.

I went to Paris to see Denongrais   Madame la Police had been interfering with business   she made up her mind to sell her property and to retire with her cuckold of a husband to her native village for she'd put by quite a bit in the course of her work   I was
all for it   She said to me   I see clearly from what you've just said that you never loved
me   She was right for never had a woman touched my heart except for sensual pleasure
and nothing else   I promised her to come say my farewells and they've yet to be said

   Since it was the good season we went to Champigny and went with some friends of
mine to what are called *guinguettes* [open-air cafés with music and dancing — Trans.]
Sundays and holidays we went to dance in front of the castle and other days usually with
the people from the *guinguette* we played tennis or went visiting the local festivals   One
holiday in a village one league from Montigny people were playing tennis on the square
when Du Tillet showed up accompanied by the lord the magistrate or sheriff and the
priest   I heard somebody say   That's the Parisian over there I wondered what this was
all about   It's because they know you're good at tennis said my friend   they're going to
propose a match   In fact six young men came and politely gave each of us a racket   My
friend said no since he didn't know how to play but he said   But as for my friend he'll
give you a good show   I declined   They insisted   the lord the sheriff and the priest
joined in   I played   applause   hands were heard to clap   They took us to the castle
(and) gave us refreshment

   I was greatly applauded   I promised again that the fellows from Montigny and I
would be waiting for them next Sunday   People came from all around   I was all over
the court and we had a good time   we won and whatever else they were well enter-
tained   My friend went all out because M Trudaine had wanted to see me play and
when I passed in front of him he and the people around him said to me Courage   So I
answered that that was one thing I wasn't lacking

   One day I followed the game warden   Since I had no rifle I let him run all over
the fields and went to a village where I had seen the curate pay his respects to M Trudaine   who recognized me   and said I was pretty nimble at tennis and took me to his
presbytery for a drink

   After some idle talk we finally got onto the subject of religion   We talked about
the mysteries of the sacraments . . . I spoke passionately about the sufferings that had
been inflicted on men who worshiped the same God except for a few matters of
opinion   And (I said that) the Roman religion should be tolerant if it followed the
maxims of its lawgiver   that because of its mysteries it was absurd and that all mysteries
were in my opinion nothing but lies   And that so long as they sold indulgences and gave
remission for sins in exchange for money   fear of hell which was like purgatory just an
invention of the first impostors   that Jesus had never spoken of purgatory   And that all
those sacraments were nothing but pure inventions to make money and impress the vulgar   And that he himself who was a very intelligent man was not capable of making his
God   chewing him and then swallowing him   That we mistreated those peoples who
did not share our belief (and who) according to the Church should have been damned
because all the priests went around saying   Outside the Church there is no salvation
And that we accused those who worship idols of being idolators when we prostrate ourselves before statues   We even worship a piece of dough which we eat in the firm belief
that it is God   And those idolators only worship all those things to keep from being

hurt by them and other things in the hope of getting some good out of them while we on the other hand we were real man-eaters   After praying to him and worshipping him in order to satisfy him we've got to eat him too

He answered me with objections as many others had answered me   His one and only response was to say to me   All these mysteries must be believed because the Church believes them   he said to me   My friend you are enlightened   It is necessary that for the sake of government nations live always in ignorance and credulity   I answered him So be it

DISCUSSION QUESTIONS

1. Why do you think Ménétra was so critical of the Catholic Church?

2. How do Ménétra's criticisms echo those of great Enlightenment thinkers?

3. What does the priest mean when he describes Ménétra as enlightened?

4. How would you characterize Ménétra's style of writing?

3. Reforming the Law

Cesare Beccaria, *On Crimes and Punishments* (1764)

Although French philosophes transformed Paris into the intellectual capital of the Enlightenment, they were not alone in their faith in the power of human reason to understand and reshape the world around them. Like-minded thinkers across Europe embraced the Enlightenment spirit in their own pursuit of knowledge and progress for humanity. For Cesare Beccaria (1738–1794), this pursuit centered on a critical study of existing criminal law. An Italian aristocrat and doctor of laws, Beccaria joined a circle of intellectuals in Milan committed to a broad program of reform, including the creation of a rational and centralized system of equal justice for all. One of the circle's founders was an official in a local prison with firsthand knowledge of the physical and legal plight of prisoners. In his book On Crimes and Punishments, *Beccaria takes up their cause by systematically examining the traditional legal and penal system. As he argues, many criminal justice practices not only are arbitrary, cruel, and ineffective but also do not serve the greatest public good. Such practices include the use of torture to secure confessions (discussed in the excerpt that follows), the indiscriminate power of judges, and the use of capital punishment. Beccaria analyzes these and other outmoded forms of justice, calling for change. His book had a broad influence on European law and was translated into French and English, serving as a model for legal reform.*

For the most part, men leave the care of the most important regulations either to common sense or to the discretion of individuals whose interests are opposed to those most foresighted laws which distribute benefits to all and resist the pressures to concentrate those

From Cesare Beccaria, *On Crimes and Punishments and Other Writings*, ed. Richard Bellamy (Cambridge: Cambridge University Press, 1995), 7–8, 39–44.

benefits in the hands of a few, raising those few to the heights of power and happiness, and sinking everyone else in feebleness and poverty. It is, therefore, only after they have experienced thousands of miscarriages in matters essential to life and liberty, and have grown weary of suffering the most extreme ills, that men set themselves to right the evils that beset them and to grasp the most palpable truths which, by virtue of their simplicity, escape the minds of the common run of men who are not used to analyzing things, but instead passively take on a whole set of second-hand impressions of them derived more from tradition than from enquiry.

If we open our history books we shall see that the laws, for all that they are or should be contracts amongst free men, have rarely been anything but the tools of the passions of a few men or the offspring of a fleeting and haphazard necessity. They have not been dictated by a cool observer of human nature, who has brought the actions of many men under a single gaze and has evaluated them from the point of view of whether or not they conduce to *the greatest happiness shared among the greater number.* Blessed are those very few nations which have not waited for the slow succession of coincidence and contingencies to bring about some tentative movement towards the good from out of the extremities of evil, but which have sped with good laws through the intervening stages. And that philosopher who had the courage to scatter out among the multitudes from his humble, despised study the first seeds of those beneficial truths that would be so long in bearing fruit, deserves the gratitude of all humanity.

We have discovered the true relations between sovereign and subjects and between nation and nation. Commerce has been stimulated by philosophic truths disseminated by the press, and there is waged among nations a silent war by trade, which is the most humane sort of war and more worthy of reasonable men. Such is the progress we owe to the present enlightened century. But there are very few who have scrutinized and fought against the savagery and the disorderliness of the procedures of criminal justice, a part of legislation which is so prominent and so neglected in almost the whole of Europe. How few have ascended to general principles to expose and root out the errors that have built up over the centuries, so curbing, as far as it is within the power of disseminated truths to do, the all too free rein that has been given to misdirected force, which has, up to now, provided an entrenched and legitimized example of cold-blooded atrocity. And yet, the groans of the weak, sacrificed to cruel indifference and to wealthy idleness, the barbarous tortures that have been elaborated with prodigal and useless severity, to punish crimes unproven or illusory, the horrors of prison, compounded by that cruelest tormentor of the wretched, uncertainty, ought to have shaken into action that rank of magistrates who guide the opinions and minds of men.

Of Torture

The torture of a criminal while his trial is being put together is a cruelty accepted by most nations, whether to compel him to confess a crime, to exploit the contradictions he runs into, to uncover his accomplices, to carry out some mysterious and incomprehensible metaphysical purging of his infamy, [or, lastly, to expose other crimes of which he is guilty but with which he has not been charged].

No man may be called guilty before the judge has reached his verdict; nor may society withdraw its protection from him until it has been determined that he has broken the terms of the compact by which that protection was extended to him. By what right, then, except that of force, does the judge have the authority to inflict punishment on a citizen while there is doubt about whether he is guilty or innocent? This dilemma is not a novelty: either the crime is certain or it is not; if it is certain, then no other punishment is called for than what is established by law and other torments are superfluous because the criminal's confession is superfluous; if it is not certain, then an innocent man should not be made to suffer, because, in law, such a man's crimes have not been proven. Furthermore, I believe it is a willful confusion of the proper procedure to require a man to be at once accuser and accused, in such a way that physical suffering comes to be the crucible in which truth is assayed, as if such a test could be carried out in the sufferer's muscles and sinews. This is a sure route for the acquittal of robust ruffians and the conviction of weak innocents. Such are the evil consequences of adopting this spurious test of truth, but a test worthy of a cannibal, that the ancient Romans, for all their barbarity on many other counts, reserved only for their slaves, the victims of a fierce and overrated virtue.

What is the political purpose of punishment? The instilling of terror in other men. But how shall we judge the secret and secluded torture which the tyranny of custom visits on guilty and innocent alike? It is important that no established crime go unpunished; but it is superfluous to discover who committed a crime which is buried in shadows. A misdeed already committed, and for which there can be no redress, need be punished by a political society only when it influences other people by holding out the lure of impunity. If it is true that, from fear or from virtue, more men observe the laws than break them, the risk of torturing an innocent ought to be accounted all the greater, since it is more likely that any given man has observed the laws than that he has flouted them.

Another absurd ground for torture is the purging of infamy, that is, when a man who has been attainted by the law has to confirm his own testimony by the dislocation of his bones. This abuse should not be tolerated in the eighteenth century. It presupposes that pain, which is a sensation, can purge infamy, which is a mere moral relation. . . .

The third ground for torture concerns that inflicted on suspected criminals who fall into inconsistency while being investigated, as if both the innocent man who goes in fear and the criminal who wishes to cover himself would not be made to fall into contradiction by fear of punishment, the uncertainty of the verdict, the apparel and magnificence of the judge, and by their own ignorance, which is the common lot both of most knaves and of the innocent; as if the inconsistencies into which men normally fall even when they are calm would not burgeon in the agitation of a mind wholly concentrated on saving itself from a pressing danger.

. . . Every act of our will is always proportional to the force of the sensory impression which gives rise to it; and the sensibility of every man is limited. Therefore, the impression made by pain may grow to such an extent that, having filled the whole of the sensory field, it leaves the torture victim no freedom to do anything but choose the quickest route to relieving himself of the immediate pain. . . . And thus the sensitive but guiltless man will admit guilt if he believes that, in that way, he can make the pain stop. All distinctions between the guilty and the innocent disappear as a consequence of the use of the very means which was meant to discover them.

This truth is also felt, albeit indistinctly, by those very people who apparently deny it. No confession made under torture can be valid if it is not given sworn confirmation when it is over; but if the criminal does not confirm his crime, he is tortured afresh. Some learned men and some nations do not allow this vicious circle to be gone round more than three times; other nations and other learned men leave it to the choice of the judge, in such a way that, of two men equally innocent or equally guilty, the hardy and enduring will be acquitted and the feeble and timid will be convicted by virtue of the following strict line of reasoning: *I, the judge, had to find you guilty of such and such a crime; you, hardy fellow, could put up with the pain, so I acquit you; you, feeble fellow, gave in, so I convict you. I know that the confession extorted from you in the midst of your agonies would carry no weight, but I shall torture you afresh if you do not confirm what you have confessed.*

A strange consequence which necessarily follows from the use of torture is that the innocent are put in a worse position than the guilty. For, if both are tortured, the former has everything against him. Either he confesses to the crime and is convicted, or he is acquitted and has suffered an unwarranted punishment. The criminal, in contrast, finds himself in a favorable position, because if he staunchly withstands the torture he must be acquitted and so has commuted a heavier sentence into a lighter one. Therefore, the innocent man cannot but lose and the guilty man may gain.

DISCUSSION QUESTIONS

1. According to Beccaria, why is torture a customary practice?
2. Why doesn't he agree with this practice? What is the basis of his reasoning? Do you find it convincing? Why or why not?
3. What similarities and/or differences do you see between Beccaria's recommendations for reform and practices in contemporary criminal justice systems?
4. In what ways does Beccaria's choice of language reflect fundamental Enlightenment ideas?

4. Reforming Commerce

Adam Smith, *An Inquiry into the Nature and Causes of the Wealth of Nations* (1776)

Although philosophes embraced human reason as an essential tool of understanding, their views on what reason revealed varied widely. Rousseau trained his lens on the origins of government and society, Beccaria on crimes and punishments. The work of Scottish philosopher Adam Smith (1723–1790) is an example of another, equally enduring approach. A professor of moral philosophy with interests in law and economics, Smith, too, was concerned with how to promote the good of society, specifically through the "progress of opulence" that was so visible in the eighteenth-century economic boom. He set forth his

From Adam Smith, *An Inquiry into the Nature and Causes of the Wealth of Nations*, 2nd ed., vol. 2 (Oxford: Clarendon Press, 1880), 25–30.

explanation in masterful fashion in An Inquiry into the Nature and Causes of the Wealth of Nations *published in 1776. The excerpt here reveals one of the pillars of Smith's argument, namely, that economic markets should be left to their own devices, free from the government regulations that prevailed in his day. In this way, Smith declared, individual self-interest "led by an invisible hand" of competition could come to the fore, which was naturally compatible with society's general welfare.*

By restraining, either by high duties, or by absolute prohibitions, the importation of such goods from foreign countries as can be produced at home, the monopoly of the home market is more or less secured to the domestic industry employed in producing them. . . .

That this monopoly of the home market frequently gives great encouragement to that particular species of industry which enjoys it, and frequently turns towards that employment a greater share of both the labor and stock of the society than would otherwise have gone to it, cannot be doubted. But whether it tends either to increase the general industry of the society, or to give it the most advantageous direction, is not, perhaps, altogether so evident.

The general industry of the society never can exceed what the capital of the society can employ. As the number of workmen that can be kept in employment by any particular person must bear a certain proportion to his capital, so the number of those that can be continually employed by all the members of a great society, must bear a certain proportion to the whole capital of that society, and never can exceed that proportion. No regulation of commerce can increase the quantity of industry in any society beyond what its capital can maintain. It can only divert a part of it into a direction into which it might not otherwise have gone; and it is by no means certain that this artificial direction is likely to be more advantageous to the society than that into which it would have gone of its own accord.

Every individual is continually exerting himself to find out the most advantageous employment for whatever capital he can demand. It is his own advantage, indeed, and not that of the society, which he has in view. But the study of his own advantage naturally or rather necessarily, leads him to prefer that employment which is most advantageous to the society.

First, every individual endeavors to employ his capital as near home as he can, and consequently as much as he can in the support of domestic industry; provided always that he can thereby obtain the ordinary, or not a great deal less than the ordinary, profits of stock. . . .

. . . Home is in this manner the center, if I may say so, round which the capitals of the inhabitants of every country are continually circulating, and towards which they are always tending, though by particular causes they may sometimes be driven off and repelled from it towards more distant employments. But a capital employed in the home trade, it has already been shown, necessarily puts into motion a greater quantity of domestic industry, and gives revenue and employment to a greater number of the inhabitants of the country, than an equal capital employed in the foreign trade of consumption; and one employed in the foreign trade of consumption has the same advantage over an equal capital employed in the carrying trade. Upon equal, or only nearly equal profits, therefore, every individual naturally inclines to employ his capital in the manner in which it is likely to afford the greatest support to domestic industry, and to give revenue and employment to the greatest number of people of his own country.

Secondly, every individual who employs his capital in the support of domestic industry, necessarily endeavors so to direct that industry, that its produce may be of the greatest possible value.

The produce of industry is what it adds to the subject or materials upon which it is employed. In proportion as the value of this produce is great or small, so will likewise be the profits of the employer. But it is only for the sake of profit that any man employs a capital in the support of industry; and he will always, therefore, endeavor to employ it in the support of that industry of which the produce is likely to be of the greatest value, or to exchange for the greatest quantity either of money or of other goods.

But the annual revenue of every society is always precisely equal to the exchangeable value of the whole annual produce of its industry, or rather is precisely the same thing with that exchangeable value. As every individual, therefore, endeavors as much as he can both to employ his capital in the support of domestic industry, and so to direct that industry that its produce may be of the greatest value, every individual necessarily labors to render the annual revenue of the society as great as he can. He generally, indeed, neither intends to promote the public interest, nor knows how much he is promoting it. By preferring the support of domestic to that of foreign industry, he intends only his own security; and by directing that industry in such a manner as its produce may be of the greatest value, he intends only his own gain, and he is in this, as in many other cases, led by an invisible hand to promote an end which was no part of his intention. Nor is it always the worse for the society that it was no part of it. By pursuing his own interest he frequently promotes that of the society more effectually than when he really intends to promote it. . . .

What is the species of domestic industry which his capital can employ, and of which the produce is likely to be of the greatest value, every individual, it is evident, can, in his local situation, judge much better than any statesman or lawgiver can do for him. The statesman, who should attempt to direct private people in what manner they ought to employ their capitals, would not only load himself with a most unnecessary attention, but assume an authority which could safely be trusted, not only to no single person, but to no council or senate whatever, and which would nowhere be so dangerous as in the hands of a man who had folly and presumption enough to fancy himself fit to exercise it.

To give the monopoly of the home market to the produce of domestic industry, in any particular art or manufacture, is in some measure to direct private people in what manner they ought to employ their capitals, and must, in almost all cases, be either a useless or a hurtful regulation. If the produce of domestic can be brought there as cheap as that of foreign industry, the regulation is evidently useless. If it cannot, it must generally be hurtful. It is the maxim of every prudent master of a family, never to attempt to make at home what it will cost him more to make than to buy. . . .

What is prudence in the conduct of every private family, can scarce be folly in that of a great kingdom. If a foreign country can supply us with a commodity cheaper than we ourselves can make it, better buy it of them with some part of the produce of our own industry, employed in a way in which we have some advantage. The general industry of the country, being always in proportion to the capital which employs it, will not thereby be diminished, no more than that of the above-mentioned artificers, but only left to find out the way in which it can be employed with the greatest advantage. It is certainly not employed to the greatest advantage, when it is thus directed towards an object which it can buy cheaper than it can make. The value of its annual produce is certainly more or less diminished, when it is thus turned away from producing commodities evidently of more value than the commodity which it is directed to produce. According to the supposition, that commodity could be purchased from foreign countries cheaper than it can be made at home. It could, therefore, have been purchased with a part only of the commodities, or, what is the same thing, with a part only of the price of the commodities, which the industry employed by an equal capital would have produced at home, had it been left to follow its natural course. The industry of the country, therefore, is thus turned away from a more to a less advantageous employment, and the exchangeable value of its annual produce, instead of being increased, according to the intention of the lawgiver, must necessarily be diminished by every such regulation.

DISCUSSION QUESTIONS

1. Why does Smith argue against the regulation of commerce? What evidence does he cite to support his argument?

2. Why does Smith think that allowing individuals to pursue economic gain freely is advantageous to society as a whole?

3. How does this excerpt support the view held by scholars that Smith helped to lay the theoretical foundations of modern capitalist society?

4. How does Smith reflect broader Enlightenment ideas?

5. Enlightened Monarchy

Frederick II, *Political Testament* (1752)

The Enlightenment's triumph is perhaps best reflected in the politics of the second half of the eighteenth century. Rather than working to suppress the philosophes' calls for change, rulers across continental Europe embraced them as a means of enhancing their power and prestige. They did so at their own discretion, however, and often with an iron hand, as the case of King Frederick II of Prussia (r. 1740–1786) vividly reveals. A devotee of the Enlightenment as well as an exemplary soldier and statesman, Frederick transformed Prussia into a leading European state during his reign. In his Political Testament *of 1752, excerpted here, he outlines his political philosophy, which blended Enlightenment ideals with an uncompromising view of his own power.*

One must attempt, above all, to know the special genius of the people which one wants to govern in order to know if one must treat them leniently or severely, if they are inclined to revolt . . . to intrigue. . . .

From George L. Mosse, Rondo E. Cameron, Henry Bertram Hill, and Michael B. Petrovich, eds., *Europe in Review* (Chicago: Rand McNally and Company, 1957), 111–12.

[The Prussian nobility] has sacrificed its life and goods for the service of the state, its loyalty and merit have earned it the protection of all its rulers, and it is one of the duties [of the ruler] to aid those [noble] families which have become impoverished in order to keep them in possession of their lands: for they are to be regarded as the pedestals and the pillars of the state. In such a state no factions or rebellions need be feared . . . it is one goal of the policy of this state to preserve the nobility.

A well conducted government must have an underlying concept so well integrated that it could be likened to a system of philosophy. All actions taken must be well reasoned, and all financial, political and military matters must flow towards one goal: which is the strengthening of the state and the furthering of its power. However, such a system can flow but from a single brain, and this must be that of the sovereign. Laziness, hedonism, and imbecility, these are the causes which restrain princes in working at the noble task of bringing happiness to their subjects . . . a sovereign is not elevated to his high position, supreme power has not been confined to him in order that he may live in lazy luxury, enriching himself by the labor of the people, being happy while everyone else suffers. The sovereign is the first servant of the state. He is well paid in order that he may sustain the dignity of his office, but one demands that he work efficiently for the good of the state, and that he, at the very least, pay personal attention to the most important problems. . . .

You can see, without doubt, how important it is that the King of Prussia govern personally. Just as it would have been impossible for Newton to arrive at his system of attractions if he had worked in harness with Leibnitz and Descartes, so a system of politics cannot be arrived at and continued if it has not sprung from a single brain. . . . All parts of the government are inexorably linked with each other. Finance, politics, and military affairs are inseparable; it does not suffice that one be well administered; they must all be . . . a Prince who governs personally, who has formed his [own] political system, will not be handicapped when occasions arise where he has to act swiftly: for he can guide all matters towards the end which he has set for himself. . . .

Catholics, Lutherans, Reformed, Jews, and other Christian sects live in this state, and live together in peace: if the sovereign, actuated by a mistaken zeal, declares himself for one religion or another, parties will spring up, heated disputes ensue, little by little persecutions will commence, and, in the end, the religion persecuted will leave the fatherland and millions of subjects will enrich our neighbors by their skill and industry.

It is of no concern in politics whether the ruler has a religion or whether he has none. All religions, if one examines them, are founded on superstitious systems, more or less absurd. It is impossible for a man of good sense, who dissects their contents, not to see their error; but these prejudices, these errors and mysteries were made for men, and one must know enough to respect the public and not to outrage its faith, whatever religion be involved.

DISCUSSION QUESTIONS

1. Based on this excerpt, in what ways does the term *enlightened despot* apply to Frederick II? How is he enlightened? How is he despotic?

2. What reasons does Frederick advance in favor of religious tolerance?

3. According to Frederick, what should be the one goal of government?

6. Racism and the Enlightenment

SOURCES IN CONVERSATION | David Hume, *Of National Characters* (1754), and Robert Hancock, *The Tea Party* (1756–1757)

The promise of the Enlightenment coexisted side by side with a darker reality: slavery. Foreign trade boomed in the eighteenth century, fueled by the importation of millions of enslaved African people to work the colonial plantations that produced goods for the European market. The British Empire took the lead in the transatlantic slave trade, which had a direct impact on both intellectual and material culture. Scottish philosopher David Hume (1711–1776) was a close friend of Adam Smith, and they both worked to observe and understand the world around them. For Hume, this included examining the different "species" of men and variations among them. Following trends in Enlightenment science, Hume believed that nature was an inherently hierarchical system waiting to be discovered, ordered, and classified. The excerpt below is from a 1758 edition of his essay "Of National Characters." This edition includes a footnote, not found in the first edition, that Hume first added to the second edition in 1754 and retained with slight alterations through subsequent editions. It asserts his view that whites are naturally superior to all other "breeds" of men, notably "negroes," whom he singles out by name. Hume's belief in white superiority was not unique, nor was it confined to his educated audience. Engraver Robert Hancock's (1730–1817) image, known as The Tea Party, *was the most popular of all ceramic transfer-print designs during the second half of the eighteenth century. Transfer printing was a new and inexpensive way to decorate porcelain, making it affordable to a broader clientele. Hancock perfected the process, and* The Tea Party *was reproduced on a variety of objects, notably tea utensils, such as the tea saucer here. Hancock's design portrays a fashionable couple in a garden seated in front of a table laid out for tea. To their left, a black boy wearing a turban bows as he pours water from a kettle into a teapot. To their right, a small dog sits by the woman's side. As tea from China and sugar from the West Indies became more widely available in England, the practice of tea drinking grew in popularity while remaining intimately connected to the labor of enslaved people and to the new global economy.*

Of National Characters

The vulgar are very apt to carry all *national characters* to extremes; and having once established it as a principle, that any people are knavish, or cowardly, or ignorant, they will admit of no exception, but comprehend every individual under the same character. Men of sense condemn these undistinguishing judgments; though at the same time, they allow, that each nation has a peculiar set of manners, and that some particular qualities are more frequently to be met with among one people than among their neighbors. The common people in Switzerland have surely more probity than those of

---

Adapted from David Hume, *Essays and Treatises on Several Subjects,* new ed. (London: Printed for A. Millar; and A. Kincaid and A. Donaldson, at Edinburgh, 1758), 119, 121, 122, 124, 125.

the same rank in Ireland; and every prudent man will, from that circumstance alone, make a difference in the trust which he reposes in each. . . .

Different reasons are assigned for these *national characters*; while some account for them from *moral* and others from *physical* causes. By *moral* causes, I mean all circumstances, which are fitted to work on the mind as motives or reasons, and which render a peculiar set of manners habitual to us. Of this kind are, the nature of the government, the revolutions of public affairs, the plenty or penury in which the people live, the situation of the nation with regard to its neighbors, and such like circumstances. By *physical* causes, I mean those qualities of the air and climate, which are supposed to work insensibly on the temper, by altering the tone and habit of the body, and giving a particular complexion, which tho' reflection and reason may sometimes overcome, yet will it prevail among the generality of mankind, and have an influence on their manners.

That the character of a nation will very much depend on *moral* causes must be evident to the most supersicial observer; since a nation is nothing but a collection of individuals, and the manners of individuals are frequently determined by these causes. As poverty and hard labor debase the minds of the common people, and render them unfit for any science and ingenious profession; so where any government becomes very oppressive to all its subjects, it must have a proportional effect on their temper and genius, and must banish all the liberal arts from among them.

As to *physical causes,* I am inclined to doubt altogether of their operation in this particular; nor do I think, that men owe any thing of their temper or genius to the air, food, or climate. I confess, that the contrary opinion may justly, at first sight, seem very probable; since we find, that these circumstances have an influence over every other animal, and that even those creatures, which are fitted to live in all climates, such as dogs, horses, etc. do not attain the same perfection in all. The courage of bull-dogs and game-cocks seems peculiar to England. Flanders is remarkable for large and heavy horses: Spain for horses light, and of good mettle. And any breed of these creatures, transported from one country into another, will soon lose the qualities, which they derived from their native climate. It may be asked, why not the same with men?

There are few questions more curious than this, or which will occur oftener in our enquiries concerning human affairs; and therefore it may be proper to give it a serious examination.

The human mind is of a very imitative nature; nor is it possible for any set of men to converse often together, without acquiring a similitude of manners, and communicating to each other their vices as well as virtues. The propensity to company and society is strong in all rational creatures; and the same disposition, which gives us this propensity, makes us enter deeply into each other's sentiments, and causes like passions and inclinations to run, as it were by contagion, through the whole club or knot of companions. Where a number of men are united into one political body, the occasions of their intercourse must be so frequent, for defence, commerce, and government, that, together with the same speech or language, they must contract a resemblance in their manners, and have a common or national character, as well as a personal one, peculiar to each individual. Now though nature produces all kinds of temper and understanding in great abundance, it follows not that she always produces them in like proportions, and that in every society the ingredients of industry and indolence, valor and cowardice, humanity and brutality, wisdom and folly, will be mixed after the same manner. In the infancy of society, if any of these dispositions be found in greater abundance than the rest, it will naturally prevail in the composition, and give a tincture to the national character.

If the characters of men depended on the air and climate, the degrees of heat and cold should naturally be expected to have a mighty influence; since nothing has a greater effect on all plants and irrational animals. And indeed there is some reason to think, that all the nations, which live beyond the polar circles or betwixt the tropics, are inferior to the rest of the species, and are utterly incapable of all the higher attainments of the human mind. The poverty and misery of the northern inhabitants of the globe, and the indolence of the southern from their few necessities, may, perhaps, account for this remarkable difference, without having recourse to *physical* causes. This however is certain, that the characters of nations are very promiscuous in the temperate climates, and that almost all the general observations, which have been formed of the more southern or more northern nations in these climates, are found to be uncertain and fallacious. [Originally in a footnote] I am apt to suspect the negroes, and in general all the other species of men (for there are four or five different kinds) to be naturally inferior to the whites. There never was a civilized nation of any other complexion than white, nor even any individual eminent either in action or speculation. No ingenious manufactures amongst them, no arts, no sciences. On the other hand, the most rude and barbarous of the whites, such as the ancient Germans, the present Tartars, have still something eminent about them, in their valour, form of government, or some other particular. Such a uniform and constant difference could not happen, in so many countries and ages, if nature had not made an original distinction betwixt these breeds of men. Not to mention our colonies, there are negroe slaves dispersed all over Europe, of which none ever discovered any symptoms of ingenuity; though low people, without education, will start up amongst us, and distinguish themselves in every profession. In Jamaica indeed they talk of one negroe as a man of parts and learning; but 'tis likely he is admired for very slender accomplishments, like a parrot, who speaks a few words plainly.

Bowl and saucer, 1756–57. Worcester porcelain factory, engraved by Robert Hancock / Victoria and Albert Museum, London, UK / V & A Images, London / Art Resource, NY

DISCUSSION QUESTIONS

1. According to Hume, what reasons have people provided to explain differences among peoples and cultures in both the past and the present?

2. Why does Hume give more weight to "moral" than to "physical" causes of difference? What role does nature play in his view, and how does this account for what he describes as whites' superiority?

3. Look closely at Hancock's design, noting especially the positioning of the three figures. What is the visual focal point of the image, and what does this suggest about popular representations of black people at the time?

4. What underlying assumptions about racial diversity do Hume's essay and Hancock's design share? Based on these similarities, what broader conclusions can you draw about the role race played in eighteenth-century English society and culture?

COMPARATIVE QUESTIONS

1. How do Ménétra's and Frederick II's attitudes toward organized religion overlap? What does this suggest about Ménétra as an exception to the rule that the lower classes had little contact with Enlightenment ideas?

2. What similarities and differences do you see between Frederick II's and Beccaria's views on the basis of good government?

3. In what ways do the documents by Rousseau, Beccaria, Smith, and Frederick II reflect Enlightenment thinkers' intense interest in the relationship between the individual and secular society?

4. Among the hallmarks of Enlightenment writers was their optimism about human nature and its capacity to change for the better. What evidence of such optimism do you see in the works excerpted in this chapter? What works complicate or contradict this optimism? Based on the selections in this chapter, what conclusions can you draw about the promises and limitations of the Enlightenment?

The Cataclysm
of Revolution
1789–1799

When the Estates General convened at Versailles in May 1789, no one could have foreseen what lay ahead: ten years of upheaval that established the model of modern
revolution and set the course of modern politics. The following documents illuminate
the French Revolution in the making, from the politically charged months preceding
the convocation of the Estates General to the formation of a republic and a government of terror designed to destroy enemies of the Revolution both within and without.
At each stage, the revolutionaries remained committed to the Enlightenment principle
of using reason to reshape society and government. The second document, a political
cartoon of the Old Regime, visually brings to life why so many people clamored for
change. Even so, they were not always in control of events either in France or beyond,
as peasants, working-class city folk, women, and even enslaved people from the French
colony of St. Domingue (modern-day Haiti) rose up with their own demands, taking the
Revolution in even more radical directions.

1. Defining the Nation
Abbé Sieyès, *What Is the Third Estate?* (1789)

*Although in 1788 King Louis XVI (r. 1774–1792) agreed to call the Estates General, he left
a thorny procedural question for the deputies to answer: Would the assembly vote by order
or by head? The debate over this question galvanized the nation in the months preceding the
opening of the Estates General in May 1789, thanks in part to pamphlets like the one that
follows. Written by a middle-class clergyman, Abbé Emmanuel-Joseph Sieyès (1748–1836),
this pamphlet's message was clear: the privileged few should not determine the nation's
future, as a traditional vote by order would ensure, by allowing the clergy and nobility to*

From Lynn Hunt, ed. and trans., *The French Revolution and Human Rights: A Brief Documentary
History* (Boston: Bedford/St. Martin's, 1996), 65–70.

join forces, the blocking of any decision contrary to their liking. Rather, government should rest in the hands of the people whose labor and skills sustain society, the Third Estate. In forging his argument, Sieyès forcefully condemned traditional political and social structures while granting the Third Estate a voice on the national stage.

The plan of this work is quite simple. We must ask ourselves three questions.

1. What is the Third Estate? Everything.
2. What has it been until now in the political order? Nothing.
3. What does it want? To become something. . . .

What does a Nation require to survive and prosper? *Private* employment and *public* offices.

Private employment includes four classes of work:

1. Since the land and water provide the raw material for the needs of mankind, the first class, in logical order, includes all those families attached to work in the countryside.

2. Between the initial sale of raw materials and their consumption or usage as finished goods, labor of various sorts adds more value to these goods. In this way human industry manages to improve on the blessings of Nature and to multiply the value of the raw materials two, ten, or a hundredfold. Such is the second class of work.

3. Between production and consumption, as also between the different stages of production, there are a host of intermediary agents, useful both to producers and consumers; these are the merchants and wholesale traders. Wholesale traders constantly weigh demand according to place and time and speculate on the profit that they can make on storage and transport; merchants actually sell the goods on the markets, whether wholesale or retail. This type of utility designates the third class of work.

4. Besides these three classes of hard-working and useful Citizens who occupy themselves with the *things* fit to be consumed or used, society also needs a multitude of private occupations and services *directly* useful or agreeable to the *person*. This fourth class embraces all those occupations from the most distinguished scientific and liberal professions down to the least esteemed domestic servants.

These are the kinds of work that sustain society. Who carries them out? The Third Estate.

In the present state of affairs public offices can also be ranked in four well-known categories: the Sword [the army], the Robe [the courts], the Church, and the Administration. Detailed analysis is not necessary to show that the Third Estate makes up everywhere 19/20ths of their number, except that it is charged with all the really hard work, all the work that the privileged order refuses to perform. Only the lucrative and most honored places are taken by the members of the privileged order. Should we praise them for this? We could do so only if the Third [Estate] was unwilling or unable to fill these offices. We know the truth of the matter, but the Third Estate has nonetheless been excluded. They are told, "Whatever your services, whatever your talents, you will only go so far and no further. Honors are not for your sort." A few rare exceptions, noteworthy as they are bound to be, are only a mockery, and the language encouraged on these exceptional occasions is but an additional insult.

If this exclusion is a social crime committed against the Third Estate, can we say at least that it is useful to the public good? Ah! Are the effects of monopoly now known? If it discourages those whom it pushes aside, does it not also render those it favors less competent? Is it not obvious that every piece of work kept out of free competition will be made more expensively and less well?

When any office is deemed the prerogative of a separate order among the citizens, has no one noticed that a salary has to be paid not only to the man who does the work but also to all those of the same caste who do not and even to entire families of both those who work and those who do not? Has no one noticed that this state of affairs, so abjectly respected among us, nonetheless seems contemptible and shameful in the history of ancient Egypt and in the stories of voyages to the Indies? But let us leave aside those considerations which though broadening our purview and perhaps enlightening would only slow our pace. It suffices here to have made the point that the supposed usefulness of a privileged order to the public service is nothing but a mirage; that without that order, all that is most arduous in this service is performed by the Third Estate; that without the privileged the best places would be infinitely better filled; that such places should naturally be the prize and reward for recognized talents and services; and that if the privileged have succeeded in usurping all the lucrative and honored posts, this is at once an odious iniquity committed against the vast majority of the citizenry and an act of treason against the public good.

Who therefore dares to say that the Third Estate does not contain within itself all that is needed to form a complete Nation? The Third Estate is like a strong and robust man with one arm still in chains. If we remove the privileged order, the Nation will not be something less but something more. Thus, what is the Third Estate? All, but an all that is shackled and oppressed. What would it be without the privileged order? All, but an all that is free and flourishing. Nothing can be done without it [the Third Estate]; everything would be infinitely better without the other two orders.

It does not suffice to have demonstrated that the privileged, far from being useful to the Nation, can only weaken and harm it; it must be proved further that the noble order[1] is not even part of society itself: It may very well be a burden for the Nation but it cannot be a part of it.

---

[1] [Sieyès's own note] I do not speak of the clergy here. In my way of thinking, the clergy is not an order but rather a profession charged with a public service. In the clergy, it is not the person who is privileged but the office, which is very different. . . . The word *caste* refers to a class of men who, without functions and without usefulness and by the sole fact that they exist, enjoy the privileges attached to their person. From this point of view, which is the true one in my opinion, there is only one order, that of the nobility. They are truly a people apart but a false people, which not being able to exist by itself by reason of its lack of useful organs, attaches itself to a real Nation like those plant growths which can only survive on the sap of the plants that they tire and suck dry. The Clergy, the Robe, the Sword, and the Administration are four classes of public trustees that are necessary everywhere. Why are they accused in France of *aristocraticism*? It is because the noble caste has usurped all the good positions; it has done so as if this was a patrimonial property exploited for its personal profit rather than in the spirit of social welfare.

First, it is not possible to assign a place to the caste of nobles among the many elements that make up a Nation. I know that there are too many individuals whose infirmities, incapacity, incurable laziness, or excessively bad morals make them essentially foreigners to the work of society. The exception and the abuse always accompany the rule, especially in a vast empire. But at least we can agree that the fewer the abuses, the better ordered the state. The worst-off state of all would be the one in which not only isolated individual cases but also an entire class of citizens would glory in inactivity amidst the general movement and would contrive to consume the best part of what is produced without having contributed anything to its making. Such a class is surely foreign to the Nation because of its *idleness*.

The noble order is no less foreign amongst us by reason of its *civil* and *public* prerogatives.

What is a Nation? A body of associates living under a *common* law and represented by the same *legislature*.

Is it not more than certain that the noble order has privileges, exemptions, and even rights that are distinct from the rights of the great body of citizens? Because of this, it does not belong to the common order, it is not covered by the law common to the rest. Thus its civil rights already make it a people apart inside the great Nation. It is truly *imperium in imperio* [a law unto itself].

As for its *political* rights, the nobility also exercises them separately. It has its own representatives who have no mandate from the people. Its deputies sit separately, and even when they assemble in the same room with the deputies of the ordinary citizens, the nobility's representation still remains essentially distinct and separate: it is foreign to the Nation by its very principle, for its mission does not emanate from the people, and by its purpose, since it consists in defending, not the general interest, but the private interests of the nobility.

The Third Estate therefore contains everything that pertains to the Nation and nobody outside of the Third Estate can claim to be part of the Nation. What is the Third Estate? EVERYTHING. . . .

By Third Estate is meant the collectivity of citizens who belong to the common order. Anybody who holds a legal privilege of any kind leaves that common order, stands as an exception to the common law, and in consequence does not belong to the Third Estate. . . . It is certain that the moment a citizen acquires privileges contrary to common law, he no longer belongs to the common order. His new interest is opposed to the general interest; he has no right to vote in the name of the people. . . .

What is the will of a Nation? It is the result of individual wills, just as the Nation is the aggregate of the individuals who compose it. It is impossible to conceive of a legitimate association that does not have for its goal the common security, the common liberty, in short, the public good. No doubt each individual also has his own personal aims. He says to himself, "protected by the common security, I will be able to peacefully pursue my own personal projects, I will seek my happiness where I will, assured of encountering only those legal obstacles that society will prescribe for the common interest, in which I have a part and with which my own personal interest is so usefully allied." . . .

Advantages which differentiate citizens from one another lie outside the purview of citizenship. Inequalities of wealth or ability are like the inequalities of age, sex, size, etc.

In no way do they detract from the *equality* of citizenship. These individual advantages no doubt benefit from the protection of the law; but it is not the legislator's task to create them, to give privileges to some and refuse them to others. The law grants nothing; it protects what already exists until such time that what exists begins to harm the common interest. These are the only limits on individual freedom. I imagine the law as being at the center of a large globe; we the citizens, without exception, stand equidistant from it on the surface and occupy equal places; all are equally dependent on the law, all present it with their liberty and their property to be protected; and this is what I call the *common rights* of citizens, by which they are all alike. All these individuals communicate with each other, enter into contracts, negotiate, always under the common guarantee of the law. If in this general activity somebody wishes to get control over the person of his neighbor or usurp his property, the common law goes into action to repress this criminal attempt and puts everyone back in their place at the same distance from the law. . . .

It is impossible to say what place the two privileged orders ought to occupy in the social order: this is the equivalent of asking what place one wishes to assign to a malignant tumor that torments and undermines the strength of the body of a sick person. It must be *neutralized*. We must re-establish the health and working of all the organs so thoroughly that they are no longer susceptible to these fatal schemes that are capable of sapping the most essential principles of vitality.

DISCUSSION QUESTIONS

1. What is the traditional status of the Third Estate? How does Sieyès want to change it, and why?

2. Why do you think Sieyès was so critical of nobility in particular? What do these criticisms reveal about his political principles?

3. How effective do you think this pamphlet is as a work of political propaganda, and why?

2. The People under the Old Regime

Political Cartoon (1815)

This cartoon depicts a man carrying three figures on his back. Chained and bloodied, the man struggles beneath the weight not only of the riders' rotund physiques but also of the numerous privileges they enjoy, as recorded on the papers each holds in his hand. In the front sits an aristocrat, or perhaps Louis XVI himself, brandishing a whip and his claim to feudal rights. A bishop clings to his shoulder, wielding his own set of powers: the Inquisition and the annual church tax (dîme). Behind him sits a judge, resplendent in his robe, who trumpets the nobility's domination of the regional courts (parlements). Their beast of burden is none other than the French people, symbolically depicted here as the naked and emaciated man whom the riders control with reins, chains, and a blindfold. Although this cartoon was first published in 1815, it captures the mood of thousands of French men and women on the eve of the Revolution just as powerfully as Sieyès and other pamphleteers had done in words.

Bettmann/Getty Images

DISCUSSION QUESTIONS

1. What is the primary message of this cartoon?

2. What images in particular do you think convey this message most effectively, and why?

3. In what ways do these images reflect the mixture of social and political conflicts that ultimately helped to fuel the French Revolution?

3. Establishing Rights

National Assembly, *The Declaration of the Rights of Man and of the Citizen* (1789)

Promulgated by the fledgling National Assembly in August 1789, the Declaration of the Rights of Man and of the Citizen *gave the Revolution a clear sense of purpose and direction after the dizzying series of events of that summer. In it, the delegates set forth the guiding principles of the new government, echoing many of the ideals of influential eighteenth-century thinkers. The document also marked the definitive end of the Old Regime by presenting the protection of individual rights, not royal prerogative, as the cornerstone of political authority. The deputies' work was not done, however, for they regarded the declaration as a preliminary step toward their primary goal: to write a constitution for the country that would transform it into an enlightened constitutional monarchy. This goal was met with the Constitution of 1791, to which the declaration was attached.*

The representatives of the French people, organized as a National Assembly, believing that the ignorance, neglect, or contempt of the rights of man are the sole cause of public calamities and of the corruption of governments, have determined to set forth in a solemn declaration the natural, inalienable, and sacred rights of man, in order that this declaration, being constantly before all the members of the social body, shall remind them continually of their rights and duties; in order that the acts of the legislative power, as well as those of the executive power, may be compared at any moment with the objects and purposes of all political institutions and may thus be more respected; and, lastly, in order that the grievances of the citizens, based hereafter upon simple and incontestable principles, shall tend to the maintenance of the constitution and redound to the happiness of all. Therefore the National Assembly recognizes and proclaims, in the presence and under the auspices of the Supreme Being, the following rights of man and of the citizen:

Article 1. Men are born and remain free and equal in rights. Social distinctions may be founded only upon the general good.

2. The aim of all political association is the preservation of the natural and imprescriptible rights of man. These rights are liberty, property, security, and resistance to oppression.

3. The principle of all sovereignty resides essentially in the nation. No body nor individual may exercise any authority which does not proceed directly from the nation.

4. Liberty consists in the freedom to do everything which injures no one else; hence the exercise of the natural rights of each man has no limits except those which assure to the other members of the society the enjoyment of the same rights. These limits can only be determined by law.

5. Law can only prohibit such actions as are hurtful to society. Nothing may be prevented which is not forbidden by law, and no one may be forced to do anything not provided for by law.

From James Harvey Robinson, *Readings in European History*, vol. 2 (Boston: Ginn and Company, 1906), 409–11.

6. Law is the expression of the general will. Every citizen has a right to participate personally, or through his representative, in its formation. It must be the same for all, whether it protects or punishes. All citizens, being equal in the eyes of the law, are equally eligible to all dignities and to all public positions and occupations, according to their abilities, and without distinction except that of their virtues and talents.

7. No person shall be accused, arrested, or imprisoned except in the cases and according to the forms prescribed by law. Any one soliciting, transmitting, executing, or causing to be executed, any arbitrary order, shall be punished. But any citizen summoned or arrested in virtue of the law shall submit without delay, as resistance constitutes an offense.

8. The law shall provide for such punishments only as are strictly and obviously necessary, and no one shall suffer punishment except it be legally inflicted in virtue of a law passed and promulgated before the commission of the offense.

9. As all persons are held innocent until they shall have been declared guilty, if arrest shall be deemed indispensable, all harshness not essential to the securing of the prisoner's person shall be severely repressed by law.

10. No one shall be disquieted on account of his opinions, including his religious views, provided their manifestation does not disturb the public order established by law.

11. The free communication of ideas and opinions is one of the most precious of the rights of man. Every citizen may, accordingly, speak, write, and print with freedom, but shall be responsible for such abuses of this freedom as shall be defined by law.

12. The security of the rights of man and of the citizen requires public military forces. These forces are, therefore, established for the good of all and not for the personal advantage of those to whom they shall be intrusted.

13. A common contribution is essential for the maintenance of the public forces and for the cost of administration. This should be equitably distributed among all the citizens in proportion to their means.

14. All the citizens have a right to decide, either personally or by their representatives, as to the necessity of the public contribution; to grant this freely; to know to what uses it is put; and to fix the proportion, the mode of assessment and of collection and the duration of the taxes.

15. Society has the right to require of every public agent an account of his administration.

16. A society in which the observance of the law is not assured, nor the separation of powers defined, has no constitution at all.

17. Since property is an inviolable and sacred right, no one shall be deprived thereof except where public necessity, legally determined, shall clearly demand it, and then only on condition that the owner shall have been previously and equitably indemnified.

DISCUSSION QUESTIONS

1. In delineating the rights of the individual, how did the National Assembly respond to Enlightenment writers' calls for reforms?

2. According to this document, what are the fundamental roles of government and the individual citizen?

3. How does the document define political sovereignty, and how is this definition related to the deputies' collective sense of identity and purpose?

4. A Call for Women's Inclusion

SOURCES IN CONVERSATION | Olympe de Gouges, *Declaration of the Rights of Woman* (1791) and Mary Wollstonecraft, *A Vindication of the Rights of Woman* (1792)

Despite its call to reshape society for everyone's betterment, the National Assembly did not extend its revolutionary ideal of equality to women. The rights of man were for man alone, echoing the dominant view that women were emotionally and intellectually incapable of participating in politics. Not only were women denied the right to vote, but they also lacked legal equality within marriage, the right to divorce, and the right to own property. French writer and political activist Olympe de Gouges (1748–1793) refused to accept the status quo. Drawing on Enlightenment ideals and a well-established French feminist tradition, de Gouges took the title of the Declaration of the Rights of Man and of the Citizen *at face value and directly challenged its exclusion of women by writing a declaration for them. Even women less radical than de Gouges embraced her message. They organized festivals of freedom, workshops, and clubs and offered prizes for recitations of the declaration. English writer and educator Mary Wollstonecraft (1759–1797) was equally disappointed in the National Assembly's failure to break with traditional views on women, and she too used the printed word as a call to action with her book* A Vindication of the Rights of Woman. *For her, society's narrow expectations for women were the product of time-bound prejudices and false assumptions. Women had the same capacity to reason as men, Wollstonecraft proclaimed; they simply needed to be educated properly to break free and claim their full humanity as wives, mothers, and citizens. Wollstonecraft had made up for her own lack of formal education in various ways, including by translating and reviewing the works of prominent Enlightenment authors, such as Kant and Rousseau. Controversial at the time of its publication in 1792, Wollstonecraft's book is regarded today as a cornerstone of modern feminism.*

Olympe de Gouges, *Declaration of the Rights of Woman*

Man, are you capable of being just? It is a woman who poses the question; you will not deprive her of that right at least. Tell me, what gives you sovereign empire to oppress my sex? Your strength? Your talents? Observe the Creator in his wisdom; survey in all her grandeur that nature with whom you seem to want to be in harmony, and give me, if you dare, an example of this tyrannical empire. Go back to animals, consult the elements, study plants, finally glance at all the modifications of organic matter, and surrender to the evidence when I offer you the means; search, probe, and distinguish, if you can, the sexes in the administration of nature. Everywhere you will find them mingled; everywhere they cooperate in harmonious togetherness in this immortal masterpiece.

From Darline Gay Levy, Harriet Branson Applewhite, and Mary Durham Johnson, eds. and trans., *Women in Revolutionary Paris, 1789–1795* (Chicago: University of Illinois Press, 1979), 89–92, and Mary Wollstonecraft, *A Vindication of the Rights of Woman*, ed. Miriam Brody (New York: Penguin Books, 2004), 13–14, 28, 48–49.

Man alone has raised his exceptional circumstances to a principle. Bizarre, blind, bloated with science and degenerated — in a century of enlightenment and wisdom — into the crassest ignorance, he wants to command as a despot a sex which is in full possession of its intellectual faculties; he pretends to enjoy the Revolution and to claim his rights to equality in order to say nothing more about it.

Declaration of the Rights of Woman and the Female Citizen

For the National Assembly to decree in its last sessions, or in those of the next legislature:

Preamble

Mothers, daughters, sisters [and] representatives of the nation demand to be constituted into a national assembly. Believing that ignorance, omission, or scorn for the rights of woman are the only causes of public misfortunes and of the corruption of governments, [the women] have resolved to set forth in a solemn declaration the natural, inalienable, and sacred rights of woman in order that this declaration, constantly exposed before all the members of the society, will ceaselessly remind them of their rights and duties; in order that the authoritative acts of women and the authoritative acts of men may be at any moment compared with and respectful of the purpose of all political institutions; and in order that citizens' demands, henceforth based on simple and incontestable principles, will always support the constitution, good morals, and the happiness of all.

Consequently, the sex that is as superior in beauty as it is in courage during the sufferings of maternity recognizes and declares in the presence and under the auspices of the Supreme Being, the following Rights of Women and of Female citizens.

Article I

Woman is born free and lives equal to man in her rights. Social distinctions can be based only on the common utility.

Article II

The purpose of any political association is the conservation of the natural and impre-scriptible rights of woman and man; these rights are liberty, property, security, and especially resistance to oppression.

Article III

The principle of all sovereignty rests essentially with the nation, which is nothing but the union of woman and man; no body and no individual can exercise any authority which does not come expressly from it [the nation].

Article IV

Liberty and justice consist of restoring all that belongs to others; thus, the only limits on the exercise of the natural rights of woman are perpetual male tyranny; these limits are to be reformed by the laws of nature and reason.

Article V

Laws of nature and reason proscribe all acts harmful to society; everything which is not prohibited by these wise and divine laws cannot be prevented, and no one can be constrained to do what they do not command.

Article VI

The law must be the expression of the general will; all female and male citizens must contribute either personally or through their representatives to its formation; it must be the same for all: male and female citizens, being equal in the eyes of the law, must be equally admitted to all honors, positions, and public employment according to their capacity and without other distinctions besides those of their virtues and talents.

Article VII

No woman is an exception; she is accused, arrested, and detained in cases determined by law. Women, like men, obey this rigorous law.

Article VIII

The law must establish only those penalties that are strictly and obviously necessary, and no one can be punished except by virtue of a law established and promulgated prior to the crime and legally applicable to women.

Article IX

Once any woman is declared guilty, complete rigor is [to be] exercised by the law.

Article X

No one is to be disquieted for his very basic opinions; woman has the right to mount the scaffold; she must equally have the right to mount the rostrum, provided that her demonstrations do not disturb the legally established public order.

Article XI

The free communication of thoughts and opinions is one of the most precious rights of woman, since that liberty assures the recognition of children by their fathers. Any female citizen thus may say freely, I am the mother of a child which belongs to you, without being forced by a barbarous prejudice to hide the truth; [an exception may be made] to respond to the abuse of this liberty in cases determined by the law.

Article XII

The guarantee of the rights of woman and the female citizen implies a major benefit; this guarantee must be instituted for the advantage of all, and not for the particular benefit of those to whom it is entrusted.

Article XIII

For the support of the public force and the expenses of administration, the contributions of woman and man are equal; she shares all the duties [*corvées*] and all the painful tasks; therefore, she must have the same share in the distribution of positions, employment, offices, honors, and jobs [*industrie*].

Article XIV

Female and male citizens have the right to verify, either by themselves or through their representatives, the necessity of the public contribution. This can only apply to women if they are granted an equal share, not only of wealth, but also of public administration, and in the determination of the proportion, the base, the collection, and the duration of the tax.

Article XV

The collectivity of women, joined for tax purposes to the aggregate of men, has the right to demand an accounting of his administration from any public agent.

Article XVI

No society has a constitution without the guarantee of rights and the separation of powers; the constitution is null if the majority of individuals comprising the nation have not cooperated in drafting it.

Article XVII

Property belongs to both sexes whether united or separate; for each it is an inviolable and sacred right; no one can be deprived of it, since it is the true patrimony of nature, unless the legally determined public need obviously dictates it, and then only with a just and prior indemnity.

Mary Wollstonecraft, *A Vindication of the Rights of Woman*

My own sex, I hope, will excuse me, if I treat them like rational creatures, instead of flattering their *fascinating* graces, and viewing them as if they were in a state of perpetual childhood, unable to stand alone. I earnestly wish to point out in what true dignity and human happiness consists—I wish to persuade women to endeavour to acquire strength, both of mind and body, and to convince them that the soft phrases, susceptibility of heart, delicacy of sentiment, and refinement of taste, are almost synonymous with epithets of weakness, and that those beings who are only the objects of pity and that kind of love, which has been termed its sister, will soon become objects of contempt.

Dismissing then those pretty feminine phrases, which the men condescendingly use to soften our slavish dependence, and despising that weak elegancy of mind, exquisite sensibility, and sweet docility of manners, supposed to be the sexual characteristics of the weaker vessel, I wish to shew that elegance is inferior to virtue, that the first object of laudable ambition is to obtain a character as a human being, regardless of the distinction of sex; and that secondary views should be brought to this simple touchstone.

. . . To account for, and excuse the tyranny of man, many ingenious arguments have been brought forward to prove, that the two sexes, in the acquirement of virtue, ought to aim at attaining a very different character: or, to speak explicitly, women are not allowed to have sufficient strength of mind to acquire what really deserves the name of virtue. Yet it should seem, allowing them to have souls, that there is but one way appointed by Providence to lead *mankind* to either virtue or happiness.

If then women are not a swarm of ephemeron triflers, why should they be kept in ignorance under the specious name of innocence? Men complain, and with reason, of the follies and caprices of our sex, when they do not keenly satirize our headstrong passions and groveling vices. — Behold, I should answer, the natural effect of ignorance! The mind will ever be unstable that has only prejudices to rest on, and the current will run with destructive fury when there are no barriers to break its force. Women are told from their infancy, and taught by the example of their mothers, that a little knowledge of human weakness, justly termed cunning, softness of temper, *outward* obedience, and a scrupulous attention to a puerile kind of propriety, will obtain for them the protection of man; and should they be beautiful, every thing else is needless, for, at least, twenty years of their lives.

. . . If, I say, for I would not impress by declamation when Reason offers her sober light, if they be really capable of acting like rational creatures, let them not be treated like slaves; or, like the brutes who are dependent on the reason of man, when they associate with him; but cultivate their minds, give them the salutary, sublime curb of principle, and let them attain conscious dignity by feeling themselves only dependent on God. Teach them, in common with man, to submit to necessity, instead of giving, to render them more pleasing, a sex to morals.

Further, should experience prove that they cannot attain the same degree of strength of mind, perseverance, and fortitude, let their virtues be the same in kind, though they may vainly struggle for the same degree; and the superiority of man will be equally clear, if not clearer; and truth, as it is a simple principle, which admits of no modification, would be common to both. Nay, the order of society as it is at present regulated would not be inverted, for woman would then only have the rank that reason assigned her, and arts could not be practised to bring the balance even, much less to turn it.

These may be termed Utopian dreams. — Thanks to that Being who impressed them on my soul, and gave me sufficient strength of mind to dare to exert my own reason, till, becoming dependent only on him for the support of my virtue, I view, with indignation, the mistaken notions that enslave my sex.

I love man as my fellow; but his sceptre, real, or usurped, extends not to me, unless the reason of an individual demands my homage; and even then the submission is to reason, and not to man. In fact, the conduct of an accountable being must be regulated by the operations of its own reason; or on what foundation rests the throne of God?

It appears to me necessary to dwell on these obvious truths, because females have been insulated, as it were; and, while they have been stripped of the virtues that should clothe humanity, they have been decked with artificial graces that enable them to exercise a short-lived tyranny. Love, in their bosoms, taking place of every nobler passion, their sole ambition is to be fair, to raise emotion instead of inspiring respect; and this ignoble desire, like the servility in absolute monarchies, destroys all strength of character. Liberty is the mother of virtue, and if women be, by their very constitution, slaves, and not allowed to breathe the sharp invigorating air of freedom, they must ever languish like exotics, and be reckoned beautiful flaws in nature.

DISCUSSION QUESTIONS

1. De Gouges passionately argues that women and men should have the same inalienable and sacred rights as guaranteed by law. What rights for women does she delineate specifically in her declaration, and why?

2. How does Wollstonecraft describe the stereotypical woman of the time? What traits did men value in women, and why? How does Wollstonecraft's argument seek to counter such stereotypes?

3. How do de Gouges and Wollstonecraft persuade the reader that their views are not simply in the best interest of women but of society in general? What do their arguments have in common, and where do they differ?

5. Defending Terror

Maximilien Robespierre, *Report on the Principles of Political Morality* (1794)

Despite the momentous events of the first two years of the Revolution, even more radical changes were yet to come. With pressures mounting at home and the threat of war looming abroad, in 1792 the National Convention abolished the monarchy and established the first French Republic. A year later, the government set up the Committee of Public Safety to defend the Revolution from its enemies. To this end, the committee instituted a set of emergency measures known as the Terror to crush all forms of dissent. Maximilien Robespierre (1758–1794), the leader of the committee, was a driving force behind the radicalization of the Revolution. In a speech delivered to the National Convention on February 5, 1794, excerpted here, he set forth his political vision. As he argued, virtue was the soul of the republic. With the republic fighting for its very survival, terror flowed from virtue in the form of swift and firm justice; neither could succeed without the other. At the time, Robespierre and his allies were the targets of increasingly strong criticism, for many believed that the Terror had achieved its goals and should now be dismantled. Robespierre met his critics head-on, holding up terror as the sword of liberty.

What is the goal toward which we are heading? The peaceful enjoyment of liberty and equality; the reign of that eternal justice whose laws have been inscribed, not in marble and stone, but in the hearts of all men, even in that of the slave who forgets them and in that of the tyrant who denies them.

We seek an order of things in which all the base and cruel passions are enchained, all the beneficent and generous passions are awakened by the laws; where ambition becomes the desire to merit glory and to serve our country; where distinctions are born only of equality itself; where the citizen is subject to the magistrate, the magistrate to the people, and the people to justice; where our country assures the well-being of each individual, and where each individual proudly enjoys our country's prosperity and glory; where

From Richard Bienvenu, ed., *The Ninth of Thermidor: The Fall of Robespierre* (New York: Oxford University Press, 1968), 33–36, 38–39.

every soul grows greater through the continual flow of republican sentiments, and by the need of deserving the esteem of a great people; where the arts are the adornments of the liberty which ennobles them and commerce the source of public wealth rather than solely the monstrous opulence of a few families.

In our land we want to substitute morality for egotism, integrity for formal codes of honor, principles for customs, a sense of duty for one of mere propriety, the rule of reason for the tyranny of fashion, scorn of vice for scorn of the unlucky, self-respect for insolence, grandeur of soul for vanity, love of glory for the love of money, good people in place of good society. We wish to substitute merit for intrigue, genius for wit, truth for glamor, the charm of happiness for sensuous boredom, the greatness of man for the pettiness of the great, a people who are magnanimous, powerful, and happy, in place of a kindly, frivolous, and miserable people — which is to say all the virtues and all the miracles of the republic in place of all the vices and all the absurdities of the monarchy.

We want, in a word, to fulfill nature's desires, accomplish the destiny of humanity, keep the promises of philosophy, absolve providence from the long reign of crime and tyranny. Let France, formerly illustrious among the enslaved lands, eclipsing the glory of all the free peoples who have existed, become the model for the nations, the terror of oppressors, the consolation of the oppressed, the ornament of the world — and let us, in sealing our work with our blood, see at least the early dawn of universal bliss — that is our ambition, that is our goal.

What kind of government can realize these wonders? Only a democratic or republican government — these two words are synonyms, despite the abuses in common speech, because an aristocracy is no closer than a monarchy to being a republic. Democracy is not a state in which the people, continually meeting, regulate for themselves all public affairs, still less is it a state in which a tiny fraction of the people, acting by isolated, hasty, and contradictory measures, decide the fate of the whole society. Such a government has never existed, and it could exist only to lead the people back into despotism.

Democracy is a state in which the sovereign people, guided by laws which are of their own making, do for themselves all that they can do well, and by their delegates do all that they cannot do for themselves.

It is therefore in the principles of democratic government that you should seek the rules for your political conduct.

But, in order to lay the foundations of democracy among us and to consolidate it, in order to arrive at the peaceful reign of constitutional laws, we must finish the war of liberty against tyranny and safely cross through the storms of the revolution: that is the goal of the revolutionary system which you have put in order. You should therefore still base your conduct upon the stormy circumstances in which the republic finds itself; and the plan of your administration should be the result of the spirit of revolutionary government, combined with the general principles of democracy.

Now, what is the fundamental principle of popular or democratic government, that is to say, the essential mainspring which sustains it and makes it move? It is virtue. I speak of the public virtue which worked so many wonders in Greece and Rome and which ought to produce even more astonishing things in republican France — that virtue which is nothing other than the love of the nation and its laws.

But as the essence of the republic or of democracy is equality, it follows that love of country necessarily embraces the love of equality.

There are important consequences to be drawn immediately from the principles we have just explained.

Since the soul of the Republic is virtue, equality, and since your goal is to found, to consolidate the Republic, it follows that the first rule of your political conduct ought to be to relate all your efforts to maintaining equality and developing virtue; because the first care of the legislator ought to be to fortify the principle of the government. Thus everything that tends to excite love of country, to purify morals, to elevate souls, to direct the passions of the human heart toward the public interest, ought to be adopted or established by you. Everything which tends to concentrate them in the abjection of selfishness, to awaken enjoyment for petty things and scorn for great ones, ought to be rejected or curbed by you. Within the scheme of the French revolution, that which is immoral is impolitic, that which is corrupting is counter-revolutionary. Weakness, vice, and prejudices are the road to royalty. Dragged too often, perhaps, by the weight of our former customs, as much as by the imperceptible bent of human frailty, toward false ideas and faint-hearted sentiments, we have less cause to guard ourselves against too much energy than against too much weakness. The greatest peril, perhaps, that we have to avoid is not that of zealous fervor, but rather of weariness in doing good works and of timidity in displaying our own courage. Maintain, then, the sacred power of the republican government, instead of letting it decline. I do not need to say that I have no wish here to justify any excess. The most sacred principles can indeed be abused. It is up to the wisdom of the government to pay heed to circumstances, to seize the right moments, to choose the proper means; because the manner of preparing great things is an essential part of the talent for performing them, just as wisdom is itself an element of virtue.

We deduce from all this a great truth — that the characteristic of popular government is to be trustful towards the people and severe towards itself.

Here the development of our theory would reach its limit, if you had only to steer the ship of the Republic through calm waters. But the tempest ranges, and the state of the revolution in which you find yourselves imposes upon you another task.

This great purity of the French revolution's fundamental elements, the very sublimity of its objective, is precisely what creates our strength and our weakness: our strength, because it gives us the victory of truth over deception and the rights of public interest over private interests; our weakness, because it rallies against us all men who are vicious, all those who in their hearts plan to despoil the people, and all those who have despoiled them and want impunity, and those who reject liberty as a personal calamity, and those who have embraced the revolution as a livelihood and the Republic as if it were an object of prey. Hence the defection of so many ambitious or greedy men who since the beginning have abandoned us along the way, because they had not begun the voyage in order to reach the same goal. One could say that the two contrary geniuses that have been depicted competing for control of the realm of nature, are fighting in this great epoch of human history to shape irrevocably the destiny of the world, and that France is the theater of this mighty struggle. Without, all the tyrants encircle you; within, all the friends of tyranny conspire — they will conspire until crime has been robbed of hope. We must smother the internal and external enemies of the Republic or perish with them. Now, in this situation, the first maxim of your policy ought to be to lead the people by reason and the people's enemies by terror.

If the mainspring of popular government in peacetime is virtue, amid revolution it is at the same time [both] virtue and *terror*: virtue, without which terror is fatal; terror, without which virtue is impotent. Terror is nothing but prompt, severe, inflexible justice; it is therefore an emanation of virtue. It is less a special principle than a consequence of the general principle of democracy applied to our country's most pressing needs.

It has been said that terror was the mainspring of despotic government. Does your government, then, resemble a despotism? Yes, as the sword which glitters in the hands of liberty's heroes resembles the one with which tyranny's lackeys are armed. Let the despot govern his brutalized subjects by terror; he is right to do this, as a despot. Subdue liberty's enemies by terror, and you will be right, as founders of the Republic. The government of the revolution is the despotism of liberty against tyranny.

DISCUSSION QUESTIONS

1. According to Robespierre, what is the central goal of the Revolution?

2. Describe Robespierre's notion of virtue. How is it related to his vision for the Revolution's future?

3. In Robespierre's view, what methods can governments use to defend virtue, and why?

4. Historians have long debated whether the radical Revolution marked the beginning of true democracy or justified totalitarianism. Based on Robespierre's speech, what evidence do you find to support these two contradictory ideas?

6. Liberty for All?

Decree of General Liberty (August 29, 1793) and Bramante Lazzary, *General Call to Local Insurgents* (August 30, 1793)

In declaring that men are born free and equal in rights, the National Convention unleashed a debate with momentous consequences. Not only did women like Olympe de Gouges agitate for inclusion in the revolutionary ideal of equality, so too did other groups without representation. These included free and enslaved blacks and in the French colony of St. Domingue. News of the Revolution's progress traveled quickly to the island, prompting enslaved people in the north to launch an insurrection against their white masters in August 1791. Violence worsened when the royalist government of Spain joined forces with the rebels to destroy France's hold on the colony. To deal with the crisis and secure the insurgents' support, the newly elected Legislative Assembly granted civil and political rights to free blacks in what became known as the Law of April 4. The French commissioners managing the situation in St. Domingue knew that the law did not go far enough, however, if France wanted to regain control. They thus took matters into their own hands, issuing the Decree of General Liberty on August 29, 1793. The decree succeeded in swaying some rebels to join the French side, including Bramante Lazzary, who made a general call to local insurgents to join the French. Lazzary's exact status

---

From H. Pauléus Sannon, *Histoire de Toussaint Louverture* (Port-au-Prince, Haiti: Imprimerie Aug. A. Heraux, 1938), 1:146ff, and Bramante Lazzary to Toussaint L'Ouverture, Archives Nationales, DXXV 23, 231, letter 98, trans. Laurent DuBois and John D. Garrigus in *Slave Revolution in the Caribbean, 1789–1804* (New York: Bedford/St. Martin's, 2006).

is unclear; he may have been enslaved or been a free man of color. Regardless, he welcomed the commissioners' call for unity under the banner of the liberty for all men regardless of their skin color. Propelled by these and other events, the National Convention voted to follow suit, abolishing slavery throughout the French Empire in February 1794.

Decree of General Liberty

August 29, 1793

Men are born and remain free and equal in rights; citizens, this is France's gospel. It is high time that it be proclaimed in all areas of the republic.

Sent by the nation to Saint-Domingue as civil commissioners, our mission was to enforce the law of April 4, to see it applied in all its force, and gradually, smoothly, without rupture, to prepare the general emancipation of the slaves.

Upon our arrival, we found a horrible division among the whites who, separated by interest and opinion, agreed only on a single point: to maintain the slavery of the *nègres* forever and therefore to prohibit any system of liberty or even improvement of their fate.

In order to foil malicious persons and to reassure everyone, since they all feared any sudden action, we declared that we believed slavery was necessary for agriculture.

What we said was true, citizens; at that time slavery was as essential to the continuation of work as it was to keeping the colonists faithful to France. A group of ferocious tyrants still ruled Saint-Domingue, men who publicly preached that one's skin color should be a sign of power or condemnation. These were men like those who condemned the unfortunate Ogé[1] or the creators and members of those notorious military tribunals who filled the towns with gallows and torture racks in order to sacrifice Africans and men of color to their own foul pretensions. The colony was still full of these bloodthirsty men. If by some great foolhardiness, we had then broken the chains that bound slaves to their masters, undoubtedly their first reaction would have been to throw themselves upon their persecutors, and, in their justifiable rage, they might easily have confounded innocent with guilty people. At that time, we did not have the legal authority to decide the status of the Africans; we would have been disloyal and in violation of the law had we done so.

Today the situation is quite different. The slave traders and cannibals are gone. Some of them have died, victims of their impotent rage, while others have sought safety by fleeing to foreign countries. Those whites who remain believe in France's laws and values.

The men of April 4[2] make up the majority of the [remaining] population; these are men to whom you owe your freedom, the first to show you what it is to have the courage to fight for natural and human rights. These men were so proud of their independence that they chose to lose their property rather than suffer the shame of putting on their

---

[1]Vincent Ogé was a rich free man of color from Cap Français, the commercial capital of Saint-Domingue. He was executed in 1791 for leading an insurrection in support of allowing free people of color to vote in local elections. [Ed.]

[2]The men of color given political rights by the April 4, 1792, decree.

old shackles. Never forget, citizens, that they gave you the weapons that conquered your liberty; never forget that you fought for the French Republic, that of all the whites in the universe, the only ones that are your friends are the Frenchmen of Europe.

The French Republic wants all men to be free and equal with no color distinctions. Kings can only be content when they are surrounded by slaves; they are the ones who sold you to the whites on the African coast; they are the tyrants in Europe who want this vile trade to continue. The republic adopts you among its children; these kings wanted only to load you down with chains or eliminate you.

The representatives of this very republic were the ones who rescued you by untying the hands of the civil commissioners and giving them authority to make provisional changes in the slave regime.

This regime is going to be changed; a new order of things will be born, and the old slavery will disappear. Yet do not think that the liberty that you will enjoy means laziness and inactivity. In France, everyone is free and everyone works; in Saint-Domingue under these same laws, you will follow the same model. After returning to your old work crews or your former owners, you will be paid for your work; you will no longer suffer the humiliating punishments previously inflicted upon you; you will no longer be property, as before. You will be your own master and live contented.

Since you have chosen to become citizens of the French nation, you must also be the zealous defender of its laws; you will undoubtedly defend the interests of the republic against kings, more out of gratitude for the benefits she has heaped upon you than to preserve your own independence. Liberty has brought you from nothingness into existence; show that you are worthy of her. Renounce laziness forever as if it were a crime. Have the courage to want to be a people, and soon you will be equal to the nations of Europe. Your detractors and your tyrants maintain that an African who is set free will never work again. Prove them wrong. Work twice as hard to win the prize that awaits you. Let your activity prove to France that, by including you on her side, she has truly increased her capacities and resources.

And you, citizens misled by the vile royalists, you who took up the flags and uniforms of the cowardly Spanish to fight blindly against your own interests, against the freedom of your women and children, open your eyes at last to the enormous advantages that the republic offers you. The kings promise you liberty, but do you see them giving this to their subjects? Do the Spanish free their own slaves? No, surely not. To the contrary, they are likely to weigh you down with chains as soon as they no longer need your services. Aren't they the ones who turned Ogé over to his killers? What misfortune you suffer! If France returned to its kings, the [royalist] émigrés would turn on you. They flatter you today, but they would be the first to torture you.

Given this situation, the civil commissioner, reflecting on the petition signed by individuals assembled in a meeting, exercising the powers given him by Article 3 of the law passed by the National Convention last March 5:

Orders the following, to be carried out in the northern province [of Saint-Domingue].

First Article: The Declaration of the Rights of Man and Citizen will be printed, published, and displayed everywhere it is needed.

2. All the nègres and mixed blood people currently in slavery are declared free to enjoy all the rights of French citizens; they are nevertheless subject to the regime described in the following articles. . . .

5. Servants of either sex can be hired by their masters and mistresses only for three months, and this for a salary that they will fix according to the wishes of each.

6. Former house slaves working for persons who are older than sixty, or sick, or for nursing infants less than ten years old, are not free to leave them. Their salary is set at 1 *portuguaise* (8 *gourdes*)[3] per month for wet nurses and 6 *portuguaise* for the others, for men and women alike. . . .

9. The *nègres* currently working on the plantations of their former masters are required to remain there. They will work in agriculture.

10. The enlisted fighters who are serving in army units or in forts will be allowed to establish themselves on plantations for agricultural work by first obtaining a furlough from their leader or an order from us, to be delivered if they find a willing man to replace them.

11. The former field hands will be obliged to work for a year, during which time they can change plantations only by permission of a justice of the peace.

12. The profits of each plantation will be divided into three equal portions after taxes are deducted from the whole amount. One-third will remain with the owner of the land. He will have access to another third to cover the costs of planting. The remaining third will be divided between the field workers in a manner to be set. . . .

In addition, the field workers will have their own provision grounds; they will be divided equally between each family, according to the quality of the land and the amount needed. . . .

27. Punishment by the whip is absolutely forbidden; for violations of discipline it will be replaced by the stocks for one, two, or three days, according to the severity of the case. The most severe punishments will be fines, up to complete loss of salary.

28. For civil crimes, the former slaves will be judged like other French citizens.

29. Field hands cannot be forced to work on Sunday. . . .

31. Women who are seven months pregnant will not work and will only return to the fields two months after their deliveries.

32. Field hands can change plantations for health reasons or for an incompatible personality at the request of the crew in which they work. These affairs will be subject to the decision of a justice of the peace and his counselors.

33. On the fifteenth day after the publication of this proclamation, all men who do not own property and are neither in the military, nor working in agriculture, nor employed in someone's home, within the time limits set above, or are found to be vagrants, will be arrested and put in prison.

34. Women who do not have an obvious source of income, who are not working in agriculture or employed in someone's home, within the time limits set above, or are found to be vagrants, will be arrested and put in prison.

35. The men and women imprisoned in these cases for the first time will be held for a month. The second time they will be held for three months, and the third time they will be sentenced to a public work detail for one year.

---

[3]The *portuguaise* and the *gourde* were, respectively, Portuguese and Spanish coins that circulated widely in the Caribbean in the eighteenth century. Just before the Revolution, one gourde, equal to 8½ colonial livres, would buy a medium-size table or rent a coastal trading boat for two days.

36. Persons working in agriculture and household workers will not leave their employment for any reason without permission of the city or town government where they live. . . .

Bramante Lazzary, Commander of the Camps of the Tannerie and Lacombe

August 30, 1793, year 2 of the Republic[4]

To my brothers and friends in rebellion in the northern province
Can there be any greater happiness for us than to see ourselves all united together and enjoying a good and sweet natural liberty that France has given us?

At last, my friends, general liberty has been proclaimed on the island; it has given us our well-being and made us all children of the law. It is to them, the civil commissioners, to whom France gave its power, it is to them, my brothers, that we owe our legitimate happiness; it is to them and only to them that France had confided it to grant it to us. As soon as you receive my letter, you must gather together and present yourself to the representatives of the nation, and swear to be loyal to the nation and to die for the safety of our country, to march under the national flag, which is the sign of our union, which finally announces the reunion of the three colors.

Our flag makes it clear that our liberty depends on these three colors; white, mulatto, black. We are fighting for these three colors. The nobility and the Spaniards want us to have only the white in order to bring us back to the old order. But no, we are French; we are fighting for our freedom; we want to live free or die, that is the motto of all good French republicans.

You fought for something that now has been legitimately granted to us, so let us unite as your brothers from Limbé and Morne Rouge have, to form a single and same family, to march against those who wish to attack our liberty. Spain has joined a conflict that it made you think it would support. But remember, my brothers, that they will not do so for as long as they tell you. They will bite their thumbs, like the aristocrats of Le Cap who have gone to their side. France is more powerful than you think and has already made itself respected by several crowns, and Spain will be pinched in its turn. And France will also punish those to whom it has offered happiness but who pretend they do not know the law. . . .

DISCUSSION QUESTIONS

1. How does the Decree of General Liberty draw on the language of the French Revolution to make its case for emancipation?

2. How does Lazzary's call to insurgents echo the same language? How does he draw a distinction between republican and royal government?

---

[4]Lazzary is combining the Gregorian calendar, which he uses for the day and month, with the Republican calendar, which he uses for the year. The calendar began with "Year 1" in September 1792, with the establishment of the French Republic, and subsequent calendar years began on the same date.

3. What does the decree suggest about how Europeans viewed Africans at the time? How was the content of the decree crafted to counter these views?

4. In what ways does the decree address concerns about the impact the end of slavery would have on the plantation economy?

COMPARATIVE QUESTIONS

1. In what ways does the message of the political cartoon echo that of Sieyès in his pamphlet? How did the *Declaration of the Rights of Man and of the Citizen* address such concerns? Why did people like Olympe de Gouges insist that the Declaration did not go far enough?

2. Based on Robespierre's speech, how did the Terror undermine the basic tenets of the *Declaration of the Rights of Man and of the Citizen*?

3. In what ways were de Gouges in France, Wollstonecraft in England, and free and enslaved people of color in the French colonies fighting similar battles? What do their arguments about the nature of human rights have in common, and where do they diverge?

4. Taken collectively, how do these documents allow us to chart the course that the Revolution took between 1789 and 1794?

Napoleon and the Revolutionary Legacy
1800–1830

The end of the Terror in 1794 opened a new chapter in European history — one marked by the extraordinary rise of Napoleon Bonaparte (1769–1821). Between 1795 and 1799, Napoleon transformed himself from a humble artillery officer in the revolutionary army into the ruler of France. Document 1 describes a key stage in this transformation: Napoleon's invasion of Egypt in 1798. Although the campaign ultimately failed, it foreshadowed Napoleon's subsequent successful conquest of large parts of Europe. Document 2 represents one of the most enduring methods he used to achieve his goals: the establishment of a uniform code of civil law. Later, Napoleon's defeat in the Battle of the Nations in 1813 set the stage for a new era in European politics. Napoleon's enemies met at the Congress of Vienna to negotiate the terms of peace united by their singular desire to restore the old order. Document 3 reveals the allied powers in action as they worked to restore traditional authority through the force of arms and conservative ideology. Yet, as Document 4 indicates, the revolutionary legacy was still a powerful force threatening the status quo. Documents 5 and 6 reflect the cultural response to the shifting European landscape — romanticism — which strove to strip away artifice and expose truth as revealed in nature and the imagination. In doing so, romantic artists exposed the profound tension, characteristic of the postrevolutionary age, between the desire for stability and the desire to stretch the limits of human creativity.

1. Napoleon in Egypt
The Chronicle of Abd al-Rahman al-Jabartî (1798)

While the Directory government that came to power in 1795 worked to establish order in France, Napoleon (1769–1821) continued the Revolution's policy of conquest and annexation abroad, first in Italy (1796–1797) and then in Egypt (1798–1801). At the time,

Egypt was France's most important trading partner outside of the Caribbean; it was also a key base for challenging British interests in Asia. Egyptian historian Abd al-Rahman al-Jabartî's (1753–c. 1826) account of the first six months of the French invasion offers an Egyptian perspective of Napoleon. In the excerpt here, Jabartî views Napoleon's actions skeptically through the lens of his own culture. His skepticism proved well founded, for Napoleon failed to colonize Egypt. Even so, he retained his reputation as a great military leader, preparing the way for his mastery of France and ultimately most of western Europe.

On Monday news arrived that the French had reached Damanhur and Rosetta, bringing about the flight of their inhabitants to Fuwwa and its surroundings. Contained in this news was mention of the French sending notices throughout the country demanding impost for the upkeep of the military. Furthermore they printed a large proclamation in Arabic, calling on the people to obey them and to raise their "Bandiera." In this proclamation were inducements, warnings, all manner of wiliness and stipulations. Some copies were sent from the provinces to Cairo and its text is:

In the name of God, the Merciful, the Compassionate. There is no god but God. He has no son, nor has He an associate in His Dominion.

On behalf of the French Republic which is based upon the foundation of liberty and equality, General Bonaparte, Commander-in-Chief of the French armies makes known to all the Egyptian people that for a long time the Sanjaqs[1] who lorded it over Egypt have treated the French community basely and contemptuously and have persecuted its merchants with all manner of extortion and violence. Therefore the hour of punishment has now come.

Unfortunately this group of Mamlūks,[2] imported from the mountains of Circassia and Georgia have acted corruptly for ages in the fairest land that is to be found upon the face of the globe. However, the Lord of the Universe, the Almighty, has decreed the end of their power.

O ye Egyptians, they may say to you that I have not made an expedition hither for any other object than that of abolishing your religion; but this is a pure falsehood and you must not give credit to it, but tell the slanderers that I have not come to you except for the purpose of restoring your rights from the hands of the oppressors and that I more than the Mamlūks, serve God. . . .

And tell them also that all people are equal in the eyes of God and the only circumstances which distinguish one from the other are reason, virtue, and knowledge. But amongst the Mamlūks, what is there of reason, virtue, and knowledge, which would distinguish them from others and qualify them alone to possess everything which sweetens life in this world? Wherever fertile land is found it is appropriated to the Mamlūks; and the handsomest female slaves, and the best horses, and the most desirable

---

From Shmuel Moreh, trans., *Napoleon in Egypt: Al-Jabartî's Chronicle of the French Occupation, 1798* (Princeton, NJ: Markus Wiener, 1993), 24–33.

[1]**Sanjaqs:** Provincial governors in the Ottoman Empire.
[2]**Mamlūks:** Descendants of medieval slave-soldiers who enjoyed considerable political power until the French invasion.

dwelling-places, all these belong to them exclusively. If the land of Egypt is a fief of the Mamlūks, let them then produce the title-deed, which God conferred upon them. But the Lord of the Universe is compassionate and equitable toward mankind, and with the help of the Exalted, from this day forward no Egyptian shall be excluded from admission to eminent positions nor from acquiring high ranks, therefore the intelligent and virtuous and learned ("*ulamā*") amongst them, will regulate their affairs, and thus the state of the whole population will be rightly adjusted. . . .

Blessing on blessing to the Egyptians who will act in concert with us, without any delay, for their condition shall be rightly adjusted, and their rank raised. Blessing also, upon those who will abide in their habitations, not siding with either of the two hostile parties, yet when they know us better, they will hasten to us with all their hearts. But woe upon woe to those who will unite with the Mamlūks and assist them in the war against us, for they will not find the way of escape, and no trace of them shall remain. . . .

Here is an explanation of the incoherent words and vulgar constructions which he put into this miserable letter.

His statement "In the name of God, the Merciful, the Compassionate. There is no god but God. He has no son, nor has He an associate in His Dominion." In mentioning these three sentences there is an indication that the French agree with the three religions, but at the same time they do not agree with them, not with any religion. They are consistent with the Muslims in stating the formula "In the name of God," in denying that He has a son or an associate. They disagree with the Muslims in not mentioning the two Articles of Faith, in rejecting the mission of Muhammad, and the legal words and deeds which are necessarily recognized by religion. They agree with the Christians in most of their words and deeds, but disagree with them by not mentioning the Trinity, and denying the mission and furthermore in rejecting their beliefs, killing the priests and destroying the churches. Then, their statement "On behalf of the French Republic, etc.," that is, this proclamation is sent from their Republic, that means their body politic, because they have no chief or sultan with whom they all agree, like others, whose function is to speak on their behalf. For when they rebelled against their sultan six years ago and killed him, the people agreed unanimously that there was not to be a single ruler but that their state, territories, laws, and administration of their affairs, should be in the hands of the intelligent and wise men among them. They appointed persons chosen by them and made them heads of the army, and below them generals and commanders of thousands, two hundreds, and tens, administrators and advisers, on condition that they were all to be equal and none superior to any other in view of the equality of creation and nature. They made this the foundation and basis of their system. This is the meaning of their statement "based upon the foundation of liberty and equality." . . . They follow this rule: great and small, high and low, male and female are all equal. Sometimes they break this rule according to their whims and inclinations or reasoning. Their women do not veil themselves and have no modesty; they do not care whether they uncover their private parts. Whenever a Frenchman has to perform an act of nature he does so wherever he happens to be, even in full view of people, and he goes away as he is, without washing his private parts after defecation. If he is a man of taste and refinement he wipes himself with whatever he finds, even with a paper with writing on it, otherwise he remains as he is. They have intercourse with any woman who pleases them and vice versa. Sometimes one of their women goes into a barber's shop, and invites him to shave her pubic hair. If he wishes he can take his fee in kind. It is their custom to shave both their moustaches and beard. Some of them leave the hair of their cheeks only. . . .

His saying *qad hattama* etc. (has decreed) shows that they are appointing themselves controllers of God's secrets, but there is no disgrace worse than disbelief. . . .

His statement *wa-qnln li'l-muftariyīn* (but tell the slanderers) is the plural of *muftari* (slanderer) which means liar, and how worthy of this description they are. The proof of that is his saying "I have not come to you except for the purpose of restoring your rights from the hands of the oppressors," which is the first lie he uttered and a falsehood which he invented. Then he proceeds to something even worse than that, may God cast him into perdition, with his words: "I more than the Mamlūks serve God. . . ." There is no doubt that this is a derangement of his mind, and an excess of foolishness. . . .

His saying [all people] are equal in the eyes of God the Almighty, this is a lie and stupidity. How can this be when God has made some superior to others as is testified by the dwellers in the Heavens and on the Earth? . . .

May God hurry misfortune and punishment upon them, may He strike their tongues with dumbness, may He scatter their hosts, and disperse them, confound their intelligence, and cause their breath to cease. He has the power to do that, and it is up to Him to answer.

DISCUSSION QUESTIONS

1. What strategy did Napoleon use in his proclamation to garner the support of the Egyptian people?

2. What does this strategy suggest about Napoleon's personal ambitions and method of rule?

3. Why is Jabartî critical of Napoleon's intentions, as stated in his proclamation?

4. What do Jabartî's criticisms suggest about the differences between French and Egyptian cultures at the time?

2. Codifying French Law

Napoleon Bonaparte, *The Civil Code* (1804)

Despite the failure of the Egyptian campaign, Napoleon's reputation remained untarnished. Disillusioned with the revolutionary government, his supporters orchestrated a coup in 1799, installing him as the head of the French government. Once in power, Napoleon consolidated his position, ultimately crowning himself emperor in 1804. Through the same blend of authoritarian policies and revolutionary principles he displayed in Egypt, Napoleon worked

---

From E. A. Arnold, ed. and trans., *A Documentary Survey of Napoleonic France* (Lanham, MD: University Press of America, 1994), 151–64, quoted in *Sources of Western Society: Since 1300*, ed. Amy R. Caldwell et al. (Boston: Bedford/St. Martin's, 2011), 346–50.

to restructure French legal, political, and social institutions. His efforts included the codification of French law, a process that the National Assembly had initiated years earlier. Completed in 1804, the Civil Code replaced a patchwork of Roman, customary, and canon law with a single, uniform body of civil law. The code comprises three sections pertaining to people, property (predominantly understood as land), and the acquisition of property. The excerpts below are from the first and third parts. On the one hand, the code protected core gains of the French Revolution by promising equality before the law. On the other, it reinforced patriarchal authority by undermining the rights of women in both public and private spheres. As Napoleon's armies racked up victory after victory across western Europe, the code was imposed as a cornerstone of French rule, ensuring its influence for decades to come.

Preliminary Title: Of the Publication, Effect, and Application of the Laws in General

1. The laws are executory throughout the whole French territory, by virtue of the promulgation thereof made by the First Consul. They shall be executed in every part of the Republic, from the moment at which their promulgation can have been known. The promulgation made by the First Consul shall be taken to be known in the department which shall be the seat of government, one day after the promulgation; and in each of the other departments, after the expiration of the same interval augmented by one day for every ten myriameters[1] (about twenty ancient leagues[2]) between the town in which the promulgation shall have been made, and the chief place of each department.

2. The law ordains for the future only; it has no retrospective operation.

3. The laws of police and public security bind all the inhabitants of the territory. Immovable property, although in the possession of foreigners, is governed by the French law. The laws relating to the condition and privileges of persons govern Frenchmen, although residing in a foreign country....

6. Private agreements must not contravene the laws which concern public order and good morals.

Book I: Of Persons

Title I: Of the Enjoyment and Privation of Civil Rights

1. The exercise of civil rights is independent of the quality of citizen, which is only acquired and preserved conformably to the constitutional law....

8. Every Frenchman shall enjoy civil rights.

---

[1]**myriameters**: Ten thousand meters, or ten kilometers. One of the Revolution's accomplishments was to replace the many local systems of measurement in France with a unified, easy-to-use metric system.

[2]**leagues**: Roman leagues; about two kilometers. The Roman Empire's systems of measurement survived long after its political structure crumbled.

Chapter VI: Of the Respective Rights and Duties of Married Persons

212. Married persons owe to each other fidelity, succor, assistance.

213. The husband owes protection to his wife, the wife obedience to her husband.

214. The wife is obliged to live with her husband, and to follow him to every place where he may judge it convenient to reside: the husband is obliged to receive her, and to furnish her with every necessity for the wants of life, according to his means and station.

215. The wife cannot plead in her own name, without the authority of her husband, even though she should be a public trader, or noncommunicant, or separate in property.

216. The authority of the husband is not necessary when the wife is prosecuted in a criminal manner, or relating to police.

217. A wife, although noncommunicant or separate in property, cannot give, pledge, or acquire by free or chargeable title, without the concurrence of her husband in the act, or his consent in writing.

218. If the husband refuses to authorize his wife to plead in her own name, the judge may give her authority.

219. If the husband refuses to authorize his wife to pass an act, the wife may cause her husband to be cited directly before the court of the first instance, of the circle of their common domicil[e], which may give or refuse its authority, after the husband shall have been heard, or duly summoned before the chamber of council.

220. The wife, if she is a public trader, may, without the authority of her husband, bind herself for that which concerns her trade; and in the said case she binds also her husband, if there be a community between them. She is not reputed a public trader if she merely retails goods in her husband's trade, but only when she carries on a separate business.

221. When the husband is subjected to a condemnation, carrying with it an afflictive or infamous punishment, although it may have been pronounced merely for coutumacy,[3] the wife, though of age, cannot, during the continuance of such punishment, plead in her own name or contract, until after authority given by the judge, who may in such case give his authority without hearing or summoning the husband. . . .

226. The wife may make a will without the authority of her husband.

Title VI: Of Divorce

Section II: Of the Provisional Measures to Which the Petition for Cause Determinate May Give Rise

267. The provisional management of the children shall rest with the husband, petitioner, or defendant, in the suit for divorce, unless it be otherwise ordered for the greater advantage of the children, on petition of either the mother, or the family, or the government commissioner.

---

[3]**contumacy:** Refusal to obey legal authority.

271. Every obligation contracted by the husband at the expense of the community, every alienation made by him of immovable property dependent upon it, subsequent to the date of the order mentioned in article 238, shall be declared void, if proof be given, moreover, that it has been made or contracted in fraud of the rights of the wife.

Title IX: Of Paternal Power

375. A father who shall have cause of grievous dissatisfaction at the conduct of a child, shall have the following means of correction.

376. If the child has not commenced his sixteenth year, the father may cause him to be confined for a period which shall not exceed one month; and to this effect the president of the court of the circle shall be bound, on his petition, to deliver an order of arrest.

377. From the age of sixteen years commenced to the majority or emancipation, the father is only empowered to require the confinement of his child during six months at the most; he shall apply to the president of the aforesaid court, who, after having conferred thereon with the commissioner of government, shall deliver an order of arrest or refuse the same, and may in the first case abridge the time of confinement required by the father.

379. The father is always at liberty to abridge the duration of the confinement by him ordered or required. If the child after his liberation fall into new irregularities, his confinement may be ordered anew, according to the manner prescribed in the preceding articles.

Book III: Modes of Acquiring Property

Title I: Of Successions

818. The husband may, without the concurrence of his wife, claim a distribution of objects movable or immovable fallen to her and which come into community; with respect to objects which do not come into community, the husband cannot claim the distribution thereof without the concurrence of his wife; he can only demand a provisional distribution in case he has a right to the enjoyment of her property. The co-heirs of the wife cannot claim final distribution without suing the husband and his wife.

Title II: Donations and Wills

905. A married woman cannot make donation during life without the assistance or the special consent of her husband, or without being thereto authorized by the law, conformably to what is prescribed by articles 217 and 219, under the title "Of Marriage." She shall not need either the consent of her husband, or the authorization of the law, in order to dispose by will.

Chapter IV: Of Donations during Life

Section II: Of the Administration of the Community, and of the Effect of the Acts of Either of the Married Parties Relating to the Conjugal Union

1421. The husband alone administers the property of the community. He may sell it, alienate and pledge it without the concurrence of his wife.

1424. Fines incurred by the husband for a crime not importing civil death, may be sued for out of the property of the community, saving the compensation due to the wife; such as are incurred by the wife cannot be put in execution except out of her bare property in her personal goods, so long as the community continues.

1427. The wife cannot bind herself nor engage the property of the community, even to free her husband from prison, or for the establishment of their children in case of her husband's absence, until she shall have been thereto authorized by the law.

1428. The husband has the management of all the personal property of the wife. He may prosecute alone all possessory actions and those relating to movables, which belong to his wife. He cannot alienate the personal immovables of his wife without her consent. He is responsible for all waste in the personal goods of his wife, occasioned by the neglect of conservatory acts.

DISCUSSION QUESTIONS

1. Viewed as a whole, how do these laws blend traditional and revolutionary principles? What specific examples can you cite?

2. What segments of French society do you think benefited the most from these laws? What does this suggest about Napoleon's vision for an ordered state?

3. Why might these laws have placed so much emphasis on marriage and family? What does this emphasis suggest about the broader roles marriage and family played in French society?

3. The Conservative Order

Prince Klemens von Metternich, *Results of the Congress at Laybach* (1821)

Upon Napoleon's defeat in 1813, the allied powers met at the Congress of Vienna in 1814–1815 to establish the political landscape of post-Napoleonic Europe. Here they adopted a two-pronged strategy firmly rooted in conservative doctrine. First, they determined the boundaries of European states and restored as many nations as possible to their former rulers; then they agreed to convene periodic meetings, or congresses, to confront any future threats to order. Austria's chief negotiator, Prince Klemens von Metternich (1773–1859), was the mastermind of the congress system and a chief spokesperson for conservatism. In the excerpt that follows, Metternich assumes both roles as he writes to Tsar Alexander I of Russia about the results of the Congress at Laybach in 1821. The major powers had assembled at Laybach to discuss an uprising to secure a constitution in the kingdom of Naples. Along with

From Klemens von Metternich, *Memoirs of Prince Metternich*, vol. 3, 1815–1829, ed. Richard Metternich, trans. Mrs. Alexander Napier (New York: Howard Fertig, 1970; reprint of 1881 edition), 535–39.

Alexander, the Austrian emperor and the king of Naples also agreed to armed intervention to suppress the revolt. Metternich praises Alexander for his decision while clearly enumerating his own political principles, which favored monarchies over republics, tradition over revolution.

Before the separation of the monarchs and their Cabinets, may I be permitted to place in the hands of your Imperial Majesty one word of gratitude and homage? Of gratitude, Sire, for you deserve it, not on my part, nor on that of Austria, but from society at large.

You must do me the justice to admit that I discerned long ago the evil which has been lately unmasked with such awful intensity. You must also remember, Sire, that, although I knew the evil, I did not despair of the remedy. This remedy has begun to take effect; it is the intimate moral union between your Imperial Majesty and your august allies, each being free in his actions. The merit, Sire, belongs to you: for your situation was the most free, and certainly not so near to the danger as that of the other monarchs. Your Imperial Majesty has done an immense good; your conscience must tell you so; and that is the only recompense which a good man earnestly seeks after; it is the only one which can reach the man placed by providence above other men.

There is but one act of homage which I consider worthy of your Imperial Majesty. Placed as I am between the Emperor, my master, and your Imperial Majesty, grave duties rest upon me. The first is perhaps the most difficult — that of seeking and finding the truth. The day when I lose confidence in my own calculations I shall regard myself as guilty in the eyes of my master and those of your Imperial Majesty. My homage, Sire, must simply be to tell you all my thoughts.

Society would have been irretrievably lost but for the measures which have been taken during the last few months. These measures could not have arrested its fall unless they had rested on the most correct principles. Such being the case, the dawn of a better future begins to appear: the day will succeed if we continue to walk on in the path in which we have placed ourselves. One single false principle, and the night will be upon us, and chaos will succeed that night.

There are two means of enabling us to continue in this path: — Reciprocal and unrestrained confidence, and a frank understanding of the principles on which our conduct must be grounded.

This confidence, Sire, is what the mind has most difficulty in seizing. It has been, and would for ever have been, an insurmountable difficulty, if Providence had not created two sovereigns such as your Imperial Majesty and the Emperor Francis. You know each other perfectly, and this is ever necessary to a good understanding.

To establish for the future that perfect agreement of conduct so decisive for the fate of Europe, it is necessary to lay the foundation as simply as possible on clear, precise principles, and to secure their application by reciprocal engagements no less clear and precise. A great distance separates us, and this inconvenience we must remedy.

I will now state the principles, and point out the engagements to be made.

It is demonstrated that a vast and dangerous conspiracy has since 1814 acquired sufficient strength and means of action to enable it to seize upon a number of places in the public administration. This conspiracy was less evident to the eyes of the world as long as it did not court discovery, and contented itself with the domain of theory. In that domain nothing is surprising: discussions, pretensions, contradictions belong to it by full right. From the day that I saw sound doctrines attacked with impunity, and observed that they ran the risk of being suppressed altogether, I recognized revolution, with its inevitable consequences, disorder, anarchy, and death, where others saw only light fighting with prejudice. Up to that time the conspiracy had only reconnoitered its ground and prepared it. It has grown, and it must grow, thanks to the instruments which a too deplorable folly has allowed it to create for itself.

It has not been slow in descending from the intellectual sphere into that of material facts. One word was sufficient to gain public favor. That word was Constitution, of all words the least precise, the most open to variety of interpretation, and the easiest to make popular, for it acts on the mass of the people through their hopes. Tell men that by means of a single word you will ensure them their rights, a liberty which the mass always confound with license, a career for their ambition, and success in all their enterprises, and you will have no trouble in making them listen to you. The mass once agitated, they give up everything: they listen, but do not care to comprehend. When the people do really comprehend, they are the first to re-establish order.

This ground taken, as the last resource, authority has been attacked. The factious have had recourse to arms; triumph seemed to them quite certain.

The clear and precise aim of the factious is one and uniform. It is the overthrow of everything legally existing. The ambitious and successful are always impatient and ardent in their demands. Every day in a revolution is equivalent to the career of a man. The day past is nothing, the present day is everything, and that will be nothing tomorrow. Influence, place, fortune, all that human passions most covet, are suspended and attached to the tree of liberty like prizes on the pole at a fair. The people do not want urging to flock to it in crowds. Go to the fair they must, and to get there everything must be overturned.

The principle which the monarchs must oppose to this plan of universal destruction is the preservation of everything legally existing. The only way to arrive at this end is by allowing no innovations.

Your Imperial Majesty knows me well enough to be assured that no person is farther removed than I am from any narrow views of administration. It is simply the attainment of real good that I desire, and on every occasion consider my duty to maintain. But the more positive I am of this the more I am convinced that it is impossible at the same time to preserve and to reform with any justice or reason when the mass of the people is in agitation; it is then like an individual in a state of irritation, threatened with fever, or already yielding to its ravages.

Let the Governments govern, and authority be something more than a name, for it is nothing without power.

By ruling, it really ameliorates the situation, but let authority remove nothing from the foundations on which it rests; let it act, but not concede. It should exercise its rights, but not discuss them. It should be just (and to be so it must be strong), and should respect all rights as it would have its own respected.

In one word, Sire, let us be conservative; let us walk steadily and firmly on well-known paths; let us not deviate from those lines in word or deed: we shall thus be strong, and shall come at last to a time when improvements may be made with as much chance of success as there is now certainty of failure.

DISCUSSION QUESTIONS

1. What does this document reveal about the inner workings of the congress system and the reasons for its success?

2. According to Metternich, what are the underlying principles that should guide the system, and why? If applied in practice, what benefits do they provide for society?

3. What specific aspects of the revolutionary legacy does Metternich target for criticism? What dangers does he think they pose? How should governments respond?

4. Challenge to Autocracy

Peter Kakhovsky, *The Decembrist Insurrection in Russia* (1825)

Guided by the Laybach agreement, the Austrians quickly suppressed the uprising in Naples, but challenges to the conservative order continued to loom on the horizon. Across Europe, people longing for constitutional rights and national independence chafed under the Vienna settlement and joined secret societies to agitate for change. When Tsar Alexander I died unexpectedly in December 1825, Russia became embroiled in the turmoil. Secret societies took this opportunity to orchestrate a revolt of the army at St. Petersburg on December 14 against Alexander's brother Nicholas as the new tsar. They favored Alexander's other brother, Constantine, who they thought would promote constitutional reform but who had, in fact, refused the crown. Nicholas I (r. 1825–1855) suppressed the uprising the same day. Peter Kakhovsky (1797–1826) was among the captured rebel leaders who were interrogated by a special committee set up for the investigation and eradication of secret societies in Russia. As the committee was preparing its final report for the tsar, Kakhovsky wrote this letter in February 1826 to one of the committee's members, General V. Levashev, defending his cause. Kakhovsky's impassioned words did nothing to change either his fate or that of Russia, however. He was executed in July, and for the remainder of his reign Nicholas kept a tight lid on all forms of dissent.

Your Excellency,
Dear Sir!

The uprising of December 14 is a result of causes related above. I see, Your Excellency, that the Committee established by His Majesty is making a great effort to discover all the members of the secret Society. But the government will not derive any notable benefit from that. We were not trained within the Society but were already ready to work when we joined it. The origin and the root of the Society one must seek in the spirit of the time and in our state of mind. I know a few belonging to the secret Society but am inclined to think the membership is not very large. Among my many acquaintances who do not adhere to the secret societies very few are opposed to my opinions. Frankly I state that among thousands of young men there are hardly a hundred who do not passionately long

From Anatole G. Mazour, *The First Russian Revolution, 1825* (Stanford, CA: Stanford University Press, 1961, 1937), 274–77.

for freedom. These youths, striving with pure and strong love for the welfare of their Fatherland, toward true enlightenment, are growing mature.

The people have conceived a sacred truth — that they do not exist for governments, but that governments must be organized for them. This is the cause of struggle in all countries; peoples, after tasting the sweetness of enlightenment and freedom, strive toward them; and governments, surrounded by millions of bayonets, make efforts to repel these peoples back into the darkness of ignorance. But all these efforts will prove in vain; impressions once received can never be erased. Liberty, that torch of intellect and warmth of life, was always and everywhere the attribute of peoples emerged from primitive ignorance. We are unable to live like our ancestors, like barbarians or slaves.

But even our ancestors, though less educated, enjoyed civil liberty. During the time of Tsar Aleksei Mikhailovich the National Assembly, including representatives of various classes of the people, still functioned and participated in important affairs of the State. In his reign five such Assemblies were summoned. Peter I, who killed everything national in the State, also stamped out our feeble liberty. This liberty disappeared outwardly but lived within the hearts of true citizens; its advancement was slow in our country. Wise Catherine II expanded it a little; Her Majesty inquired from the Petersburg Free Economic Society concerning the value and consequences of the emancipation of peasants in Russia. This great beneficial thought lived in the heart of the Empress, whom the people loved. Who among Russians of her day and time could have read her INSTRUCTION without emotion? The INSTRUCTION alone redeems all the shortcoming of that time, characteristic of that century.

Emperor Alexander promised as much; he, it could be said, enormously stirred the minds of the people toward the sacred rights of humanity. Later he changed his principles and intentions. The people became frightened, but the seed had sprouted and the roots grew deep. So rich with various revolutions are the latter half of the past century and the events of our own time that we have no need to refer to distant ones. We are witnesses of great events. The discovery of the New World and the United States, by virtue of its form of government, have forced Europe into rivalry with her. The United States will shine as an example even to distant generations. The name of Washington, the friend and benefactor of the people, will pass from generation to generation; the memory of his devotion to the welfare of the Fatherland will stir the hearts of citizens. In France the revolution which began so auspiciously turned, alas, at the end from a lawful into a criminal one. However, not the people but court intrigues and politics were responsible for that. The revolution in France shook all the thrones of Europe and had a greater influence upon the governments and peoples than the establishment of the United States.

The dominance of Napoleon and the war of 1813 and 1814 united all the European nations, summoned by their monarchs and fired by the call to freedom and citizenship. By what means were countless sums collected among citizens? What guided the armies? They preached freedom to us in Manifestoes, Appeals, and in Orders! We were lured and, kindly by nature, we believed, sparing neither blood nor property. Napoleon was overthrown! The Bourbons were called back to the throne of France and, submitting to circumstances, gave that brave, magnanimous nation a constitution, pledging themselves to forget that past. The Monarchs united into a Holy Alliance; congresses sprang into existence, informing the nations that they were assembled to reconcile all classes and introduce political freedom. But the aim of these congresses was soon revealed; the nations learned how greatly they had been deceived. The Monarchs thought only of how to retain their unlimited power, to support their shattered thrones, and to extinguish the last spark of freedom and enlightenment.

Offended nations began to demand what belonged to them and had been promised to them — chains and prisons became their lot! Crowns transgressed their pledges, the constitution of France was violated at its very base. Manuel, the representative of the people, was dragged from the Chamber of Deputies by gendarmes! Freedom of the press was restricted, the army of France, against its own will, was sent to destroy the lawful liberty of Spain. Forgetting the oath given by Louis XVIII, Charles X compensates *émigrés* and for that purpose burdens the people with new taxes. The government interferes with the election of deputies, and in the last elections, among the deputies only thirty-three persons were not in the service and payment of the King, the rest being sold to the Ministers. The firm, courageous Spanish people at the cost of blood rose for the liberty of their country, saved the King, the Monarchy, and the honor of the Fatherland; of their own volition the people themselves received Ferdinand as King. The King took the oath to safeguard the rights of the people. As early as the year 1812, Alexander I recognized the constitution of Spain.

Then the Alliance itself assisted France by sending her troops, and thus aided in dishonoring her army in the invasion of Spain. Ferdinand, arrested in Cadiz, was sentenced to death. He summoned Riego, swore to be once more loyal to the constitution and to expel the French troops from his territory, and begged Riego to spare his life. Honest men are apt to be trustful. Riego gave guaranty to the Cortes for the King, and he was freed. And what was the first step of Ferdinand? By his order Riego was seized, arrested, poisoned and, half-alive, that saint-martyr hero who renounced the throne offered to him, friend of the people, savior of the King's life, by the King's order is now taken through the streets of Madrid in the shameful wagon pulled by a donkey, and is hanged like a criminal. What an act! Whose heart would not shudder at it? Instead of the promised liberty the nations of Europe found themselves oppressed and their educational facilities curtailed. The prisons of Piedmont, Sardinia, Naples, and, in general, of the whole of Italy and Germany were filled with chained citizens. The lot of the people became so oppressive that they began to regret the past and to bless the memory of Napoleon the conqueror! These are the incidents which enlightened their minds and made them realize that it was impossible to make agreements with Sovereigns. . . .

The story told to Your Excellency that, in the uprising of December 14 the rebels were shouting "Long live the Constitution!" and that the people were asking "What is Constitution, the wife of His Highness the Grand Duke?" is not true. It is an amusing invention. We knew too well the meaning of a constitution and we had a word that would equally stir the hearts of all classes — LIBERTY!

. . .

The events of December are calamitous for us and, of course, must be distressing to the Emperor. Yet the events of this date should be fortunate for His Imperial Highness. After all, it was necessary sometime for the Society to begin its activities, but hardly could it have been so precipitate as in this instance. I swear to God, I wish the kind Sovereign prosperity! May God aid him in healing the wounds of our Fatherland and to become a friend and benefactor of the people. . . .

Most obedient and devoted servant of Your Excellency,

Peter Kakhovsky

DISCUSSION QUESTIONS

1. Why does Kakhovsky begin by denying broad membership in secret societies? What point is he trying to make about the source of Russians' political discontent?

2. How does Kakhovsky portray the Vienna settlement and its impact on European society and politics?

3. Kakhovsky was well versed in political history and had traveled widely in Europe before the Decembrist revolt. How did this knowledge and experience shape his views? What does this suggest about the power of the revolutionary legacy in post-Napoleonic Europe?

5. The Romantic Imagination

SOURCES IN CONVERSATION | Joseph M. W. Turner, *Transept of Tintern Abbey* (c. 1794) and William Wordsworth, *Lines Written a Few Miles above Tintern Abbey* (1798)

The political and social unrest of the first half of the nineteenth century found cultural expression in the artistic movement known as romanticism. As a whole, the movement challenged classical aesthetic conventions and instead embraced emotion, nature, and creativity. Painting and poetry were especially vibrant vehicles for the romantic sensibility, as displayed in these two sources. English painter Joseph M. W. Turner (1775–1851) and poet William Wordsworth (1770–1850) were contemporaries who had both come of age during the French Revolution. Like many others at the time, they traveled in search of scenery manifesting their idealized view of nature as an antidote to the cold heart of reason. The growing tourism industry was happy to oblige, organizing "picturesque" tours throughout Great Britain, including to Tintern Abbey along the River Wye. Long abandoned and in ruins, the abbey was a popular site for tourists seeking to experience a place that nature had made her own. Turner visited the abbey in 1792 and 1793, composing on-the-spot drawings upon which this watercolor is based. William Wordsworth likewise visited the region several times, including with his sister in 1798 as part of a walking tour. He captured his thoughts and impressions in the poem below, pondering his own mortality and the permanence of nature.

From William Wordsworth, "Lines Composed a Few Miles above Tintern Abbey: On Revisiting the Banks of the Wye during a Tour, July 12, 1798," in *European Romanticism: A Brief History with Documents*, ed. Warren Breckman (Boston: Bedford/St. Martin's, 2008), 71–75.

Transept of Tintern Abbey, Monmouthshire, c. 1794, by Joseph Turner (1775–1851) / Ashmolean Museum, University of Oxford, UK/Bridgeman Images

Five years have past; five summers, with the length
Of five long winters! and again I hear
These waters, rolling from their mountain-springs
With a soft inland murmur. — Once again
Do I behold these steep and lofty cliffs,
That on a wild secluded scene impress
Thoughts of more deep seclusion; and connect
The landscape with the quiet of the sky.
The day is come when I again repose
Here, under this dark sycamore, and view
These plots of cottage-ground, these orchard-tufts,
Which at this season, with their unripe fruits,
Are clad in one green hue, and lose themselves
'Mid groves and copses. Once again I see
These hedge-rows, hardly hedge-rows, little lines
Of sportive wood run wild: these pastoral farms,
Green to the very door; and wreaths of smoke
Sent up, in silence, from among the trees!
With some uncertain notice, as might seem
Of vagrant dwellers in the houseless woods,
Or of some Hermit's cave, where by his fire
The Hermit sits alone.
                              These beauteous forms,
Through a long absence, have not been to me
As is a landscape to blind man's eye:
But oft, in lonely rooms, and 'mid the din
Of towns and cities, I have owed to them
In hours of weariness, sensations sweet,
Felt in the blood, and felt along the heart;
And passing even into my purer mind,
With tranquil restoration: — feelings too
Of unremembered pleasure: such, perhaps,
As have no slight or trivial influence
On that best portion of a good man's life,
His little, nameless, unremembered, acts
Of kindness and of love. Nor less, I trust,
To them I may have owed another gift,
Of aspect more sublime; that blessed mood,
In which the burthen of the mystery,
In which the heavy and the weary weight
Of all this unintelligible world,
Is lightened: — that serene and blessed mood,
In which the affections gently lead us on, —
Until, the breath of this corporeal frame
And even the motion of our human blood
Almost suspended, we are laid asleep

In body, and become a living soul:
While with an eye made quiet by the power
Of harmony, and the deep power of joy,
We see into the life of things.
                              If this
Be but a vain belief, yet, oh! how oft —
In darkness and amid the many shapes
Of joyless daylight; when the fretful stir
Unprofitable, and the fever of the world,
Have hung upon the beatings of my heart—
How oft, in spirit, have I turned to thee,
O sylvan Wye! thou wanderer thro' the woods,
How often has my spirit turned to thee!
    And now, with gleams of half-extinguished thought,
With many recognitions dim and faint,
And somewhat of a sad perplexity,
The picture of the mind revives again:
While here I stand, not only with the sense
Of present pleasure, but with pleasing thoughts
That in this moment there is life and food
For future years. And so I dare to hope,
Though changed, no doubt, from what I was when first
I came among these hills; when like a roe
I bounded o'er the mountains, by the sides
Of the deep rivers, and the lonely streams,
Wherever nature led: more like a man
Flying from something that he dreads, than one
Who sought the thing he loved. For nature then
(The coarser pleasures of my boyish days,
And their glad animal movements all gone by)
To me was all in all. — I cannot paint
What then I was. The sounding cataract
Haunted me like a passion: the tall rock,
The mountain, and the deep and gloomy wood,
Their colours and their forms, were then to me
An appetite; a feeling and a love,
That had no need of a remoter charm,
By thought supplied, nor any interest
Unborrowed from the eye. — That time is past,
And all its aching joys are now no more,
And all its dizzy raptures. Not for this
Faint I, nor mourn nor murmur; other gifts
Have followed; for such loss, I would believe,
Abundant recompense. For I have learned
To look on nature, not as in the hour
Of thoughtless youth; but hearing oftentimes

The still, sad music of humanity,
Nor harsh nor grating, though of ample power
To chasten and subdue. And I have felt
A presence that disturbs me with the joy
Of elevated thoughts; a sense sublime
Of something far more deeply interfused,
Whose dwelling is the light of setting suns,
And the round ocean and the living air,
And the blue sky, and in the mind of man;
A motion and a spirit, that impels
All thinking things, all objects of all thought,
And rolls through all things. Therefore am I still
A lover of the meadows and the woods,
And mountains; and of all that we behold
From this green earth; of all the mighty world
Of eye, and ear, — both what they half create,
And what perceive; well pleased to recognise
In nature and the language of the sense,
The anchor of my purest thoughts, the nurse,
The guide, the guardian of my heart, and soul
Of all my moral being.
                                        Nor perchance,
If I were not thus taught, should I the more
Suffer my genial spirits to decay:
For thou art with me here upon the banks
Of this fair river; thou my dearest Friend,
My dear, dear Friend; and in thy voice I catch
The language of my former heart, and read
My former pleasures in the shooting lights
Of thy wild eyes. Oh! yet a little while
May I behold in thee what I was once,
My dear, dear Sister! and this prayer I make,
Knowing that Nature never did betray
The heart that loved her; 'tis her privilege,
Through all the years of this our life, to lead
From joy to joy: for she can so inform
The mind that is within us, so impress
With quietness and beauty, and so feed
With lofty thoughts, that neither evil tongues,
Rash judgments, nor the sneers of selfish men,
Nor greetings where no kindness is, nor all
The dreary intercourse of daily life,
Shall e'er prevail against us, or disturb
Our cheerful faith, that all which we behold
Is full of blessings. Therefore let the moon
Shine on thee in thy solitary walk;

And let the misty mountain-winds be free
To blow against thee: and, in after years,
When these wild ecstasies shall be matured
Into a sober pleasure; when thy mind
Shall be a mansion for all lovely forms,
Thy memory be as a dwelling-place
For all sweet sounds and harmonies; oh! then,
If solitude, or fear, or pain, or grief,
Should be thy portion, with what healing thoughts
Of tender joy wilt thou remember me,
And these my exhortations! Nor, perchance —
If I should be where I no more can hear
Thy voice, nor catch from thy wild eyes these gleams
Of past existence — wilt thou then forget
That on the banks of this delightful stream
We stood together; and that I, so long
A worshipper of Nature, hither came
Unwearied in that service; rather say
With warmer love — oh! with far deeper zeal
Of holier love. Nor wilt thou then forget,
That after many wanderings, many years
Of absence, these steep woods and lofty cliffs,
And this green pastoral landscape, were to me
More dear, both for themselves and for thy sake!

DISCUSSION QUESTIONS

1. Describe the overall impressions created by Turner's watercolor. What details stand out to you, and why?

2. How does Wordsworth describe nature in his poem? What influence does it play on his creative process?

3. Promoters of "picturesque" tourism in this period highlighted the contrast between natural beauty and man-made structures. In what ways are both Turner's watercolor and Wordsworth's poem built around a similar contrast?

6. Musical Romanticism

Reviews of Beethoven's Works (1799, 1812)

Romantic artists' desire to push aesthetic boundaries in this period extended to music as well. German composer Ludwig van Beethoven (1770–1827) was extremely influential in this process because of his extraordinary musical diversity and creative imagination. The

From *The Critical Reception of Beethoven's Compositions*, vol. I, ed. and trans. Wayne M. Senner (Lincoln: University of Nebraska Press, 1999), 142–43, 203.

critical reception of Beethoven's works allows us to see Beethoven through his contemporaries' eyes. Some viewed his ability to defy traditional musical categories as a weakness; others, by contrast, praised it as the very embodiment of genius. This tension between old and new, past and present, reflected broader tensions within European society in the wake of the French Revolution and Napoleonic domination. The two reviews below appeared during Beethoven's lifetime in the most influential music journal of the early nineteenth century, Allgemeine musikalische Zeitung. Closely allied with the music scene in Vienna, the journal had a network of correspondents in hundreds of communities across Germany. Its success went hand in hand with the growth of the public's interest in and the availability of music concerts such as the ones reviewed here.

Three Piano Sonatas in C Minor, F Major, and D Major
(October 9, 1799)

It cannot be denied that Mr. v. B. is a man of genius, has originality, and goes entirely his own way. In addition, his unusual thoroughness in the higher manner of writing and his own extraordinary command of the instrument he writes for unquestionably assure him of his rank among the best keyboard composers and performers of our time. His abundance of ideas, which a striving genius usually is unable to constrain as soon as it seizes upon a subject suitable for representation, too often still causes him to pile up ideas without restraint and to arrange them by means of a bizarre manner so as to bring about an obscure artificiality or an artificial obscurity, which is disadvantageous rather than advantageous to the effect of the entire piece.

Fantasy such as Beethoven possesses in no common degree, supported especially by such excellent knowledge, is something very valuable and indeed indispensable for a composer who feels within himself the dedication to become a greater artist and who disdains superficial and conventional composition. Rather, he wants to put forth something that has an inner, powerful vitality, which entices the connoisseur to a more frequent repetition of his work. However, in all arts there is an overabundance that derives from a too great and frequent craving for effect and learnedness, just as there is a clarity and charm that can well exist in conjunction with any thoroughness and diversity of composition (this word is used entirely in the general artistic sense).

This reviewer, who after having attempted gradually to accustom himself to Beethoven's manner, is beginning to value him more than before and cannot therefore suppress the wish that it might please this fanciful composer to allow himself to be guided throughout his works by a certain economy, which is, of course, more advantageous than the opposite. Indeed, this wish is intensified even more by the present work, which is clearer and therefore more beautiful than many of his other sonatas and remaining fortepiano pieces, although they do not thereby lose any of their thoroughness.

There are undoubtedly few artists to whom one must exclaim: save your treasures and be thrifty with them! For not many artists abound in ideas and are skilled in their combinations. It is therefore less a direct censure of Mr. v. B. here than a well-meant acclamation, which retains something honorable even if it does censure. . . .

News: Munich (February 19, 1812)

A Grand Symphony in D by Beethoven opened the first concert, given on 9 December. The works of this artist, unique in his own way, are as yet not well enough known here. People are accustomed to Haydn's and Mozart's works and should not be surprised if these rare products of Beethoven, which diverge so greatly from what is customary, don't always produce their effect upon the listener. This is not the place to evaluate this manner of composition. However, that a glowing fantasy, a high flight of powerful and ingenious harmonies prevails in it throughout, is admitted even by those who hold clarity and song-fulness to be the highest degree of art. Incidentally, the Andante of this symphony never-theless leaves nothing left to be desired in this respect. Certainly, the minuet and the final Allegro have a very bizarre quality. However, when the humor of so many of our writers attracts us, why do we want to expect the composer, who lays claim to the entire as yet so little charted domain of music, to stick only to customary forms? Why do we expect him always only to flatter the ear, never to un-settle us, and raise us above the customary, even if somewhat forcefully?

DISCUSSION QUESTIONS

1. What is the basis of the first reviewer's criticism of Beethoven's sonatas? What does this suggest about why some people resisted novelty and change in this period?

2. The second reviewer likewise acknowledges Beethoven's novelty. Does he cast it in a positive light or a negative light for his readers? What does he hope they will take away from his review about Beethoven's talents as a composer?

3. In what ways can the second review be seen as a response to the first despite the many years separating the two? What does this suggest about the public's acceptance of romanticism's ideals over time?

COMPARATIVE QUESTIONS

1. Al-Jabartî was highly critical of the French in Egypt because, from his perspective, they embraced the ideals of equality and liberty yet often placed restrictions on their mean-ings in practice. In what ways do the laws in the Civil Code support this view? What does this suggest about contradictions in Napoleon's method of rule and their long-term consequences?

2. Compare the political principles of Metternich and Kakhovsky. How did they differ? How were their differences rooted in the legacy of the French Revolution and Napoleonic conquests?

3. Kakhovsky targets Tsar Alexander's political views as a cause of the Decembrist rebel-lion. How did Metternich seek to shape these views and their translation into practice?

4. What do the Turner, Wordsworth, and Beethoven sources suggest about broader changes in popular culture in the early nineteenth century? In what ways did their work tap into these changes and channel them in new directions?

Industrialization and Social Ferment
1830–1850

T he nineteenth century was a time of momentous economic and social change as factories sprang up across much of Europe and railroad tracks crisscrossed the landscape. Although Britain initially led the way in industrial growth, the continent soon began to catch up. For the middle classes, industrialization opened a door to new riches and prestige. By contrast, for the men, women, and children who labored in factories and mines, it meant little more than a life of drudgery, poverty, and often extreme physical hardship. Documents 1 and 2 expose industrialization's effects on the everyday world, from the grueling regime of factory work to the demands of running the ideal middle-class household. Documents 3 and 4 demonstrate that, as industrialization picked up pace, people became increasingly aware of its human costs and the need to address them. Some social critics promoted reform within existing governmental structures; others sought to abolish them completely, giving rise to one of the most significant ideological consequences of the new age, the birth of communism. Yet the immediate impact of communism was far less visible than the effects of other forms of social and political ferment, as Documents 5 and 6 suggest. Against this backdrop, Europe's place in the world also underwent a shift. As Document 7 reveals, Europeans adopted new political and economic strategies overseas that laid the foundations for imperialism.

1. Establishing New Work Habits
Factory Rules in Berlin (1844)

Industrialization did not simply create new social classes, new jobs, and new problems; it also created new work habits regimented by the pace of machines and the time clock. It fell on factory owners and managers to instill these habits in the workforce to ensure efficient

From Sidney Pollard and C. Holmes, *Documents of European Economic History*, vol. I: *The Process of Industrialization, 1750–1870* (New York: St. Martin's Press, 1968), 534–36.

and consistent levels of production. This was no easy task because most people, whether former peasants or skilled workers, were traditionally accustomed to controlling their own time. The list of rules distributed to the employees of the Foundry and Engineering Works of the Royal Overseas Trading Company in Berlin provides a telling example of one approach to this challenge. This document also illustrates the spread of industrialization eastward across continental Europe.

In every large works, and in the co-ordination of any large number of workmen, good order and harmony must be looked upon as the fundamentals of success, and therefore the following rules shall be strictly observed.

Every man employed in the concern named below shall receive a copy of these rules, so that no one can plead ignorance. Its acceptance shall be deemed to mean consent to submit to its regulations.

(1) The normal working day begins at all seasons at 6 a.m. precisely and ends, after the usual break of half an hour for breakfast, an hour for dinner and half an hour for tea, at 7 p.m., and it shall be strictly observed.

Five minutes before the beginning of the stated hours of work until their actual commencement, a bell shall ring and indicate that every worker employed in the concern has to proceed to his place of work, in order to start as soon as the bell stops.

The doorkeeper shall lock the door punctually at 6 a.m., 8.30 a.m., 1 p.m., and 4.30 p.m.

Workers arriving 2 minutes late shall lose half an hour's wages; whoever is more than 2 minutes late may not start work until after the next break, or at least shall lose his wages until then. Any disputes about the correct time shall be settled by the clock mounted above the gatekeeper's lodge.

These rules are valid both for time and for piece-workers, and in cases of breaches of these rules, workmen shall be fined in proportion to their earnings. The deductions from the wage shall be entered in the wage-book of the gatekeeper whose duty they are; they shall be unconditionally accepted as it will not be possible to enter into any discussions about them.

(2) When the bell is rung to denote the end of the working day, every workman, both on piece and on day-wage, shall leave his workshop and the yard, but is not allowed to make preparations for his departure before the bell rings. Every breach of this rule shall lead to a fine of five silver groschen to the sick fund. Only those who have obtained special permission by the overseer may stay on in the workshop in order to work. — If a workman has worked beyond the closing bell, he must give his name to the gatekeeper on leaving, on pain of losing his payment for the overtime.

(3) No workman, whether employed by time or piece, may leave before the end of the working day, without having first received permission from the overseer and having given his name to the gatekeeper. Omission of these two actions shall lead to a fine of ten silver groschen payable to the sick fund.

(4) Repeated irregular arrival at work shall lead to dismissal. This shall also apply to those who are found idling by an official or overseer, and refuse to obey their order to resume work.

(5) Entry to the firm's property by any but the designated gateway, and exit by any prohibited route, e.g., by climbing fences or walls, or by crossing the Spree, shall be

punished by a fine of fifteen silver groschen to the sick fund for the first offences, and dismissal for the second.

(6) No worker may leave his place of work otherwise than for reasons connected with his work.

(7) All conversation with fellow-workers is prohibited; if any worker requires information about his work, he must turn to the overseer, or to the particular fellow-worker designated for the purpose.

(8) Smoking in the workshops or in the yard is prohibited during working hours; anyone caught smoking shall be fined five silver groschen for the sick fund for every such offence.

(9) Every worker is responsible for cleaning up his space in the workshop, and if in doubt, he is to turn to his overseer. — All tools must always be kept in good condition, and must be cleaned after use. This applies particularly to the turner, regarding his lathe.

(10) Natural functions must be performed at the appropriate places, and whoever is found soiling walls, fences, squares, etc., and similarly, whoever is found washing his face and hands in the workshop and not in the places assigned for the purpose, shall be fined five silver groschen for the sick fund.

(11) On completion of his piece of work, every workman must hand it over at once to his foreman or superior, in order to receive a fresh piece of work. Pattern makers must on no account hand over their patterns to the foundry without express order of their supervisors. No workman may take over work from his fellow-workman without instruction to that effect by the foreman.

(12) It goes without saying that all overseers and officials of the firm shall be obeyed without question, and shall be treated with due deference. Disobedience will be punished by dismissal.

(13) Immediate dismissal shall also be the fate of anyone found drunk in any of the workshops.

(14) Untrue allegations against superiors or officials of the concern shall lead to stern reprimand, and may lead to dismissal. The same punishment shall be meted out to those who knowingly allow errors to slip through when supervising or stocktaking.

(15) Every workman is obliged to report to his superiors any acts of dishonesty or embezzlement on the part of his fellow workmen. If he omits to do so, and it is shown after subsequent discovery of a misdemeanor that he knew about it at the time, he shall be liable to be taken to court as an accessory after the fact and the wage due to him shall be retained as punishment. Conversely, anyone denouncing a theft in such a way as to allow conviction of the thief shall receive a reward of two Thaler, and, if necessary, his name shall be kept confidential. — Further, the gatekeeper and the watchman, as well as every official, are entitled to search the baskets, parcels, aprons, etc. of the women and children who are taking dinners into the works, on their departure, as well as search any worker suspected of stealing any article whatever. . . .

(18) Advances shall be granted only to the older workers, and even to them only in exceptional circumstances. As long as he is working by the piece, the workman is entitled merely to his fixed weekly wage as subsistence pay; the extra earnings shall be paid out only on completion of the whole piece contract. If a workman leaves before his piece contract is completed, either of his own free will, or on being dismissed as punishment, or because of illness, the partly completed work shall be valued by the general manager with

the help of two overseers, and he will be paid accordingly. There is no appeal against the decision of these experts.

(19) A free copy of these rules is handed to every workman, but whoever loses it and requires a new one, or cannot produce it on leaving, shall be fined 2½ silver groschen, payable to the sick fund.

DISCUSSION QUESTIONS

1. As delineated in the rules, what new modes of discipline did factory work require, and why?
2. What was the principal method used to encourage compliance with these rules?
3. Based on this document, how would you describe a typical day for the workers in this factory?

2. New Rules for the Middle Class

Sarah Stickney Ellis,
Characteristics of the Women of England (1839)

As more working-class women toiled in factories, the growing ranks of middle-class women faced their own challenges. Many social commentators expected middle-class women to focus on their homes and families, thereby transforming them into bastions of order, tranquillity, and proper behavior. Writers such as Sarah Stickney Ellis (1812–1872) offered ample advice on fulfilling such expectations. Published in 1839, The Women of England was the first in Ellis's series of hugely successful conduct guides for women. In the following excerpt, she discusses a range of topics to help her female readers cultivate their "highest attributes" as pillars of family life, which, Ellis argues, required unwavering self-sacrifice and service. Her words portray the domestic ideal that, in reality, eluded many women, either by choice or by circumstance. Even so, the book reveals much about changing attitudes toward women during the industrial age.

Perhaps it may be necessary to be more specific in describing the class of women to which this work relates. It is, then, strictly speaking, to those who belong to that great mass of the population of England which is connected with trade and manufactures; — or, in order to make the application more direct, to that portion of it who are restricted to the services of from one to four domestics, — who, on the one hand, enjoy the advantages of a liberal education, and, on the other, have no pretension to family rank. . . .

It is from the class of females above described, that we naturally look for the highest tone of moral feeling, because they are at the same time removed from the pressing necessities of absolute poverty, and admitted to the intellectual privileges of the great; and thus, while they enjoy every facility in the way of acquiring knowledge, it is their still higher privilege not to be exempt from the domestic duties which call forth the best energies of the female character.

From Sarah Stickney Ellis, *The Women of England: Their Social Duties and Domestic Habits* (New York: Henry G. Langley, 1844), 8–10.

Where domestics abound, and there is a *hired* hand for every kindly office, it would be a work of supererogation for the mistress of the house to step forward, and assist with her own; but where domestics are few, and the individuals who compose the household are thrown upon the consideration of the mothers, wives, and daughters for their daily comfort, innumerable channels are opened for the overflow of those floods of human kindness, which it is one of the happiest and most ennobling duties of woman to administer to the weary frame, and to pour into the wounded mind.

It is perhaps the nearest approach we can make towards any thing like a definition of what is most striking in the characteristics of the women of England, to say, that the nature of their domestic circumstances is such as to invest their characters with the three-fold recommendation of *promptitude in action, energy of thought, and benevolence of feeling.* With all the responsibilities of family comfort and social enjoyment resting upon them, and unaided by those troops of menials who throng the halls of the affluent and the great, they are kept alive to the necessity of making their own personal exertions conducive to the great end of promoting the happiness of those around them. They cannot sink into supineness, or suffer any of their daily duties to be neglected, but some beloved member of the household is made to feel the consequences, by enduring inconveniences which it is alike their pride and their pleasure to remove. The frequently recurring avocations of domestic life admit of no delay. When the performance of any kindly office has to be asked for, solicited, and re-solicited, it loses more than half its charm. It is therefore strictly in keeping with the fine tone of an elevated character to be beforehand with expectation, and thus to show, by the most delicate yet most effectual of all human means, that the object of attention, even when unheard and unseen, has been the subject of kind and affectionate solicitude.

By experience in these apparently minute affairs, a woman of kindly feeling and properly disciplined mind, soon learns to regulate her actions also according to the principles of true wisdom, and hence arises that energy of thought for which the women of England are so peculiarly distinguished. Every passing event, however insignificant to the eye of the world, has its crisis, every occurrence its emergency, every cause its effect; and upon these she has to calculate with precision, or the machinery of household comfort is arrested in its movements, and thrown into disorder.

Woman, however, would but ill supply the place appointed her by Providence, were she endowed with no other faculties than those of promptitude in action and energy of thought. Valuable as these may be, they would render her but a cold and cheerless companion, without the kindly affections and tender offices that sweeten human life. It is a high privilege, then, which the women of England enjoy, to be necessarily, and by the force of circumstances, thrown upon their affections, for the rule of their conduct in daily life. "What shall I do to gratify myself — to be admired — or to vary the tenor of my existence?" are not the questions which a woman of right feelings asks on first awaking to the avocations of the day. Much more congenial to the highest attributes of woman's character, are inquiries such as these: "How shall I endeavor through this day to turn the time, the health, and the means permitted me to enjoy, to the best account? — Is any one sick? I must visit their chamber without delay, and try to give their apartment an air of comfort, by arranging such things as the wearied nurse may not have thought of. Is any one about to set off on a journey? I must see that the early meal is spread, or prepare it with my own hands, in order that the servant, who was working last night, may profit by unbroken rest. Did I fail in what was kind or considerate to any of the family yesterday? I will meet her this morning with a cordial welcome, and show, in the most delicate way I can, that I am anxious to atone for the past. Was any one exhausted by the last day's exertion? I will be an hour before them this morning, and let them see that their labor is so much in advance. Or, if nothing extraordinary occurs to claim my attention, I will meet the family with a consciousness that, being the least engaged of any member of it, I am consequently the most at liberty to devote myself to the general good of the whole, by cultivating cheerful conversation, adapting myself to the prevailing tone of feeling, and leading those who are least happy, to think and speak of what will make them more so."

Who can believe that days, months, and years spent in a continual course of thought and action similar to this, will not produce a powerful effect upon the character, and not only upon the individual who thinks and acts alone, but upon all to whom her influence extends? In short, the customs of English society have so constituted women the guardians of the comfort of their homes, that, like the Vestals of old, they cannot allow the lamp they cherish to be extinguished, or to fail for want of oil, without an equal share of degradation attaching to their names.

In other countries, where the domestic lamp is voluntarily put out, in order to allow the women to resort to the opera, or the public festival, they are not only careless about their home comforts, but necessarily ignorant of the high degree of excellence to which they might be raised. In England there is a kind of science of good household management, which, if it consisted merely in keeping the house respectable in its physical character, might be left to the effectual working out of hired hands; but, happily for the women of England, there is a philosophy in this science, by which all their highest and best feelings are called into exercise. Not only must the house be neat and clean, but it must be so ordered as to suit the tastes of all, as far as may be, without annoyance or offence to any. Not only must a constant system of activity be established, but peace must be preserved, or happiness will be destroyed. Not only must elegance be called in, to adorn and beautify the whole, but strict integrity must be maintained by the minutest calculation as to lawful means, and self, and self-gratification, must be made the yielding point in every disputed case. Not only must an appearance of outward order and comfort be kept up, but around every domestic scene there must be a strong wall of confidence, which no internal suspicion can undermine, no external enemy break through.

DISCUSSION QUESTIONS

1. How does Ellis define middle-class English women, and why does she address her book specifically to them?

2. According to Ellis, what are a middle-class woman's principal domestic duties, and why are they important?

3. What do a woman's domestic duties suggest about the status of middle-class women in English society at the time?

3. The Division of Labor

SOURCES IN CONVERSATION | *Testimony Gathered by Ashley's Mines Commission* (1842) and *Punch* Magazine, *Capital and Labour* (1843)

Coal-fired steam engines were at the heart of the Industrial Revolution. They fueled the rapid spread of railroads and new textile machinery, which in turn fueled an increased demand for coal. Miners, young and old, worked under extremely difficult conditions to keep pace. This was especially true in Britain, the hub of the Industrial Revolution, where the output of coal and iron doubled between 1830 and 1850. The miners' plight sparked calls for reform, with the government often taking the lead. In 1842, Anthony Ashley Cooper headed a series of parliamentary hearings to gather firsthand accounts of the working conditions in the mines, particularly regarding the use of child labor. Below are excerpts from testimony heard by the commission describing the dismal realities of the mining industry. The "Capital and Labour" cartoon appeared in the British magazine Punch *the following year to coincide with Parliament's ongoing investigation into the employment of children in the workplace. As it suggests, people recognized not only that industrialization was built on the backs of workers but also that it profoundly altered traditional socioeconomic relations, with capitalistic "money men" exploiting human labor for monetary gain.*

Sarah Gooder, Aged 8 Years

I'm a trapper[1] in the Gawber pit. It does not tire me, but I have to trap without a light and I'm scared. I go at four and sometimes half past three in the morning, and come out at five and half past. I never go to sleep. Sometimes I sing when I've light, but not in the dark; I dare not sing then. I don't like being in the pit. I am very sleepy when I go sometimes in the morning. I go to Sunday-schools and read *Reading Made Easy*. She knows her letters and can read little words. They teach me to pray. She repeated the Lord's Prayer, not very perfectly, and ran on with the following addition: — "God bless my father and mother, and sister and brother, uncles and aunts and cousins, and everybody else, and God bless me and make me a good servant. Amen." I have heard tell of Jesus many a time. I don't know why he came on earth, I'm sure, and I don't know why he died, but he had stones for his head to rest on. I would like to be at school far better than in the pit.

Thomas Wilson, Esq., of the Banks, Silkstone, Owner of Three Collieries[2]

. . . The employment of females of any age in and about the mines is most objectionable, and I should rejoice to see it put an end to; but in the present feeling of the colliers,

From Jonathan F. Scott and Alexander Baltzly, *Readings in European History Since 1814* (New York: Appleton-Century-Crofts, Inc., 1958), 87–90; and Michael Freeman, *Railways and the Victorian Imagination* (New Haven: Yale University Press, 1999), plate 108. © *Punch* Magazine, 1843.

[1]**trapper:** A job, always performed by young children, that involved sitting in a hole hollowed out for them, where they could open trapdoors to allow coal wagons to pass through the mine. [Ed.]
[2]**colliery:** A coal mine and its physical plant, including buildings. [Ed.]

no individual would succeed in stopping it in a neighbourhood where it prevailed, because the men would immediately go to those pits where their daughters would be employed. The only way effectually to put an end to this and other evils in the present colliery system is to elevate the minds of the men; and the only means to attain this is to combine sound moral and religious training and industrial habits with a system of intellectual culture much more perfect than can at present be obtained by them.

I object on general principles to government interference in the conduct of any trade, and I am satisfied that in mines it would be productive of the greatest injury and injustice. The art of mining is not so perfectly understood as to admit of the way in which a colliery shall be conducted being dictated by any person, however experienced, with such certainty as would warrant an interference with the management of private business. I should also most decidedly object to placing collieries under the present provisions of the Factory Act with respect to the education of children employed therein. First, because, if it is contended that coal-owners, as employers of children, are bound to attend to their education, this obligation extends equally to all other employers, and therefore it is unjust to single out one class only; secondly, because, if the legislature asserts a right to interfere to secure education, it is bound to make that interference general; and thirdly, because the mining population is in this neighbourhood so intermixed with other classes, and is in such small bodies in any one place, that it would be impossible to provide separate schools for them.

Isabella Read, 12 Years Old, Coal-Bearer

Works on mother's account, as father has been dead two years. Mother bides at home, she is troubled with bad breath, and is very weak in her body from early labour. I am wrought with sister and brother, it is very sore work; cannot say how many rakes or journeys I make from pit's bottom to wall face and back, thinks about 30 or 25 on the average; the distance varies from 100 to 250 fathom.

I carry about 1 cwt.³ and a quarter on my back; have to stoop much and creep through water, which is frequently up to the calves of my legs. When first down fell frequently asleep while waiting for coal from heat and fatigue.

I do not like the work, nor do the lassies, but they are made to like it. When the weather is warm there is difficulty in breathing, and frequently the lights go out.

Isabel Wilson, 38 Years Old, Coal Putter [hauler]

When women have children thick (fast) they are compelled to take them down early, I have been married 19 years and have had 10 bairns; seven are in life. When on Sir John's work was a carrier of coals, which caused me to miscarry five times from the strains, and was ill after each. Putting is not so oppressive; last child was born on Saturday morning, and I was at work on the Friday night.

Once met with an accident; a coal brake my cheek-bone, which kept me idle some weeks.

I have wrought below 30 years, and so has the guid man; he is getting touched in the breath now.

---

³One hundredweight (cwt.) equals 100 pounds. [Ed.]

None of the children read, as the work is not regular. I did read once, but not able to attend to it now; when I go below lassie 10 years of age keeps house and makes the broth or stir-about.

Nine sleep in two bedsteads; there did not appear to be any beds, and the whole of the other furniture consisted of two chairs, three stools, a table, a kail-pot and a few broken basins and cups. Upon asking if the furniture was all they had, the guid wife said, furniture was of no use, as it was so troublesome to flit with.

Patience Kershaw, Aged 17

My father has been dead about a year; my mother is living and has ten children, five lads and five lasses; the oldest is about thirty, the youngest is four; three lasses go to mill; all the lads are colliers, two getters and three hurriers[4]; one lives at home and does nothing; mother does nought but look after home.

All my sisters have been hurriers, but three went to the mill. Alice went because her legs swelled from hurrying in cold water when she was hot. I never went to day-school; I go to Sunday-school, but I cannot read or write; I go to pit at five o'clock in the morning and come out at five in the evening; I get my breakfast of porridge and milk first; I take my dinner with me, a cake, and eat it as I go; I do not stop or rest any time for the purpose; I get nothing else until I get home, and then have potatoes and meat, not every day meat. I hurry in the clothes I have now got on, trousers and ragged jacket; the bald place upon my head is made by thrusting the corves; my legs have never swelled, but sisters' did when they went to mill; I hurry the corves a mile and more under ground and back; they weigh 300 cwt.; I hurry 11 a-day; I wear a belt and chain at the workings to get the corves out; the getters that I work for are naked except their caps; they pull off all their clothes; I see them at work when I go up; sometimes they beat me, if I am not quick enough, with their hands; they strike me upon my back; the boys take liberties with me sometimes they pull me about; I am the only girl in the pit; there are about 20 boys and 15 men; all the men are naked; I would rather work in mill than in coal-pit.

This girl is an ignorant, filthy, ragged, and deplorable-looking object, and such an one as the uncivilized natives of the prairies would be shocked to look upon.

Mary Barrett, Aged 14

I have worked down in pit five years; father is working in next pit; I have 12 brothers and sisters — all of them but one live at home; they weave, and wind, and hurry, and one is a counter, one of them can read, none of the rest can, or write; they never went to day-school, but three of them go to Sunday-school; I hurry for my brother John, and come down at seven o'clock about; I go up at six, sometimes seven; I do not like working in pit, but I am obliged to get a living; I work always without stockings, or shoes, or trousers; I wear nothing but my chemise; I have to go up to the headings with the men; they are all naked there; I am got well used to that, and don't care now much about it; I was afraid at first, and did not like it; they never behave rudely to me; I cannot read or write.

---

[4]**hurrier**: Job involving pulling carts, called corves, filled with coal to the mine's surface. The worker was typically harnessed to the cart for this purpose. [Ed.]

Capital and Labour

CAPITAL AND LABOUR.

Universal History Archive / Universal Images Group / Shutterstock

DISCUSSION QUESTIONS

1. How does the top portion of the cartoon portray the lifestyle of British capitalists? What images stand out in particular?

2. How does this portrait contrast to that of the people shown in the bottom portion? What connections do you see between the images here and the testimony gathered by Ashley's Mines Commission?

3. What is the relationship between the top and bottom parts of the cartoon? How are their meanings interdependent?

4. What Is the Proletariat?

Friedrich Engels,
Draft of a Communist Confession of Faith (1847)

When Friedrich Engels (1820–1895) composed the following draft of a communist "confession of faith" in 1847, the Industrial Revolution was in full swing in Great Britain and rapidly gaining ground on the continent. Engels observed the impact of this process on the working class with a critical eye. Two years earlier, he had joined forces with another critic of industrialization, Karl Marx (1818–1883). Together they launched an ideological revolution with the publication of the Communist Manifesto in 1848, which set forth a new understanding of industrial society and its problems and proposed a new set of solutions centered on the abolition of capitalist, "private" property. Engels's "confession of faith" illuminates key landmarks on his and Marx's intellectual journey, for it was among the materials Marx used to compose the manifesto. The confession was debated and approved in 1847 at the first congress of the Communist League. Although the first six questions reveal Engels's debt to the utopian principle of the community of property, those remaining reflect his and Marx's distinct historical vision.

Draft of a Communist Confession of Faith

June 9, 1847

QUESTION 1: *Are you a Communist?*

ANSWER: Yes.

QUESTION 2: *What is the aim of the Communists?*

ANSWER: To organize society in such a way that every member of it can develop and use all his capabilities and powers in complete freedom and without thereby infringing the basic conditions of this society.

QUESTION 3: *How do you wish to achieve this aim?*

ANSWER: By the elimination of private property and its replacement by community of property.

QUESTION 4: *On what do you base your community of property?*

ANSWER: Firstly, on the mass of productive forces and means of subsistence resulting from the development of industry, agriculture, trade and colonization, and on the possibility inherent in machinery, chemical, and other resources of their infinite extension.

Secondly, on the fact that in the consciousness or feeling of every individual there exist certain irrefutable basic principles which, being the result of the whole of historical development, require no proof.

QUESTION 5: *What are such principles?*

ANSWER: For example, every individual strives to be happy. The happiness of the individual is inseparable from the happiness of all, etc.

QUESTION 6: *How do you wish to prepare the way for your community of property?*

ANSWER: By enlightening and uniting the proletariat.

QUESTION 7: *What is the proletariat?*

ANSWER: The proletariat is that class of society which lives exclusively by its labor and not on the profit from any kind of capital; that class whose weal and woe, whose life and death, therefore, depend on the alternation of times of good and bad business; in a word, on the fluctuations of competition.

QUESTION 8: *Then there have not always been proletarians?*

From John E. Toews, ed., *The Communist Manifesto with Related Documents* (Boston: Bedford/ St. Martin's, 1999), 99–104.

ANSWER: No. There have always been poor and working classes; and those who worked were almost always the poor. But there have not always been proletarians, just as competition has not always been free.

QUESTION 9: *How did the proletariat arise?*

ANSWER: The proletariat came into being as a result of the introduction of the machines which have been invented since the middle of the last century and the most important of which are: the steam-engine, the spinning machine, and the power loom. These machines, which were very expensive and could therefore only be purchased by rich people, supplanted the workers of the time, because by the use of machinery it was possible to produce commodities more quickly and cheaply than could the workers with their imperfect spinning wheels and hand-looms. The machines thus delivered industry entirely into the hands of the big capitalists and rendered the workers' scanty property which consisted mainly of their tools, looms, etc., quite worthless, so that the capitalist was left with everything, the worker with nothing. In this way the factory system was introduced. Once the capitalists saw how advantageous this was for them, they sought to extend it to more and more branches of labor. They divided work more and more between the workers so that workers who formerly had made a whole article now produced only a part of it. Labor simplified in this way produced goods more quickly and therefore more cheaply and only now was it found in almost every branch of labor that here also machines could be used. As soon as any branch of labor went over to factory production it ended up, just as in the case of spinning and weaving, in the hands of the big capitalists, and the workers were deprived of the last remnants of their independence. We have gradually arrived at the position where almost *all* branches of labor are run on a factory basis. This has increasingly brought about the ruin of the previously existing middle class, especially of the small master craftsmen, completely transformed the previous position of the workers, and two new classes which are gradually swallowing up all other classes have come into being, namely:

I. The class of the big capitalists, who in all advanced countries are in almost exclusive possession of the means of subsistence and those means (machines, factories, workshops, etc.) by which these means of subsistence are produced. This is the *bourgeois* class, or the *bourgeoisie*.

II. The class of the completely propertyless, who are compelled to sell their labor to the first class, the bourgeois, simply to obtain from them in return their means of subsistence. Since the parties to this trading in labor are not *equal*, but the bourgeois have the advantage, the propertyless must submit to the bad conditions laid down by the bourgeois. This class, dependent on the bourgeois, is called the class of the *proletarians* or the *proletariat*.

QUESTION 10: *In what way does the proletarian differ from the slave?*

ANSWER: The slave is sold once and for all, the proletarian has to sell himself by the day and by the hour. The slave is the property of one master and for that very reason has a guaranteed subsistence, however wretched it may be. The proletarian is, so to speak, the slave of the entire bourgeois *class*, not of one master, and therefore has no guaranteed subsistence, since nobody buys his labor if he does not need it.[...]

QUESTION 11: *In what way does the proletarian differ from the serf?*

ANSWER: The serf has the piece of land, that is, of an instrument of production, in return for handing over a greater or lesser portion of the yield. The proletarian works with instruments of production which belong to someone else who, in return for his labor, hands over to him a portion, determined by competition, of the products. In the case of the serf, the share of the laborer is determined by his own labor, that is, by himself. In the case of the proletarian it is determined by competition, therefore in the first place by the bourgeois. The serf has guaranteed subsistence, the proletarian has not.[...]

QUESTION 12: *In what way does the proletarian differ from the handicraftsman?*

ANSWER: As opposed to the proletarian, the so-called handicraftsman, who still existed nearly everywhere during the last century and still exists here and there, is at most a *temporary* proletarian. His aim is to acquire capital himself and so to exploit other workers. He can often achieve this aim where the craft guilds still exist or where freedom to follow a trade has not yet led to the organization of handwork on a factory basis and to intense competition. But as soon as the factory system is introduced into handwork and competition is in full swing, this prospect is eliminated and the handicraftsman becomes more and more a proletarian. The handicraftsman therefore frees himself *either* by becoming a bourgeois or in general passing over into the middle class, *or*, by becoming a proletarian as a result of competition (as now happens in most cases) and joining the movement of the proletariat — i.e., the more or less conscious communist movement.

QUESTION 13: *Then you do not believe that community of property has been possible at any time?*

ANSWER: No. Communism has only arisen since machinery and other inventions made it possible to hold out the prospect of an all-sided development, a happy existence, for all members of society. Communism is the theory of a liberation which was not possible for the slaves, the serfs, or the handicraftsmen, but only for the proletarians and hence it belongs of necessity to the 19th century and was not possible in any earlier period.

QUESTION 14: *Let us go back to the sixth question. As you wish to prepare for community of property by the enlightening and uniting of the proletariat, then you reject revolution?*

ANSWER: We are convinced not only of the uselessness but even of the harmfulness of all conspiracies. We are also aware that revolutions are not made deliberately and arbitrarily but that everywhere and at all times they are the necessary consequence of circumstances which are not in any way whatever dependent either on the will or on the leadership of individual parties or of whole classes. But we also see that the development of the proletariat in almost all countries of the world is forcibly repressed by the possessing classes and that thus a revolution is being forcibly worked for by the opponents of communism. If, in the end, the oppressed proletariat is thus driven into a revolution, then we will defend the cause of the proletariat just as well by our deeds as now by our words.

QUESTION 15: *Do you intend to replace the existing social order by community of property at one stroke?*

ANSWER: We have no such intention. The development of the masses cannot be ordered by decree. It is determined by the development of the conditions in which these masses live, and therefore proceeds gradually.

QUESTION 16: *How do you think the transition from the present situation to commu-nity of property is to be effected?*

ANSWER: The first, fundamental condition for the introduction of community of property is the political liberation of the proletariat through a democratic constitution.

QUESTION 17: *What will be your first measure once you have established democracy?*

ANSWER: Guaranteeing the subsistence of the proletariat.

QUESTION 18: *How will you do this?*

ANSWER: I. By limiting private property in such a way that it gradually prepares the way for its transformation into social property, e.g., by progressive taxa-tion, limitation of the right of inheritance in favor of the state, etc., etc.

II. By employing workers in national workshops and factories and on national estates.

III. By educating all children at the expense of the state.

DISCUSSION QUESTIONS

1. According to Engels's confession, what were the central goals of the communists, and how did they aim to achieve them?

2. How does Engels define the proletariat, and what sets it apart from other types of workers?

3. How does Engels's confession explicitly link communist ideology to industrialization? What place did revolution have in this ideology?

5. The Promise of Emigration

Gottfried Menzel, *The United States of North America, With Special Reference to German Emigration* (1853)

Even as industrialization advanced across the continent, food shortages, overpopulation, and unemployment plagued much of Europe. The result was an unprecedented era of mass migration, particularly from agricultural regions in the east that were largely isolated from industrial markets and susceptible to famine. Between 1840 and 1860, 4.2 million people left Europe to forge new lives in the United States. In the 1840s alone, 400,000 German immigrants seeking a better life arrived on American shores. As German emigration picked up pace, so too did the publication of guides and advice books promoting migration and the United States in glowing terms. After visiting the United States in the early 1840s, German botanist Gottfried Menzel (1798–1889) tapped into this trend with his guidebook

Gottfried Menzel, *The United States of North America, with Special Reference to German Emigra-tion (1853)*. From "What Does North America Offer to the German Emigrant?" in Edith Abbott, ed., *Historical Aspects of the Immigration Problem: Select Documents* (Chicago: University of Chicago Press, 1987), 137–42.

The United States of North America. *Originally published in German in Berlin in 1853, the book offered a more tempered view than many of its competitors on both the benefits and the pitfalls awaiting German immigrants in North America.*

In Germany as in most of the European states many people are dissatisfied with the state organization and institutions. They feel themselves hampered by the government, complain of lack of freedom, of too much government, and the like, and direct their gaze to the free states of the great North American Republic, as the land of desired freedom. . . .

Much greater is the number of those who leave their fatherland on account of the poverty of its material resources and in order to better their condition in America. For many people industrial conditions in Germany are such that you cannot blame them for emigrating when they learn that in North America there are far greater productive natural resources and that work has a greater value than in Germany.

He who in Germany has to suffer from want and misery, or must expect these in the near future, finds that hope of better fortune overcomes his attachment to the fatherland. He easily separates himself from his old home and wanders to a distant land believing that he will find life more favorable there.

That it is easier to make a living in America cannot be denied; but it is a matter of regret that those who could better their condition in this way frequently lack the means. Many people who take this risk find only their misfortune or ruin. The numbers of those who return to Germany from America prove that many are not successful there. . . .

Therefore everyone who is thinking of emigrating to America should take care to determine whether or not he is fit for America. He should carefully weigh what he leaves here against what he may find there, lest he should be guilty of too great haste or light-mindedness and make a mistake that he may regret only too soon and bitterly. . . .

A great many books about emigration to America have been written, and every year new ones appear. . . . A book written against emigration, or one advising emigration only for the few, would have little charm and would find few purchasers. But as soon as a book appears which describes the land to which the emigrant would go as a land of paradise, then it is sold and read diligently, and thousands are moved in this way to become emigrants. Many a book on emigration very truly describes what is good and what is agreeable in America, but passes over in silence the disadvantages or disagreeable features of American life. Through this one-sided presentation of American conditions many are lured to emigrate. It is obvious that the countless speculators who every year gain many millions of emigrants will make a great effort to bring to the attention of the people many books through which the desire for emigration is awakened and increased. They are themselves completely indifferent to the fate of the emigrants, and if emigration turns out to be for their ruin they do not care. . . .

What Does North America Offer That Is Good?

This great country offers its inhabitants noteworthy advantages which may be summarized as follows:

Although the citizens of the United States are not, as is popularly supposed, free from taxes, yet the taxes on land and cattle which the farmer has to pay are not high, and artisans pay no taxes on their business.

The citizens are, during a certain age, under obligation to serve in the militia, but except in the case of war this is rarely asked of them except perhaps for suppression of a riot. For regular military service volunteers are always available, since they are well paid. The quartering of soldiers in time of peace is not allowed.

Complete freedom in the trades and professions, hunting and fishing is allowed to everyone....

There is no difference in rank. The terms "upper class" and "lower class" have no significance. The public official has no advantage not shared by the farmer, the merchant, or the teamster.

North America, as a country with fertile land still partly unoccupied, a country thinly populated with flourishing trade and general freedom of trade, offers far greater and more abundant means of livelihood than Germany.

Labor there has a high, and cost of living a lower, value; therefore on the whole the people are far less oppressed by want and need and the tormenting anxiety for one's daily bread.

Against the advantages just enumerated . . . the following disadvantages will not please those who are eager to emigrate....

The German in America is a complete stranger. Everything is strange, the country, the climate, laws, and customs. One ought to realize what it means to be an alien in a far distant land. More than this, the German in America is despised as alien, and he must often hear the nickname "Dutchman,"[1] at least until he learns to speak English fluently. It is horrible what the German immigrants must endure from the Americans, Irish, and English. I was more than once a witness to the way German immigrants were forced by the American captain or pilot with terrible brutality, kicking, etc., to carry wood from the shore to the boat, although they had paid their full fare and had not been engaged for those duties. Only in the places where the Germans are in the majority does the newly arrived immigrant find, after all the hardships of the journey, an endurable existence. The Americans are accustomed to alter their behavior to him only after he has become Americanized. The rabble who also emigrated from Germany in former times have brought the German name into discredit.

The educational institutions are, in America, defective and expensive or they are completely lacking. Therefore parents can give their children the necessary education only through great sacrifices or, in case they are poor, the children must be allowed to run wild....

The majority of the Germans emigrating to America wish to seek their fortunes in agriculture. But the purchase of land has its dangers and difficulties. The price of the land is, in proportion to its productivity, not so low as is generally believed. To establish a farm on new and uncultivated land is for the newcomer an almost impossible task....

I have been approached since my return from North America by a large number of persons for information concerning conditions there and for advice concerning their projected plan of emigration. Either because of their personal qualifications or circumstances, hardly one-fourth of these people could be advised with confidence to undertake this important step. I found most of them unsuitable for emigration for the following more or less serious reasons:

---

[1]Dutchman: Derived from the German word for German, *Deutsch*, pronounced "doitch." [Ed.]

A weak constitution or shattered health. — The emigrant to America needs a strong and healthy body.

Advanced age. — The man who is already over forty years of age, unless he has some sons who can help him with their labor, cannot count upon success and prosperity in America.

Childlessness with somewhat advanced age. — What will a married couple do when their capacity to labor disappears with the years? They could not earn enough when young to support them in later years. If they have a substantial property to bring over from Germany, then emigration would be a very unwise step for them, since for the man without employment living is much higher in America than in Europe, especially if one needs servants or cannot do without the comforts and luxuries of life.

Lack of experience in the field of labor on the part of those who expect to establish their fortunes there through hard labor. — The duties of the agriculturists, as well as the occupations of the artisan, involve heavy labor. Many harbor the delusion that they are already accustomed to the labor required there, or that they will easily learn it if they have worked a little here in this country. But he who has not from his youth up been performing continuously the most severe labor, so much the more will he lack, in America, where work is harder, the necessary strength and ability. He will certainly not be a competent and contented workingman. In America . . . labor is much more severe and much more work is required for the higher wages he receives than is usual in Germany. Those who spent their youth in schools, offices, or in other sedentary work, play in America a very sad and pitiable rôle.

A slow easy-going habit of living a life of ease and comfort. — One may find in the great cities of North America all the comforts and conveniences which European cities offer, but in America they are only for the few — for the rich — and to this class German emigrants do not usually belong. Not many persons in America can command even the comforts of the ordinary citizen of Europe. Many people seek compensation in whiskey for their many privations and hardships and this is the way to certain ruin.

Destitution. — If the passage for a single emigrant costs only 50 thaler, at least as much again must be counted for the land journey here and in America. Unfortunately this amount is beyond the reach of those who would have the best chance of improving their condition in America. The artisan, even though he cannot carry on his business there independently but must work in great workshops and factories must often make yet a further land journey in order to find the most suitable place, and he needs, especially if he has a family, a not inconsiderable amount of money. Seldom is a place found in the vicinity of the port of arrival where places are not already filled with laborers. If the means of traveling are not available, he falls into difficulties and distress, is obliged to sell the effects he brought with him for a trifling sum, or considers himself fortunate if he finds a job anywhere at the lowest wage — a wage that will barely keep him and his family from hunger. Those who wish to move on to the land should not come to America without capital unless they are young, strong, and eager to work. It is necessary to earn the means to independence through service or through daily labor which is, to be sure, not easy, but is surer than to purchase immediately an independent position with money brought from Germany.

DISCUSSION QUESTIONS

1. As described by Menzel, what types of Germans typically emigrated to the United States, and what were their motives?

2. In Menzel's view, what advantages did the United States offer German emigrants? What obstacles should they expect to face?

3. According to historians, in the mid-nineteenth century Europe was in a period of profound social, economic, and political transition. What evidence does Menzel's guidebook offer to support this claim?

6. Demanding Political Freedom

Address by the Hungarian Parliament (March 14, 1848) and *Demands of the Hungarian People* (March 15, 1848)

As word of the February Revolution in Paris spread, it inspired people seeking change to stage public demonstrations across Europe, including in Hungary. Long under Habsburg control, in the 1830s a growing segment of the Hungarian population advocated for national self-determination. They faced stiff opposition, however, from the absolutist, autocratic court in Vienna. When protests there prompted the Austrian emperor Ferdinand to agree to a series of concessions, including forming a constitutional government, the Hungarian Parliament wasted no time in stepping up the pressure for reform. On March 14, it met in Pozsony near Vienna and approved the following address to Ferdinand, written by Magyar nationalist Lajos Kossuth (1802–1894). Inspired by the news, thousands of demonstrators took to the streets in Budapest, the Hungarian capital, calling for Hungary's liberation from Habsburg tyranny. With the crowd's support, a group of university students composed the twelve-point demands of the Hungarian people. Although the ensuing revolution was ultimately crushed, in 1991 the National Assembly of Hungary designated March 15 as one of three national days commemorating Hungary's statehood.

Address by the Hungarian Parliament

Your Majesty, — events which have recently transpired impose upon us the imperative duty of directing your attention to those exigencies which our fidelity towards the reigning house, the legal relations of the monarchy at large, and our love for our country prescribe. Reverting to the history of the past, we are reminded that for three centuries not only have we been hindered from giving free development to the constitutional spirit of our country, in accordance with the demands of the time, but our most zealous efforts have with difficulty succeeded in preserving it. The cause of this has been that the government of Your

From G. A. Kertesz, ed., *Documents in the Political History of the European Continent 1815–1939* (London: Oxford University Press, 1968), 123–26.

Majesty has not followed a constitutional direction, and consequently has been at variance with the independent character of our Government. This alone has hitherto prevented the development of the constitutional system in Hungary; and it is clear that unless the direction be changed, and Your Majesty's Government is made to harmonize with constitutional principles, the throne of Your Majesty, no less than the monarchy itself, endeared to us by virtue of the Pragmatic Sanction,[1] will be placed in a state of perplexity and danger, the end of which we cannot foresee, and which must entail unspeakable misery upon our country. Having been called together by Your Majesty for the purpose of carrying out measures of reform, we have resolved that upon the basis of an equal taxation we will take our share in those public burdens by which the expenses of the municipal administration have hitherto been defrayed, and provide for what farther shall be required. We have also resolved to free the country from feudal burdens, indemnifying at the same time the proprietors of the soil; and thus, by reconciling the interests of the people and the nobility, to strengthen the throne of Your Majesty, and establish it upon the well being of the country at large. One of the most important of our tasks is to alleviate the burdens of the peasantry, as regards the quarterings and the necessary provisions for the soldiery. Believing in the necessity of reform, as regards the municipalities of the towns and districts, we are likewise of opinion that the time has arrived for granting political rights to the people. The country has a right to expect measures to be carried out for raising our industrial resources, our commerce, and our agriculture. At the same time the spirit of our constitution demands free development under a true representative system, and the intellectual interests of the nation likewise demand support, based upon freedom. Our military institutions require a thorough reform, — a reform the urgency of which is pressed upon us by a regard to Your Majesty's throne and the safety of our country. We cannot longer consent to a postponement of the constitutional application of the state revenues of Hungary, and the rendering an exact account of the revenue and expenditure. In entertaining several of these questions it becomes requisite, from our relations with the hereditary provinces, to reconcile as far as possible our mutual interests, and reserving in all cases our national rights and independence, we readily offer to those countries the hand of brotherhood. We are moreover convinced, that all measures proposed as aids to our constitutional progress, and to the elevation of the moral and material condition of our country, can only attain real value and vitality when a national government shall exist independent of foreign influence, which may give its sanction to such measures; and which, based on true constitutional principles, shall be responsible to the nation, the voice of which it will duly represent. For these reasons it is that we consider the conversion of the present system of a government by boards and commissions into a responsible Hungarian ministry, the chief condition, the most essential guarantee of all measures of reform.

Demands of the Hungarian People

1. Freedom of the press; abolition of censorship.

2. A responsible ministry with its seat in the capital.[2]

---

[1] A law of 1722 which regulated the succession and the relationship of Hungary with the Austrian provinces.

[2] The government was conducted from offices in Vienna.

3. An annual parliament in Budapest.[3]

4. Political and religious equality before the law.

5. A national guard.

6. Taxes to be paid by all.[4]

7. Abolition of serfdom.

8. Jury system. Equality of representation.

9. A national bank.

10. The military to take an oath to the constitution; Hungarian soldiers not to be stationed abroad, foreign soldiers to be removed.

11. Political prisoners to be freed.

12. Union with Transylvania.[5]

DISCUSSION QUESTIONS

1. What are the key reforms proposed in the address by the Hungarian Parliament? How do they reflect both liberal and nationalist ideals prevalent throughout much of Europe at the time?

2. In what ways do the March 15 demands build on these reforms and seek to translate them into practice?

3. Do you see any similarities between these demands and contemporary expectations regarding the basis of democratic governments and the rights of their citizens?

7. Imperialism and Opium

Commissioner Lin, *Letter to Queen Victoria* (1839)

The Industrial Revolution was not the only factor reshaping the European economy in the first half of the nineteenth century. With the abolition of slavery by Great Britain and many other nations, European governments shifted focus away from their Caribbean plantation colonies toward new colonies in Asia and Africa. British merchants took the lead in opening up China to trade with the West, armed with an extremely addictive commodity: opium. They justified the importation of the drug into China with the argument

---

From William H. McNeill and Mitsuko Iriye, eds., *Modern Asia and Africa* (New York: Oxford University Press, 1971), 113–18.

[3]Parliament met at Pozsony, near Vienna, and not at the capital, Budapest.

[4]Up to this time the nobility and the gentry were exempt from taxation.

[5]Transylvania, part of the Hungarian kingdom since the tenth century, had been governed as a separate entity for several centuries. Although many Magyars lived in Transylvania, the majority in the region were not Magyar. [Ed.]

that it was a legitimate commercial enterprise. The Chinese government held a different view, however, as the letter below reveals. The Chinese emperor had appointed Lin Tse-hsü (1785–1850) to address the opium problem, which he proposed to do with a two-pronged strategy: cutting off the supply of opium and punishing all users and sellers, including foreign traders. Lin wrote to British Queen Victoria (r. 1837–1901) seeking support for this policy. There is no evidence that she ever received his letter, excerpted here, but it was published later in the London Times. *Ultimately, Britain waged the first of two Opium Wars (1839–1842) to secure the continuation of the opium trade and gain a territorial foothold in the region.*

We find that your country is distant from us, . . . that your foreign ships come hither striving the one with the other for our trade, and for the simple reason of their strong desire to reap a profit. Now, out of the wealth of our Inner Land, if we take a part to bestow upon foreigners from afar, it follows, that the immense wealth which the said foreigners amass, ought properly speaking to be portion of our own native Chinese people. By what principle of reason then, should these foreigners send in return a poisonous drug, which involves in destruction those very natives of China? Without meaning to say that the foreigners harbor such destructive intentions in their hearts, we yet positively assert that from their inordinate thirst after gain, they are perfectly careless about the injuries they inflict upon us! And such being the case, we should like to ask what has become of that conscience which heaven has implanted in the breasts of all men?

We have heard that in your own country opium is prohibited with the utmost strictness and severity: — this is a strong proof that you know full well how hurtful it is to mankind. Since then you do not permit it to injure your own country, you ought not to have the injurious drug transferred to another country, and above all others, how much less to the Inner Land! Of the products which China exports to your foreign countries, there is not one which is not beneficial to mankind in some shape or other. There are those which serve for food, those which are useful, and those which are calculated for re-sale; — but all are beneficial. . . .

On the other hand, the things that come from your foreign countries are only calculated to make presents of, or serve for mere amusement. It is quite the same to us if we have them, or if we have them not. If then these are of no material consequence to us of the Inner Land, what difficulty would there be in prohibiting and shutting our market against them? It is only that our heavenly dynasty most freely permits you to take off her tea, silk, and other commodities, and convey them for consumption everywhere, without the slightest stint or grudge, for no other reason, but that where a profit exists, we wish that it be diffused abroad for the benefit of all the earth!

Your honorable nation takes away the products of our central land, and not only do you thereby obtain food and support for yourselves, but moreover, by re-selling these products to other countries you reap a threefold profit. Now if you would only not sell opium, this threefold profit would be secured to you: how can you possibly consent to forego it for a drug that is hurtful to men, and an unbridled craving after gain that seems to know no bounds! Let us suppose that foreigners came from another country, and brought opium into England, and seduced the people of your country to smoke it, would not you, the sovereign of the said country, look upon such a procedure with anger, and in your just indignation endeavor to get rid of it? Now we have always heard that your highness possesses a most kind and benevolent heart, surely then you are incapable of doing or causing to be done unto another, that which you should not wish another to do unto you! . . .

Suppose the subject of another country were to come to England to trade, he would certainly be required to comply with the laws of England, then how much more does this apply to us of the celestial empire! Now it is a fixed statute of this empire, that any native Chinese who sells opium is punishable with death, and even he who merely smokes it, must not less die. Pause and reflect for a moment: if you foreigners did not bring the opium hither, where should our Chinese people get it to re-sell? It is your foreigners who involve our simple natives in the pit of death, and are they alone to be permitted to escape alive? If so much as one of those deprive one of our people of his life, he must forfeit his life in requital for that which he has taken: — how much more does this apply to him who by means of opium destroys his fellow-men? Does the havoc which he commits stop with a single life? Therefore it is that those foreigners who now import opium into the Central Land are condemned to be beheaded and strangled by the new statute. . . .

Our celestial empire rules over ten thousand kingdoms! Most surely do we possess a measure of godlike majesty which you cannot fathom! Still we cannot bear to slay or exterminate without previous warning, and it is for this reason that we now clearly make known to you the fixed laws of our land. If the foreign merchants of your said honorable nation desire to continue their commercial intercourse, they then must tremblingly obey our recorded statutes, they must cut off for ever the source from which the opium flows, and on no account make an experiment of our laws in their own persons! Let then your highness punish those of your subjects who may be criminal, do not endeavor to screen or conceal them, and thus you will secure peace and quietness to your possessions, thus will you more than ever display a proper sense of respect and obedience, and thus may we unitedly enjoy the common blessing of peace and happiness.

DISCUSSION QUESTIONS

1. How does Lin describe economic relations between Britain and China? Which country benefits the most according to his view? Why is this important to his argument against the import of opium?

2. Why does Lin set opium apart from the other goods imported by Britain into China? How does he describe the drug's effects on the Chinese people?

3. Why does Lin accuse the British government of hypocrisy in its attitudes toward opium?

4. How would you describe Lin's tone in this letter? What does it suggest about how he viewed Western culture in general?

COMPARATIVE QUESTIONS

1. How do Ellis's conduct guide, the Berlin factory rules, and the testimony before Ashley's Mines Commission reflect the regimentation of daily life that characterized industrial society?

2. What do Ashley's Mines Commission, the *Punch* cartoon, Engels, and Menzel suggest about the broader social, political, and economic changes reshaping Europe at this time?

3. In what ways do Engels, Menzel, and the Hungarian revolutionaries offer their contemporaries an alternative vision of society to the one portrayed in the other documents in this chapter? What similarities and/or differences do you see among their visions, and how might you account for them?

4. Based on the first five documents, how did the Industrial Revolution create a new social and economic order in Europe? What does Commissioner Lin's letter suggest about the impact of these changes on China?

Politics and Culture of the Nation-State
1850–1870

The second half of the nineteenth century marked the dawning of a new age in European politics and culture. After the failed revolutions of 1848–1849, politicians, artists, intellectuals, and the general public cast aside the promises of idealists and claimed to see society as it really was: combative, competitive, and inherently disordered. To master this unruly scene and strengthen state power from above, European leaders embraced tough-minded politics (Realpolitik). With the rise of Realpolitik came the decline of the concert of Europe, which had favored a balance of power over national aspirations. Document 1 reflects Russia's response to this changing landscape as the country struggled to modernize. Documents 2 and 3 allow us to see two masters of Realpolitik at work — Italian count Camillo di Cavour (1810–1861) and Prussian politician Otto von Bismarck (1815–1898). The writings of Herbert Spencer (1820–1903) and Charles Darwin (1809–1882) illustrate the growing prominence of the natural sciences at the time, as documents 4 and 5 illustrate. Spencer proposed the idea of evolution before Darwin and used it as a lens for understanding the development of both nature and society. Darwin's research gave further scientific credence to this idea, suggesting that human beings had evolved from more primitive life-forms. Together, their work helped to lay the foundations of a school of thought known as Social Darwinism; its proponents maintained that only the toughest and most advanced societies would prosper, leaving the "unfit" to fend for themselves.

1. Ending Serfdom in Russia
Peter Kropótkin, *Memoirs of a Revolutionist* (1861)

Largely engineered by French emperor Napoleon III to advance his territorial ambitions, the Crimean War (1853–1856) opened the door to a major shift in the distribution of European power. With the death toll mounting at the hands of France and its allies, Russia asked for peace.

From Peter Kropótkin, *Memoirs of a Revolutionist* (New York: Horizon Press, 1968), 133–36.

Russia's defeat marked the end of its role as a mainstay of the concert of Europe and also revealed the country's inability to compete in the rapidly changing industrial world. Among Russia's greatest liabilities was the institution of serfdom — binding the peasant population to the land — which inhibited the growth of a modern labor force and fostered widespread discontent. After years of discussion and debate, Russian tsar Alexander II (r. 1855–1881) chose a momentous solution to combat these problems: on March 3, 1861, he issued the Emancipation Manifesto, officially abolishing serfdom. In the following excerpt from his memoirs published in 1899, Prince Peter Kropótkin (1842–1921) provides a firsthand glimpse of how people in St. Petersburg reacted to the emancipation decree and of its impact on one of his family estates. At the time, Kropótkin was a student at a select military school in St. Petersburg, the Corps of Pages, and he later gained fame as a revolutionary and anarchist.

I was at the corps, having to take part in the military parade at the riding-school. I was still in bed, when my soldier servant, Ivánoff, dashed in with the tea tray, exclaiming, "Prince, freedom! The manifesto is posted on the Gostínoi Dvor" (the shops opposite the corps).

"Did you see it yourself?"

"Yes. People stand round; one reads, the others listen. It *is* freedom!"

In a couple of minutes I was dressed, and out. A comrade was coming in.

"Kropótkin, freedom!" he shouted. "Here is the manifesto. My uncle learned last night that it would be read at the early mass at the Isaac Cathedral; so we went. There were not many people there; peasants only. The manifesto was read and distributed after the mass. They well understood what it meant. When I came out of the church, two peasants, who stood in the gateway, said to me in such a droll way, 'Well, sir? now — all gone?'" And he mimicked how they had shown him the way out. Years of expectation were in that gesture of sending away the master.

I read and re-read the manifesto. It was written in an elevated style by the old Metropolitan of Moscow, Philarète, but with a useless mixture of Russian and Old Slavonian which obscured the sense. . . . Notwithstanding all this, one thing was evident: serfdom was abolished, and the liberated serfs would get the land and their homesteads. They would have to pay for it, but the old stain of slavery was removed. They would be slaves no more; the reaction had *not* got the upper hand.

We went to the parade; and when all the military performances were over, Alexander II, remaining on horseback, loudly called out, "The officers to me!" They gathered round him, and he began, in a loud voice, a speech about the great event of the day.

"The officers . . . the representatives of the nobility in the army" — these scraps of sentences reached our ears — "an end has been put to centuries of injustice . . . I expect sacrifices from the nobility . . . the loyal nobility will gather round the throne" . . . and so on. Enthusiastic hurrahs resounded amongst the officers as he ended.

We ran rather than marched back on our way to the corps, — hurrying to be in time for the Italian opera, of which the last performance in the season was to be given that afternoon; some manifestation was sure to take place then. Our military attire was flung off with great haste, and several of us dashed, light-footed, to the sixth-story gallery. The house was crowded.

During the first entr'acte the smoking-room of the opera filled with excited young men, who all talked to one another, whether acquainted or not. We planned at once to return to the hall, and to sing, with the whole public in a mass choir, the hymn "God Save the Tsar."

However, sounds of music reached our ears, and we all hurried back to the hall. The band of the opera was already playing the hymn, which was drowned immediately in enthusiastic hurrahs coming from all parts of the hall. I saw Bavéri, the conductor of the band, waving his stick, but not a sound could be heard from the powerful band. Then Bavéri stopped, but the hurrahs continued. I saw the stick waved again in the air; I saw the fiddle-bows moving, and musicians blowing the brass instruments, but again the sound of voices overwhelmed the band. Bavéri began conducting the hymn once more, and it was only by the end of that third repetition that isolated sounds of the brass instruments pierced through the clamor of human voices.

The same enthusiasm was in the streets. Crowds of peasants and educated men stood in front of the palace, shouting hurrahs, and the Tsar could not appear without being fol-lowed by demonstrative crowds running after his carriage....

Where were the uprisings which had been predicted by the champions of slavery? Conditions more indefinite than those which had been created by the Polozhénie (the emancipation law) could not have been invented. If anything could have provoked revolts, it was precisely the perplexing vagueness of the conditions created by the new law. And yet, except in two places where there were insurrections, and a very few other spots where small disturbances entirely due to misunderstandings and immediately appeased took place, Russia remained quiet, — more quiet than ever. With their usual good sense, the peasants had understood that serfdom was done away with, that "freedom had come," and they accepted the conditions imposed upon them, although these conditions were very heavy.

I was in Nikólskoye in August, 1861, and again in the summer of 1862, and I was struck with the quiet, intelligent way in which the peasants had accepted the new con-ditions. They knew perfectly well how difficult it would be to pay the redemption tax for the land, which was in reality an indemnity to the nobles in lieu of the obligations of serfdom. But they so much valued the abolition of their personal enslavement that they accepted the ruinous charges — not without murmuring, but as a hard necessity — the moment that personal freedom was obtained. For the first months they kept two holi-days a week, saying that it was a sin to work on Friday; but when the summer came they resumed work with even more energy than before.

When I saw our Nikólskoye peasants, fifteen months after the liberation, I could not but admire them. Their inborn good nature and softness remained with them, but all traces of servility had disappeared. They talked to their masters as equals talk to equals, as if they never had stood in different relations.

DISCUSSION QUESTIONS

1. As described by Kropótkin, how did people react to the emancipation decree?

2. According to Kropótkin, how did the decree challenge traditional social boundaries?

3. How does Kropótkin describe Alexander II, and what do you think his description suggests about the tsar's power at the time?

2. Fighting for Italian Nationalism

Camillo di Cavour, *Letter to King Victor Emmanuel* (July 24, 1858)

*As prime minister of the northern Italian kingdom of Piedmont-Sardinia, Camillo di Cavour was among the most skilled practitioners of Realpolitik in mid-nineteenth-century Europe. Politically fragmented, Italy had long been a battleground for European rulers, sowing the seeds of the movement for Italian unification (*Risorgimento*). Cavour capitalized on this movement to guide Italy down the path of nationhood. His target was Austria, which dominated most of the peninsula. His strategy was to draw them into war with the help of French emperor Napoleon III. To this end, Cavour met secretly with Napoleon in July 1858. In the letter excerpted here, Cavour summarizes the terms of their agreement for the Piedmontese king Victor Emmanuel II (r. Italy 1861–1878). It reflects Cavour's pragmatic, calculated approach to the unification process, which culminated in 1861 with the formal establishment of the united kingdom of Italy.*

As soon as I entered the Emperor's study, he raised the question which was the purpose of my journey. He began by saying that he had decided to support Piedmont with all his power in a war against Austria, provided that the war was undertaken for a nonrevolutionary end which could be justified in the eyes of diplomatic circles — and still more in the eyes of French and European public opinion.

Since the search for a plausible excuse presented our main problem before we could agree, I felt obliged to treat that question before any others. . . . The Emperor came to my aid, and together we set ourselves to discussing each state in Italy, seeking grounds for war. It was very hard to find any. After we had gone over the whole peninsula without success, we arrived at Massa and Carrara, and there we discovered what we had been so ardently seeking. After I had given the Emperor a description of that unhappy country, of which he already had a clear enough idea anyway, we agreed on instigating the inhabitants to petition Your Majesty, asking protection and even demanding the annexation of the Duchies to Piedmont. This Your Majesty would decline, but you would take note of the Duke of Modena's oppressive policy and would address him a haughty and menacing note. The Duke, confident of Austrian support, would reply impertinently. Thereupon Your Majesty would occupy Massa, and the war could begin.

As it would be the Duke of Modena who would look responsible, the Emperor believes the war would be popular not only in France, but in England and the rest of Europe, because the Duke is considered, rightly or wrongly, the scapegoat of despotism. . . .

The Emperor readily agreed that it was necessary to drive the Austrians out of Italy once and for all, and to leave them without an inch of territory south of the Alps or west of the Isonzo. But how was Italy to be organized after that? After a long discussion, which I spare Your Majesty, we agreed more or less to the following principles, recognizing that they were subject to modification as the course of the war might determine. The valley

From Denis Mack Smith, ed., *The Making of Italy, 1796–1870* (New York: Harper & Row, 1968), 238–42.

of the Po, the Romagna, and the Legations would form a kingdom of Upper Italy under the House of Savoy. Rome and its immediate surroundings would be left to the Pope. The rest of the Papal States, together with Tuscany, would form a kingdom of central Italy. The Neapolitan frontier would be left unchanged. These four Italian states would form a confederation on the pattern of the German Bund, the presidency of which would be given to the Pope to console him for losing the best part of his estates.

This arrangement seemed to me fully acceptable. Your Majesty would be legal sovereign of the richest and most powerful half of Italy, and hence would in practice dominate the whole peninsula.

After we had settled the fate of Italy, the Emperor asked me what France would get, and whether Your Majesty would cede Savoy and the County of Nice. I answered that Your Majesty believed in the principle of nationalities and realized accordingly that Savoy ought to be reunited with France; and that consequently you were ready to make this sacrifice. . . .

Then we proceeded to examine how the war could be won, and the Emperor observed that we would have to isolate Austria so that she would be our sole opponent. That was why he deemed it so important that the grounds for war be such as would not alarm the other continental powers. Better still if they were also popular in England. He seemed convinced that what we had decided would fulfill this double purpose. The Emperor counts positively on England's neutrality; he advised me to make every effort to influence opinion in that country to compel the government (which is a slave to public opinion) not to side with Austria. He counts, too, on the antipathy of the Prince of Prussia toward the Austrians to keep Prussia from deciding against us. As for Russia, Alexander has repeatedly promised not to oppose Napoleon's Italian projects. Unless the Emperor is deluding himself, which I am not inclined to believe after all he told me, it would simply be a matter of a war between France and ourselves on one side and Austria on the other.

The Emperor nevertheless believes that, even reduced to these proportions, there remain formidable difficulties. There is no denying that Austria is very strong. . . .

Once agreed on military matters, we equally agreed on the financial question, and I must inform Your Majesty that this is what chiefly preoccupies the Emperor. Nevertheless he is ready to provide us with whatever munitions we need, and to help us negotiate a loan in Paris. As for contributions from other Italian provinces in money and material, the Emperor believes we should insist on something, but use great caution. All these questions which I here relate to you as briefly as possible were discussed with the Emperor from eleven o'clock in the morning to three o'clock in the afternoon.

DISCUSSION QUESTIONS

1. Why did Napoleon III agree to help Cavour in planning Piedmont's war against Austria? What did each seek to gain through the agreement?

2. Why did Cavour and Napoleon think it important to consider public opinion in devising the grounds for war?

3. How did the two men think Italy should be organized after the war? What does this reveal about the methods of state building in the mid-nineteenth century?

3. Realpolitik and Otto von Bismarck

Rudolf von Ihering, *Two Letters* (1866)

Like Cavour, Prussian prime minister Otto von Bismarck (1815–1898) embraced the principles of Realpolitik. Through his military and diplomatic strategies, Bismarck took advantage of the collapse of the concert of Europe and made the dream of a united Germany a reality. Bismarck had many detractors, however, including liberals like jurist Rudolf von Ihering (1818–1892). In the excerpts here from two letters he wrote in 1866, von Ihering provides a contemporary assessment of Realpolitik in action during the war with Austria, a pivotal period in Bismarck's quest for German unification. The war erupted in June 1866, and by early July, Prussia was triumphant. At first, Bismarck's tactics shocked von Ihering. Yet the allure of German unity proved irresistible to him and other liberals, and they soon embraced the sense of military superiority that came to define German nationalism.

(*To J. Glaser, Giessen, 1 May.*) . . . Never, probably, has a war been incited so shamelessly and with such horrifying frivolity as the one that Bismarck is currently trying to start against Austria. My innermost feelings are revolted by this violation of every legal and moral principle. God knows I am no friend of Austria; on the contrary, I have always been regarded as one of her enemies — that is to say of her political system, not of the Austrian people whom I have learned to love . . . — ; I am devoted to the idea of Prussian influence in north Germany, even though I have little sympathy for the present political system in Prussia. But I would rather cut off my hand than to use it in such a disgusting operation as Prussian policy is now launching against Austria — the common sense of any honest man cannot even comprehend the depths of this perfidy. We ask ourselves in amazement: is it really true that what the whole world knows to be lies can be proclaimed from on high as the truth? Austria is supposed to be mobilizing against Prussia! Any child knows that the opposite is the case. . . . The saddest thing about it all is that once the struggle is under way principles of right and wrong must come in absolutely tragic conflict with interests. Whom should we wish victorious, Austria or Prussia? We have no choice, we must come down on the side of the *unjust* cause, because we cannot tolerate the possibility of Austria gaining the upper hand in Germany. Everyone here detests this war, nobody can be comfortable with the idea that it will have the result that we *must* desire — the hegemony of Prussia. That is our situation. Germans taking up arms against Germans, civil war, a plot of three or four Powers against one, with not even an appearance of legality, without popular participation, created by a few diplomats alone, a conspiracy against your poor country, which causes even the enemies of Austria to sympathize with her and in which they would have to desire her victory — if this victory did not mean our own ruin! . . . The war would be unthinkable if Austria had not for decades been doing everything to make it impossible even for her friends in Germany to take sides with her and putting the most menacing weapons in the hands of her enemies. . . . Everyone agrees on the crying

---

From Walter Michael Simon, *Germany in the Age of Bismarck* (London: Allen and Unwin, 1968), 110–13.

injustice that is being done to Austria, and yet, as I say, thousands here would not lift a finger for her cause, people feel that that would mean turning against one's own cause; for with very few exceptions the general opinion here is that the free development of Germany would be incompatible with Austrian supremacy. This may be wrong, but I am merely stating the fact. There is just as little affection for the German princes: here also one finds the same collision between undoubted historical justice and a total inability to work up any enthusiasm for it. It is sad to be in conflict with one's own feelings — we ought to desire victory for the just cause in this instance too, but we cannot!

(*To B. Windscheid, Giessen, 19 August.*) . . . I think I must be dreaming when I think of how much has happened in the short space of a few weeks; it seems that it must be years. I am only now gradually coming to my senses again; at one time I was quite dizzy from the pace of events. What a surging of emotions — of deep fear, anxious hesitation, joyous exultation, apprehensive suspense, furious indignation, profound pity, and in the end once more a rejoicing of the soul, an ecstasy of happiness such as my heart has never before known! Oh, my dear friend, what enviable luck to be living at this time, to have seen this turning-point in German history with which there has been nothing to compare for a thousand years. For years I have envied the Italians that they succeeded in what seemed for us to lie only in the distant future, I have wished for a German Cavour and Garibaldi as Germany's political messiah. And overnight he has appeared in the person of the much-abused Bismarck. Should we not think we are dreaming if the impossible becomes possible? Like you I was afraid at the prospect of war, I was convinced of the notion that the Austrians, experienced in the practical school of war, would be superior to the Prussians. Has intelligence and moral energy ever in history celebrated such a triumph over crude force? There is something wonderful about this spirit that animates little Prussia, this spirit that lifts us all out of a state of impotence and ignominy and gives to the name of Germany in Europe a lustre and a tone that it has not had for a thousand years. I bow before the genius of Bismarck, who has achieved a masterpiece of political planning and action such as are only rarely to be found in history. How marvelously the man spun all the threads of the great web, how firmly and safely so that none of them broke, how precisely he knew and used all the ways and means — his king, Napoleon, his army, the administration, Austria and her forces — in short, a masterpiece of calculation. I have forgiven the man everything he has done up to now, more, I have convinced myself that it was necessary; what seemed to us, the uninitiated, as criminal arrogance has turned out in the end to have been an indispensable means to the goal. He is one of the greatest men of the century; it is a real revelation to have lived at the same time as such a man; a man of action like that, not heedless action but action inspired and prepared both politically and morally, is worth a hundred men of liberal principles and of powerless honesty!

Nine weeks ago I should not have believed that I would write a paean of praise to Bismarck, but I cannot help myself! I leave it to my stubborn colleagues from Swabia and Bavaria to abuse him, to concentrate everything disgusting they can think of on the name of Bismarck. Incorrigible doctrinaires! For years, they have yelled and drunk themselves hoarse for German unity, and when someone comes on the scene and achieves the impossible by transferring German unity from a book of student songs into reality they cry "crucify him."

DISCUSSION QUESTIONS

1. What does von Ihering reveal about Bismarck's political methods in these two letters?
2. Why do you think von Ihering was conflicted in his attitudes about these methods?
3. How do von Ihering's opinions change between the time he wrote the first and second letters, and what do you think accounts for this change?

4. Social Evolution

Herbert Spencer, *Progress: Its Law and Cause* (1857)

As Otto von Bismarck (1815–1898) and other practitioners of Realpolitik were transforming European political views in the late nineteenth century, British philosopher and sociologist Herbert Spencer (1820–1903) was transforming social views. Trained as an engineer during Britain's industrial boom times, Spencer was a man of wide-ranging interests who, after a stint as a journalist, devoted himself full-time to writing in 1853. Guided by a deeply ingrained faith in the notion of progress and in the ability of science to expose its inner workings, he devoted much of his work to synthesizing the findings of different branches of science and applying them to the social world. The excerpt below from an article he published in 1857, "Progress: Its Law and Cause," provides insight into his reasoning and its broader implications. Here he argues that processes of continuous change from homogeneity to heterogeneity shape both nature and human civilization. Spencer thereby helped prepare the way for Darwin's own conclusions regarding biological evolution and their usefulness for understanding the way society functioned.

The current conception of Progress is somewhat shifting and indefinite [...]. Only those changes are held to constitute progress which directly or indirectly tend to heighten human happiness. And they are thought to constitute progress simply *because* they tend to heighten human happiness. But rightly to understand Progress, we must inquire what is the nature of these changes, considered apart from our interests. Ceasing, for example, to regard the successive geological modifications that have taken place in the Earth, as modifications that have gradually fitted it for the habitation of Man, and as *therefore* a geological progress, we must seek to determine the character common to these modifications — the law to which they all conform. And similarly in every other case. Leaving out of sight concomitants and beneficial consequences, let us ask what Progress is in itself.

In respect to that progress which individual organisms display in the course of their evolution, this question has been answered. . . . In its primary stage, every germ consists of a substance that is uniform throughout, both in texture and chemical composition. The first step in its development is the appearance of a difference between two parts of

From Herbert Spencer, "Progress: Its Law and Cause," *The Westminster Review* 67 (April 1857): 445–47, 451, 453–56.

this substance; or, as the phenomenon is described in physiological language — a differentiation. Each of these differentiated divisions presently begins itself to exhibit some contrast of parts; and by these secondary differentiations become as definite as the original one. This process is continuously repeated — is simultaneously going on in all parts of the growing embryo; and by endless multiplication of these differentiations there is ultimately produced that complex combination of tissues and organs constituting the adult animal or plant. This is the course of evolution followed by all organisms whatever. It is settled beyond dispute that organic progress consists in a change from the homogeneous to the heterogeneous.

Now, we propose in the first place to show, that this law of organic progress is the law of all progress. Whether it be in the development of the Earth, in the development of Life upon its surface, the development of Society, of Government, of Manufactures, of Commerce, of Language, Literature, Science, Art, this same evolution of the simple into the complex, through a process of continuous differentiation, holds throughout. From the earliest traceable cosmical changes down to the latest results of civilization, we shall find that the transformation of the homogeneous into the heterogeneous, is that in which Progress essentially consists. . . .

Whether an advance from the homogeneous to the heterogeneous is or is not displayed in the biological history of the globe, it is clearly enough displayed in the progress of the latest and most heterogeneous creature — Man. It is alike true that, during the period in which the Earth has been peopled, the human organism has become more heterogeneous among the civilized divisions of the species; and that the species, as a whole, has been growing more heterogeneous in virtue of the multiplication of races and the differentiation of these races from each other. . . .

On passing from Humanity under its individual form, to Humanity as socially embodied, we find the general law still more variously exemplified. The change from the homogeneous to the heterogeneous is displayed equally in the evolution of civilization as a whole, and in the progress of every tribe or nation; and is still going on with increasing rapidity. As we see in still existing barbarous tribes, society in its first and lowest form is a homogeneous aggregation of individuals having like powers and performing like functions: the only marked differentiation of function being that which accompanies difference of sex. Every man is warrior, hunter, fisherman, tool-maker, builder; every woman performs the same drudgeries; every family is self-sufficing, and, save for purposes of aggression and defence, might as well live apart from the rest. Very early, however, in the process of social evolution, we find an incipient differentiation between the governing and the governed. Some kind of chieftainship seems almost co-ordinate with the first advance from the state of separate wandering families to that of a nomadic tribe. The authority of the strongest makes itself felt among a body of savages as in a herd of animals, or a posse of schoolboys. At first, however, it is indefinite, uncertain, — is shared by others of scarcely inferior power, and is unaccompanied by any difference in occupation or style of living: the first ruler kills his own game, makes his own weapons, builds his own hut, and, economically considered, does not differ from others of his tribe. Gradually, as the tribe progresses, the contrast between the governing and the governed grows more marked. Supreme power becomes hereditary in one family; the head of that family ceasing to provide for his own wants, is served by others; and he begins to assume the sole office of ruling. At the same time there has been arising a co-ordinate species of government — that of Religion. . . . Thus, no sooner does the originally homogeneous social mass become definitely differentiated into the governed and the governing parts, than this last exhibits an incipient differentiation into religious and secular — Church and State; while at the same time there begins to be differentiated from both, that less concrete species of government which rules the daily intercourse of individuals — a species of government which, as we may see in heralds' colleges, in books of the peerage, in masters of ceremonies, is not without a certain embodiment of its own. Each of these is itself subject to successive differentiations. In the course of ages, there arises, as among ourselves, a highly complex political organization of monarch, ministers, lords, and commons, with their subordinate administrative departments, courts of justice, revenue offices, &c., supplemented in the provinces by municipal governments, county governments, parish, or union governments — all of them more or less elaborated. By its side there grows up a highly complex religious organization, with its various grades of officials. . . . And at the same time there is developed a highly complex aggregation of customs, manners, and temporary fashions, enforced by society at large, and serving to control those minor transactions between man and man which are not regulated by civil and religious law. Moreover it is to be observed that this ever-increasing heterogeneity in the governmental appliances of each nation, has been accompanied by an increasing heterogeneity in the governmental appliances of different nations: all of which are more or less unlike in their political systems and legislation, in their creeds and religious institutions, in their customs and ceremonial usages.

Simultaneously there has been going on a second differentiation of a still more familiar kind; that, namely, by which the mass of the community has become segregated into distinct classes and orders of workers. While the governing part has been undergoing the complex development above described, the governed part has been undergoing an equally complex development, which has resulted in that minute division of labour characterizing advanced nations. It is needless to trace out this progress from its first stages, up through the caste divisions of the East and the incorporated guilds of Europe, to the elaborate producing and distributing organization existing among ourselves. Political economists have made familiar to all, the evolution which, beginning with a tribe whose members severally perform the same actions each for himself, ends with a civilized community whose members severally perform different actions for each other; and they have further explained the evolution through which the solitary producer of any one commodity, is transformed into a combination of producers who, united under a master, take separate parts in the manufacture of such commodity. But there are yet other and higher phases of this advance from the homogeneous to the heterogeneous in the industrial structure of the social organism. Long after considerable progress has been made in the division of labour among different classes of workers, there is still little or no division of labour among the widely separated parts of the community: the nation continues comparatively homogeneous in the respect that in each district the same occupations are pursued. But when roads and other means of transit become numerous and good, the different districts begin to assume different functions, and to become mutually dependent. The calico manufacture locates itself in this county, the woollen-cloth manufacture in that; silks are produced here, lace there; stockings in one place, shoes in another;

pottery, hardware, cutlery, come to have their special towns; and ultimately every locality becomes more or less distinguished from the rest by the leading occupation carried on in it. Nay, more, this subdivision of functions shows itself not only among the different parts of the same nation, but among different nations. That exchange of commodities which free-trade promises so greatly to increase, will ultimately have the effect of specializing, in a greater or less degree, the industry of each people. So that beginning with a barbarous tribe, almost if not quite homogeneous in the functions of its members, the progress has been, and still is, towards an economic aggregation of the whole human race, growing ever more heterogeneous in respect of the separate functions assumed by separate nations, the separate functions assumed by the local sections of each nation, the separate functions assumed by the many kinds of makers and traders in each town, and the separate functions assumed by the workers united in producing each commodity.

Not only is the law thus clearly exemplified in the evolution of the social organism, but it is exemplified with equal clearness in the evolution of all products of human thought and action; whether concrete or abstract, real or ideal.

DISCUSSION QUESTIONS

1. What does Spencer mean by the word *evolution*? What are its key features in his view?
2. How does he apply the idea of evolution to society in general? Why does he think doing so is essential to reshaping people's conception of progress?
3. What examples does Spencer cite to validate his argument? In what ways does his approach reflect the growing importance of science and scientific understanding in this era of nation building?

5. The Science of Man

SOURCES IN CONVERSATION | Charles Darwin, *The Descent of Man* (1871) and *Figaro's London Sketch Book of Celebrities* (1874)

Herbert Spencer may have been the most prominent advocate of evolutionary theory in the mid-nineteenth century, but he would soon share the stage with English naturalist Charles Darwin (1809–1882). Building on Spencer's views and grounding them in his own biological research, in 1859 Darwin published On the Origin of Species, *in which he argued that animal species evolved over time through a process of natural selection by which the strongest and most well adapted to any given environment survived. The biblical story of creation had no place in Darwin's conclusions, and this incited considerable debate. Not only did Darwin's book appear in multiple editions in multiple languages, its ideas also found expression in*

From Charles Darwin, *The Descent of Man and Selection in Relation to Sex* (New York: D. Appleton and Company, 1896), 606–9, 612–13, 618–19.

everyday culture, notably printed cartoons and caricatures published in popular illustrated journals and magazines. The debate intensified twelve years later when Darwin applied his theory of evolution directly to humans in The Descent of Man and Selection in Relation to Sex, *excerpted here. After its publication, humorists saw an opportunity they could not pass up, frequently caricaturing Darwin as an ape. The image below, published in 1874 in* Figaro's London Sketch Book of Celebrities, *is representative of this type of visual commentary. Darwin is shown holding up a mirror to an ape seated at his side, with lines printed below from two Shakespearean plays intended to reinforce the image's message.*

The main conclusion here arrived at, and now held by many naturalists who are well competent to form a sound judgment, is that man is descended from some less highly organized form. The grounds upon which this conclusion rests will never be shaken, for the close similarity between man and the lower animals in embryonic development, as well as in innumerable points of structure and constitution, both of high and of the most trifling importance, — the rudiments which he retains, and the abnormal reversions to which he is occasionally liable, — are facts which cannot be disputed. They have long been known, but until recently they told us nothing with respect to the origin of man. Now when viewed by the light of our knowledge of the whole organic world, their meaning is unmistakable. The great principle of evolution stands up clear and firm, when these groups of facts are considered in connection with others such as the mutual affinities of the members of the same group, their geographical distribution in past and present times, and their geological succession. It is incredible that all these facts should speak falsely. He who is not content to look, like a savage, at the phenomena of nature as disconnected, cannot any longer believe that man is the work of a separate act of creation. . . .

We have seen that man incessantly presents individual differences in all parts of his body and in his mental faculties. These differences or variations seem to be induced by the same general causes, and to obey the same laws as with the lower animals. In both cases similar laws of inheritance prevail. Man tends to increase at a greater rate than his means of subsistence; consequently he is occasionally subjected to a severe struggle for existence, and natural selection will have effected whatever lies within its scope. . . .

Through the means just specified, aided perhaps by others as yet undiscovered, man has been raised to his present state. But since he attained to the rank of manhood, he has diverged into distinct races, or as they may be more fitly called, subspecies. Some of these, such as the Negro and European, are so distinct that, if specimens had been brought to a naturalist without any further information, they would undoubtedly have been considered by him as good and true species. Nevertheless all the races agree in so many unimportant details of structure and in so many mental peculiarities, that these can be accounted for only by inheritance from a common progenitor; and a progenitor thus characterized would probably deserve to rank as man. . . .

By considering the embryological structure of man, — the homologies which he presents with the lower animals, — the rudiments which he retains, — and the reversions to which he is liable, we can partly recall in imagination the former condition of our early progenitors; and can approximately place them in their proper place in the zoological series. We thus learn that man is descended from a hairy, tailed quadruped, probably arboreal in its habits, and an inhabitant of the Old World. . . .

The belief in God has often been advanced as not only the greatest, but the most complete of all the distinctions between man and the lower animals. It is however impossible, . . . to maintain that this belief is innate or instinctive in man. On the other hand a belief in all-pervading spiritual agencies seems to be universal; and apparently follows from a considerable advance in man's reason, and from a still greater advance in his faculties of imagination, curiosity and wonder. I am aware that the assumed instinctive belief in God has been used by many persons as an argument for His existence. But this is a rash argument, as we should thus be compelled to believe in the existence of many cruel and malignant spirits, only a little more powerful than man; for the belief in them is far more general than in a beneficent Deity. The idea of a universal and beneficent Creator does not seem to arise in the mind of man, until he has been elevated by long-continued culture. . . .

I am aware that the conclusions arrived at in this work will be denounced by some as highly irreligious; but he who denounces them is bound to show why it is more irreligious to explain the origin of man as a distinct species by descent from some lower form, through the laws of variation and natural selection, than to explain the birth of the individual through the laws of ordinary reproduction. The birth both of the species and of the individual are equally parts of that grand sequence of events, which our minds refuse to accept as the result of blind chance. The understanding revolts at such a conclusion. . . .

The main conclusion arrived at in this work, namely that man is descended from some lowly organized form, will, I regret to think, be highly distasteful to many. But there can hardly be a doubt that we are descended from barbarians. The astonishment which I felt on first seeing a party of Fuegians on a wild and broken shore will never be forgotten by me, for the reflection at once rushed into my mind — such were our ancestors. These men were absolutely naked and bedaubed with paint, their long hair was tangled, their mouths frothed with excitement, and their expression was wild, startled, and distrustful. They possessed hardly any arts, and like wild animals lived on what they could catch; they had no government, and were merciless to every one not of their own small tribe. He who has seen a savage in his native land will not feel much shame, if forced to acknowledge that the blood of some more humble creature flows in his veins. For my own part I would as soon be descended from that heroic little monkey, who braved his dreaded enemy in order to save the life of his keeper, or from that old baboon, who descending from the mountains, carried away in triumph his young comrade from a crowd of astonished dogs — as from a savage who delights to torture his enemies, offers up bloody sacrifices, practices infanticide without remorse, treats his wives like slaves, knows no decency, and is haunted by the grossest superstitions.

Man may be excused for feeling some pride at having risen, though not through his own exertions, to the very summit of the organic scale; and the fact of his having thus risen, instead of having been aboriginally placed there, may give him hope for a still higher destiny in the distant future. But we are not here concerned with hopes or fears, only with the truth as far as our reason permits us to discover it; and I have given the evidence to the best of my ability. We must, however, acknowledge, as it seems to me, that man with all his noble qualities, with sympathy which feels for the most debased, with benevolence which extends not only to other men but to the humblest living creature, with his god-like intellect which has penetrated into the movements and constitution of the solar system — with all these exalted powers — Man still bears in his bodily frame the indelible stamp of his lowly origin.

THE
LONDON SKETCH BOOK.

PROF. DARWIN.

This is the ape of form.
Love's Labor Lost, act 5, scene 2.

Some four or five descents since.
All's Well that Ends Well, act 3, sc. 7.

DISCUSSION QUESTIONS

1. What evidence does Darwin supply to support his theory of human evolution? How does he emphasize realism and concrete facts in making his argument?

2. How does Darwin's evidence call into question the relationship between religion and science?

3. What similarities do you see between Darwin's and the ape's physical appearance in the cartoon? Why do you think the cartoonist made this stylistic choice? What message does it convey?

4. Scholars argue that cartoons such as this one simplified the complexity of Darwin's theory of human evolution for the general public. What connections can you find between the cartoon's overall message and Darwin's argument in *The Descent of Man*?

COMPARATIVE QUESTIONS

1. How would you compare the political methods and goals of Alexander II, Cavour, and Bismarck?

2. Why did these methods and goals help to end the concert of Europe?

3. How do Spencer's and Darwin's ideas support the principles of Realpolitik?

4. What do these documents reveal about how Europeans built a sense of national identity in the late nineteenth century?

Empire, Industry, and Everyday Life
1870–1890

The dual phenomena of industry and empire transformed Europe and the world during the late nineteenth century. With domestic industries booming, European leaders looked abroad for new markets and raw materials. The widespread belief that a nation's imperial holdings were an indication of its strength and racial superiority also fueled the quest for empire. As documents 1 to 3 show, this quest was a source of both unity and discord among Europeans and the indigenous peoples under their political control. Document 4 illuminates Germany's especially striking success in melding industrial growth and imperial expansion, which raised concerns throughout Europe, particularly in Great Britain. Document 5 points to the political repercussions of economic development as workers joined together to demand a say in the workplace. Industry and empire found artistic expression as well. Heavily influenced by Asian art and architecture, some visual artists abandoned tradition to depict scenes from nature and society as they appeared at any given moment. In the process, they also set their work apart from the photographic realism of the camera, a popular industrial invention. Document 6 allows us to see this creative process through the eyes of French painter Edgar Degas (1834–1917).

1. Defending Conquest
Jules Ferry, *Speech before the French National Assembly* (1883)

French politician Jules Ferry (1832–1893) fueled his country's quest to compete in the continent's race to conquer foreign territory in the closing decades of the nineteenth century. While serving two terms as premier during the Third Republic, Ferry took the lead in

From Ralph A. Austin, ed., *Modern Imperialism: Western Overseas Expansion and Its Aftermath, 1776–1965* (Lexington, MA: D. C. Heath, 1969), 69–74.

France's colonial expansion in Africa and Asia. Yet not everyone embraced his imperialist policies, including his conservative and socialist colleagues within the government. In the following speech, delivered before the National Assembly in July 1883, Ferry faced his opponents head-on, defending not only the political and economic necessity of French expansionism but also its moral justness. At the same time, his critics voiced their views, revealing the basis of their anticolonial sentiment.

M. JULES FERRY: Gentlemen, it embarrasses me to make such a prolonged demand upon the gracious attention of the Chamber, but I believe that the duty I am fulfilling upon this platform is not a useless one. It is as strenuous for me as for you, but I believe that there is some benefit in summarizing and condensing, in the form of arguments, the principles, the motives, and the various interests by which a policy of colonial expansion may be justified; it goes without saying that I will try to remain reasonable, moderate, and never lose sight of the major continental interests which are the primary concern of this country. What I wish to say, to support this proposition, is that in fact, just as in word, the policy of colonial expansion is a political and economic system; I wish to say that one can relate this system to three orders of ideas: economic ideas, ideas of civilization in its highest sense, and ideas of politics and patriotism.

In the area of economics, I will allow myself to place before you, with the support of some figures, the considerations which justify a policy of colonial expansion from the point of view of that need, felt more and more strongly by the industrial populations of Europe and particularly those of our own rich and hard working country: the need for export markets. Is this some kind of chimera? Is this a view of the future or is it not rather a pressing need, and, we could say, the cry of our industrial population? I will formulate only in a general way what each of you, in the different parts of France, is in a position to confirm. Yes, what is lacking for our great industry, drawn irrevocably on to the path of exportation by the [free trade] treaties of 1860, what it lacks more and more is export markets. Why? Because next door to us Germany is surrounded by barriers, because beyond the ocean, the United States of America has become protectionist, protectionist in the most extreme sense, because not only have these great markets, I will not say closed but shrunk, and thus become more difficult of access for our industrial products, but also these great states are beginning to pour products not seen heretofore onto our own markets. . . .

I say that I know very well the thoughts of the economists [...]. They say to us, "The true export markets are the commercial treaties which furnish and assure them." Gentlemen, I do not look down upon commercial treaties: if we could return to the situation which existed after 1860, if the world had not been subjected to that economic revolution which is the product of the development of science and the speeding up of communications, if this great revolution had not intervened, I would gladly take up the situation which existed after 1860. It is quite true that in that epoch the competition of grain from Odessa did not ruin French agriculture, that the grain of America and of India did not yet offer us any competition; at that moment we were living under the regime of commercial treaties, not only with England, but with the other great powers, with Germany, which had not yet become an industrial power. I do not look down upon them, these treaties; I had the honor of negotiating some of less importance than those of 1860; but gentlemen, in order to make treaties, it is necessary to have two parties: one does not make treaties with the United States; this is the conviction which has grown among those who have attempted to open some sort of negotiations in this quarter, whether officially or officiously.

Gentlemen, there is a second point, a second order of ideas to which I have to give equal attention, but as quickly as possible, believe me; it is the humanitarian and civilizing side of the question. On this point the honorable M. Camille Pellatan has jeered in his own refined and clever manner; he jeers, he condemns, and he says, "What is this civilization which you impose with cannonballs? What is it but another form of barbarism? Don't these populations, these inferior races, have the same rights as you? Aren't they masters of their own houses? Have they called upon you? You come to them against their will, you offer them violence, but not civilization." There, gentlemen, is the thesis; I do not hesitate to say that this is not politics, nor is it history: it is political metaphysics. ["Ah, Ah," *on far left*].

... Gentlemen, I must speak from a higher and more truthful plane. It must be stated openly that, in effect, superior races have rights over inferior races. [*Movement on many benches on the far left.*]

M. JULES MAIGNE: Oh! You dare to say this in the country which has proclaimed the rights of man!

M. DE GUILLOUTET: This is a justification of slavery and the slave trade!

M. JULES FERRY: If M. Maigne is right, if the declaration of the rights of man was written for the blacks of equatorial Africa, then by what right do you impose regular commerce upon them? They have not called upon you.

M. RAOUL DUVAL: We do not want to impose anything upon them. It is you who wish to do so!

M. JULES MAIGNE: To propose and to impose are two different things!

M. GEORGES PERIN: In any case, you cannot bring about commerce by force.

M. JULES FERRY: I repeat that superior races have a right, because they have a duty. They have the duty to civilize inferior races. . . . [*Approbation from the left. New interruptions from the extreme left and from the right.*]

That is what I have to answer M. Pelletan in regard to the second point upon which he touched.

He then touched upon a third, more delicate, more serious, and upon which I ask your permission to express myself quite frankly. It is the political side of the question. The honorable M. Pelletan, who is a distinguished writer, always comes up with remarkably precise formulations. I will borrow from him the one which he applied the other day to this aspect of colonial policy.

"It is a system," he says, "which consists of seeking out compensations in the Orient with a circumspect and peaceful seclusion which is actually imposed upon us in Europe."

I would like to explain myself in regard to this. I do not like this word, "compensation," and, in effect, not here but elsewhere it has often been used in a treacherous way. If what is being said or insinuated is that any government in this country, any Republican minister could possibly believe that there are in any part of the world compensations for the disasters which we have experienced, an injury is being inflicted . . . and an injury undeserved by that government. [*Applause at the center and left.*] I will ward off this injury with all the force of my patriotism! [*New applause and bravos from the same benches.*]

Gentlemen, there are certain considerations which merit the attention of all patriots. The conditions of naval warfare have been profoundly altered. ["Very true! Very true!"]

At this time, as you know, a warship cannot carry more than fourteen days' worth of coal, no matter how perfectly it is organized, and a ship which is out of coal is a derelict on the surface of the sea, abandoned to the first person who comes along. Thence the necessity of having on the oceans provision stations, shelters, ports for defense and rev-ictualling. [*Applause at the center and left. Various interruptions.*] And it is for this that we needed Tunisia, for this that we needed Saigon and the Mekong Delta, for this that we need Madagascar, that we are at Diégo-Suarez and Vohemar [two Madagascar ports] and will never leave them! [*Applause from a great number of benches.*] Gentlemen, in Europe as it is today, in this competition of so many rivals which we see growing around us, some by perfecting their military or maritime forces, others by the prodigious development of an ever growing population; in a Europe, or rather in a universe of this sort, a policy of peaceful seclusion or abstention is simply the highway to decadence! Nations are great in our times only by means of the activities which they develop; it is not simply "by the peaceful shining forth of institutions" [*Interruptions on the extreme left and right*] that they are great at this hour.

As for me, I am astounded to find the monarchist parties becoming indignant over the fact that the Republic of France is following a policy which does not confine itself to that ideal of modesty, of reserve, and, if you will allow me the expression, of bread and butter [*Interruptions and laughter on the left*] which the representatives of fallen monar-chies wish to impose upon France. [*Applause at the center.*]

. . . [The Republican Party] has shown that it is quite aware that one cannot impose upon France a political ideal conforming to that of nations like independent Belgium and the Swiss Republic; that something else is needed for France: that she cannot be merely a free country, that she must also be a great country, exercizing all of her rightful influence over the destiny of Europe, that she ought to propagate this influence throughout the world and carry everywhere that she can her language, her customs, her flag, her arms, and her genius. [*Applause at center and left.*]

DISCUSSION QUESTIONS

1. Why does Ferry consider colonial expansion to be an economic necessity?

2. Aside from its economic benefits, why is colonial expansion justified according to Ferry?

3. How does Ferry appeal to nationalist sentiment to defend his imperialist stance, and why?

4. What is the basis of his critics' arguments against imperialism?

2. Subverting Empire

Imperial Federation Map of the World (1886)

As European powers rushed to expand their imperial holdings, maps became a popular vehicle for engaging public interest in the race for empire. The map below was produced in 1886 to commemorate a London exhibition showcasing the wealth and industry of the British Empire and was included as a large colored supplement for an illustrated weekly newspaper, The Graphic. The map depicts the world with British territories colored pink, connected by a web of maritime trade routes. Statistical tables appear next to each major colony with information on its area, population, and volume of trade. A small inset map in the top right shows the scope of British landholdings a century earlier. Elaborate illustrations portraying the colonies' inhabitants frame the map, with Britannia center among them, seated on top of a globe. In its visual display of British imperial might, the map is typical of others published in this period. Yet the recent identification of the map's illustrator, Walter Crane (1845–1915), suggests a more complex message. While Crane produced a variety of commercial artwork, he was most well known as a socialist artist. For him, imperialism in its current form was a capitalist tool of enslavement; he believed instead that imperialism should be used to advance the socialist vision of an international commonwealth. The caps worn by the figures holding the banners "freedom," "fraternity," and "federation" at the top of the map tip Crane's hand — they mimic the style of cap worn by liberated slaves in ancient Rome, which became a broadly used anticolonial symbol in the nineteenth century.

Royal Geographical Society, London, UK / Bridgeman Images

DISCUSSION QUESTIONS

1. What details of the map and its border illustrations stand out to you in particular, and why?

2. What do these details suggest about the mechanisms by which Britain and other European countries gained control of foreign territories?

3. At first glance, in what ways could this map be interpreted as a classic representation of nineteenth-century imperialism? How does the identity of its creator complicate this interpretation? What does this suggest about the range of attitudes toward imperialism at the time?

3. Resisting Imperialism

Ndansi Kumalo, *His Story* (1890s)

In the closing decades of the nineteenth century, European nations competed for direct control of larger and larger regions of the world. Competition in Africa was especially fierce, often with tragic results for Africans and their ways of life. The document below, an excerpt from an interview with Ndansi Kumalo, reveals this process unfolding during the 1890s. African by birth, in the 1930s Ndansi Kumalo was invited to participate in the making of a film on the life of British imperialist Cecil Rhodes (1853–1902). While completing the film in England, he recounted his life story to the English Africanist Margery Perham. At the time of the events Ndansi Kumalo described to her, Rhodes had claimed a huge tract of interior Africa, dubbed "Rhodesia" in his honor, for the English crown. Ndansi Kumalo and his people, Ndebele pastoralists living in southeastern Africa, were swept up in Rhodes's and other European immigrants' scramble for power and resources. Ndansi Kumalo had been raised a warrior to guard Ndebele land; thus, he and other Ndebele fought back against the European incursion. War broke out in 1893 and again in 1897, both times ending in the Ndebele's defeat. The British repaid the Ndebele for their resistance by relegating them to a reservation.

We were terribly upset and very angry at the coming of the white men, for Lobengula[1] had sent to the Queen in England and he was under her [the Queen of England's] protection and it was quite unjustified that white men should come with force into our country.[2] . . . Lobengula had no war in his heart: he had always protected the white men and been good to them. If he had meant war, would he have sent our regiments far away to the north at this moment? As far as I know the trouble began in this way.

From Margery Perham, ed., *Ten Africans* (Chicago: Northwestern University Press, 1971), 69–75.

[1]**Lobengula:** The Ndebele chieftain. [Ed.]

[2]Lobengula signed an agreement with Cecil Rhodes in 1888 in which the British government guaranteed that there would be no English settlers on Ndebele land or an intrusion on Lobengula's authority. When Lobengula failed to press the English to uphold the agreement, many of his warriors began to agitate for war against the Europeans. [Ed.]

Gandani, a chief who was sent out, reported that some of the Mashona[3] had taken the king's cattle; some regiments were detailed to follow and recover them. They followed the Mashona to Ziminto's people [Victoria district]. Gandani had strict instructions not to molest the white people established in certain parts and to confine himself to the people who had taken the cattle. The commander was given a letter which he had to produce to the Europeans and tell them what the object of the party was. But the members of the party were restless and went without reporting to the white people and killed a lot of Mashonas. The pioneers were very angry and said, "You have trespassed into our part." [This was in 1893.] They went with the letter, but only after they had killed some people, and the white men said, "You have done wrong, you should have brought the letter first and then we should have given you permission to follow the cattle." The commander received orders from the white people to get out, and up to a certain point which he could not possibly reach in the time allowed. A force followed them up and they defended themselves. When the pioneers turned out there was a fight at Shangani and at Bembezi.

. . . The next news was that the white people had entered Bulawayo; the King's kraal[4] had been burnt down and the King had fled. Of the cattle very few were recovered; most fell into the hands of the white people. Only a very small portion were found and brought to Shangani where the King was, and we went there to give him any assistance we could. I did not catch up with the King; he had gone on ahead. Three of our leaders mounted their horses and followed up the King and he wanted to know where his cattle were; they said they had fallen into the hands of the whites, only a few were left. He said, "Go back and bring them along." But they did not go back again; the white forces had occupied Bulawayo and they went into the Matoppos. Then the white people came to where we were living and sent word round that all chiefs and warriors should go into Bulawayo and discuss peace, for the King had gone and they wanted to make peace. The first order we got was, "When you come in, come in with cattle so that we can see that you are sincere about it." The white people said, "Now that your King has deserted you, we occupy your country. Do you submit to us?" What could we do? "If you are sincere, come back and bring in all your arms, guns and spears." We did so. . . .

So we surrendered to the white people and were told to go back to our homes and live our usual lives and attend to our crops. But the white men sent native police who did abominable things; they were cruel and assaulted a lot of our people and helped themselves to our cattle and goats. These policemen were not our own people; anybody was made a policeman. We were treated like slaves. They came and were overbearing and we were ordered to carry their clothes and bundles. They interfered with our wives and our daughters and molested them. In fact, the treatment we received was intolerable. We thought it best to fight and die rather than bear it. How the rebellion started I do not know; there was no organization, it was like a fire that suddenly flames up. We had been flogged by native police and then they rubbed salt water in the wounds.

---

[3]**Mashona**: Fellow pastoralists who lived under Ndebele control. [Ed.]
[4]**kraal**: A rural village, typically encircled by a stockade, where the king resided. [Ed.]

There was much bitterness because so many of our cattle were branded and taken away from us; we had no property, nothing we could call our own. We said, "It is no good living under such conditions; death would be better — let us fight." Our King gone, we had submitted to the white people and they ill-treated us until we became desperate and tried to make an end of it all. We knew that we had very little chance because their weapons were so much superior to ours. But we meant to fight to the last, feeling that even if we could not beat them we might at least kill a few of them and so have some sort of revenge.

I fought in the rebellion. We used to look out for valleys where the white men were likely to approach. We took cover behind rocks and trees and tried to ambush them. We were forced by the nature of our weapons not to expose ourselves. I had a gun, a breech-loader. They — the white men — fought us with big guns and Maxims[5] and rifles.

I remember a fight in the Matoppos when we charged the white men. There were some hundreds of us; the white men also were many. We charged them at close quarters: we thought we had a good chance to kill them but the Maxims were too much for us. . . .

We were still fighting when we heard that Mr. Rhodes was coming and wanted to make peace with us. It was best to come to terms he said, and not go shedding blood like this on both sides. The older people went to meet him. Mr. Rhodes came and they had a discussion and our leaders came back and discussed amongst themselves and the people. Then Mr. Rhodes came again and we agreed at last to terms of peace.

So peace was made. Many of our people had been killed, and now we began to die of starvation; and then came the rinderpest[6] and the cattle that were still left to us perished. We could not help thinking that all these dreadful things were brought by the white people. We struggled, and the Government helped us with grain; and by degrees we managed to get crops and pulled through. Our cattle were practically wiped out, but a few were left and from them we slowly bred up our herds again. We were offered work in the mines and farms to earn money and so were able to buy back some cattle. At first, of course, we were not used to going out to work, but advice was given that the chief should advise the young people to go out to work, and gradually they went. At first we received a good price for our cattle and sheep and goats. Then the tax came. It was 10s. a year. Soon the Government said, "That is too little, you must contribute more; you must pay £1." We did so. Then those who took more than one wife were taxed; 10s. for each additional wife. The tax is heavy, but that is not all. We are also taxed for our dogs; 5s. for a dog. Then we were told we were living on private land; the owners wanted rent in addition to the Government tax; some 10s. some £1, some £2 a year. After that we were told we had to dip our cattle and pay 1s. per head per annum.

Would I like to have the old days back? Well, the white men have brought some good things. For a start, they brought us European implements — ploughs; we can buy European clothes, which are an advance. The Government have arranged for education

---

[5]The Maxim gun was an early version of a machine gun. [Ed.]
[6]**rinderpest:** A highly infectious disease of cattle. [Ed.]

and through that, when our children grow up, they may rise in status. We want them to be educated and civilized and make better citizens. Even in our own time there were troubles, there was much fighting and many innocent people were killed. It is infinitely better to have peace instead of war, and our treatment generally by the officials is better than it was at first. But, under the white people, we still have our troubles. Economic conditions are telling on us very severely. We are on land where the rainfall is scanty, and things will not grow well. In our own time we could pick our own country, but now all the best land has been taken by the white people. We get hardly any price for our cattle; we find it hard to meet our money obligations. If we have crops to spare we get very little for them; we find it difficult to make ends meet and wages are very low. When I view the position, I see that our rainfall has diminished, we have suffered drought and have poor crops and we do not see any hope of improvement, but all the same our taxes do not diminish. We see no prosperous days ahead of us.

DISCUSSION QUESTIONS

1. How would you describe the Ndebele's lifestyle before the arrival of the Europeans?

2. What social and economic changes did the Europeans initiate when they gained control of the region and its people?

3. What do these changes suggest about British tactics for expanding their footing in Africa?

4. How would you describe Ndansi Kumalo's attitudes toward Europeans? Why does he characterize their arrival as a mixed blessing?

4. Global Competition

Ernest Edwin Williams, *Made in Germany* (1896)

In the closing decades of the nineteenth century, Germany emerged as a new, seemingly unstoppable economic force. It enjoyed astounding industrial growth throughout this period and gained a substantial share of European export markets. Many people in Great Britain observed these events with dismay, seeing Germany as a threat not only to their country's long-standing industrial dominance but also to its national identity as a world power. Journalist Ernest Edwin Williams (1866–1935) fanned the flames of such fears in Made in Germany, *published in 1896. Drawing on a dizzying array of statistics, Williams painted a menacing picture of the omnipresence of German products in his readers' everyday lives. He hoped that his bleak portrait would prompt Parliament to adopt measures to protect and enhance British trade. Although his message went unheeded, it evidently struck a chord, for the book went through six printings in its first year.*

From Ernest Edwin Williams, *Made in Germany*, 4th ed. (London: William Heinemann, 1896), 1–2, 7–12, 18.

The Departing Glory

Preliminary

The Industrial Supremacy of Great Britain has been long an axiomatic commonplace; and it is fast turning into a myth, as inappropriate to fact as the Chinese Emperor's computation of his own status. This is a strong statement. But it is neither wide nor short of the truth. The industrial glory of England is departing, and England does not know it. There are spasmodic outcries against foreign competition, but the impression they leave is fleeting and vague. The phrase, "Made in Germany," is raw material for a jape at the pantomime, or is made the text for a homily by the official guardians of some particular trade, in so far as the matter concerns themselves. British Consuls, too, send words of warning home, and the number of these is increasing with significant frequency. But the nation at large is yet as little alive to the impending danger as to the evil already wrought. The man in the shop or the factory has plenty to say about the Armenian Question and the House of Lords, but about commercial and industrial matters which concern him vitally he is generally much less eloquent. The amount of interest evinced by the amateur politician seems invariably to advance with the remoteness of the matter from his daily bread. It is time to disturb the fatal torpor: even though the moment be, in one sense, unhappily chosen. The pendulum between depression and prosperity has swung to the latter, and manufacturers and merchants are flushed with the joyful contemplation of their order-books. Slackness has given way to briskness; the lean years have been succeeded by a term of fat ones. The prophet of evil commands his most attentive audiences when the times are with him. When they are good — though the good be fleeting — his words are apt to fall unheeded. . . .

As It Was

There was a time when our industrial empire was unchallenged. It was England which first emerged from the Small-Industry stage. She produced the Industrial Revolution about the middle of the last century, and well-nigh until the middle of this she developed her multitude of mills, and factories, and mines, and warehouses, undisturbed by war at home, and profiting by wars abroad. The great struggles which drained the energies of the Continental nations, sealed her industrial supremacy, and made her absolute mistress of the world-market. Thanks to them, she became the Universal Provider. English machinery, English pottery, English hardware, guns, and cutlery, English rails and bridge-work, English manufactures of well-nigh every kind formed the material of civilization all over the globe. She covered the dry land with a network of railways, and the seas were alive with her own ships freighted with her own merchandise. Between 1793 and 1815 the value of her exports had risen from £17,000,000 to £58,000,000. Her industrial dominion was immense, unquestioned, unprecedented in the history of the human race; and not unnaturally we have come to regard her rule as eternal. But careless self-confidence makes not for Empire. While she was throwing wide her gates to the world at large, her sisters were building barriers of protection against her; and, behind those barriers, and aided often by State subventions, during the middle and later years of the century, they have developed industries of their own. Of course, this was to a certain extent inevitable. England could not hope for an eternal monopoly of the world's manufactures; and industrial growths abroad do not of necessity sound the knell of her greatness. But she must discriminate in her equanimity. And most certainly she must discriminate against Germany. For Germany has entered into a deliberate and deadly rivalry with her, and is battling with might and main for the extinction of her supremacy. . . .

The German Revolution

Up to a couple of decades ago, Germany was an agricultural State. Her manufactures were few and unimportant; her industrial capital was small; her export trade was too insignificant to merit the attention of the official statistician; she imported largely for her own consumption. Now she has changed all that. Her youth has crowded into English houses, has wormed its way into English manufacturing secrets, and has enriched her establishments with the knowledge thus purloined. She has educated her people in a fashion which has made it in some branches of industry the superior, and in most the equal of the English. Her capitalists have been content with a simple style, which has enabled them to dispense with big immediate profits, and to feed their capital. They have toiled at their desks, and made their sons do likewise; they have kept a strict controlling hand on all the strings of their businesses; they have obtained State aid in several ways — as special rates to shipping ports; they have insinuated themselves into every part of the world — civilized, barbarian, savage — learning the languages, and patiently studying the wants and tastes of the several peoples. Not content with reaping the advantages of British colonization — this was accomplished with alarming facility — Germany has "protected" the simple savage on her own account, and the Imperial Eagle now floats on the breezes of the South Sea Islands, and droops in the thick air of the African littoral. Her diplomatists have negotiated innumerable commercial treaties. The population of her cities has been increasing in a manner not unworthy of England in the Thirties and Forties. Like England, too, she is draining her rural districts for the massing of her children in huge factory towns. Her yards (as well as those of England) too, are ringing with the sound of hammers upon ships being builded for the transport of German merchandise. Her agents and travelers swarm through Russia, and wherever else there is a chance of trade on any terms — are even supplying the foreigner with German goods *at a loss*, that they may achieve their purpose in the end. In a word, an industrial development, unparalleled, save in England a century ago, is now her portion. A gigantic commercial State is arising to menace our prosperity, and contend with us for the trade of the world. . . .

Made in Germany

The phrase is fluent in the mouth: how universally appropriate it is, probably no one who has not made a special study of the matter is aware. Take observations, Gentle Reader, in your own surroundings: the mental exercise is recommended as an antidote to that form of self-sufficiency which our candid friends regard as indigenous to the

British climate. Your investigations will work out somewhat in this fashion. You will find that the material of some of your own clothes was probably woven in Germany. Still more probably is it that some of your wife's garments are German importations; while it is practically beyond a doubt that the magnificent mantles and jackets wherein her maids array themselves on their Sundays out are German-made and German-sold, for only so could they be done at the figure. Your governess's *fiancé* is a clerk in the City; but he also was made in Germany. The toys, and the dolls, and the fairy books which your children maltreat in the nursery are made in Germany: nay, the material of your favorite (patriotic) newspaper had the same birthplace as like as not. Roam the house over, and the fateful mark will greet you at every turn, from the piano in your drawing-room to the mug on your kitchen dresser, blazoned though it be with the legend, *A Present from Margate*. Descend to your domestic depths, and you shall find your very drain-pipes German made. You pick out of the grate the paper wrappings from a book consignment, and they also are "Made in Germany." You stuff them into the fire, and reflect that the poker in your hand was forged in Germany. As you rise from your hearthrug you knock over an ornament on your mantlepiece; picking up the pieces you read, on the bit that formed the base, "Manufactured in Germany." And you jot your dismal reflections down with a pencil that was made in Germany. At midnight your wife comes home from an opera which was made in Germany, has been here enacted by singers and conductor and players made in Germany, with the aid of instruments and sheets of music made in Germany. You go to bed, and glare wrathfully at a text on the wall; it is illuminated with an English village church, and it was "Printed in Germany." If you are imaginative and dyspeptic, you drop off to sleep only to dream that St. Peter (with a duly stamped halo round his head and a bunch of keys from the Rhineland) has refused you admission into Paradise, because you bear not the Mark of the Beast upon your forehead, and are not of German make. But you console yourself with the thought that it was only a Bierhaus Paradise any way; and you are awakened in the morning by the sonorous brass of a German band.

Is the picture exaggerated? Bear with me, while I tabulate a few figures from the Official Returns of Her Majesty's Custom House, where, at any rate, fancy and exaggeration have no play. In '95 Germany sent us linen manufactures to the value of £91,257; cotton manufactures to the value of £536,471; embroidery and needlework to the value of £11,309; leather gloves to the value of £27,934 (six times the amount imported six years earlier); and woolen manufactures to the value of £1,016,694. Despite the exceeding cheapness of toys, the value of German-made playthings for English nurseries amounted, in '95, to £459,944. In the same year she sent us books to the value of £37,218, and paper to the value of £586,835. For musical instruments we paid her as much as £563,018; for china and earthenware £216,876; for prints, engravings, and photographs, £111,825. This recital of the moneys which *in one year* have come out of John Bull's pocket for the purchase of his German-made household goods is, I submit disproof enough of any charge of alarmism. For these articles, it must be remembered, are not like oranges and guano. They are not products which we must either import or lack: — *they all belong to the category of English manufactures*, the most important of them, indeed, being articles in the preparation of which Great Britain is held pre-eminent. The total value of manufactured goods imported into the United Kingdom by Germany rose from £16,629,987 in '83 to £21,632,614 in '93: an increase of 30.08 per cent. . . .

The Significance of These Facts

These are the sober — to believers in our eternal rule, the sobering — facts. They are picked almost at random from a mass of others of like import, and I think they are sufficient to prove that my general statements are neither untrue nor unduly emphatic. And yet the data needed for the purpose of showing the parlous condition into which our trade is drifting are still largely to seek. Germany is yet in her industrial infancy; and the healthiest infant can do but poor battle against a grown man. England, with her enormous capital, and the sway she has wielded for a century over the world-market, is as that strong man. Now, to tell a strong man, conscious of his strength to an over-ween-ing degree, that he is in peril from a half-grown youngster, is to invite his derision; and yet if a strong man, as the years advance on him, neglect himself and abuse his strength, he may fall before an energetic stripling. Germany has already put our trade in a bad way; but the worst lies in the future, and it is hard to convince the average Englishman of this. He will admit that Germany's trade has increased, and that at many points it hits our own; but here his robust insularity asserts itself. Germany has not the capital, he will tell you; her workmen are no workmen at all; her capitalists and her managers are poor bureaucratic plodders; the world will soon find out that her products are not of English make, and so forth. And he goes on vocalizing *Rule Britannia* in his best commercial prose.

DISCUSSION QUESTIONS

1. According to Williams, what are the secrets of Germany's economic "revolution"?
2. Why does he regard Germany's industrial success as a cause for alarm, particularly in Great Britain?
3. What does this excerpt suggest about industrial growth during this period and its impact on international relations?

5. The Advance of Unionism

Margaret Bondfield, *A Life's Work* (1948)

Despite the explosive industrial growth of the last third of the nineteenth century, life for European workers was still a struggle. They remained vulnerable to economic exploitation and fluctuations in the faster-paced, more competitive, and more complex marketplace. Workers began to take matters into their own hands by organizing formal unions to fight for better working conditions. Although men dominated the trade union movement, women

From Margaret Bondfield, *A Life's Work* (London: Hutchinson & Co., 1948), 27–29, 36.

found a place there too, as the following excerpt from the autobiography of Margaret Bondfield (1873–1954) reveals. The daughter of a lace factory worker, Bondfield went to work at age fourteen as a draper's assistant. With the rise of consumer capitalism, shop assisting was among the fastest-growing employment opportunities for women. The long days and low wages prompted Bondfield to join the newly established National Union for Shop Assistants in 1894, launching her lifelong commitment to political activism.

London: By dint of rigid economy, at the end of five years of shop life in Brighton I had saved £5, which seemed to me great wealth; but the material side of life did not bother me much. I had reached a stage in my spiritual pilgrimage which I must needs travel alone. Religion had become something personal, to be accepted or rejected; at home it was like the air — it permeated our lives, but was not discussed. I could no longer passively accept contemporary opinion on business morality, to which I applied the harsh judgments of the very young. The outward and visible sign of my protest was a sudden move to London. It was undoubtedly *the* turning-point in my life. But for that I might have become a successful business woman!

For the next three months I was nearer to starvation than at any time since. I learned the bitterness of a hopeless search for work. The kindness of a landlady who trusted me kept me going when I was penniless, and until I got a job.

In those days the seekers after work had no Labor Exchange to help them. The best plan was to visit the wholesale firms in the City and get information about vacancies from the commercial travelers, and then journey as fast as the old horse buses allowed — perhaps right across London — only to find a queue of 150 to 200 applicants already there. Before we had stood in the queue for long a notice would be put up: "No good waiting any longer — place filled."

I have taken the whole of Oxford Street, going into every shop walking West on the one side, and every shop on the other side coming back on the chance that there might be a vacancy. I was not tall enough. I remember one man saying to me, "We never engage anyone under five feet eight inches."

Even today those first months in the great city searching for work carry the shadow of a nightmare; but finally I got a job — only to find that conditions, which I had thought peculiar to the Brighton shop, were almost universal. . . . !

A small thing led me to another adventure of faith. I was hungry and I went across to Fitzroy Street to buy a penn'orth of fish and a ha'p'orth of chips, served to me in a newspaper; munching my feast, I strolled around Fitzroy Square reading the paper, in which was a letter from James Macpherson, Secretary of the National Union of Shop Assistants, Warehousemen and Clerks, urging shop assistants to join together to fight against the wretched conditions of employment. I was working about sixty-five hours a week for between £15 and £25 per annum, living in. Here I felt was the right thing to do, and at once I joined up.

My brother Frank was in London, working at Clement's House Printing Works, where he was "Father of the Chapel" and a member of the Union committee to negotiate terms for the introduction of the Linotype. He encouraged my Trade Union activities. This was a happy time for me.

My Union officers gave me all the work I could do in my scant leisure, and every kind of encouragement. They elected me on to the district council, and once I attended a national conference. For the next two years the Union utilized me for platform work in an ever-increasing degree.

Encouraged by T. Spencer Jones, the editor of our little Union paper, I ventured first to undertake reports of meetings, and later to write a few short stories under the pen-name of Grace Dare. It was quite impossible for me to write in the presence of any who might know what I was doing, and as I had not one inch of space I could call my own, I would wait till one or two of my room-mates were asleep, and then stealthily, with the feeling of a conspirator, and knowing that I was committing an offense for which I could be heavily fined, I would light my halfpenny dip, hiding its glare by means of a towel thrown over the back of a chair, and set to work on my monthly article.

If my room-mates woke they were kind enough not to remember it the next morning, and although this surreptitious writing was kept up for about two years, I do not think any breach of rules was ever reported to the firm.

In those early days — 1894 to 1896 — executive committee meetings of my Union were called for Sundays, the only possible day. The committee members had often to travel long distances on night trains, arriving early on Sunday morning, sitting for the transaction of business in a stuffy room, clouded with tobacco smoke, starting back again on Sunday night to be in time for business at 7.30 or 8 a.m. on Monday; they were the pioneers, and to me they were heroes, for they had only bare expenses from the Union. . . . "Death to the Living-in System," "Abolish Fines and Deductions," "Reduce the Hours Worked in Shops," were the slogans. We had no delusions about the size of the job. We frankly told our audiences that we invited them to share in hard work for the next ten years in building up the membership. We were about 2,000 strong in a trade employing 750,000 people. "Come, pioneers! O pioneers!" we sang, and they were coming! . . .

From this time on I just lived for the Trade Union Movement. I concentrated on my job.

This concentration was undisturbed by love affairs. I had seen too much — too early — to have the least desire to join in the pitiful scramble of my work-mates. The very surroundings of shop life accentuated the desire of most shop girls to get married. Long hours of work and the living-in system deprived them of the normal companionship of men in their leisure hours, and the wonder is that so many of the women continued to be good and kind, and self-respecting, without the incentive of a great cause, or of any interest outside their job.

Many of them would toil after business hours to make their clothes, so that, from their small salaries, they could help some member of their family. Some women, much older than myself, would look forward to marriage with hope and dread — hope of economic security, and dread of the unknown ordeal of childbirth. Through what sex knowledge I was able to pass on, Mrs. Martindale resolved their fears, but it was not at all easy to transmit to them the reverence for motherhood, which I had seen at its best and highest, but which to them was too often linked with the obscene.

I had no vocation for wifehood or motherhood, but an urge to serve the Union — an urge which developed into "a sense of oneness with our kind."

DISCUSSION QUESTIONS

1. According to Bondfield, what was life like for her and her coworkers?

2. What traditional female roles did Bondfield reject to devote herself fully to union activities?

3. What does Bondfield reveal about the role of literacy and the press in working-class collective action?

6. Artistic Expression

SOURCES IN CONVERSATION | Edgar Degas, *Notebooks* (1863–1884)

Visual artists were not immune to the changes unfolding around them in late nineteenth-century Europe. Beginning in the 1850s, many artists turned away from classical and romantic conventions and portrayed the world in realistic and graphic ways. Some artists pushed the boundaries of tradition further still with a new style called impressionism. Impressionists were equally fascinated with their immediate surroundings but also focused on the light, color, and movement of a single moment. Edgar Degas (1834–1917) embodied this shift in the visual arts. A classically trained draftsman, Degas began his professional career in Paris in 1859, painting portraits and historical subjects. For Degas, the pull of convention was ultimately no match for the novel artistic influences energizing the Parisian art scene at the time, notably Japanese prints, photography, and the fledgling impressionist movement. The impact on Degas was profound. By the late 1860s, he had turned his eye to depicting modern life in motion. The excerpts and pencil drawing of ballet dancers rehearsing from his private notebooks capture his artistic creativity and driving desire to portray local scenes and individuals one moment and one action at a time.

From Degas's Notebook: 1878–1884

For a portrait, make someone pose on the ground floor and work on the first floor to get used to keeping hold of the forms and expressions and never draw or paint *immediately.*

For the Newspaper cut a lot. Of a dancer do either the arms or the legs or the back. Do the shoes — the hands — of the hairdresser — the badly cut coiffure . . . , bare feet in dance, action, etc., etc.

Do every kind of worn object placed, accompanied in such a way that they have the life of the man or the woman; corsets which have just been taken off, for example — and which keep the form of the body, etc., etc.

From Linda Nochlin, ed., *Impressionism and Post-Impressionism, 1874–1904* (Englewood Cliffs, NJ: Prentice-Hall, 1966), 61–63.

Series on instruments and instrumentalists, their shapes, twisting of the hands and arms and neck of the violinist, for example, puffing out and hollowing of the cheeks of bassoons, oboes, etc.

Do a series in aquatint on *mourning* (different blacks), black veils of deep mourning (floating on the face), black gloves, carriages in mourning, carriage of the Funeral Company, carriages like Venetian gondolas.

On smoke, smoke of smokers, pipes, cigarettes, cigars, smoke of locomotives, of high chimneys, factories, steamboats, etc. Destruction of smoke under the bridges. Steam.

On the evening. Infinite subjects. In the cafés, different values of the glass-shades reflected in the mirrors.

On the bakery, the bread: series on journeymen bakers, seen in the cellar itself or through the air vents from the street. Colors of pink flour — lovely curves of pie, still lifes on the different breads, large, oval, fluted, round, etc. Experiment, in color, on the yellows, pinks, grey-whites of breads. Perspective views of rows of breads. Charming layout of bakeries. Cakes, the wheat, the mills, the flour, the sacks, the market-porters.

No one has ever done monuments or houses from below, from beneath, up close as one sees them going by in the streets.

DISCUSSION QUESTIONS

1. What subjects intrigued Degas as an artist? Why was he interested in portraying them from so many different viewpoints and positions? How does this interest find visual expression in the pencil sketch?

2. Although Degas disliked the label "impressionist," what evidence do you see of impressionism's influence on his ideas about visual art?

3. How did the changing economic and social scene in Paris at the time influence Degas's interests and approach?

The J. Paul Getty Museum, Los Angeles / Digital image courtesy of the Getty's Open Content Program

COMPARATIVE QUESTIONS

1. According to Ferry and Williams, what factors are key to a nation's strength, and why are they important? In what ways do these factors find visual expression in the Imperial Federation Map?

2. What do Ferry, Williams, and the Imperial Federation Map suggest about changes in Europe's place within the world at large?

3. How do you think Ndansi Kumalo would have reacted to Ferry's defense of colonial expansion?

4. What do Williams, Bondfield, and Degas reveal about the impact of industrialization on everyday life and culture in Europe?

Modernity and the Road to War
1890–1914

A s the twentieth century dawned, Europeans had cause for both elation and fear. On the one hand, many enjoyed unprecedented prosperity: Europe's industrial and tech-nological forces continued to grow, and European nations controlled most of the world's surface. On the other, domestic and international tensions abounded: at home, people struggled to navigate the hazards of modern life, while abroad nation-states faced mount-ing competition and dissent in their quest for imperial glory. Documents 1 to 5 illustrate the disorder and chaos that seemed to lurk around every corner — in the family, in mass politics, even in one's own dreams and sexuality. At the same time, the foundations of nationalism had changed as European powers jockeyed for position both within Europe and beyond. For many citizens, pride in their nation rested not in its democratic institu-tions but in its military might. Document 6 reveals just how pervasive a pro-war spirit was at the time, setting the stage for a war of unprecedented destruction, World War I.

1. Racialized Ideas of Evolution
Sir Francis Galton, *Eugenics:*
Its Definition, Scope, and Aims (1904) and
International Eugenics Conference Poster (c. 1921)

As Europe's falling birthrate sparked concerns that Anglo-Saxons were committing "race suicide" by not having enough children, marriage and sexuality came under the public spot-light. Social Darwinists were especially vocal in their warnings of racial decay. Among the most well known of these was Charles Darwin's cousin, Sir Francis Galton (1822–1911), who

From Francis Galton, "Eugenics: Its Definition, Scope, and Aims," *The American Journal of Sociology* 10, no. 1 (July 1904): 1–5.

reasoned that society's efforts to protect the weakest, most vulnerable members of humanity were in fact at odds with natural selection — meaning that far from evolving to become a stronger and more talented people, society risked reverting toward mediocrity. His solution was eugenics, a term Galton coined to define "the study of the Agencies under social control, that improve or impair the racial qualities of future generations either physically or mentally." He actively promoted his views, including through the talk excerpted here delivered to the Sociological Society in London in May 1904; it was printed a month later in The American Journal of Sociology. *In 1907, academic friends of Galton's joined with middle-class professional men interested in eugenics to form the Eugenics Education Society, electing Galton as their first president. Their aim was practical rather than scholarly: to spread the wisdom of eugenics as widely as possible in society, with the intention of improving the population as a whole. The society also convened the first of three International Eugenics Congresses in 1912, helping to popularize their ideas internationally and increase scholarly interest in eugenics. An image of eugenics as a tree of knowledge, reproduced here, was used at both the second and the third International Eugenics Congresses and shows how the movement envisioned itself as a logical outgrowth of scientific research.*

Eugenics: Its Definition, Scope, and Aims

Eugenics is the science which deals with all influences that improve the inborn qualities of a race; also with those that develop them to the utmost advantage. . . .

A considerable list of qualities can easily be compiled that nearly everyone except "cranks" would take into account when picking out the best specimens of his class. It would include health, energy, ability, manliness, and courteous disposition. Recollect that the natural differences between dogs are highly marked in all these respects, and that men are quite as variable by nature as other animals of like species. Special aptitudes would be assessed highly by those who possessed them, as the artistic faculties by artists, fearlessness of inquiry and veracity by scientists, religious absorption by mystics, and so on. . . . They would have more of those qualities that are needed in a state — more vigor, more ability, and more consistency of purpose. . . .

Let us for a moment suppose that the practice of eugenics should hereafter raise the average quality of our nation . . . and consider the gain. The general tone of domestic, social, and political life would be higher. The race as a whole would be less foolish, less frivolous, less excitable, and politically more provident than now. . . . We should be better fitted to fulfil our vast imperial opportunities. Lastly, men of an order of ability which is now very rare would become more frequent, because, the level out of which they rose would itself have risen.

The aim of eugenics is to bring as many influences as can be reasonably employed, to cause the useful classes in the community to contribute *more* than their proportion to the next generation.

The course of procedure that lies within the functions of a learned and active society, such as the sociological may become, would be somewhat as follows:

1. Dissemination of a knowledge of the laws of heredity, so far as they are surely known, and promotion of their further study. . . .

2. Historical inquiry into the rates with which the various classes of society (classified according to civic usefulness) have contributed to the population at various times, in ancient and modern nations. . . .

3. Systematic collection of facts showing the circumstances under which large and thriving families have most frequently originated; in other words, the *conditions* of eugenics.

International Eugenics Conference Poster

'A decade of progress in Eugenics', Scientific / Wellcome Collection CCBY

The definition of a thriving family, that will pass muster for the moment at least, is one in which the children have gained distinctly superior positions to those who were their classmates in early life. Families may be considered "large" that contain not less than three adult male children. . . .

4. Influences affecting marriage. . . . The passion of love seems so overpowering that it may be thought folly to try to direct its course. But plain facts do not confirm this view. Social influences of all kinds have immense power in the end, and they are very various. If unsuitable marriages from the eugenic point of view were banned socially, or even regarded with the unreasonable disfavor which some attach to cousin-marriages, very few would be made. . . .

5. Persistence in setting forth the national importance of eugenics. There are three stages to be passed through: (1) It must be made familiar as an academic question, until its exact importance has been understood and accepted as a fact. (2) It must be recognized as a subject whose practical development deserves serious consideration. (3) It must be introduced into the national conscience, like a new religion.

DISCUSSION QUESTIONS

1. According to Galton, what specific steps should be taken to promote eugenics and apply its principles to society?

2. How does the tree in the poster visualize Galton's understanding of the relationship between different academic disciplines and the practice of eugenics?

3. What parallels can be drawn between the turn-of-the-century interest in eugenics and present-day speculation about the possibilities of genetic engineering?

2. Tapping the Human Psyche

Sigmund Freud, *The Interpretation of Dreams* (1900)

The fast-paced and conflict-ridden nature of life in industrial Europe undermined many people's optimism about their own and society's future. Austrian doctor Sigmund Freud (1856–1939) developed the method of psychoanalysis to tap into and cure such anxieties. After studying medicine in Vienna, in 1886 Freud opened his own practice to treat patients with nervous disorders. His clinical experience was the basis for his lifelong commitment to the scientific study of the human unconscious. In 1900, he published his most well-known work, The Interpretation of Dreams, *excerpted here. In it, he described dreams as windows into an individual's irrational desires and inner conflicts. Only by drawing out dreams' hidden meanings could a person expose the roots of his or her psychological problems. Psychoanalysis was designed to do just that, thereby laying the foundation of modern psychology.*

From A. A. Brill, trans. and ed., *The Basic Writings of Sigmund Freud* (New York: The Modern Library, 1938), 183, 188, 191–94, 208–9.

Furthermore, in arguing that scientists could — and should — study the human psyche, Freud further blurred the boundaries between public and private life.

In the following pages, I shall demonstrate that there is a psychological technique which makes it possible to interpret dreams, and that on the application of this technique, every dream will reveal itself as a psychological structure, full of significance, and one which may be assigned to a specific place in the psychic activities of the waking state. Further, I shall endeavor to elucidate the processes which underlie the strangeness and obscurity of dreams, and to deduce from these processes the nature of the psychic forces whose conflict or co-operation is responsible for our dreams. . . .

I am proposing to show that dreams are capable of interpretation; and any contributions to the solution of the problem which have already been discussed will emerge only as possible by-products in the accomplishment of my special task. On the hypothesis that dreams are susceptible of interpretation, I at once find myself in disagreement with the prevailing doctrine of dreams . . . for "to interpret a dream" is to specify its "meaning," to replace it by something which takes its position in the concatenation of our psychic activities as a link of definite importance and value. But, as we have seen, the scientific theories of the dream leave no room for a problem of dream-interpretation; since, in the first place, according to these theories, dreaming is not a psychic activity at all, but a somatic process which makes itself known to the psychic apparatus by means of symbols. . . .

I have, however, come to think differently. . . . I must insist that the dream actually does possess a meaning, and that a scientific method of dream-interpretation is possible. I arrived at my knowledge of this method in the following manner:

For years I have been occupied with the solution of certain psychopathological structures — hysterical phobias, obsessional ideas, and the like — with therapeutic intentions. . . . In the course of these psychoanalytic studies, I happened upon the question of dream-interpretation. My patients, after I had pledged them to inform me of all the ideas and thoughts which occurred to them in connection with a given theme, related their dreams, and thus taught me that a dream may be interpolated in the psychic concatenation, which may be followed backwards from a pathological idea into the patient's memory. The next step was to treat the dream itself as a symptom, and to apply to it the method of interpretation which had been worked out for such symptoms.

For this a certain psychic preparation on the part of the patient is necessary. A twofold effort is made, to stimulate his attentiveness in respect of his psychic perceptions, and to eliminate the critical spirit in which he is ordinarily in the habit of viewing such thoughts as come to the surface. For the purpose of self-observation with concentrated attention it is advantageous that the patient should take up a restful position and close his eyes; he must be explicitly instructed to renounce all criticism of the thought-formations which he may perceive. He must also be told that the success of the psychoanalysis depends upon his noting and communicating everything that passes through his mind, and that he must not allow himself to suppress one idea because it seems to him unimportant or irrelevant to the subject, or another because it seems nonsensical. He must preserve an absolute impartiality in respect to his ideas; for if he is unsuccessful in finding the desired solution of the dream, the obsessional idea, or the like, it will be because he permits himself to be critical of them. . . .

As will be seen, the point is to induce a psychic state which is in some degree analogous, as regards the distribution of psychic energy (mobile attention), to the state of the mind before falling asleep — and also, of course, to the hypnotic state. On falling asleep the "undesired ideas" emerge, owing to the slackening of a certain arbitrary (and, of course, also critical) action, which is allowed to influence the trends of our ideas; we are accustomed to speak of fatigue as the reason of this slackening; the emerging undesired ideas are changed into visual and auditory images. In the condition which it utilized for the analysis of dreams and pathological ideas, this activity is purposely and deliberately renounced, and the psychic energy thus saved (or some part of it) is employed in attentively tracking the undesired thoughts which now come to the surface. . . .

The first step in the application of this procedure teaches us that one cannot make the dream as a whole the object of one's attention, but only the individual components of its content. If I ask a patient who is as yet unpracticed: "What occurs to you in connection with this dream?" he is unable, as a rule, to fix upon anything in his psychic field of vision. I must first dissect the dream for him; then, in connection with each fragment, he gives me a number of ideas which may be described as the "thoughts behind" this part of the dream. In this first and important condition, then, the method of dream-interpretation which I employ diverges from the popular, historical and legendary method of interpretation by symbolism and approaches more nearly to the second or "cipher method." Like this, it is an interpretation in detail, not *en masse*; like this, it conceives the dream, from the outset, as something built up, as a conglomerate of psychic formations. . . .

When, after passing through a narrow defile, one suddenly reaches a height beyond which the ways part and a rich prospect lies outspread in different directions, it is well to stop for a moment and consider whither one shall turn next. We are in somewhat the same position after we have mastered this first interpretation of a dream. We find ourselves standing in the light of a sudden discovery. The dream is not comparable to the irregular sounds of a musical instrument, which, instead of being played by the hand of a musician, is struck by some external force; the dream is not meaningless, not absurd, does not presuppose that one part of our store of ideas is dormant while another part begins to awake. It is a perfectly valid psychic phenomenon, actually a wish-fulfilment; it may be enrolled in the continuity of the intelligible psychic activities of the waking state; it is built up by a highly complicated intellectual activity. . . .

It is easy to show that the wish-fulfilment in dreams is often undisguised and easy to recognize, so that one may wonder why the language of dreams has not long since been understood. There is, for example, a dream which I can evoke as often as I please, experimentally, as it were. If, in the evening, I eat anchovies, olives, or other strongly salted foods, I am thirsty at night, and therefore I wake. The waking, however, is preceded by a dream, which has always the same content, namely, that I am drinking. I am drinking long draughts of water; it tastes as delicious as only a cool drink can taste when one's throat is parched; and then I wake, and find that I have an actual desire to drink. The cause of this dream is thirst, which I perceive when I wake. From this sensation arises the wish to drink and the dream shows me this wish as fulfilled. It thereby serves a function, the nature of which I soon surmise. I sleep well, and am not accustomed to being waked by a bodily need. If I succeed in appeasing my thirst by means of the dream that I am drinking, I need not wake up in order to satisfy my thirst. It is thus a *dream of convenience*. The dream takes the place of action, as elsewhere in life.

DISCUSSION QUESTIONS

1. How did Freud's theory of dream interpretation reject contemporary scientific views about dreams?

2. What does Freud mean when he describes dreams as "wish-fulfilment"?

3. According to Freud, what is the relationship between a person's dreams and his or her waking state?

3. The Dreyfus Affair

Émile Zola, *"J'accuse!"* (January 13, 1898)

At the close of the nineteenth century, more and more Europeans embraced militant nationalism and anti-Semitism as weapons against the struggles of modern society. The combination of these forces fueled what became a defining event of the period, the Dreyfus Affair. In 1894, a Jewish captain in the French army, Alfred Dreyfus (1859–1935), was accused of spying for Germany. A military memorandum (bordereau) discovered by a secret agent in the German embassy in Paris formed the centerpiece of the military's case. Despite Dreyfus's protestations of innocence, he was convicted and imprisoned on Devil's Island. The case receded from public view for nearly two years until new evidence pointed to the real traitor, Ferdinand Walsin-Esterhazy. Forced to open an investigation, the army desperately sought a way to protect its prestige and reputation. Its efforts culminated on January 12, 1898, when a panel of military judges found Esterhazy not guilty after a two-day trial conducted behind closed doors. Among Dreyfus's most ardent champions was French writer Émile Zola (1840–1902), who drafted the letter excerpted here in response to the trial. The day after the verdict, Zola's letter appeared in 300,000 copies of a special edition of the Parisian newspaper L'Aurore. Because of Zola's popularity and his willingness to name names, his letter transformed the Dreyfus case into an international affair.

Monsieur le Président,

Will you allow me, out of my gratitude for the gracious manner in which you once granted me an audience, to express my concern for your well-deserved glory? Will you allow me to tell you that although your star has been in the ascendant hitherto, it is now in danger of being dimmed by the most shameful and indelible of stains?

You have emerged unscathed from libelous slurs, you have won the people's hearts. You are the radiant center of our apotheosis, for the Russian alliance has been indeed, for France, a patriotic celebration. And now you are about to preside over our World Fair. What a solemn triumph it will be, the crowning touch on our grand century of diligent labor, truth and liberty. But what a blot on your name (I was about to say, on your reign) this abominable Dreyfus Affair is! A court martial, acting on orders, has just dared to acquit such a man as Esterhazy. Truth itself and justice itself have been slapped in the face.

From Alain Pagès, ed., *The Dreyfus Affair, "J'Accuse" and Other Writings*, trans. Eleanor Levieux (New Haven, CT: Yale University Press, 1996), 43–47, 50–53.

And now it is too late, France's cheek has been sullied by that supreme insult, and History will record that it was during your Presidency that such a crime against society was committed.

They have dared to do this. Very well, then, I shall dare too. I shall tell the truth, for I pledged that I would tell it, if our judicial system, once the matter was brought before it through the normal channels, did not tell the truth, the whole truth. It is my duty to speak up; I will not be an accessory to the fact. If I were, my nights would be haunted by the specter of that innocent man so far away, suffering the worst kind of torture as he pays for a crime he did not commit.

And it is to you, M. le Président, that I will shout out the truth with all the revulsion of a decent man. To your credit, I am convinced that you are unaware of the truth. And to whom should I denounce the evil machinations of those who are truly guilty if not to you, the First Magistrate in the land? . . .

Ah, for anyone who knows the true details of the first affair, what a nightmare it is! Major du Paty de Clam arrests Dreyfus and has him placed in solitary confinement. He rushes to the home of Madame Dreyfus and terrifies her, saying that if she speaks up, her husband is lost. Meanwhile the unfortunate man is tearing out his hair, clamoring his innocence. And that is how the investigation proceeded, as in some fifteenth-century chronicle, shrouded in mystery and a wealth of the wildest expedients, and all on the basis of a single, childish accusation, that idiotic bordereau, which was not only a very ordinary kind of treason but also the most impudent kind of swindle, since almost all of the so-called secrets that had supposedly been turned over to the enemy were of no value. I dwell on this point because this is the egg from which the real crime — the dreadful denial of justice which has laid France low — was later to hatch. I would like to make it perfectly clear how the miscarriage of justice came about, how it is the product of Major du Paty de Clam's machinations, how General Mercier and Generals de Boisdeffre and Gonse came to be taken in by it and gradually became responsible for this error and how it is that later they felt they had a duty to impose it as the sacred truth, a truth that will not admit of even the slightest discussion. At the beginning, all they contributed was negligence and lack of intelligence. The worst we can say is that they gave in to the religious passions of the circles they move in and the prejudices wrought by esprit de corps. They let stupidity have its way.

But now, here is Dreyfus summoned before the court martial. The most utter secrecy is demanded. They could not have imposed stricter silence and been more rigorous and mysterious if a traitor had actually opened our borders to the enemy and led the German Emperor straight to Notre Dame. The entire nation is flabbergasted. Terrible deeds are whispered about, monstrous betrayals that scandalize History itself, and of course the nation bows to these rumors. No punishment can be too severe; the nation will applaud the traitor's public humiliation; the nation is adamant: the guilty man shall remain on the remote rock where infamy has placed him and he shall be devoured by remorse. But then, those unspeakable accusations, those dangerous accusations that might inflame all of Europe and had to be so carefully concealed behind the closed doors of a secret session — are they true? No, they are not! There is nothing behind all that but the extravagant, demented flights of fancy of Major du Paty de Clam. It's all a smokescreen with just one purpose: to conceal a cheap novel of the most outlandish sort. And to be convinced of this, one need only examine the formal indictment that was read before the court martial.

How hollow that indictment is! Is it possible a man has been found guilty on the strength of it? Such iniquity is staggering. I challenge decent people to read it: their hearts will leap with indignation and rebellion when they think of the dis-proportionate price Dreyfus is paying so far away on Devil's Island. So Dreyfus speaks several languages, does he? This is a crime. Not one compromising paper was found in his home? A crime. He occasionally pays a visit to the region he hails from? A crime. He is a hard-working man, eager to know everything? A crime. He does not get flustered? A crime. He does get flustered? A crime. And how naively it is worded! How baseless its claims are! They told us he was indicted on fourteen different counts but in the end there is actually only one: that famous bordereau; and we even find out that the experts did not all agree, that one of them, M. Gobert, was subjected to some military pressure because he dared to come to a different conclusion from the one they wanted him to reach. We were also told that twenty-three officers had come and testified against Dreyfus. We still do not know how they were questioned, but what is certain is that not all of their testimony was negative. Besides, all of them, you will notice, came from the offices of the War Department. This trial is a family conclave; they all *belong*. We must not forget that. It is the General Staff who wanted this trial; it is they who judged Dreyfus; and they have just judged him for the second time....

... And what makes the whole business all the more odious and cynical is that they are lying with impunity and there is no way to convict them. They turn France inside out, they shelter behind the legitimate uproar they have caused, they seal mouths by making hearts quake and perverting minds. I know of no greater crime against society.

These, M. le Président, are the facts that explain how a miscarriage of justice has come to be committed. And the evidence as to Dreyfus's character, his financial situation, his lack of motives, the fact that he has never ceased to clamor his innocence — all these demonstrate that he has been a victim of Major du Paty de Clam's overheated imagination, and of the clericalism that prevails in the military circles in which he moves, and of the hysterical hunt for "dirty Jews" that disgraces our times....

. . .

As I have already shown, the Dreyfus Affair was the affair of the War Office: an officer from the General Staff denounced by his fellow officers on the General Staff, sentenced under pressure from the Chiefs of the General Staff. And I repeat, he cannot emerge from his trial innocent without all of the General Staff being guilty. Which is why the War Office employed every means imaginable — campaigns in the press, statements and innuendoes, every type of influence — to cover Esterhazy, in order to convict Dreyfus a second time.... Where, oh where is a strong and wisely patriotic ministry that will be bold enough to overhaul the whole system and make a fresh start? I know many people who tremble with alarm at the thought of a possible war, knowing what hands our national defense is in! and what a den of sneaking intrigue, rumor-mongering and back-biting that sacred chapel has become — yet that is where the fate of our country is decided! People take fright at the appalling light that has just been shed on it all by the Dreyfus Affair, that tale of human sacrifice! Yes, an unfortunate, a "dirty Jew" has been sacrificed. Yes, what an accumulation of madness, stupidity, unbridled imagination, low police tactics, inquisitorial and tyrannical methods this handful of officers have got away with!

They have crushed the nation under their boots, stuffing its calls for truth and justice down its throat on the fallacious and sacrilegious pretext that they are acting for the good of the country!

And they have committed other crimes. They have based their action on the foul press and let themselves be defended by all the rogues in Paris — and now the rogues are triumphant and insolent while law and integrity go down in defeat. It is a crime to have accused individuals of rending France apart when all those individuals ask for is a generous nation at the head of the procession of free, just nations — and all the while the people who committed that crime were hatching an insolent plot to make the entire world swallow a fabrication. It is a crime to lead public opinion astray, to manipulate it for a death-dealing purpose and pervert it to the point of delirium. It is a crime to poison the minds of the humble, ordinary people, to whip reactionary and intolerant passions into a frenzy while sheltering behind the odious bastion of anti-Semitism. France, the great and liberal cradle of the rights of man, will die of anti-Semitism if it is not cured of it. It is a crime to play on patriotism to further the aims of hatred. And it is a crime to worship the saber as a modern god when all of human science is laboring to hasten the triumph of truth and justice. . . .

That, M. le Président, is the plain truth. It is appalling. It will remain an indelible blot on your term as President. Oh, I know that you are powerless to deal with it, that you are the prisoner of the Constitution and of the people nearest to you. But as a man, your duty is clear, and you will not overlook it, and you will do your duty. Not for one minute do I despair that truth will triumph. I am confident and I repeat, more vehemently even than before, the truth is on the march and nothing shall stop it. The Affair is only just beginning, because only now have the positions become crystal clear: on the one hand, the guilty parties, who do not want the truth to be revealed; on the other, the defenders of justice, who will give their lives to see that justice is done. I have said it elsewhere and I repeat it here: if the truth is buried underground, it swells and grows and becomes so explosive that the day it bursts, it blows everything wide open along with it. Time will tell; we shall see whether we have not prepared, for some later date, the most resounding disaster.

. . .

But this letter has been a long one, M. le Président, and it is time to bring it to a close.

I accuse Lt-Col du Paty de Clam of having been the diabolical agent of a miscarriage of justice (though unwittingly, I am willing to believe) and then of having defended his evil deed for the past three years through the most preposterous and most blameworthy machinations.

I accuse General Mercier of having been an accomplice, at least by weak-mindedness, to one of the most iniquitous acts of this century.

I accuse General Billot of having had in his hands undeniable proof that Dreyfus was innocent and of having suppressed it, of having committed this crime against justice and against humanity for political purposes, so that the General Staff, which had been compromised, would not lose face.

I accuse Generals de Boisdeffre and Gonse of having been accomplices to this same crime, one out of intense clerical conviction, no doubt, and the other perhaps because of the esprit de corps which makes the War Office the Holy of Holies and hence unattackable.

I accuse General de Pellieux and Major Ravary of having led a villainous inquiry, by which I mean a most monstrously one-sided inquiry, the report on which, by Ravary, constitutes an imperishable monument of naive audacity.

I accuse the three handwriting experts, Messrs Belhomme, Varinard, and Couard, of having submitted fraudulent and deceitful reports — unless a medical examination concludes that their eyesight and their judgment were impaired.

I accuse the War Office of having conducted an abominable campaign in the press (especially in *L'Eclair* and *L'Echo de Paris*) in order to cover up its misdeeds and lead public opinion astray.

Finally, I accuse the first court martial of having violated the law by sentencing a defendant on the basis of a document which remained secret, and I accuse the second court martial of having covered up that illegal action, on orders, by having, in its own turn, committed the judicial crime of knowingly acquitting a guilty man.

In making these accusations, I am fully aware that my action comes under Articles 30 and 31 of the law of 29 July 1881 on the press, which makes libel a punishable offense. I deliberately expose myself to that law.

As for the persons I have accused, I do not know them; I have never seen them; I feel no rancor or hatred towards them. To me, they are mere entities, mere embodiments of social malfeasance. And the action I am taking here is merely a revolutionary means to hasten the revelation of truth and justice.

I have but one goal: that light be shed, in the name of mankind which has suffered so much and has the right to happiness. My ardent protest is merely a cry from my very soul. Let them dare to summon me before a court of law! Let the inquiry be held in broad daylight!

I am waiting.

M. le Président, I beg you to accept the assurance of my most profound respect.

DISCUSSION QUESTIONS

1. According to Zola, what motivated the army officers' actions against Dreyfus?
2. What does Zola mean when he describes Dreyfus's conviction and Esterhazy's acquittal as "crimes against society"?
3. Why do you think Zola felt compelled to publicize his views?
4. Many scholars argue that with the rise of mass politics during the late nineteenth century, the press played an increasingly important role in everyday life. In what ways do the form and content of Zola's letter support this argument?

4. Militant Suffrage

Emmeline Pankhurst, *Speech from the Dock* (1908)

By granting working-class men the vote in 1884, the British government hoped to make politics more unified and orderly. Yet the realization of such hopes proved elusive, in part because a new political foe had appeared on the scene: the women's suffrage movement. The founder of the Women's Social and Political Union (WSPU), Emmeline Pankhurst

(1858–1928), was among the most influential voices of the movement. Although women in Britain had long been fighting for rights, the expansion of the male electorate further accentuated their political exclusion. In the following speech before a police court judge, Pankhurst defends the WSPU's tactics, which had become increasingly militant since its inception in 1903. She and two colleagues had been arrested for distributing a leaflet encouraging her supporters "to rush the House of Commons," and they faced a prison sentence for refusing to "bind themselves over" — in other words, to promise to behave properly. Pankhurst's speech reflects her belief that the WSPU's struggle was more than a quest for the vote; it was a war against a patriarchal society.

Ever since my girlhood, a period of about 30 years, I have belonged to organizations to secure for women that political power which I have felt was essential to bringing about those reforms which women need. I have tried constitutional methods. I have been womanly. When you spoke to some of my colleagues the day before yesterday about their being unwomanly, I felt that bitterness which I know every one of them felt in their hearts. We have tried to be womanly, we have tried to use feminine influence, and we have seen that it is of no use. Men who have been impatient have invariably got reforms for their impatience. And they have not our excuse for being impatient. . . .

Now, while I share in the feeling of indignation which has been expressed to you by my daughter, I have lived longer in the world than she has. Perhaps I can look round the whole question better than she can, but I want to say here, deliberately, to you, that we are here today because we are driven here. We have taken this action, because as women — and I want you to understand it is as women we have taken this action — it is because we realize that the condition of our sex is so deplorable that it is our duty even to break the law in order to call attention to the reasons why we do so.

I do not want to say anything which may seem disrespectful to you, or in any way give you offense, but I do want to say that I wish, sir, that you could put yourself into the place of women for a moment before you decide upon this case. My daughter referred to the way in which women are huddled into and out of these police-courts without a fair trial. I want you to realize what a poor hunted creature, without the advantages we have had, must feel.

I have been in prison. I was in Holloway Gaol for five weeks. I was in various parts of the prison. I was in the hospital, and in the ordinary part of the prison, and I tell you, sir, with as much sense of responsibility as if I had taken the oath, that there were women there who have broken no law, who are there because they have been able to make no adequate statement.

You know that women have tried to do something to come to the aid of their own sex. Women are brought up for certain crimes, crimes which men do not understand — I am thinking especially of infanticide — they are brought before a man judge, before a jury of men, who are called upon to decide whether some poor, hunted woman is guilty of murder or not. I put it to you, sir, when we see in the papers, as we often do, a case similar to that of Daisy Lord, for whom a great petition was got up in this country, I want you to realize how we women feel, because we are women, because we are not men, we need some legitimate influence to bear upon our law-makers.

From Emmeline Pankhurst, "Speech from the Dock [Police Court]," in *Votes for Women* (October 29, 1908), 1.

Now, we have tried every way. We have presented larger petitions than were ever presented for any other reform; we have succeeded in holding greater public meetings than men have ever had for any reform, in spite of the difficulty which women have in throwing off their natural diffidence, that desire to escape publicity which we have inherited from generations of our foremothers; we have broken through that. We have faced hostile mobs at street corners, because we were told that we could not have that representation for our taxes which men have won unless we converted the whole of the country to our side. Because we have done this, we have been misrepresented, we have been ridiculed, we have had contempt poured upon us. The ignorant mob at the street corner has been incited to offer us violence, which we have faced unarmed and unprotected by the safe-guards which Cabinet Ministers have. We know that we need the protection of the vote even more than men have needed it.

I am here to take upon myself now, sir, as I wish the prosecution had put upon me, the full responsibility for this agitation in its present phase. I want to address you as a woman who has performed the duties of a woman, and, in addition, has performed the duties which ordinary men have had to perform, by earning a living for her children, and educating them. In addition to that, I have been a public officer. I enjoyed for 10 years an official post under the Registrar, and I performed those duties to the satisfaction of the head of the department. After my duty of taking the census was over, I was one of the few Registrars who qualified for a special bonus, and was specially praised for the way in which the work was conducted. Well, sir, I stand before you, having resigned that office when I was told that I must either do that or give up working for this movement.

I want to make you realize that it is a point of honor that if you decide — as I hope you will not decide — to bind us over, that we shall not sign any undertaking, as the Member of Parliament did who was before you yesterday. Perhaps his reason for signing that undertaking may have been that the Prime Minister had given some assurance to the people he claimed to represent that something should be done for them. We have no such assurance. Mr. Birrell told the women who questioned him the other day that he could not say that anything would be done to give an assurance to the women that their claims should be conceded. So, sir, if you decide against us today, to prison we must go, because we feel that we should be going back to the hopeless condition this movement was in three years ago if we consented to be bound over to keep the peace which we have never broken, and so, sir, if you decide to bind us over, whether it is for three or six months, we shall submit to the treatment, the degrading treatment, that we have submitted to before.

Although the Government admitted that we are political offenders, and, therefore, ought to be treated as political offenders are invariably treated, we shall be treated as pick-pockets and drunkards; we shall be searched. I want you, if you can, as a man, to realize what it means to women like us. We are driven to do this, we are determined to go on with agitation, because we feel in honor bound. Just as it was the duty of your forefathers, it is our duty to make this world a better place for women than it is today. . . .

This is the only way we can get that power which every citizen should have of deciding how the taxes she contributes to should be spent, and how the laws she has to obey should be made, and until we get that power we shall be here — we are here today, and we shall come here over and over again. You must realize how futile it is to settle this question by binding us over to keep the peace. You have tried it; it has failed. Others have tried to do it, and have failed. If you had power to send us to prison, not for six months, but for six years, for 16 years, or for the whole of our lives, the Government must not think that they can stop this agitation. It will go on.

I want to draw your attention to the self-restraint which was shown by our followers on the night of the 13th, after we had been arrested. It only shows that our influence over them is very great, because I think that if they had yielded to their natural impulses, there might have been a breach of the peace on the evening of the 13th. They were very indignant, but our words have always been, "be patient, exercise self-restraint, show our so-called superiors that the criticism of women being hysterical is not true; use no violence, offer yourselves to the violence of others." We are going to win. Our women have taken that advice; if we are in prison they will continue to take that advice.

Well, sir, that is all I have to say to you. We are here not because we are law-breakers; we are here in our efforts to become law-makers.

DISCUSSION QUESTIONS

1. How did the WSPU's tactics challenge conventional notions of proper behavior for women at the time?

2. According to Pankhurst, why was the WSPU forced to adopt such tactics?

3. Why did she think that women had both a right to and a need for political enfranchisement?

5. Imperialism and Anti-Imperialism

SOURCES IN CONVERSATION | Rudyard Kipling, *The White Man's Burden* and *Editorial from the* San Francisco Call (1899)

Another factor contributing to people's sense of unease in the late nineteenth century was an increasingly loud debate over the merits of imperialism. This debate was not confined to European shores; it also exploded onto the American scene when the United States gained control of Puerto Rico, Guam, and the Philippines in February 1899 after its victory in the Spanish-American War. Rudyard Kipling (1865–1936) published the poem "The White Man's Burden" in London and U.S. newspapers in direct response to the fledging status of the United States as an imperial power. He urged Americans to share the "burden" — of implanting Western civilization among the "new-caught, sullen peoples" of East Asia — already shouldered by Europe. Born in British India and the son of a civil servant, Kipling was well versed in the ways of empire building and had already made a name for himself as the author of The Jungle Book, *among other works. The poem elicited a swift response across the United States, including the anti-imperialist editorial, which appeared in the* San Francisco Call, *that follows the poem.*

From *Rudyard Kipling's Verse: Inclusive Edition (1885–1918)* (New York: Doubleday, 1927), 371–72; "The White Man's Burden," *San Francisco Call* (Feb. 7, 1899). Reprinted on www.boon docksnet.com/ai/, Jim Zwick, ed., *Anti-Imperialism in the United States.*

The White Man's Burden

Take up the White Man's burden —
    Send forth the best ye breed —
Go bind your sons to exile
    To serve your captives' need;
To wait in heavy harness,
    On fluttered folk and wild —
Your new-caught, sullen peoples,
    Half-devil and half-child.

Take up the White Man's Burden —
    In patience to abide,
To veil the threat of terror
    And check the show of pride;
By open speech and simple,
    An hundred times made plain,
To seek another's profit,
    And work another's gain.

Take up the White Man's burden —
    The savage wars of peace —
Fill full the mouth of Famine
    And bid the sickness cease;
And when your goal is nearest
    The end for others sought,
Watch Sloth and heathen Folly
    Bring all your hope to nought.

Take up the White Man's burden —
    No tawdry rule of kings,
But toil of serf and sweeper —
    The tale of common things.
The ports ye shall not enter,
    The roads ye shall not tread,
Go make them with your living,
    And mark them with your dead.

Take up the White Man's burden —
    And reap his old reward:
The blame of those ye better,
    The hate of those ye guard —
The cry of hosts ye humor
    (Ah, slowly!) toward the light: —
"Why brought ye us from bondage,
    Our loved Egyptian night?"

Take up the White Man's burden —
　　Ye dare not stoop to less —
Nor call too loud on Freedom
　　To cloak your weariness;
By all ye cry or whisper,
　　By all ye leave or do,
The silent, sullen peoples
　　Shall weigh your Gods and you.

Take up the White Man's burden —
　　Have done with childish days —
The lightly proffered laurel,
　　The easy, ungrudged praise.
Comes now, to search your manhood
　　Through all the thankless years,
Cold, edged with dear-bought wisdom,
　　The judgment of your peers!

Editorial from the *San Francisco Call*

Rudyard Kipling has joined the ranks of those eminent British jingoes who are trying to induce the United States to help Great Britain in her imperial schemes by taking part in the Oriental imbroglio. Chamberlain and Balfour have enticed us with lofty oratory. Kipling wooes us with a song published in The Call of Sunday.

The title of the ballad is "The White Man's Burden." Mr. Kipling sings:

Take up the White Man's burden —
　　Have done with childish days —
The lightly proffered laurel,
　　The easy, ungrudged praise;
Comes now, to search your manhood
　　Through all the thankless years,
Cold, edged with dear-bought wisdom,
　　The judgment of your peers!

By way of further information as to what we shall have to do when we have done with childish days and set about winning the approving judgment of our peers with their cold, edged, dear-bought wisdom, the poet, drawing an easy lesson from the experience of Great Britain, adds:

Take up the White Man's Burden —
　　Send forth the best ye breed —
Go, bind your sons to exile
　　To serve your captives' need;

To wait, in heavy harness,
    On fluttered folk and wild —
Your new-caught sullen peoples,
    Half-devil and half-child.

It seems we are to infer from this that if we do not consent to send forth the best we breed to serve in exile amid the jungles of tropic islands for the noble purpose of imposing American law and civilization upon the mongrel races, half devil and half child, we shall lose the esteem of European powers now engaged in that task, and possibly the esteem of Mr. Kipling also. It is a dilemma from which we cannot escape. Fate has ordained it and face it we must.

We might be more willing to enter upon the imperial task if our British cousins were not so outspoken in their eagerness to get us to do so. Their willingness to have us share the glory of civilizing the Orient awakens a suspicion that the glory is not altogether a profitable one. Great Britain evidently has more than she can carry and would like to divide the glory with us.

The invitation to take part is flattering to our pride, but not attractive to our common sense. We have a pretty heavy white man's burden at home and it will take something more than a song even from so strong a singer as Kipling to coax us to go to the Orient in search of an increase.

In all seriousness the eagerness of Chamberlain, Balfour, and other British leaders to get the United States involved in the affairs of the Orient and indirectly made a party to all European squabbles, is a significant sign of the times, and ought to be a sufficient warning to all intelligent Americans to avoid imperialism as they would a plague.

The pursuit of imperialism has raised up antagonists to Great Britain in every part of the world; it has imposed upon her people a heavy burden of debt and taxation; it has disturbed her politics by the continual menace of war and thus prevented the accomplishment of many needed reforms at home; and finally it has brought her into a position where without an ally she is confronted by a hostile world and is in danger of having her commerce, and perhaps even her empire, swept away at the first outbreak of war.

Rightly considered the white man's burden is to set and keep his own house in order. It is not required of him to upset the brown man's house under pretense of reform and then whip him into subjugation whenever he revolts at the treatment.

DISCUSSION QUESTIONS

1. How does Kipling define the "White Man's burden"? What duties does he think this "burden" entails?

2. What kind of portrait does Kipling paint of non-Western peoples?

3. According to the author of the editorial from the *San Francisco Call*, why should Americans reject Kipling's appeal and avoid imperialism "as they would a plague"?

4. In what ways do these two sources expose the paradoxes of the new imperialism?

6. Exalting War

Heinrich von Treitschke, *Place of Warfare in the State* (1897–1898) and Henri Massis and Alfred de Tarde, *The Young People of Today* (1912)

As the nineteenth century came to a close, competitive nationalism in preparation for war gripped much of Europe. Against this backdrop, people from all walks of life, including the intellectual elite, embraced war as a necessary, even desirable, reality in the modern age. The two documents here give voice to this pro-war spirit on the eve of World War I. The first is an excerpt from a series of lectures by German historian Heinrich von Treitschke (1834–1896), who taught a popular course on politics at the University of Berlin. The course lectures were compiled after his death from the notebooks of his students and published in two volumes. Entrenched in a climate of military buildup and competition for empire, Treitschke devoted much of his teaching to supporting his nation. The second document comes from an opinion poll conducted among male students at various elite educational institutions in Paris. It was first published in a Paris newspaper in 1912. Although purported to be an objective survey, the poll was shaped by the authors' own views of the characteristics separating modern students from the preceding generation, notably their exaltation of war as the most noble of human virtues.

Place of Warfare in the State

One must certainly, when considering war, remember that it does not always appear as a judgment of God; there are also temporary results, but the life of a people is reckoned by centuries. The decisive verdict can only be obtained by the review of great epochs. A State like Prussia, which was freer and more rational than the French, might owing to momentary exhaustion be brought near annihilation, but it would then call to mind its inner life, and would thus regain its superiority. One must say with the greatest determination: War is for an afflicted people the only remedy. When the State exclaims: My very existence is at stake! then social self-seeking must disappear and all party hatred be silent. The individual must forget his own *ego* and feel himself a member of the whole, he must recognize how negligible is his life compared with the good of the whole. Therein lies the greatness of war that the little man completely vanishes before the great thought of the State. The sacrifice of nationalities for one another is nowhere invested with such beauty as in war. At such a time the corn is separated from the chaff. . . .

It is indeed political idealism which fosters war, whereas materialism rejects it. What a perversion of morality to want to banish heroism from human life. The heroes of a people are the personalities who fill the youthful souls with delight and enthusiasm; and amongst authors, we as boys and youths admire most those whose words sound like a

---

From German Emperor et al., *Germany's War Mania* (New York: Dodd, Mead and Company Publishers, 1915), 221–22, 224, 226–27; and John W. Boyer and Jan Goldstein, eds., *Readings in Western Civilization*, Volume 9: *Twentieth-Century Europe* (Chicago: University of Chicago Press, 1987), 26–27.

flourish of trumpets. He who cannot take pleasure therein, is too cowardly to take up arms himself for his fatherland. All appeal to Christianity in this matter is perverted. The Bible states expressly that the man in authority shall wield the sword; it states likewise that: "Greater love hath no man than this that he giveth his life for his friend." Those who preach the nonsense about everlasting peace do not understand the life of the Aryan race, the Aryans are before all brave. They have always been men enough to protect by the sword what they had won by the intellect. . . . Thus to a noble nation, heroism and the maintenance of physical strength and of moral courage are essential.

To the historian who lives in the realms of the Will, it is quite clear that the further-ance of an everlasting peace is fundamentally reactionary. He sees that to banish war from history would be to banish all progress and becoming. It is only the periods of exhaustion, weariness and mental stagnation that have dallied with the dream of everlasting peace. . . .

War and conquest are therefore the most important State builders. The rule of the founding of States by the Sword is preponderant; and we observe here in modern history the unceasing impetus towards a great national empire-building from a little centre, which at first arises merely from the bare instinct of force, but by degrees, becoming conscious, it finds in the recognition of a common nationality the requisite unifying force. Thus England's Unity began with Wessex. This united Anglo-Saxon kingdom then conquered Scotland and Ireland and endowed them with Anglo-Saxon culture. The development of France was similar. Here from Isle de France, in a similar manner, the microcosm of the ethno-graphical conditions of Gaul, arose the unity of the land. In Spain from Castile; and in Russia from the realm of Rurik grew by degrees the great Muscovite Empire. . . .

We, on the other hand, are finding out to-day what opportunities we have neglected. The results of the last half century are frightful: during that period England has conquered the world. The Continent had no time in consequence of its continual restlessness to cast its eyes over the seas, where England was grasping everything for herself. Germany had to miss and sleep through that just because she was much too busy with her neighbours and with her own home struggles. Beyond a doubt a great colonial development is a great blessing to a nation. And that is the short sightedness of our opponents of colonial devel-opment, that they cannot see this. The whole position of Germany depends partly upon this factor — how many millions of men in the future will speak the German language. . . .

Consequently, that colonization which retains a homogeneous nationality has become, for the future of the world, a factor of enormous significance. On it will depend the extent to which each nation will share in the domination of the world by the white races. It is quite thinkable that it might come to pass that a country possessing no colonies might cease to be numbered amongst the Great Powers in Europe, however powerful it might once have been. For this reason we dare not drift into that condition of torpor which is the result of a continental policy, and the issue of our next successful war must, if possible, be the acquisition of a colony of some sort.

The Young People of Today

Consider something even more significant. Students of advanced rhetoric in Paris, that is, the most cultivated elite among young people, declare that they find in warfare an aes-thetic ideal of energy and strength. They believe that "France needs heroism in order to live." "Such is the faith," comments Monsieur Tourolle, "which consumes modern youth."

How many times in the last two years have we heard this repeated: "Better war than this eternal waiting!" There is no bitterness in this avowal, but rather a secret hope. . . .

War! The word has taken on a sudden glamour. It is a youthful word, wholly new, adorned with that seduction which the eternal bellicose instinct has revived in the hearts of men. These young men impute to it all the beauty with which they are in love and of which they have been deprived by ordinary life. Above all, war, in their eyes, is the occasion for the most noble of human virtues, those which they exalt above all others: energy, mastery, and sacrifice for a cause which transcends ourselves. With William James, they believe that life "would become odious if it offered neither risks nor rewards for the courageous man."

A professor of philosophy at the Lycée Henri IV confided to us: "I once spoke about war to my pupils. I explained to them that there were unjust wars, undertaken out of anger, and that it was necessary to justify the bellicose sentiment. Well, the class obviously did not follow me; they rejected that distinction."

Read this passage from a letter written to us by a young student of rhetoric, Alsatian in origin. "The existence that we lead does not satisfy us completely because, even if we possess all the elements of a good life, we cannot organize them in a practical, immediate deed that would take us, body and soul, and hurl us outside of ourselves. One event only will permit that deed — war; and hence we desire it. It is in the life of the camps, it is around the fire that we will experience the supreme expansion of those French powers that are within us. Our intellect will no longer be troubled in the face of the unknowable, since it will be able to concentrate itself entirely on a present duty from which uncertainty and hesitation are excluded."

Above all, perhaps, how can one ignore the success that accounts of our colonialists have had among the young intellectuals under consideration here? The expeditions of Moll, Lenfant, and Baratier arouse their enthusiasm; they search in their own unperilous existences for a moral equivalent to these bold destinies; they attempt to transpose this intrepid valor into their inner lives.

Some go further: their studies completed, they satisfy their taste for action in colonial adventures. It is not enough for them to learn history: they are making it. A young student from the Normale, Monsieur Klipfell, who received his teaching degree in literature in July of 1912, requested to be assigned to active service in Morocco, as a member of the Expeditionary Corps. We can cite many a similar example. One thinks of Jacques Violet, a twenty-year-old officer, who died so gloriously at Ksar-Teuchan, in Adrar: he was killed at the head of his men, at the moment of victory, in a grove of palm trees; among his belongings, they found a pair of white gloves and a copy of *Servitude and Military Grandeur*; it was thus that he went into combat.

Need we recall the adventures of the colonial military artillery lieutenant Ernest Psichari, the grandson of Renan, who abandoned his studies at the Sorbonne, along with the thesis he had begun on the bankruptcy of idealism, in order to lead a French operation in the African bush. "Africa," he wrote, "is one of the last places where our finest sentiments can still be affirmed, where the last robust consciences have hope of finding an outlet for their activity." He adds: "From extreme barbarism we passed into a condition of extreme civilization. . . . But who knows whether, by one of the reversals common in human history, we will not return to the point from which we began? The moment will come when benevolence ceases to be fruitful and becomes enfeebling and cowardly."

For such young men, fired by patriotic faith and the cult of military virtues, only the occasion for heroism is lacking.

DISCUSSION QUESTIONS

1. According to Treitschke, why is war a necessary agent of statecraft and national pride? In what ways do the students in the French poll reflect similar sentiments?
2. Based on these documents, how did imperialism contribute to people's glorification of war?
3. How do these documents cast light on the factors that contributed to the outbreak of World War I?

COMPARATIVE QUESTIONS

1. What might contemporary readers have found unsettling about the idea that women should have the right to vote or that dreams could reveal one's innermost desires? How do both ideas represent a blurring of traditional boundaries between public and private life? How did Galton's idea of eugenics use new scientific ideas to reinforce these traditional boundaries?
2. In the opening paragraphs of his letter, Zola mocks militant nationalism as part of his call for a return to a government based on honesty, tolerance, and the rule of law. Based on the attitudes of the Parisian students surveyed in the 1912 opinion poll, do you think that in the long run the French government heeded his call?
3. How did Treitschke's and Kipling's attitudes toward imperialism overlap? Why did the *San Francisco Call*'s editorial challenge such views? What does this suggest about the perils of imperialism at the end of the nineteenth century?
4. In what ways do the documents in this chapter challenge such liberal political values as equal citizenship, tolerance, and the rule of law?

World War I and Its Aftermath
1914–1929

Contemporaries dubbed World War I the "Great War" with good reason. Over the course of four years, millions died in battle — victims of advanced military technologies, outdated tactics, wretched leadership, and a desire for total victory. Document 1 allows us to see these horrors through two soldiers' eyes. Document 2 reveals that civilians contributed to the staggering death toll, for it was they who manufactured the grenades, rifles, and other weapons used at the front with such devastating effects. Yet the war's legacy did not stop there. Civilian protests against the war unleashed the Russian Revolution, which transformed the world's political landscape. Document 3 illuminates the ideology of the founder of the Soviet state, V. I. Lenin (1870–1924), on the eve of the revolution. To the west, governments faced their own challenges as they struggled under the weight of postwar reconstruction and popular discontent. As documents 4 and 5 attest, among the people who capitalized on these troubled times were Benito Mussolini (1883–1945) and Adolf Hitler (1889–1945), who ushered in a new age of violent dictatorship in Europe.

1. The Horrors of War
Fritz Franke and Siegfried Sassoon,
Two Soldiers' Views (1914–1918)

When war broke out in August 1914, no one foresaw the years of massive destruction and bloodshed that would follow. By late autumn, the two sides were entrenched along a line that extended from France into Belgium, and so the Western Front was born. Here millions of soldiers like Fritz Franke (1892–1915) and Siegfried Sassoon (1886–1967) faced unspeakable horrors. In the following letter written in the war's first months, Franke,

From A. F. Wedd, trans., *German Students' War Letters* (New York: E. P. Dutton, 1929), 123–25; and Siegfried Sassoon, *Collected Poems* (New York: Viking Press, 1949), 68–69.

*a medical student from Berlin, describes trench warfare as a living hell of shells and corpses.
His description also reveals what already had become and would remain the war's defining
feature in the West: immobility and stalemate. Franke paid the ultimate price for both — he
was killed in May 1915. By contrast, Sassoon, a British officer, survived and became famous
for poems like "Counter-Attack," which describes the war's misery and futility.*

Fritz Franke

Louve, November 5th, 1914

Yesterday we didn't feel sure that a single one of us would come through alive. You can't
possibly picture to yourselves what such a battle-field looks like. It is impossible to
describe it, and even now, when it is a day behind us, I myself can hardly believe that
such bestial barbarity and unspeakable suffering are possible. Every foot of ground con-
tested; every hundred yards another trench; and everywhere bodies — rows of them! All
the trees shot to pieces; the whole ground churned up a yard deep by the heaviest shells;
dead animals; houses and churches so utterly destroyed by shell-fire that they can never
be of the least use again. And every troop that advances in support must pass through a
mile of this chaos, through this gigantic burial-ground and the reek of corpses.

In this way we advanced on Tuesday, marching for three hours, a silent column, in
the moonlight, towards the Front and into a trench as Reserve, two to three hundred
yards from the English, close behind our own infantry.

There we lay the whole day, a yard and a half to two yards below the level of the
ground, crouching in the narrow trench on a thin layer of straw, in an overpowering din
which never ceased all day or the greater part of the night — the whole ground trembling
and shaking! There is every variety of sound — whistling, whining, ringing, crashing,
rolling . . . the beastly things pitch right above one and burst and the fragments buzz in
all directions, and the only question one asks is: "Why doesn't one get me?" Often the
things land within a hand's breadth and one just looks on. One gets so hardened to it that
at the most one ducks one's head a little if a great, big naval-gun shell comes a bit too near
and its grey-green stink is a bit too thick. Otherwise one soon just lies there and thinks
of other things. And then one pulls out the Field Regulations or an old letter from home,
and all at once one has fallen asleep in spite of the row.

Then suddenly comes the order: "Back to the horses. You are relieved!" And one
runs for a mile or so, mounts, and is a gay trooper once more; hola, away, through night
and mist, in gallop and in trot!

One just lives from one hour to the next. For instance, if one starts to prepare some
food, one never knows if one mayn't have to leave it behind within an hour. If you lie
down to sleep, you must always be "in Alarm Order." On the road, you have just to ride
behind the man in front of you without knowing where you are going, or at the most only
the direction for half a day.

All the same, there is a lot that is pleasant in it all. We often go careering through lovely
country in beautiful weather. And above all one acquires a knowledge of human nature! We
all live so naturally and unconventionally here, every one according to his own instincts.
That brings much that is good and much that is ugly to the surface, but in every one there
is a large amount of truth, and above all strength — strength developed almost to a mania!

Siegfried Sassoon

Counter-Attack

We'd gained our first objective hours before
While dawn broke like a face with blinking eyes,
Pallid, unshaved and thirsty, blind with smoke.
Things seemed all right at first. We held their line,
With bombers posted, Lewis guns well placed,
And clink of shovels deepening the shallow trench.
    The place was rotten with dead; green clumsy legs
    High-booted, sprawled and grovelled along the saps
    And trunks, face downward, in the sucking mud,
    Wallowed like trodden sand-bags loosely filled;
    And naked sodden buttocks, mats of hair,
    Bulged, clotted heads slept in the plastering slime.
    And then the rain began — the jolly old rain!

A yawning soldier knelt against the bank,
Staring across the morning blear with fog;
He wondered when the Allemands would get busy;
And then, of course, they started with five-nines
Traversing, sure as fate, and never a dud.
Mute in the clamor of shells he watched them burst
Spouting dark earth and wire with gusts from hell,
While posturing giants dissolved in drifts of smoke.
He crouched and flinched, dizzy with galloping fear,
Sick for escape — loathing the strangled horror
And butchered, frantic gestures of the dead.

An officer came blundering down the trench:
"Stand-to and man the fire-step!" On he went . . .
Gasping and bawling, "Fire-step . . . counter-attack!"
    Then the haze lifted. Bombing on the right
    Down the old sap: machine-guns on the left;
    And stumbling figures looming out in front.
    "O Christ, they're coming at us!" Bullets spat,
And he remembered his rifle . . . rapid fire . . .
And started blazing wildly . . . then a bang
Crumpled and spun him sideways, knocked him out
To grunt and wriggle: none heeded him; he choked
And fought the flapping veils of smothering gloom,
Lost in a blurred confusion of yells and groans . . .
Down, and down, and down, he sank and drowned,
Bleeding to death. The counter-attack had failed.

DISCUSSION QUESTIONS

1. Although they fought on opposite sides, what attributes did Franke and Sassoon share?

2. Based on Franke's and Sassoon's descriptions of the battlefront, what physical and psychological effects did trench warfare have on soldiers?

3. How does Franke's letter challenge the Allies' propaganda in which German soldiers were depicted as being devoid of humanity?

2. Mobilizing for Total War

L. Doriat, *Women on the Home Front* (1917)

The massive mobilization of the home front made World War I like no other war fought before. Across Europe, thousands of civilians poured into factories to manufacture supplies for the troops. With casualties mounting and more and more men leaving to replenish the armed forces, women became particularly vital to sustaining the wartime labor force. Consequently, new employment opportunities arose for them, especially in traditionally masculine domains such as munitions. The following interview of a French factory worker in the city of Saint-Nazaire in Brittany by journalist L. Doriat puts a human face on this aspect of the war's impact beyond the battlefield. In it, the worker, whom Doriat never identifies, reveals her sense of patriotic duty mingled with her determination not to lose her femininity amid the din and dirt of her job.

The dwelling I enter is tidy, sun lights up the main room and makes the household objects shine; everything speaks of an orderly woman who likes her home. A few flowers in a vase on the table near which she is working prove to me that I was right about the woman I've come to see. The factory has not destroyed her feminine sense of delicacy. Without a hat she seems to me younger; she is surprised to see me, she confesses, because she doubted I would come. Convalescent, she hasn't worked for a whole month, which is why I am lucky enough to find her.

"The very day after my arrival, I found work, thanks to the foreman of a factory of shells who knew my husband," she hastens to tell me. "There is no comparison between this extremely hard and much more precise work and the little toy-like petards that I was making. Here it's not sheets of white metal but big 120 shells. You must also pay much more attention, a defect is serious. The factory never stops, day and night shifts of eight alternate. It's intensive production; no mawkishness here, we are not women by the arms of the machine. Scarcely any apprenticeship, one or two days and you're set.

"I am in a workshop for tempering the steel, or rather I was — will they give me back my place and my machine when I return to the workshop? At the moment of my accident, which I'll tell you about, I was doing the shop-trial of the steel for the shell, testing

From Margaret R. Higonnet, ed., *Lines of Fire: Women Writers of World War I* (New York: Plume, 1999), 129–31.

or inspecting the casing, of course. Right after the tempering bath, when the steel is still hot and black, the other workers and I had to tap it with a buffing wheel in order to polish the steel on a small surface of the bottom and the ogive of the shell. Doing this we handle at least a thousand shells a day, and as I told you, they are big, very heavy to manipulate. Other workers take these same pieces and make a light mark on the polished area, which must not etch the steel further than a certain depth, in a kind of test; they are equipped with a graduated sheet of metal that lets them evaluate the etched lines. If the mark is too deep, the steel is too soft; if it's too shallow, it is too hard; in either case it can't be used and goes back to be recast. The inspection requires great attentiveness. A final verification is made by a controller and as we are always required to put our number on the pieces that pass through our hands, the imperfections, the errors can be traced to their authors.

"There too you don't talk, you don't even think of it. The deafening noise of the machines, the enormous heat of the ovens near which you work, the swiftness of the movements make this precision work into painful labor. When we do it at night, the glare together with the temperature of the furnace exhausts your strength and burns your eyes. In the morning when you get home, you throw yourself on your bed without even the strength to eat a bite. There are also the lathe workshops, I've never been there; many workers learn quickly to turn a shell without needing to calibrate it; some turners do piece work; they are always the ones who hurt themselves. At the job you become very imprudent, as I told you.

"However, you see, I hurt myself too. Forgetting that my buffing machine does an incalculable number of turns a second, I brushed against it with my arm. Clothing and flesh were all taken off before I even noticed. They had to scrape the bone, bandage me every day, I was afraid of an amputation, which luckily was avoided. Only in the last few days have I been able to go without a sling and use my arm; next week I go back to the workshop. I don't want them to change my job, I'm used to my machine and a fresh apprenticeship would not please me at all. I assure you, the first day I was in this noise, near these enormous blast furnaces, opposite the huge machine at which I had to work for hours, I was afraid. We are all like that, all the more so that we are not given time to reflect. You have to understand and act quickly. Those who lose their heads don't accomplish anything, but they are rare. In general, one week suffices to turn a novice into a skilled worker.

"The foremen scold now and then, but they mustn't count it against us; doesn't everyone know that a man is an apprentice before he becomes a mechanic? But at present, however simplified, however divided up the tasks may be, you become a qualified mechanic right away.

"Yet among us there are women like myself who had never done anything; others who did not know how to sew or embroider; nothing discouraged us. As for me I don't complain, this strained activity pleases me. I can thus forget my loneliness — and not having any children, what else should I do with all my time?

"When the war is over, I will look for a job that corresponds better to my taste. I have enough education to become a cashier in a store. I will then be able to be neater than now, for you can't imagine what care it takes to stay more or less clean if you work in a metallurgy.

"A woman is always a woman; I suffered a lot from remaining for hours with my hands and face dirty with dust and smoke. Everything is a matter of habit; among us there are women who seem fragile and delicate — well! if you saw them at work, you would be stunned: it's a total transformation. As for me, I would never have thought I had so much stamina; when I remember that the least little errand wore me out before, I don't recognize myself. Certainly when the day or the night is over, you go home, the fatigue is great, but we are not more tired than the men are. True, we are more sober because we maintain better hygiene and as a result, our sources of energy are more rational and regular, we don't turn to alcohol for strength.

"Our sense of the present need, of the national peril, of hatred for the enemy, of the courage of our husbands and sons — all this pricks us on, we work with all our heart, with all our strength, with all our soul. It is not necessary to stimulate us, each one is conscious of the task assigned to her and in all simplicity she does it, convinced that she defends her country by forging the arms that will free it. We are very proud of being workers for the national defense."

On that proud phrase, I left this valiant woman, with a warm handshake to thank her and to express my admiration.

DISCUSSION QUESTIONS

1. What does this account suggest about women's role in the war effort?

2. How do both the interviewer and the interviewee cast light on people's fears about the war's effects on traditional gender roles?

3. In what ways does this interview reflect the national consensus supporting the war, as fostered by government-directed propaganda campaigns?

3. Revolutionary Marxism Defended

SOURCES IN CONVERSATION | Vladimir Ilyich Lenin, *The State and Revolution* (1917) and *"He Who Does Not Work Does Not Eat" Plate* (1921)

As World War I dragged on, European governments faced a new foe in civilian protests. The Russian tsar was ill equipped for this challenge, opening the door to revolution. By the fall of 1917, Vladimir Ilyich Lenin (1870–1924) had emerged as the leading voice of Russian revolutionaries. Having spent nearly a decade abroad in exile, he returned to Russia in April 1917 and immediately set to work laying out the blueprint for a one-party proletarian state. As part of this effort, he wrote The State and Revolution, *excerpted below. When Lenin and his Bolshevik party seized complete control of the government in October 1917, they set to work to realize their vision for social transformation. They abolished private property and nationalized factories, including the Imperial Porcelain Factory located on the outskirts of*

From Stepan Apresyan and Jim Riordan, trans. and eds., *V. I. Lenin: Collected Works*, vol. 25, June–September 1917 (London: Lawrence and Wishart, 1970), 13, 386–87, 396–97, 404, 413, 425–26, 455–56.

modern-day Saint Petersburg. When the Bolsheviks took over, they found a large supply of unpainted white porcelain platters, plates, cups, and saucers and soon realized their propaganda potential both at home and abroad. For the next decade, all of the porcelain decorated at the factory was used to promote revolutionary ideals, often borrowing from images and slogans found in newspapers and posters. The plate reproduced here is no exception. Its main message is conveyed in the words around the border, "He who does not work does not eat," an adaptation of a biblical verse that was incorporated into the Soviet constitution of 1918. A depiction of Lenin based on a famous sketch drawn from life by Nathan Altman (1889–1970) appears in the center. Ration cards frame Lenin on one side, and on the other side, the red star of the revolution crushes a partial image of an imperial eagle; below is inscribed the monogram for the Russian Soviet Federative Social Republic (RSFSR).

What is now happening to Marx's theory has, in the course of history, happened repeatedly to the theories of revolutionary thinkers and leaders of oppressed classes fighting for emancipation. During the lifetime of great revolutionaries, the oppressing classes constantly hounded them, received their theories with the most savage malice, the most furious hatred, and the most unscrupulous campaigns of lies and slander. After their death, attempts are made to convert them into harmless icons, to canonise them, so to say, and to hallow their *names* to a certain extent for the "consolation" of the oppressed classes and with the object of duping the latter, while at the same time robbing the revolutionary theory of its *substance*, blunting its revolutionary edge and vulgarising it. Today, the bourgeoisie and the opportunists within the labour movement concur in this doctoring of Marxism. They omit, obscure, or distort the revolutionary side of this theory, its revolutionary soul. . . .

In these circumstances, in view of the unprecedentedly widespread distortion of Marxism, our prime task is to *re-establish* what Marx really taught on the subject of the state. . . .

Let us begin with the most popular of Engels's works, *The Origin of the Family, Private Property, and the State.* . . .

Summing up his historical analysis, Engels says:

The state is, therefore, by no means a power forced on society from without. . . . Rather, it is a product of society at a certain stage of development; it is the admission that this society has become entangled in an insoluble contradiction with itself, that it has split into irreconcilable antagonisms which it is powerless to dispel. . . .

This expresses with perfect clarity the basic idea of Marxism with regard to the historical role and the meaning of the state. The state is a product and a manifestation of the irreconcilability of class antagonisms. The state arises where, when and insofar as class antagonisms objectively *cannot* be reconciled. And, conversely, the existence of the state proves that the class antagonisms are irreconcilable. . . .

It is safe to say that of this argument of Engels's, which is so remarkably rich in ideas, only one point has become an integral part of socialist thought among modern socialist parties, namely, that according to Marx the state "withers away" — as distinct from the anarchist doctrine of the "abolition" of the state. To prune Marxism to such an extent means reducing it to opportunism, for this "interpretation" only leaves a vague notion of a slow, even, gradual change, of absence of leaps and storms, of absence of revolution. The current, widespread, popular, if one may say so, conception of the "withering away" of the state undoubtedly means obscuring, if not repudiating, revolution.

Such an "interpretation," however, is the crudest distortion of Marxism, advantageous only to the bourgeoisie. . . .

In the first place, at the very outset of his argument, Engels says that, in seizing state power, the proletariat thereby "abolishes the state as state." . . . As a matter of fact, Engels speaks here of the proletarian revolution "abolishing" the *bourgeois* state, while the words about the state withering away refer to the remnants of the *proletarian* state *after* the socialist revolution. According to Engels, the bourgeois state does not "wither away," but is *"abolished"* by the proletariat in the course of the revolution. What withers away after this revolution is the proletarian state or semi-state. . . .

The proletariat needs state power, a centralised organisation of force, an organisation of violence, both to crush the resistance of the exploiters and to *lead* the enormous mass of the population — the peasants, the petty bourgeoisie, and semi-proletarians — in the work of organising a socialist economy.

By educating the workers' party, Marxism educates the vanguard of the proletariat, capable of assuming power and *leading the whole people* to socialism, of directing and organising the new system, of being the teacher, the guide, the leader of all the working and exploited people in organising their social life without the bourgeoisie and against the bourgeoisie. By contrast, the opportunism now prevailing trains the members of the workers' party to be the representatives of the better-paid workers, who lose touch with the masses, "get along" fairly well under capitalism, and sell their birthright for a mess of pottage, i.e., renounce their role as revolutionary leaders of the people against the bourgeoisie.

Marx's theory of "the state, i.e., the proletariat organised as the ruling class," is inseparably bound up with the whole of his doctrine of the revolutionary role of the proletariat in history. The culmination of this role is the proletarian dictatorship, the political rule of the proletariat. . . .

The essence of Marx's theory of the state has been mastered only by those who realise that the dictatorship of a *single* class is necessary not only for every class society in general, not only for the *proletariat* which has overthrown the bourgeoisie, but also for the entire *historical period* which separates capitalism from "classless society," from communism. Bourgeois states are most varied in form, but their essence is the same: all these states, whatever their form, in the final analysis are inevitably the *dictatorship of the bourgeoisie.* The transition from capitalism to communism is certainly bound to yield a tremendous abundance and variety of political forms, but the essence will inevitably be the same: *the dictatorship of the proletariat.* . . .

We are not utopians, we do not "dream" of dispensing *at once* with all administration, with all subordination. These anarchist dreams, based upon incomprehension of the tasks of the proletarian dictatorship, are totally alien to Marxism, and, as a matter of fact, serve only to postpone the socialist revolution until people are different. No, we want the socialist revolution with people as they are now, with people who cannot dispense with subordination, control, and "foremen and accountants."

The subordination, however, must be to the armed vanguard of all the exploited and working people, i.e., to the proletariat. A beginning can and must be made at once, overnight, to replace the specific "bossing" of state officials by the simple functions of "foremen and accountants," functions which are already fully within the ability of the average town dweller and can well be performed for "workmen's wages."

We, the workers, shall organise large-scale production on the basis of what capitalism has already created, relying on our own experience as workers, establishing strict, iron discipline backed up by the state power of the armed workers. We shall reduce the role of state officials to that of simply carrying out our instructions as responsible, revocable, modestly paid "foremen and accountants" (of course, with the aid of technicians of all sorts, types and degrees). This is *our* proletarian task, this is what we can and must *start* with in accomplishing the proletarian revolution. Such a beginning, on the basis of large-scale production, will of itself lead to the gradual "withering away" of all bureaucracy, to the gradual creation of an order — an order without inverted commas, an order bearing no similarity to wage slavery — an order under which the functions of control and accounting, becoming more and more simple, will be performed by each in turn, will then become a habit and will finally die out as the *special* functions of a special section of the population. . . .

In the usual arguments about the state, the mistake is constantly made against which Engels warned and which we have in passing indicated above, namely, it is constantly forgotten that the abolition of the state means also the abolition of democracy: that the withering away of the state means the withering away of democracy.

At first sight this assertion seems exceedingly strange and incomprehensible; indeed, someone may even suspect us of expecting the advent of a system of society in which the principle of subordination of the minority to the majority will not be observed — for democracy means the recognition of this very principle.

No, democracy is *not* identical with the subordination of the minority to the majority. Democracy is a *state* which recognises the subordination of the minority to the majority, i.e., an organisation for the systematic use of *force* by one class against another, by one section of the population against another.

We set ourselves the ultimate aim of abolishing the state, i.e., all organised and systematic violence, all use of violence against people in general. We do not expect the advent of a system of society in which the principle of subordination of the minority to the majority will not be observed. In striving for socialism, however, we are convinced that it will develop into communism and, therefore, that the need for violence against people in general, for the *subordination* of one man to another, and of one section of the population to another, will vanish altogether since people will *become accustomed* to observing the elementary conditions of social life *without violence* and *without subordination*.

"He Who Does Not Work Does Not Eat" Plate

© Sotheby's / akg-images / Newscom

DISCUSSION QUESTIONS

1. What are Lenin's attitudes toward different classes and social groups? Why are these attitudes important to understanding his vision of the state both before and after the proletarian revolution?

2. Why does the proletariat need state power according to Lenin? Why does he describe this power as a "dictatorship"?

3. What role did workers and their labor play in Lenin's vision for the Soviet state? What links can you make between his vision and the decoration of the 1921 propaganda plate?

4. At the time this plate was created, Russia was engulfed by civil war as pro- and anti-Bolshevik forces battled for control. How might this context be important to understanding the plate's design and intended message?

4. Establishing Fascism in Italy

Benito Mussolini, *The Doctrine of Fascism* (1932)

Like millions of his fellow Italians, Benito Mussolini (1883–1945) bitterly resented the outcome of World War I. The Allies had reneged on many of their territorial promises, and Italy's economy was in shambles. Mussolini tapped into these waves of discontent when, in 1919, he founded the Fascist movement, comprising former socialists, war veterans, and others who embraced the radical right as a new symbol of authority and strength. Blaming the parliamentary government for the country's ills, the Fascists marched on Rome in 1922 to take matters into their own hands. Upon the king's request, Mussolini became prime minister. This marked the beginning of Mussolini's rise to political power. The following excerpt from an article by Mussolini, first published in the Enciclopedia Italiana *in 1932, illuminates the basic ideological contours of fascism as they had developed during the first decade of his authoritarian rule.*

Fundamental Ideas

7. Against individualism, the Fascist conception is for the State; and it is for the individual in so far as he coincides with the State, which is the conscience and universal will of man in his historical existence. It is opposed to classical Liberalism, which arose from the necessity of reacting against absolutism, and which brought its historical purpose to an end when the State was transformed into the conscience and will of the people. Liberalism denied the State in the interests of the particular individual; Fascism reaffirms the State as the true reality of the individual. And if liberty is to be the attribute of the real man, and not of that abstract puppet envisaged by individualistic Liberalism, Fascism is for liberty. And for the only liberty which can be a real thing, the liberty of the State and of the individual within the State. Therefore, for the Fascist, everything is in the State, and nothing human or spiritual exists, much less has value, outside the State. In this sense Fascism is totalitarian, and the Fascist State, the synthesis and unity of all values, interprets, develops, and gives strength to the whole life of the people.

8. Outside the State there can be neither individuals nor groups (political parties, associations, syndicates, classes). Therefore Fascism is opposed to Socialism, which confines the movement of history within the class struggle and ignores the unity of classes established in one economic and moral reality in the State; and analogously it is opposed to class syndicalism. Fascism recognizes the real exigencies for which the socialist and syndicalist movement arose, but while recognizing them wishes to bring them under the control of the State and give them a purpose within the corporative system of interests reconciled within the unity of the State.

9. Individuals form classes according to the similarity of their interests, they form syndicates according to differentiated economic activities within these interests; but they form first, and above all, the State, which is not to be thought of numerically as the sum-total of individuals forming the majority of a nation. And consequently Fascism is opposed to Democracy, which equates the nation to the majority, lowering it to the level of that majority; nevertheless it is the purest form of democracy if the nation is conceived, as it should be, qualitatively and not quantitatively, as the most powerful idea (most powerful because most moral, most coherent, most true) which acts within the nation as the conscience and the will of a few, even of One, which ideal tends to become active within the conscience and the will of all — that is to say, of all those who rightly constitute a

From Michael Oakeshott, ed. and trans., *The Social and Political Doctrines of Contemporary Europe* (Cambridge: Cambridge University Press, 1947), 164–79.

nation by reason of nature, history or race, and have set out upon the same line of development and spiritual formation as one conscience and one sole will. . . .

Political and Social Doctrine

Fascism is today clearly defined not only as a regime but as a doctrine. And I mean by this that Fascism today, self-critical as well as critical of other movements, has an unequivocal point of view of its own, a criterion, and hence an aim, in face of all the material and intellectual problems which oppress the people of the world. . . .

3. Above all, Fascism, in so far as it considers and observes the future and the development of humanity quite apart from the political considerations of the moment, believes neither in the possibility nor in the utility of perpetual peace. It thus repudiates the doctrine of Pacifism — born of a renunciation of the struggle and an act of cowardice in the face of sacrifice. War alone brings up to their highest tension all human energies and puts the stamp of nobility upon the peoples who have the courage to meet it. All other trials are substitutes, which never really put a man in front of himself in the alternative of life and death. A doctrine, therefore, which begins with a prejudice in favor of peace is foreign to Fascism; as are foreign to the spirit of Fascism. . . .

5. Such a conception of life makes Fascism the precise negation of that doctrine which formed the basis of the so-called Scientific or Marxian Socialism: the doctrine of historical Materialism, according to which the history of human civilizations can be explained only as the struggle of interest between the different social groups and as arising out of change in the means and instruments of production. That economic improvements — discoveries of raw materials, new methods of work, scientific inventions — should have an importance of their own, no one denies, but that they should suffice to explain human history to the exclusion of all other factors is absurd: Fascism believes, now and always, in holiness and in heroism, that is in acts in which no economic motive — remote or immediate — plays a part. With this negation of historical materialism, according to which men would be only by-products of history, who appear and disappear on the surface of the waves while in the depths the real directive forces are at work, there is also denied the immutable and irreparable "class struggle" which is the natural product of this economic conception of history, and above all it is denied that the class struggle can be the primary agent of social changes. . . .

6. After Socialism, Fascism attacks the whole complex of democratic ideologies and rejects them both in their theoretical premises and in their applications or practical manifestations. Fascism denies that the majority, through the mere fact of being a majority, can rule human societies; it denies that this majority can govern by means of a periodical consultation; it affirms the irremediable, fruitful and beneficent inequality of men, who cannot be leveled by such a mechanical and extrinsic fact as universal suffrage. By democratic regimes we mean those in which from time to time the people is given the illusion of being sovereign, while true effective sovereignty lies in other, perhaps irresponsible and secret, forces. Democracy is a regime without a king, but with very many kings, perhaps more exclusive, tyrannical and violent than one king even though a tyrant. . . .

8. In face of Liberal doctrines, Fascism takes up an attitude of absolute opposition both in the field of politics and in that of economics. It is not necessary to exaggerate — merely for the purpose of present controversies — the importance of Liberalism in the past century, and to make of that which was one of the numerous doctrines sketched in that century a religion of humanity for all times, present and future. . . . The "Liberal" century, after having accumulated an infinity of Gordian knots, tried to untie them by the hecatomb of the World War. Never before has any religion imposed such a cruel sacrifice. Were the gods of Liberalism thirsty for blood? Now Liberalism is about to close the doors of its deserted temples because the peoples feel that its agnosticism in economics, its indifferentism in politics and in morals, would lead, as they have led, the States to certain ruin. In this way one can understand why all the political experiences of the contemporary world are anti-Liberal, and it is supremely ridiculous to wish on that account to class them outside of history; as if history were a hunting ground reserved to Liberalism and its professors, as if Liberalism were the definitive and no longer surpassable message of civilization. . . .

If it is admitted that the nineteenth century has been the century of Socialism, Liberalism, and Democracy, it does not follow that the twentieth must also be the century of Liberalism, Socialism, and Democracy. Political doctrines pass; peoples remain. It is to be expected that this century may be that of authority, a century of the "Right," a Fascist century. If the nineteenth was the century of the individual (Liberalism means individualism) it may be expected that this one may be the century of "collectivism" and therefore the century of the State. . . .

10. The keystone of Fascist doctrine is the conception of the State, of its essence, of its tasks, of its ends. For Fascism the State is an absolute before which individuals and groups are relative. Individuals and groups are "thinkable" in so far as they are within the State. The Liberal State does not direct the interplay and the material and spiritual development of the groups, but limits itself to registering the results; the Fascist State has a consciousness of its own, a will of its own, on this account it is called an "ethical" State. In 1929, at the first quinquennial assembly of the regime, I said: "For Fascism, the State is not the night-watchman who is concerned only with the personal security of the citizens; nor is it an organization for purely material ends, such as that of guaranteeing a certain degree of prosperity and a relatively peaceful social order, to achieve which a council of administration would be sufficient, nor is it a creation of mere politics with no contact with the material and complex reality of the lives of individuals and the life of peoples. The State, as conceived by Fascism and as it acts, is a spiritual and moral fact because it makes concrete the political, juridical, economic organization of the nation and such an organization is, in its origin and in its development, a manifestation of the spirit. The State is the guarantor of internal and external security, but it is also the guardian and the transmitter of the spirit of the people as it has been elaborated through the centuries in language, custom, faith. The State is not only present, it is also past, and above all future. It is the State which, transcending the brief limit of individual lives, represents the immanent conscience of the nation. The forms in which States express themselves change, but the necessity of the State remains. It is the State which educates citizens for civic virtue, makes them conscious of their mission, calls them to unity; harmonizes their interests in justice; hands on the achievements of thought in the sciences, the arts, in law, in human solidarity; it carries

men from the elementary life of the tribe to the highest human expression of power which is Empire; it entrusts to the ages the names of those who died for its integrity or in obedience to its laws; it puts forward as an example and recommends to the generations that are to come the leaders who increased its territory and the men of genius who gave it glory. When the sense of the State declines and the disintegrating and centrifugal tendencies of individuals and groups prevail, national societies move to their decline."

11. From 1929 up to the present day these doctrinal positions have been strengthened by the whole economico-political evolution of the world. It is the State alone that grows in size, in power. It is the State alone that can solve the dramatic contradictions of capitalism. What is called the crisis cannot be overcome except by the State, within the State. . . . Fascism desires the State to be strong, organic, and at the same time founded on a wide popular basis. The Fascist State has also claimed for itself the field of economics and, through the corporative, social and educational institutions which it has created, the meaning of the State reaches out to and includes the farthest off-shoots; and within the State, framed in their respective organizations, there revolve all the political, economic and spiritual forces of the nation. A State founded on millions of individuals who recognize it, feel it, are ready to serve it, is not the tyrannical State of the medieval lord. It has nothing in common with the absolutist States that existed either before or after 1789. In the Fascist State the individual is not suppressed, but rather multiplied, just as in a regiment a soldier is not weakened but multiplied by the number of his comrades. The Fascist State organizes the nation, but it leaves sufficient scope to individuals; it has limited useless or harmful liberties and has preserved those that are essential. It cannot be the individual who decides in this matter, but only the State. . . .

13. The Fascist State is a will to power and to government. In it the tradition of Rome is an idea that has force. In the doctrine of Fascism Empire is not only a territorial, military or mercantile expression, but spiritual or moral. One can think of an empire, that is to say a nation that directly or indirectly leads other nations, without needing to conquer a single square kilometer of territory. For Fascism the tendency to Empire, that is to say, to the expansion of nations, is a manifestation of vitality; its opposite, staying at home, is a sign of decadence: peoples who rise or re-rise are imperialist, peoples who die are denunciatory. Fascism is the doctrine that is most fitted to represent the aims, the states of mind, of a people, like the Italian people, rising again after many centuries of abandonment or slavery to foreigners. But Empire calls for discipline, coordination of forces, duty, and sacrifice; this explains many aspects of the practical working of the regime and the direction of many of the forces of the State and the necessary severity shown to those who would wish to oppose this spontaneous and destined impulse of the Italy of the twentieth century, to oppose it in the name of the superseded ideologies of the nineteenth, repudiated wherever great experiments of political and social transformation have been courageously attempted: especially where, as now, peoples thirst for authority, for leadership, for order. If every age has its own doctrine, it is apparent from a thousand signs that the doctrine of the present age is Fascism. That it is a doctrine of life is shown by the fact that it has resuscitated a faith. That this faith has conquered minds is proved by the fact that Fascism has had its dead and its martyrs.

Fascism henceforward has in the world the universality of all those doctrines which, by fulfilling themselves, have significance in the history of the human spirit.

DISCUSSION QUESTIONS

1. According to Mussolini, how is Fascism opposed to liberalism, democracy, and socialism? How is this opposition rooted in Mussolini's concept of the individual's role in the Fascist state?

2. What does Mussolini mean when he describes fascism as "totalitarian"?

3. As elaborated here, in what ways were Mussolini's principles rooted in the legacy of World War I?

5. A New Form of Anti-Semitism
Adolf Hitler, *Mein Kampf* (1925)

In 1923, Adolf Hitler (1889–1945) was sentenced to five years in prison at Landsberg Castle for his participation in the Beer Hall Putsch, an attempt by his National Socialist Party to overthrow the German Democratic national government. He was treated well in prison and received many guests as he strolled the castle grounds. When a friend suggested that he write his autobiography to pass the time, Hitler was skeptical; although a gifted orator, he had written very little. After Hitler's fellow inmate, Rudolf Hess (1894–1987), agreed to transcribe it for him, however, Hitler dictated the book. Originally titled Four Years of Struggle Against Lies, Stupidity, and Cowardice, *it was published in 1925 as* My Struggle (Mein Kampf). *In it, Hitler attributed most human achievements to the German race — he called it the "Aryan" race — and argued that it had a duty to dominate the planet. The Jews, conversely, were held responsible for what Hitler viewed as the world's worst problems, including communism, modern art, pornography, prostitution, and Germany's defeat in World War I.*

Nation and Race

It is idle to argue which race or races were the original representative of human culture and hence the real founders of all that we sum up under the word "humanity." It is simpler to raise this question with regard to the present, and here an easy, clear answer results. All the human culture, all the results of art, science, and technology that we see before us today, are almost exclusively the creative product of the Aryan. This very fact admits of the not unfounded inference that he alone was the founder of all higher humanity, therefore representing the prototype of all that we understand by the word "man." He is the Prometheus of mankind from whose bright forehead the divine spark of genius has sprung at all times, forever kindling anew that fire of knowledge which illumined the night of silent mysteries and thus caused man to climb the path of mastery over the other beings of this earth. . . .

The mightiest counterpart to the Aryan is represented by the Jew. . . . Not through him does any progress of mankind occur, but in spite of him. . . .

From Adolf Hitler, *Mein Kampf,* trans. Ralph Manheim (Boston: Houghton Mifflin, 1999), 290, 300, 303, 326, 643, 646, 649, 651–53.

He works systematically for revolutionization in a twofold sense: economic and political.

Around peoples who offer too violent a resistance to attack from within he weaves a net of enemies, thanks to his international influence, incites them to war, and finally, if necessary, plants the flag of revolution on the very battlefields.

In economics he undermines the states until the social enterprises which have become unprofitable are taken from the state and subjected to his financial control.

In the political field he refuses the state the means for its self-preservation, destroys the foundations of all national self-maintenance and defense, destroys faith in the leadership, scoffs at its history and past, and drags everything that is truly great into the gutter.

Culturally he contaminates art, literature, the theater, makes a mockery of natural feeling, overthrows all concepts of beauty and sublimity, of the noble and the good, and instead drags men down into the sphere of his own base nature.

Religion is ridiculed, ethics and morality represented as outmoded, until the last props of a nation in its struggle for existence in this world have fallen. . . .

Eastern Orientation or Eastern Policy

Only an adequately large space on this earth assures a nation of freedom of existence. . . .

The National Socialist movement must strive to eliminate the disproportion between our population and our area — viewing this latter as a source of food as well as a basis for power politics — between our historical past and the hopelessness of our present impotence. And in this it must remain aware that we, as guardians of the highest humanity on this earth, are bound by the highest obligation, and the more it strives to bring the German people to racial awareness so that, in addition to breeding dogs, horses, and cats, they will have mercy on their *own* blood, the more it will be able to meet this obligation.

. . . The demand for restoration of the frontiers of 1914 is a political absurdity of such proportions and consequences as to make it seem a crime. Quite aside from the fact that the Reich's frontiers in 1914 were anything but logical. For in reality they were neither complete in the sense of embracing the people of German nationality, nor sensible with regard to geo-military expediency. They were not the result of a considered political action, but momentary frontiers in a political struggle that was by no means concluded; partly, in fact, they were the results of chance. . . .

. . . Moreover, the times have changed since the Congress of Vienna: Today it is not princes and princes' mistresses who haggle and bargain over state borders; it is the inexorable Jew who struggles for his domination over the nations. No nation can remove this hand from its throat except by the sword. Only the assembled and concentrated might of a national passion rearing up in its strength can defy the international enslavement of peoples. Such a process is and remains a bloody one.

If, however, we harbor the conviction that the German future, regardless what happens, demands the supreme sacrifice, quite aside from all considerations of political expediency as such, we must set up an aim worthy of this sacrifice and fight for it. . . .

And I must sharply attack those folkish pen-pushers who claim to regard such an acquisition of soil as a "breach of sacred human rights" and attack it as such in their scribblings. One never knows who stands behind these fellows. But one thing is certain, that the confusion they can create is desirable and convenient to our national enemies. By such an attitude they help to weaken and destroy from within our people's will for the only correct way of defending their vital needs. For no people on this earth possesses so much as a square yard of territory on the strength of a higher will or superior right. Just as Germany's frontiers are fortuitous frontiers, momentary frontiers in the current political struggle of any period, so are the boundaries of other nations' living space. And just as the shape of our earth's surface can seem immutable as granite only to the thoughtless soft-head, but in reality only represents at each period an apparent pause in a continuous development, created by the mighty forces of Nature in a process of continuous growth, only to be transformed or destroyed tomorrow by greater forces, likewise the boundaries of living spaces in the life of nations.

DISCUSSION QUESTIONS

1. How do the ideas of race and land acquisition intersect in Hitler's strategy for German domination of the world?

2. In this excerpt, how does Hitler both anticipate and respond to criticism of the genocidal action he prescribes?

3. What does Hitler's response to the so-called folkish pen-pushers betray about his attitude toward parliamentary democracy?

COMPARATIVE QUESTIONS

1. In what ways did the communist and fascist ideologies offer radically different solutions to similar problems?

2. What do Franke, Sassoon, and the French factory worker reveal about the role of technology in World War I?

3. What specific facets of liberal ideology did Lenin, Mussolini, and Hitler reject, and why?

4. Compare and contrast Mussolini's conception of "vitality" with Hitler's ideas of "race." What does this suggest about the similarities and differences between German and Italian fascism?

The Great Depression and World War II
1929–1945

T he Great Depression of the 1930s ushered in an age of unprecedented violence and suffering around the globe. Millions were out of work, hungry, and disillusioned. Authoritarian leaders capitalized on the downhearted, gaining widespread support with their promises to revive the economy and to restore national glory. As document 1 shows, Joseph Stalin (1879–1953) relied on such support to transform the USSR into a leading industrial nation, often with violent consequences. The Nazi Party, led by Adolf Hitler (1889–1945), was another new political force on the horizon. Document 2 displays the Nazis' masterful use of propaganda to challenge liberal principles of freedom and natural rights. Ultimately, the combination of ideology and advanced technology that fueled Hitler's ambitions would have devastating repercussions. In 1936, when right-wing rebels staged a coup against the republican government of Spain, Hitler and fascists from elsewhere in Europe came to their aid, eager for the opportunity to test new weapons and military tactics aimed at civilians. Although the human impact of such tactics was dreadful, as document 3 reveals, no one was prepared for the scale of the slaughter that lay ahead. Western democracies responded cautiously to the Nazis, hoping to contain their aggression through a policy of appeasement rather than military might. Document 4 illustrates this policy in action at a critical juncture in Hitler's march toward war. Documents 5 and 6 expose the horrible physical and psychological toll that World War II had on the civilian population, setting a dangerous precedent for the future.

1. Collectivizing Farming

Antonina Solovieva, *Sent by the Komsomol* (1930s)

Against the backdrop of the Great Depression, Soviet leader Joseph Stalin (1879–1953) was determined to transform the USSR from a rural society to an industrial powerhouse. Stalin's authoritarian tactics epitomize the rise of totalitarian regimes in Europe in the 1930s. Under his direction, the government assumed complete control over the economy, working to expand both industrial and agricultural output at a dizzying pace. A major part of Stalin's plan to feed the growing workforce and provide much-needed exports included ending independent farming. With this goal in mind, the Communist Party leveraged support among young Soviets to recruit peasants to join collective farms. Antonina Solovieva was a member of a local branch of the communist youth organization, the Komsomol, who was assigned, with others like her, to promote collectivization in the countryside under the direction of party officials. The result was the destruction of traditional peasant life: private land was seized, and farmers were compelled to farm state property as a group. Three decades later, Solovieva wrote down her recollections as part of a popular trend in the Soviet Union at the time to memorialize the "heroic" deeds of surviving participants who had helped build the Soviet state.

"Comrade Komsomol members, we have assembled you here today because you, along with us Communists, will be going out to the countryside to help the collective farms and village Soviets get ready for the spring sowing season. The situation in the villages is alarming. As you know, the country is counting on kolkhoz grain, while kulak scoundrels are hiding and spoiling the seeds and disorganizing the peasants. Your task is to engage in mass agitational work among the village youth from the unaffiliated middle stratum[1] and to find out where the kulaks are hiding the grain and who is wrecking the agricultural machinery. On top of everything else, owing to the intimidation on the part of the kulaks and their henchmen, many of the poor households have not yet joined the collective farms. This means that you will need to talk to these people and explain party policies and collectivization to them. This is your task."

This was a huge task; were we up to it? . . .

We got to our villages however we could. . . .

There was no time to lose. After presenting their papers at the village soviet, the arriving Komsomol members would be sent to some collective farm or individual household — to the hardest possible spot. The objective was to talk individual peasants into joining the collective farm; to make sure that the collective farm was ready to begin sowing; and, most important, to find out where and by whom state grain was being hidden. Usually, our first task was to organize a group of activists (preferably from among the village youth), gain their trust, and start a frank conversation. We were quite successful, I must say. We would spend long evenings around a small table with a weakly flickering kerosene lamp at some collective farm headquarters or by a burning stove in some poor peasant's hut. Some of us would even join the peasant girls at their evening get-togethers. Usually the boys would come, too, and sing quiet songs. Whenever we found out about such get-togethers, we would show up unannounced.

From Sheila Fitzpatrick and Yuri Slezkine, eds., *In the Shadow of Revolution: Life Stories of Russian Women, from 1917 to the Second World War* (Princeton, NJ: Princeton University Press, 2000), 236–39.

[1]Peasants were officially divided into three groups based, in theory, on their wealth: the rich peasants, or "kulaks," who were considered implacably hostile to the regime; the middle peasants, who wavered between a pro- and antiregime position; and the poor peasants, who were considered to be the basis for regime support in the village.

One of our Komsomol activists, Kostia Lutkov, was particularly good at this. He acted completely natural, joking around, laughing a lot, and improvising funny rhymes. The men respected him, and the girls admired him. Sooner or later the subject of the kolkhoz would come up. Some of those who came to the get-togethers were under the kulaks' influence, but Kostia would listen patiently until everyone had spoken and then join the conversation as if he were one of them. Once a local field hand, Mitia Varlamov, asked Kostia for some tobacco. Kostia offered him some and said; "Just look at yourself, kid: your coat is all torn; you're wearing bast shoes; and your pants are made of sackcloth. Now, in the collective farm you could make some money, receive your grain ration, and even buy cologne for your evening get-togethers."

Mitia Varlamov, who was eighteen years old, looked at Kostia and asked shyly: "I can't really make that much in the kolkhoz, can I?"

"Just think about it," said Kostia. "All the land will be collectivized, so the kolkhoz will have plenty of it; all the horses will be in the same stable in the large collective farm yard; and all the machines — harvesting, sowing, and threshing — will stand next to each other in the same collective farm yard. With all that land and all those horses and machines — if you just work hard, you will be well-fed and well-dressed."

Mitia still did not get it. "But if you take all the machines away from the rich people, what are the field hands going to work on?" he asked.

"They aren't going to work for the rich people anymore," said Kostia. "In any case, most of them are already in the collective farm. The point is for you to work for yourself, not for the rich."

"And not just any old way, but on a machine," dark-eyed Nastia joined in. "Have you seen the red threshing machine they took away from Stepan last week?"

"I sure have," Mitia drawled. "Two years ago I spent the better part of the fall season threshing on that machine. Got paid peanuts for it, too." The kid looked hurt and turned away.

"That's what we're talking about," said Nastia, with a sly glance in Kostia's direction. "Just sign up, and nobody will cheat you anymore. You'll get what you earn."

The young people would leave the get-together feeling transformed, and Kostia would add new names to his list of youngsters who wished to build a new collective farm future.

It was through these young collective farm members that we were able to find out who was hiding grain and wrecking collective farm property. This information would be transmitted secretly, "through the grapevine." We would not know where the information had originated but would always check it out and, sure enough, often it would turn out to be correct. . . .

But things did not always go so smoothly. The enemy tried to retaliate whenever opportunity afforded.

Once we were taking inventory of the confiscated property of a kulak. There were four of us: Liza Korobeinikova, a former field hand and Kelchino's first Komsomol member; Sasha Kosachev, the head of the reading hut; Cherepanov, a party member and the representative of the district executive committee; and I. We were sitting at a table drawing up lists of confiscated property items. A kerosene lamp with a metal shade hung over the table.

Suddenly we heard the sound of the window breaking, and then the lamp burst into little pieces and went out. A heavy object fell onto the table. Cherepanov ordered us to sit on the floor between the windows, and then he lit a match. On the table lay a half-pint bottle filled with river sand — another kulak weapon used not infrequently to kill people.

Two days later I learned from Liza who had thrown the bottle and who the intended victim had been. It turned out that the Kosachevo kulaks were out to get Sasha. I decided to go to Kosachevo immediately — to conduct an on-the-spot investigation and to inform the appropriate authorities of the attack. Unfortunately, the chairman of the village soviet would not let me go. Then later, in 1932, I discovered that the Kosachevo kulaks had been planning to drown me in the Kama River.

DISCUSSION QUESTIONS

1. According to Solovieva, what role were she and other Komsomol members expected to play once they arrived in the villages?

2. How does Solovieva describe the *kulaks* and their influence on the local population? Why is this important to understanding the process of collectivization as a whole?

3. What strategies did Solovieva's colleague Kostia Lutkov use to convince local residents to join collective farms? What does his approach suggest about how the communist regime mobilized popular support for its policies?

2. Socialist Nationalism

Joseph Goebbels, *Nazi Propaganda Pamphlet* (1930)

Perhaps no one better personifies the power of authoritarian rulers to manipulate the minds of millions in the 1930s than Adolf Hitler (1889–1945). Key to Hitler's success was his propaganda chief, Joseph Goebbels (1895–1945). A member of the National Socialist Party since 1922, Goebbels shared Hitler's belief that the masses were easily managed if the message directed to them was simple and repetitive. To this end, Goebbels wrote pamphlets, such as the one that follows, in support of the Nazi cause. In it, he reveals the virulent anti-Semitism that shaped the Nazis' political program and set them apart from other totalitarian regimes. Goebbels's tactics helped propel Hitler to national leadership in 1933.

Why Are We Nationalists?

We are NATIONALISTS because we see in the NATION the only possibility for the protection and the furtherance of our existence.

The NATION is the organic bond of a people for the protection and defense of their lives. He is nationally minded who understands this IN WORD AND IN DEED.

Today, in GERMANY, NATIONALISM has degenerated into BOURGEOIS PATRI-OTISM, and its power exhausts itself in tilting at windmills. It says GERMANY and means MONARCHY. It proclaims FREEDOM and means BLACK-WHITE-RED.

From Louis L. Snyder, ed., *Documents of German History* (New Brunswick, NJ: Rutgers University Press, 1958), 414–16.

Young nationalism has its unconditional demands. BELIEF IN THE NATION is a matter of all the people, not for individuals of rank, a class, or an industrial clique. The eternal must be separated from the contemporary. The maintenance of a rotten industrial system has nothing to do with nationalism. I can love Germany and hate capitalism; not only CAN I do it, I also MUST do it. The germ of the rebirth of our people LIES ONLY IN THE DESTRUCTION OF THE SYSTEM OF PLUNDERING THE HEALTHY POWER OF THE PEOPLE.

WE ARE NATIONALISTS BECAUSE WE, AS GERMANS, LOVE GERMANY. And because we love Germany, we demand the protection of its national spirit and we battle against its destroyers.

Why Are We Socialists?

We are SOCIALISTS because we see in SOCIALISM the only possibility for maintaining our racial existence and through it the reconquest of our political freedom and the rebirth of the German state. SOCIALISM has its peculiar form first of all through its comradeship in arms with the forward-driving energy of a newly awakened nationalism. Without nationalism it is nothing, a phantom, a theory, a vision of air, a book. With it, it is everything, THE FUTURE, FREEDOM, FATHERLAND!

It was a sin of the liberal bourgeoisie to overlook THE STATE-BUILDING POWER OF SOCIALISM. It was the sin of MARXISM to degrade SOCIALISM to a system of MONEY AND STOMACH.

We are SOCIALISTS because for us THE SOCIAL QUESTION IS A MATTER OF NECESSITY AND JUSTICE, and even beyond that A MATTER FOR THE VERY EXISTENCE OF OUR PEOPLE.

SOCIALISM IS POSSIBLE ONLY IN A STATE WHICH IS FREE INSIDE AND OUTSIDE.

DOWN WITH POLITICAL BOURGEOIS SENTIMENT: FOR REAL NATIONALISM!

DOWN WITH MARXISM: FOR TRUE SOCIALISM!

UP WITH THE STAMP OF THE FIRST GERMAN NATIONAL SOCIALIST STATE!

AT THE FRONT THE NATIONAL SOCIALIST GERMAN WORKERS PARTY! . . .

WHY DO WE OPPOSE THE JEWS?

We are ENEMIES OF THE JEWS, because we are fighters for the freedom of the German people. THE JEW IS THE CAUSE AND THE BENEFICIARY OF OUR MISERY. He has used the social difficulties of the broad masses of our people to deepen the unholy split between Right and Left among our people. He has made two halves of Germany. He is the real cause for our loss of the Great War.

The Jew has no interest in the solution of Germany's fateful problems. He CANNOT have any. FOR HE LIVES ON THE FACT THAT THERE HAS BEEN NO SOLUTION. If we would make the German people a unified community and give them freedom before the world, then the Jew can have no place among us. He has the best trumps in his hands when a people lives in inner and outer slavery. THE JEW IS RESPONSIBLE FOR OUR MISERY AND HE LIVES ON IT.

That is the reason why we, AS NATIONALISTS and AS SOCIALISTS, oppose the Jew. HE HAS CORRUPTED OUR RACE, FOULED OUR MORALS, UNDERMINED OUR CUSTOMS, AND BROKEN OUR POWER.

THE JEW IS THE PLASTIC DEMON OF THE DECLINE OF MANKIND.

THE JEW IS UNCREATIVE. He produces nothing. HE ONLY HANDLES PRODUCTS. As long as he struggles against the state, HE IS A REVOLUTIONARY; as soon as he has power, he preaches QUIET AND ORDER, so that he can consume his plunder at his convenience.

ANTI-SEMITISM IS UN-CHRISTIAN. That means, then, that he is a Christian who looks on while the Jew sews straps around our necks. TO BE A CHRISTIAN MEANS: LOVE THY NEIGHBOR AS THYSELF! MY NEIGHBOR IS ONE WHO IS TIED TO ME BY HIS BLOOD. IF I LOVE HIM, THEN I MUST HATE HIS ENEMIES. HE WHO THINKS GERMAN MUST DESPISE THE JEWS. The one thing makes the other necessary.

WE ARE ENEMIES OF THE JEWS BECAUSE WE BELONG TO THE GERMAN PEOPLE. THE JEW IS OUR GREATEST MISFORTUNE.

It is not true that we eat a Jew every morning at breakfast.

It is true, however, that he SLOWLY BUT SURELY ROBS US OF EVERYTHING WE OWN.

THAT WILL STOP, AS SURELY AS WE ARE GERMANS.

DISCUSSION QUESTIONS

1. According to this pamphlet, what do the terms *nationalist* and *socialist* mean within the context of the Nazi Party?

2. Why do you think the pamphlet targets Jews as enemies of the German people?

3. What does the pamphlet suggest about the link between the Nazis' racial views and their goals for Germany's future?

3. The Spanish Civil War

SOURCES IN CONVERSATION | *Eyewitness Accounts of the Bombing of Guernica and Pablo Picasso, Guernica* (1937)

While the Nazis and Stalinists solidified their power, Spain was at a political crossroads. Spanish republicans had succeeded in overthrowing the monarchy in 1931 but proved ineffectual as a governing body. Right-wing forces led by Francisco Franco (1892–1975) took advantage of republicans' struggle to maintain popular support by launching an uprising of their own. Four years of civil war ensued as Spain teetered between two antithetical visions for its future, authoritarian and democratic. Fascists from other regions of Europe flocked to Franco's aid, including military personnel sent by Hitler and Mussolini. Both fascist leaders saw the civil war as a prime opportunity to test new weapons and strategies on civilian targets.

From Ronald Fraser, *Blood of Spain: An Oral History of the Spanish Civil War* (New York: Pantheon Books, 1986), 398–401.

Their involvement had devastating consequences in Guernica, a small market town in the Basque region of Spain. On April 26, 1937, several squadrons of German and Italian aircraft swooped down over the town, dropping high-explosive and incendiary bombs. The eyewitness accounts that follow vividly describe an attack that lasted for hours; by the end, the town lay in ruins, and hundreds of men, women, and children were dead. The story of Guernica made international headlines; it also served as artistic inspiration for Pablo Picasso (1881–1973), whom the Spanish republican government had commissioned four months earlier to paint a mural-size picture for display at the 1937 Paris World's Fair. The result was the modernist masterpiece Guernica, *which Picasso openly described as a work of antifascist propaganda. Beyond that, however, he never stated explicitly what his picture meant. Critical consensus holds that the bull represents Franco and the horse the Republic or "the people." Using abstract, fragmented, and overlapping geometric shapes typical of the Cubist style, Picasso surrounds the animals with images of the chaos and suffering of war — a mother clutching her limp child, a dead soldier lying on the ground, a survivor wailing in agony.*

"*Amatxu*, the church bells are ringing," Ignacia OZAMIZ's three-year-old son kept saying as, from early morning, the bells tolled out warnings of enemy planes in the vicinity. The front was barely 20 km to the east at Marquina as the crow flies. Four months pregnant, she had put her child — the youngest of four — to bed after lunch when her husband, a local blacksmith, sent her a message to go down to the shelter. People had seen a big plane — the *abuelo* — over the mountains. . . .

Monday, 26 April was market day. The livestock market had been suspended for the duration of the war, but the ordinary market, Ignacia OZAMIZ recalled, continued as usual. Father Dionisio AJANGUIZ was on his way to his home town from his parish of Aulestia, halfway to Marquina, to spend the afternoon chatting and playing cards with fellow priests. One of them, whose mother that very morning had offered them a glass of cognac each not to go to Guernica, was accompanying him. They had drunk the cognac and set out. He had taken no heed even of his own brother's admonitions; Father José AXUNGUIZ had been warning his parishioners at Marquina not to continue the traditional practice of going to Guernica on market day.

— It was an outing for the youth; buses brought people from as far away as Lequei-tio on the coast. The people lacked war training. I blame the Basque authorities. They shouldn't have allowed the practice to continue, they were responsible for a great number of deaths. Those of us who lived virtually on the front, as in Marquina, had learnt the importance of building good shelters. But in Guernica they hadn't taken adequate precautions; the shelters were rudimentary. I kept telling my mother: "Build a good one." "Poor child, poor child," was all she could say. . . .

As Father Dionisio AJANGUIZ walked into Guernica, a solitary Heinkel III flew over and dropped half a dozen bombs. "It was the people's salvation; they ran from their houses to the shelters." He was still half a kilometre from the centre when he saw nine planes appear, flying low, from the direction of the sea. He threw himself on the ground as the first bombs fell.

Hearing the explosions, Ignacia OZAMIZ, who had taken her husband's advice and gone to the shelter next to her house, thought the end had come. So did others.

— "Ignacia, where have we come to die?" the church organist from my home village said. "Here—" I replied. The shelter was packed: 150 people at least between neighbours and people who had come for the market. The bombs crashed on the near-by hospital, killing twenty-five children and two nuns. Debris fell on the shelter, and we thought it had been hit. It was little more than a roof of sandbags, narrow and short, in the patio next to our house. Soon it filled with smoke and dust. "*Amatxu*, take me out," my son began to cry in Basque. "I can't breathe. . . ."

Her eldest daughter, Manolita AGUIRRE, had gone with girlfriends to the plain that began at the edge of the town. There had been no school that day. As they were playing, they saw the planes coming. Workers shouted at them to get into the shelter close by the small-arms factory. As they ran in they heard the *tat-tat-tat* of the fighters' machine-guns. An old man pulled out a religious medallion and gave it to her to kiss. "Pray, child, pray, the planes are bombing us—"

— The fighters dived down and machine-gunned people trying to flee across the plain. The bombers were flying so low you could see the crewmen, recalled Father Dionisio AJANGUIZ. It was a magnificent clear April evening after a showery morning. . . .

The house on one side of the shelter, and then Ignacia OZAMIZ's house on the other, began to burn. The smoke poured into the shelter. Someone drove a cow in. It started to shriek.

— All the smoke came in with it. We had to keep our mouths shut, we could hardly see each other, and the smell was awful, remembered her seven-year-old daughter, KONI. I didn't think of dying, I was too young perhaps. But I thought we were going to suffocate. . . .

— People started to panic, recalled Ignacia OZAMIZ. "The house is on fire, we're going to be burnt alive," they screamed. *Gudaris* guarding the shelter let no one leave. One man tried to force his way out with his young child. "I don't care if they kill me, I can't stand it here." He was pushed back. "Keep calm," the soldiers shouted. . . .

The town was beginning to burn, the wooden rafters catching alight. After the high explosive bombs, successive waves of planes dropped incendiaries.

From the shelter of an iron-ore bore hole about a kilometre from the town, Father Dionisio AJANGUIZ saw the roofs catching alight. Even at that distance he found breathing difficult because of the smoke. He feared that at least half the town's population must have been killed. "And that's what would have happened if they had dropped the incendiaries earlier instead of towards the end." . . .

A pall of smoke rose into the sky. Between waves of bombers, Juan Manuel EPALZA, now serving in the war industries' chemical section, who by chance was lunching at a factory on the outskirts of the town, came out of an air raid shelter to look. Thoughts of Nero crossed his mind. The bombing was of a different intensity to any that he had suffered.

After some three hours it ended. As Ignacia OZAMIZ and her two children emerged from the shelter, she saw the town was alight. "Don't cry," her husband consoled her. "We've got our hands, we're unharmed, alive." But she could think only of her eldest daughter and her mother, neither of whom had been in the shelter with her. Her house in Asilo Calzado was burning from the roof. Her husband rushed in to rescue papers and money.

— "Oh, if only you'd managed to save my sewing machine," I said. He went back in. As he came down with the machine, he found the staircase alight. He threw the machine out of the window, only just managing to jump out himself. "Woman, I got your machine but it nearly cost me my life." "Why did you go up?" "To do you a pleasure." The machine broke in its fall on the air raid shelter we'd just left, but I picked up the head, and I've got it still. . . .

As her eldest daughter, Manolita, came out of the shelter on the edge of the town — where none of the industrial plants including the small-arms factory, had been hit — a wave of heat struck her face. She told a man that she had to join her parents who were in the blazing ruins she could see beyond the railway station. Together, they skirted the town along the railway track to reach the main road. A *gudari* carried her on his shoulders to reach her burning house, one of the first on the street into the centre.

Everywhere people were fleeing. The water main had been broken in the raid, and there was little to be done to put out the fire. Juana SANGRONIZ was led out of the blaze by her *novio*.[1] Crying uncontrolledly, she refused to look back at the burning town. Ignacia OZAMIZ's husband ran to rescue his crippled mother; he arrived too late. She and three other old women had been burnt alive. Leaving their house burning, the family made their way out of the town by a path known as El Agua Corriente; the main street through the centre was impassable. As they reached the higher part, they saw that the area around the oak tree had not been hit. That night, given shelter outside town at the home of the Count of Arana, one of whose sons her husband had managed earlier to get released from gaol, she had a miscarriage. Her husband took her to a relative's farm. She left her four children with her mother. Little did she think it would be three years before she saw them again.

Guernica, 1937, oil on canvas by Pablo Picasso (1881–1973) / Museo Nacional Centro de Arte Reina Sofia, Madrid, Spain / Bridgeman Images / © 2018 Estate of Pablo Picasso / Artists Rights Society, New York

[1]*novio*: Fiancé. [Ed.]

DISCUSSION QUESTIONS

1. Describe the Guernica assault as recounted by survivors and conveyed by Picasso's painting. Aside from the town's physical infrastructure, what else did the planes target?

2. Why do you think their tactics were so alarming to people at the time? Do you see elements of this alarm in the painting? What other emotions may Picasso have been trying to evoke in his viewers?

3. What impact do you think the bombing may have had on people elsewhere in Spain fighting on behalf of the republic? What does this suggest about the underlying goals of the mission?

4. In what ways were the people of Guernica ill-prepared for the attack? What does this reveal about the relative strengths and weaknesses of republican and antirepublican forces?

4. Seeking a Diplomatic Solution

Neville Chamberlain, *Speech on the Munich Crisis* (1938)

During the troubled 1930s, many Europeans' deep longing for peace clouded their ability to see the true nature of the Nazi threat. British politician Neville Chamberlain (1869–1940) was no exception. He became prime minister in 1937 when Hitler's preparations for war were well under way. After annexing Austria in March 1938, Hitler turned to his next target, Czechoslovakia. Chamberlain, Benito Mussolini (1883–1945), and French premier Edouard Daladier (1884–1970) met with Hitler in Munich in September 1938 to defuse the situation; their meeting resulted in an agreement that accepted Germany's territorial claims. In his closing speech, delivered during a debate on the agreement in the House of Commons and excerpted here, Chamberlain defended his policy of appeasement toward Hitler as the key to peace. Tragically, it was instead a prelude to war.

War today — this has been said before, and I say it again — is a different thing not only in degree, but in kind from what it used to be. We no longer think of war as it was in the days of Marlborough or the days of Napoleon or even in the days of 1914. When war starts today, in the very first hour, before any professional soldier, sailor, or airman has been touched, it will strike the workman, the clerk, the man-in-the-street or in the bus, and his wife and children in their homes. As I listened I could not help being moved, as I am sure everybody was who heard the hon. Member for Bridgeton (Mr. Maxton) when he began to paint the picture which he himself had seen and realized what it would mean in war — people burrowing underground, trying to escape from poison gas, knowing that at any hour of the day or night death or mutilation was ready to come upon them. Remembering that the dread of what might happen to them or to those dear to them might remain with fathers

From *Parliamentary Debates. Fifth Series. Volume 339. House of Commons Official Report* (London, 1938), 544–52.

and mothers for year after year — when you think of these things you cannot ask people to accept a prospect of that kind; you cannot force them into a position that they have got to accept it; unless you feel yourself, and can make them feel, that the cause for which they are going to fight is a vital cause — a cause that transcends all the human values, a cause to which you can point, if some day you win the victory, and say, "That cause is safe."

Since I first went to Berchtesgaden more than 20,000 letters and telegrams have come to No. 10, Downing Street. Of course, I have only been able to look at a tiny fraction of them, but I have seen enough to know that the people who wrote did not feel that they had such a cause for which to fight, if they were asked to go to war in order that the Sudeten Germans might not join the Reich. That is how they are feeling. That is my answer to those who say that we should have told Germany weeks ago that, if her army crossed the border of Czechoslovakia, we should be at war with her. We had no treaty obligations and no legal obligations to Czechoslovakia and if we had said that, we feel that we should have received no support from the people of this country. . . .

As regards future policy, it seems to me that there are really only two possible alternatives. One of them is to base yourself upon the view that any sort of friendly relations, or possible relations, shall I say, with totalitarian States are impossible, that the assurances which have been given to me personally are worthless, that they have sinister designs and that they are bent upon the domination of Europe and the gradual destruction of democracies. Of course, on that hypothesis, war has got to come, and that is the view — a perfectly intelligible view — of a certain number of hon. and right hon. Gentlemen in this House. I am not sure that it is not the view of some Members of the party opposite. [An HON. MEMBER: "Yes."] Not all of them. They certainly have never put it in so many words, but it is illustrated by the observations of the hon. Member for Derby (Mr. Noel-Baker), who spoke this afternoon, and who had examined the Agreement signed by the German Chancellor and myself, which he described as a pact designed by Herr Hitler to induce us to relinquish our present obligations. That shows how far prejudice can carry a man. The Agreement, as anyone can see, is not a pact at all. So far as the question of "never going to war again" is concerned, it is not even an expression of the opinion of the two who signed the paper, except that it is their opinion of the desire of their respective peoples. I do not know whether the hon. Member will believe me or attribute to me also sinister designs when I tell him that it was a document not drawn up by Herr Hitler but by the humble individual who now addresses this House.

If the view which I have been describing is the one to be taken, I think we must inevitably proceed to the next stage — that war is coming, broadly speaking, the democracies against the totalitarian States — that certainly we must arm ourselves to the teeth, that clearly we must make military alliances with any other Powers whom we can get to work with us, and that we must hope that we shall be allowed to start the war at the moment that suits us and not at the moment that suits the other side. That is what some right hon. and hon. Gentlemen call collective security. Some hon. Members opposite will walk into any trap if it is only baited with a familiar catchword and they do it when this system is called collective security. But that is not the collective security we are thinking of or did think of when talking about the system of the League of Nations. That was a sort of universal collective security in which all nations were to take their part. This plan may give you security; it certainly is not collective in any sense. It appears to me to contain all the things which the party opposite used to denounce before the War — entangling alliances, balance of power and power politics. If I reject it, as I do, it is not because I give it a label; it is because, to my mind, it is a policy of utter despair.

If that is hon. Members' conviction, there is no future hope for civilization or for any of the things that make life worth living. Does the experience of the Great War and of the years that followed it give us reasonable hope that if some new war started that would end war any more than the last one did? No. I do not believe that war is inevitable. . . . It seems to me that the strongest argument against the inevitability of war is to be found in something that everyone has recognized or that has been recognized in every part of the House. That is the universal aversion from war of the people, their hatred of the notion of starting to kill one another again. . . .

What is the alternative to this bleak and barren policy of the inevitability of war? In my view it is that we should seek by all means in our power to avoid war, by analyzing possible causes, by trying to remove them, by discussion in a spirit of collaboration and good will. I cannot believe that such a program would be rejected by the people of this country, even if it does mean the establishment of personal contact with dictators, and of talks man to man on the basis that each, while maintaining his own ideas of the internal government of his country, is willing to allow that other systems may suit better other peoples. . . .

I am told that the policy which I have tried to describe is inconsistent with the continuance, and much more inconsistent with the acceleration of our present program of arms. I am asked how I can reconcile an appeal to the country to support the continuance of this program with the words which I used when I came back from Munich the other day and spoke of my belief that we might have peace for our time. I hope hon. Members will not be disposed to read into words used in a moment of some emotion, after a long and exhausting day, after I had driven through miles of excited, enthusiastic, cheering people — I hope they will not read into those words more than they were intended to convey. I do indeed believe that we may yet secure peace for our time, but I never meant to suggest that we should do that by disarmament, until we can induce others to disarm too. Our past experience has shown us only too clearly that weakness in armed strength means weakness in diplomacy, and if we want to secure a lasting peace, I realize that diplomacy cannot be effective unless the consciousness exists, not here alone, but elsewhere, that behind the diplomacy is the strength to give effect to it…

Finally, I would like to repeat what my right hon. Friend the Chancellor of the Exchequer said yesterday in his great speech. Our policy of appeasement does not mean that we are going to seek new friends at the expense of old ones, or, indeed, at the expense of any other nations at all. I do not think that at any time there has been a more complete identity of views between the French Government and ourselves than there is at the present time. Their objective is the same as ours — to obtain the collaboration of all nations, not excluding the totalitarian States, in building up a lasting peace for Europe.

DISCUSSION QUESTIONS

1. How did Chamberlain justify his policy of appeasement?

2. According to Chamberlain, why did some people oppose a policy of appeasement?

3. What does Chamberlain's defense indicate about popular attitudes toward war and peace?

5. The Final Solution

Sam Bankhalter and Hinda Kibort,
Memories of the Holocaust (1938–1945)

When Neville Chamberlain (1869–1940) detailed the horrors that modern warfare would inflict on civilians, not even he knew how true his words would prove to be. Once the war erupted, one segment of the civilian population in particular was the target of Hitler's fury: Jews. The result was the Final Solution, a technologically and bureaucratically sophisticated system of camps for incarcerating or exterminating European Jews that the Germans put into place between 1941 and 1942. Inmates were either killed on their arrival or spared to endure a different kind of death: starvation, abuse, and overwork. The two interviews that follow allow us to see the Holocaust through the eyes of its victims. The first is that of Sam Bankhalter, who was captured by the Nazis in his native Poland and sent to Auschwitz at age fourteen. The second voice is that of Hinda Kibort, a Lithuanian who was nineteen when the Nazis began their assault on the local Jewish population. In 1944, she was deported to Stutthof, a labor camp in northern Poland.

Sam Bankhalter

Lodz, Poland

I was at camp when the Germans invaded Poland. The camp directors told us to find our own way home. We walked many miles with airplanes over our heads, dead people on the streets. At home there were blackouts. I was just a kid, tickled to death when I was issued a flashlight and gas mask. The Polish army was equipped with buggies and horses, the Germans were all on trucks and tanks. The war was over in ten days.

The Ghetto   The German occupation was humiliation from day 1. If Jewish people were wearing the beard and sidecurls, the Germans were cutting the beard, cutting the sidecurls, laughing at you, beating you up a little bit. Then the Germans took part of Lodz and put on barbed wire, and all the Jews had to assemble in this ghetto area. You had to leave in five or ten minutes or half an hour, so you couldn't take much stuff with you. . . .

Auschwitz   We were the first ones in Auschwitz. We built it. What you got for clothing was striped pants and the striped jacket, no underwear, no socks. In wintertime you put paper in your shoes, and we used to take empty cement sacks and put a string in the top, put two together, one in back and one in front, to keep warm.

If they told you to do something, you went to do it. There was no yes or no, no choices. I worked in the crematorium for about eleven months. I saw Dr. Mengele's experiments on children, I knew the kids that became vegetables. Later in Buchenwald I saw Ilse Koch with a hose and regulator, trying to get pressure to make a hole in a woman's stomach. I saw them cutting Greek people in pieces. I was in Flossenburg for two weeks, and they shot 25,000 Russian soldiers, and we put them down on wooden logs and

From Rhoda G. Lewin, *Witnesses to the Holocaust: An Oral History* (Boston: Twayne Publishers, 1990), 5–8, 50–55.

burned them. Every day the killing, the hanging, the shooting, the crematorium smell, the ovens, and the smoke going out.

I knew everybody, knew every trick to survive. I was one of the youngest in Auschwitz, and I was like "adopted" by a lot of the older people, especially the fathers. Whole families came into Auschwitz together, and you got to Dr. Mengele, who was saying "right, left, left, right," and you knew, right there, who is going to the gas chamber and who is not. Most of the men broke down when they knew their wives and their kids — three-, five-, nine-year-olds — went into the gas chambers. In fact, one of my brothers committed suicide in Auschwitz because he couldn't live with knowing his wife and children are dead.

I was able to see my family when they came into Auschwitz in 1944. I had a sister, she had a little boy a year old. Everybody that carried a child went automatically to the gas chamber, so my mother took the child. My sister survived, but she still suffers, feels she was a part of killing my mother. . . .

Looking Back   Once you start fighting for your life, all the ethics are gone. You live by circumstances. There is no pity. You physically draw down to the point where you cannot think any more, where the only thing is survival, and maybe a little hope that if I survive, I'm gonna be with my grandchildren and tell them the story.

In the camps, death actually became a luxury. We used to say, "Look at how lucky he is. He doesn't have to suffer any more."

I was a lucky guy. I survived, and I felt pretty good about it. But then you feel guilty living! My children — our friends are their "aunts" and "uncles." They don't know what is a grandfather, a grandmother, a cousin, a holiday sitting as a family.

As you grow older, you think about it, certain faces come back to you. You remember your home, your brothers, children that went to the crematorium. You wonder, how did your mother and father feel when they were in the gas chamber? Many nights I hear voices screaming in those first few minutes in the gas chamber, and I don't sleep.

I talk to a lot of people, born Americans, and they don't relate. They can't understand, and I don't blame them. Sometimes it's hard even for me to understand the truth of this whole thing. Did it really happen? But I saw it.

The majority of the people here live fairly good. I don't think there's a country in the world that can offer as much freedom as this country can offer. But the Nazi party exists here, now. This country is supplying anti-Semitic material to the whole world, printing it here and shipping it all over, and our leaders are silent, just as the world was silent when the Jews were being taken to the camps. How quick we forget.

When I sit in a plane, I see 65 percent of the people will pick up the sports page of the newspaper. They don't care what is on the front page! And this is where the danger lies. All you need is the economy to turn a little sour and have one person give out the propaganda. With 65 percent of the population the propaganda works, and then the other 35 percent is powerless to do anything about it.

Hinda Kibort

Kovno, Lithuania

When the Germans marched in in July 1941, school had let out for the summer, so our whole family was together. . . . We tried to leave the city, but it was just like you see in the documentaries — people with their little suitcases walking along highways and jumping into ditches because German planes were strafing, coming down very low, and people killed, and all this terror. German tanks overtook us, and we returned home.

The Occupation   We did not have time like the German Jews did, from '33 until the war broke out in '39, for step-by-step adjustments. For us, one day we were human, the next day we're subhuman. We had to wear yellow stars. Everybody could command us to do whatever they wanted. They would make you hop around in the middle of the street, or they made you lie down and stepped on you, or spit on you, or they tore at beards of devout Jews. And there was always an audience around to laugh. . . .

The Ghetto   In September all the Jews were enclosed in a ghetto. We lived together in little huts, sometimes two families to a room. There were no schools, no newspapers, no concerts, no theater. Officially, we didn't have any radios or books, but people brought in many books and they circulated. We also had a couple of radios and we could hear the BBC, so we were very much aware of what was going on with the war.

As long as we were strong and useful, we would survive. Everybody had to go to work except children under twelve and the elderly. There were workshops in the ghetto where they made earmuffs for the army, for instance, but mostly people went out to work in groups, with guards. A few tried to escape, but were caught.

We did not know yet about concentration camps. [. . .]

November 5, 1943, was the day all the children were taken away. They brought in Romanian and Ukrainian S.S. to do it. All five of us in our family were employed in a factory adjacent to the ghetto, so we could see through the window what was happening. They took everybody out who stayed in the ghetto — all the children, all the elderly. When we came back after work we were a totally childless society! You can imagine parents coming home to — nothing. Everybody was absolutely shattered.

People were looking for answers, for omens. They turned to seances or to heaven to look for signs. And this was the day when we heard for the first time the word *Auschwitz*. There was a rumor that the children were taken there, but we didn't know the name so we translated it as *Der Schweiz* — Switzerland. We hoped that the trains were going to Switzerland, that the children would be hostages there.

The Transport   On July 16, 1944, the rest of the ghetto were put on cattle trains, with only what we could carry. We had no bathrooms. There was a pail on one side that very soon was full. We were very crowded. The stench and the lack of water and the fear, the whole experience, is just beyond explanation. [. . .]

Labor Camp   When we arrived at Stutthof our family was separated — the men to one side of the camp, women to the other. My mother and sister and I had to undress. There were S.S. guards around, men and women. In the middle of the room was a table and an S.S. man in a white coat. We came in in batches, totally naked.

I cannot describe how you feel in a situation like this. We were searched, totally, for jewelry, gold, even family pictures. We had to stand spread-eagle and spread out our fingers. They looked through the hair, they looked into the mouth, they looked in the ears, and then we had to lie down. They looked into every orifice of the body, right in front of everybody. We were in total shock.

From this room we were rushed through a room that said above the door "shower room." There were little openings in the ceiling and water was trickling through. In the next room were piles of clothing, rags, on the floor. You had to grab a skirt, a blouse, a dress, and exchange among yourselves to find what fit. The same thing with shoes. Some women got big men's shoes. I ended up with brown suede pumps with high heels and used a rock to break off the heels, so I could march and stand in line on roll calls.

After this we went into registration and they took down your profession, scholastic background, everything. We got black numbers on a white piece of cloth that had to be sewn on the sleeve. My mother and sister and I had numbers in the 54,000s. People from all over Europe — Hungarian women and Germans, Czechoslovakia, Belgium, you name it — they were there. Children, of course, were not there. When families came with children, the children were taken right away.

As prisoners of Stutthof we were taken to outside work camps. A thousand of us women were taken to dig antitank ditches, a very deep V-shaped ditch that went for miles and miles. The Germans had the idea that Russian tanks would fall into those ditches and not be able to come up again!

When we were done, 400 of us were taken by train deeper into Germany. We ended up in tents, fifty women to a tent. We had no water for washing and not even a latrine. If at night you wanted to go, you had to call a guard who would escort you to this little field, stand there watching while you were crouching down, and then escort you back.

We were covered with lice, and we became very sick and weak. But Frau Schmidt taught us to survive. She was a chemist, and she taught us what roots or grasses we could eat that weren't poisonous. She also said that to survive we have to keep our minds occupied and not think about the hunger and cold. She made us study every day! . . .

By the middle of December we had to stop working because the snow was very deep and everything was frozen. January 20, 1945, they made a selection. The strong women that could still work would be marched out, and the sick, those who couldn't walk or who had bent backs, or who were just skeletons and too weak to work, would be left behind. My mother was selected and my sister and I decided to stay behind with her.

We were left without food, with two armed guards. We thought the guards will burn the tents, with us in them. Then we heard there was a factory where they boiled people's bodies to manufacture soap. But the next day the guards put us in formation and marched us down the highway until we came to a small town.

We were put in the jail there. There we were, ninety-six women standing in a small jail cell, with no bathroom, pressed so close together we couldn't sit down, couldn't bend down. Pretty soon everybody was hysterical, screaming. Then slowly we quieted down.

In the morning when they opened the doors, we really spilled outside! They had recruited a bunch of Polish guards and they surrounded us totally, as if in a box. So there we were, ninety-six weak, emaciated women, marching down the highway with all these guards with rifles.

Then the German guards told us to run into the woods. The snow was so deep, up to our knees, and most of us were barefoot, frozen, our feet were blistered. We couldn't really run, but we spread out in a long line, with my mother and sister and I at the very end. I was near one guard, and all of a sudden I heard the sound of his rifle going "click."

I still remember the feeling in the back of my spine, very strange and very scary. Then the guards began to shoot.

There was a terrible panic, screams. People went really crazy. The three of us always hand-held with my mother in the middle, but now she let go of us and ran toward the guards, screaming not to shoot her children. They shot her, and my sister and I grabbed each other by the hand and ran into the woods.

We could hear screaming and shooting, and then it got very quiet. We were afraid to move. The guards wore those awesome-looking black uniforms with the skull and cross-bones insignia, and every tree looked like another guard! A few women came out from behind the trees, and eventually, ten of us made it out to the highway.

With our last strength, we made it to a small Polish village about a mile away. We knocked on doors, but they didn't let us in, and they started to throw things at us. We went to the church, and the priest said he couldn't help us because the Germans were in charge.

We were so weak we just sat there on the church steps, and late in the evening the priest came with a man who told us to go hide in a barn that was empty. We did not get any other help, whatsoever, from that whole Polish village — not medical help, not a rag to cover ourselves, not even water. Nothing.

Liberation   The next morning there was a terrible battle right in front of the barn. We were so afraid. Then it got very quiet. We opened the door, and we saw Russian tanks. We were free!

The Russians put us into an empty farmhouse. They gave us Vaseline and some rags, all they had, to cover our wounds. Then they put us on trucks and took us to a town where we found a freight train and just jumped on it.

At the border Russian police took us off the train. They grilled us. "How did you survive? You must have cooperated with the Germans." It was terrible. But finally we got identity cards — in Russia, you are nobody without some kind of I.D. — and my sister and I decided to go to the small town where we had lived. We thought somebody might have survived. . . .

Looking Back   I was a prisoner from age nineteen to twenty-three. I lost my mother and twenty-eight aunts, uncles, and cousins — all killed. To be a survivor has meant to me to be a witness because being quiet would not be fair to the ones that did not survive.

There are people writing and saying the Holocaust never happened, it's a hoax, it's Jewish propaganda. We should keep talking about it, so the next generation won't grow up not knowing how a human being can turn into a beast, not knowing the danger in keeping quiet when you see something brewing. The onlooker, the bystander, is as much at fault as the perpetrator because he lets it happen. That is why I have this fear of what is called the "silent majority."

So when a non-Jewish friend or a student asks, "What can I do?" I say, when you see something anti-Semitic happen, get up and say, "This is wrong" or "I protest." Send a letter to the newspaper saying, "This should not happen in my community," and sign your name. Then maybe somebody else will be brave enough to come forward and say that he protests, too.

DISCUSSION QUESTIONS

1. According to these accounts, what role did the ghettos play in the Final Solution?

2. Based on these interviews, what was the principal difference between camps like Auschwitz and those like Stutthof?

3. What do these accounts reveal about conditions in the camps and the inmates' strategies for survival?

4. What lessons does the Holocaust hold for our own time?

6. Atomic Catastrophe
Michihiko Hachiya, *Hiroshima Diary* (August 7, 1945)

Although World War II began in Europe, in 1941 the conflict engulfed the world as Japan and the United States entered the war on opposite sides. Despite initial successes, within a year the Japanese began to lose ground to the Allies. Even so, they fought on in the face of mounting material and human costs, unwilling to surrender. Facing the prospect of a costly land invasion, on August 6, 1945, an American plane dropped a fifteen-ton atomic bomb on the Japanese city of Hiroshima, killing more than eighty thousand people, mostly civilians. Thousands more were wounded, including Dr. Michihiko Hachiya, the director of the Hiroshima Communications Hospital. Made of reinforced concrete and located approximately fifteen hundred meters from the hypocenter of the bomb, the hospital escaped destruction and was soon packed with patients. Dr. Hachiya was among them. Bedridden for several weeks, he began a journal documenting his experiences. The excerpt that follows is drawn from his entry for the day after the bomb had been dropped, when he and other survivors struggled to make sense of the unprecedented scale of destruction and human suffering around them.

Dr. Tabuchi, an old friend from Ushita, came in. His face and hands had been burned, though not badly, and after an exchange of greetings, I asked if he knew what had happened. . . .

"It was a horrible sight," said Dr. Tabuchi. "Hundreds of injured people who are trying to escape to the hills passed our house. The sight of them was almost unbearable. Their faces and hands were burnt and swollen; and great sheets of skin had peeled away from their tissues to hang down like rags on a scarecrow. They moved like a line of ants. All through the night, they went past our house, but this morning they had stopped. I found them lying on both sides of the road so thick that it was impossible to pass without stepping on them."

I lay with my eyes shut while Dr. Tabuchi was talking, picturing in my mind the horror he was describing. I neither saw nor heard Mr. Katsutani when he came in. It was not until

From Michihiko Hachiya, *Hiroshima Diary*, trans. and ed. Warner Wells, M.D. (Chapel Hill: University of North Carolina Press, 1955), 14–17, 24–25.

I heard someone sobbing that my attention was attracted, and I recognized my old friend. I had known Mr. Katsutani for many years and knew him to be an emotional person, but even so, to see him break down made tears come to my eyes. He had come all the way from Jigozen[1] to look for me, and now that he had found me, emotion overcame him.

He turned . . . and said brokenly: "Yesterday, it was impossible to enter Hiroshima, else I would have come. Even today fires are still burning in some places. You should see how the city has changed. When I reached the Misasa Bridge[2] this morning, everything before me was gone, even the castle. These buildings here are the only ones left anywhere around. The Communications Bureau seemed to loom right in front of me long before I got anywhere near here."

Mr. Katsutani paused for a moment to catch his breath and went on: "I *really* walked along the railroad tracks to get here, but even they were littered with electric wires and broken railway cars, and the dead and wounded lay everywhere. When I reached the bridge, I saw a dreadful thing. It was unbelievable. There was a man, stone dead, sitting on his bicycle as it leaned against the bridge railing. It is hard to believe that such a thing could happen!"

He repeated himself two or three times as if to convince himself that what he said was true and then continued: "It seems that most of the dead people were either on the bridge or beneath it. You could tell that many had gone down to the river to get a drink of water and had died where they lay. I saw a few live people still in the water, knocking against the dead as they floated down the river. There must have been hundreds and thousands who fled to the river to escape the fire and then drowned.

"The sight of the soldiers, though, was more dreadful than the dead people floating down the river. I came onto I don't know how many, burned from the hips up; and where the skin had peeled, their flesh was wet and mushy. They must have been wearing their military caps because the black hair on top of their heads was not burned. It made them look like they were wearing black lacquer bowls.

"And they had no faces! Their eyes, noses, and mouths had been burned away, and it looked like their ears had melted off. It was hard to tell front from back. One soldier, whose features had been destroyed and was left with his white teeth sticking out, asked me for some water, but I didn't have any. I clasped my hands and prayed for him. He didn't say anything more. His plea for water must have been his last words. The way they were burned, I wonder if they didn't have their coats off when the bomb exploded."

It seemed to give Mr. Katsutani some relief to pour out his terrifying experiences on us; and there was no one who would have stopped him, so fascinating was his tale of horror. While he was talking, several people came in and stayed to listen. Somebody asked him what he was doing when the explosion occurred.

"I had just finished breakfast," he replied, "and was getting ready to light a cigarette, when all of a sudden I saw a white flash. In a moment there was a tremendous blast. Not stopping to think, I let out a yell and jumped into an air-raid dugout. In a moment

---

[1]A village on the Inland Sea about 10 miles southwest of Hiroshima.
[2]A large bridge which crosses the Ōta River not far from the old Hiroshima Castle in the northern part of the city and only a few blocks from the Communications Hospital.

there was such a blast as I have never heard before. It was terrific! I jumped out of the dugout and pushed my wife into it. Realizing something terrible must have happened in Hiroshima, I climbed up onto the roof of my storehouse to have a look."

Mr. Katsutani became more intense and, gesticulating wildly, went on: "Towards Hiroshima, I saw a big black cloud go billowing up, like a puffy summer cloud. Knowing for sure then that something terrible had happened in the city, I jumped down from my storehouse and ran as fast as I could to the military post at Hatsukaichi.[3] I ran up to the officer in charge and told him what I had seen and begged him to send somebody to help in Hiroshima. But he didn't even take me seriously. He looked at me for a moment with a threatening expression, and then do you know what he said? He said, 'There isn't much to worry about. One or two bombs won't hurt Hiroshima.' There was no use talking to that fool!

"I was the ranking officer in the local branch of the Ex-officer's Association, but even I didn't know what to do because that day the villagers under my command had been sent off to Miyajima[4] for labor service. I looked all around to find someone to help me make a rescue squad, but I couldn't find anybody. While I was still looking for help, wounded people began to stream into the village. I asked them what had happened, but all they could tell me was that Hiroshima had been destroyed and everybody was leaving the city. With that I got on my bicycle and rode as fast as I could towards Itsukaichi. By the time I got there, the road was jammed with people, and so was every path and byway.

"Again I tried to find out what had happened, but nobody could give me a clear answer. When I asked these people where they had come from, they would point towards Hiroshima and say, 'This way.' . . .

"I saw no badly wounded or burned people around Itsukaichi, but when I reached Kusatsu, nearly everybody was badly hurt. The nearer I got to Hiroshima the more I saw until by the time I had reached Koi,[5] they were all so badly injured, I could not bear to look into their faces. They smelled like burning hair."

Mr. Katsutani paused for a moment to take a deep breath and then continued: "The area around Koi station was not burned, but the station and the houses nearby were badly damaged. Every square inch of the station platform was packed with wounded people. Some were standing; others lying down. They were all pleading for water. Now and then you could hear a child calling for its mother. It was a living hell, I tell you. It was a living hell!" . . .

All day I had listened to visitors telling me about the destruction of Hiroshima and the scenes of horror they had witnessed. I had seen my friends wounded, their families separated, their homes destroyed. I was aware of the problems our staff had to face, and I knew how bravely they struggled against superhuman odds. I knew what the patients had to endure and the trust they put in the doctors and nurses, who, could they know the truth, were as helpless as themselves.

---

[3]The next village toward Hiroshima from Jigozen.

[4]Miyajima, or "Sacred Island," one of the seven places of superlative scenic beauty in Japan, where the magnificent camphor-wood *torii* of the Itsukushima Shrine rises majestically from the sea as a gateway to the island, is plainly visible to the south of Jigozen.

[5]A railroad station on the very western limits of the city where the slopes of Chausayama merge with the Hiroshima delta.

By degrees my capacity to comprehend the magnitude of their sorrow, to share with them the pain, frustration, and horror became so dulled that I found myself accepting whatever was told me with equanimity and a detachment I would have never believed possible.

In two days I had become at home in this environment of chaos and despair.

I felt lonely, but it was an animal loneliness. I became part of the darkness of the night. There were no radios, no electric lights, not even a candle. The only light that came to me was reflected in flickering shadows made by the burning city. The only sounds were the groans and sobs of the patients. Now and then a patient in delirium would call for his mother, or the voice of one in pain would breathe out the word *eraiyo* — "the pain is unbearable; I cannot endure it!"

What kind of a bomb was it that had destroyed Hiroshima? What had my visitors told me earlier? Whatever it was, it did not make sense.

There could not have been more than a few planes. Even *my* memory would agree to that. Before the air-raid alarm there was the metallic sound of one plane and no more. Otherwise why did the alarm stop? Why was there no further alarm during the five or six minutes before the explosion occurred?

Reason as I would, I could not make the ends meet when I considered the destruction that followed. Perhaps it *was* a new weapon! More than one of my visitors spoke vaguely of a "new bomb," a "secret weapon," a "special bomb," and someone even said that the bomb was suspended from two parachutes when it burst! Whatever it was, it was beyond my comprehension. Damage of this order could have no explanation! All we had were stories no more substantial than the clouds from which we had reached to snatch them.

DISCUSSION QUESTIONS

1. How do Dr. Hachiya's friends describe the bomb's physical impact on the cityscape of Hiroshima and its residents? What images in particular stand out in their accounts?

2. Why did Dr. Hachiya find it difficult to understand what his friends described?

3. What does his confusion suggest about the nature of warfare in the new atomic era?

COMPARATIVE QUESTIONS

1. Scholars have characterized the Nazi and communist regimes as totalitarian. In what ways do Goebbels's pamphlet and Solovieva's account of collectivization support this characterization? What similarities and differences do you see?

2. How might the Spanish Civil War have represented a rehearsal for World War II? How was it different from this later conflict?

3. How did the use of the atomic bomb and the implementation of the Final Solution set World War II apart from World War I?

4. Based on survivors' accounts, what similarities and differences do you see in the circumstances and effects of violence directed at civilians during the Spanish Civil War and World War II? Do you think such accounts have any value for people today? Why or why not?

The Cold War and the Remaking of Europe
1945–1960s

D espite widespread feelings of relief and joy when World War II at last came to a close, an uncertain path lay ahead for the world. With Europe in shambles, two new super-powers emerged from the rubble: the United States and the Soviet Union. Their rivalry, known as the cold war, would shape international affairs for decades to come. Documents 1 and 2 highlight the ideological and political roots of U.S. and Soviet cold war policies. The bipolarization of world politics was not the only sign of Europe's diminished interna-tional identity, as documents 3 and 4 show. War-weary and defiant, colonial peoples from Asia to Africa successfully battled for independence from European rule. Campaigns for freedom also appeared on the horizon closer to home. As societal and governmen-tal pressures reasserted traditional boundaries between men and women, document 5 reveals that some women called for change, setting the stage for the women's liberation movement during the 1960s. Document 6 exposes the ways in which popular culture tapped into the cold war climate, notably people's anxiety regarding the omnipresent threat of nuclear annihilation.

1. Stalin and the Western Threat
The Formation of the Communist Information Bureau (Cominform) (1947)

Despite his instrumental role in defeating fascism, the head of the Soviet Union, Joseph Stalin (1879–1953), deeply mistrusted his Western allies. Convinced that their ultimate goal was to destroy communism, Stalin moved rapidly to establish a buffer zone of satellite states

From United States Senate, 81st Congress, 1st Session, Document No. 48, *North Atlantic Treaty: Documents Relating to the North Atlantic Treaty* (Washington, D.C.: U.S. Government Printing Office, 1949), 117–20.

in eastern Europe. At a meeting in September 1947, communist leaders consolidated the Soviets' hold in the East by establishing a centralized association of communist parties — the Communist Information Bureau (Cominform). As the following document justifying their actions reveals, the Cominform embodied Stalin's belief that only by coordinating their efforts could the Soviet Union and its clients defeat the "imperialist" threat. Stalin's Western rivals worked to put their own counterstrategies in place, thus hardening the battle lines of the cold war.

The representatives of the Communist Party of Yugoslavia, the Bulgarian Workers' Party (Communists), the Communist Party of Rumania, the Hungarian Communist Party, the Polish Workers' Party, the Communist Party of the Soviet Union (Bolsheviks), the Communist Party of France, the Communist Party of Czechoslovakia and the Communist Party of Italy, having exchanged views on the international situation, have agreed upon the following declaration.

Fundamental changes have taken place in the international situation as a result of the Second World War and in the post-war period.

These changes are characterized by a new disposition of the basic political forces operating in the world arena, by a change in the relations among the victor states in the Second World War, and their realignment.

While the war was on, the Allied States in the War against Germany and Japan went together and comprised one camp. However, already during the war there were differences in the Allied camp as regards the definition of both war aims and the tasks of the post-war peace settlement. The Soviet Union and the other democratic countries regarded as their basic war aims the restoration and consolidation of democratic order in Europe, the eradication of fascism and the prevention of the possibility of new aggression on the part of Germany, and the establishment of a lasting all-round cooperation among the nations of Europe. The United States of America, and Britain in agreement with them, set themselves another aim in the war: to rid themselves of competitors on the markets (Germany and Japan) and to establish their dominant position. This difference in the definition of war aims and the tasks of the post-war settlement grew more profound after the war. Two diametrically opposed political lines took shape: on the one side the policy of the USSR and the other democratic countries directed at undermining imperialism and consolidating democracy, and on the other side, the policy of the United States and Britain directed at strengthening imperialism and stifling democracy. Inasmuch as the USSR and the countries of the new democracy became obstacles to the realization of the imperialist plans of struggle for world domination and smashing of democratic movements, a crusade was proclaimed against the USSR and the countries of the new democracy, bolstered also by threats of a new war on the part of the most zealous imperialist politicians in the United States of America and Britain.

Thus two camps were formed — the imperialist and anti-democratic camp having as its basic aim the establishment of world domination of American imperialism and the smashing of democracy, and the anti-imperialist and democratic camp having as its basic aim the undermining of imperialism, the consolidation of democracy, and the eradication of the remnants of fascism.

The struggle between the two diametrically opposed camps — the imperialist camp and the anti-imperialist camp — is taking place in a situation marked by a further aggravation of the general crisis of capitalism, the weakening of the forces of capitalism and the strengthening of the forces of Socialism and democracy.

Hence the imperialist camp and its leading force, the United States, are displaying particularly aggressive activity. This activity is being developed simultaneously along all lines — the lines of strategic military measures, economic expansion and ideological struggle. The Truman-Marshall Plan is only a constituent part, the European sub-section, of the general plan for the policy of global expansion pursued by the United States in all parts of the World. The plan for the economic and political enslavement of Europe by American imperialism is being supplemented by plans for the economic and political enslavement of China, Indonesia, the South American countries. Yesterday's aggressors — the capitalist magnates of Germany and Japan — are being groomed by the United States of America for a new role, that of instruments of the imperialist policy of the United States in Europe and Asia.

The arsenal of tactical weapons used by the imperialist camp is highly diversified. It combines direct threats of violence, blackmail and extortion, every means of political and economic pressure, bribery, and utilization of internal contradictions and strife in order to strengthen its own positions, and all this is concealed behind a liberal-pacifist mask designed to deceive and trap the politically inexperienced. . . .

Under these circumstances it is necessary that the anti-imperialist, democratic camp should close its ranks, draw up an agreed program of actions and work out its own tactics against the main forces of the imperialist camp, against American imperialism and its British and French allies, against the right-wing Socialists, primarily in Britain and France.

To frustrate the plan of imperialist aggression the efforts of all the democratic anti-imperialist forces of Europe are necessary. The right-wing Socialists are traitors to this cause. With the exception of those countries of the new democracy where the bloc of the Communists and the Socialists with other democratic, progressive parties forms the basis of the resistance of these countries to the imperialist plans, the Socialists in the majority of other countries, and primarily the French Socialists and the British Labourites . . . by their servility and sycophancy are helping American capital to achieve its aims, provoking it to resort to extortion and impelling their own countries on to the path of vassal-like dependence on the United States of America.

This imposes a special task on the Communist Parties. They must take into their hands the banner of defense of the national independence and sovereignty of their countries. If the Communist Parties stick firmly to their positions, if they do not let themselves be intimidated and blackmailed, if they courageously safeguard democracy and the national sovereignty, liberty and independence of their countries, if in their struggle against attempts to enslave their countries economically and politically they be able to take the lead of all the forces that are ready to fight for honor and national independence, no plans for the enslavement of the countries of Europe and Asia can be carried into effect.

This is now one of the principal tasks of the Communist Parties.

It is essential to bear in mind that there is a vast difference between the desire of the imperialists to unleash a new war and the possibility of organizing such a war. The nations of the world do not want war. The forces standing for peace are so large and so strong that if these forces be staunch and firm in defending the peace, if they display stamina and res-olution, the plans of the aggressors will meet with utter failure. It should not be forgotten that the war danger hullabaloo raised by the imperialist agents is intended to frighten the nervous and un-stable elements and by blackmail to win concessions for the aggressor.

The principal danger for the working class today lies in underestimating their own strength and overestimating the strength of the imperialist camp. Just as the Munich pol-icy untied the hands of Hitlerite aggression in the past, so yielding to the new line in the policy of the United States and that of the imperialist camp is bound to make its inspirers still more arrogant and aggressive. Therefore, the Communist Parties must take the lead in resisting the plans of imperialist expansion and aggression in all spheres — state, politi-cal, economic, and ideological; they must close their ranks, unite their efforts on the basis of a common anti-imperialist and democratic platform and rally around themselves all the democratic and patriotic forces of the nation.

Resolution on Interchange of Experience and Coordination of Activities of the Parties Represented at the Conference

The Conference states that the absence of contacts among the Communist Parties par-ticipating at this Conference is a serious shortcoming in the present situation. Experi-ence has shown that such lack of contacts among the Communist Parties is wrong and harmful. The need for interchange of experience and voluntary coordination of action of the various Parties is particularly keenly felt at the present time in view of the grow-ing complication of the post-war international situation, a situation in which the lack of connections among the Communist Parties may prove detrimental to the working class.

In view of this, the participants in the Conference have agreed on the following:

1. To set up an Information Bureau consisting of representatives of the Communist Party of Yugoslavia, the Bulgarian Workers' Party (Communists), the Communist Party of Rumania, the Hungarian Communist Party, the Polish Workers' Party, the Communist Party of the Soviet Union (Bolsheviks), the Communist Party of France, the Communist Party of Czechoslovakia and the Communist Party of Italy.

2. To charge the Information Bureau with the organization of interchange of experi-ence, and if need be, coordination of the activities of the Communist Parties on the basis of mutual agreement.

3. The Information Bureau is to consist of two representatives from each Central Committee, the delegations of the Central Committees to be appointed and replaced by the Central Committees.

4. The Information Bureau is to have a printed organ — a fortnightly and subse-quently, a weekly. The organ is to be published in French and Russian, and when possible, in other languages as well.

5. The Information Bureau is to be located in the city of Belgrad [sic].

DISCUSSION QUESTIONS

1. According to the document, how and why did the relationship between the Soviet Union and its Western allies change during the postwar period?
2. What does the document mean when it describes the United States as an "imperialist" power?
3. What course of action does the document set forth to undermine this power, and to what end?
4. How does this document distort the reality of Soviet actions in eastern Europe?

2. Truman and the Soviet Threat

National Security Council, *Paper Number 68* (1950)

Although he had helped to end World War II, U.S. president Harry S. Truman (1945–1953) had little time to celebrate. Daunting challenges still lay ahead as the fragile wartime alliance between the United States and the Soviet Union collapsed. By 1949, the Soviet bloc in eastern Europe was firmly in place, and the threat of international communism loomed large with the triumph of Mao Zedong (1893–1976) in China. In response, Truman set out to devise a coherent strategy for combating the expansion of Soviet power. To this end, he commissioned the U.S. Departments of State and Defense to compile a report on the subject that was completed in 1950 on the eve of the outbreak of the Korean War. The classified report, excerpted here, elucidates not only the basis of U.S. cold war tactics but also the fears and perceptions underlying them.

Within the past thirty-five years the world has experienced two global wars of tremendous violence. . . . During the span of one generation, the international distribution of power has been fundamentally altered. For several centuries it had proved impossible for any one nation to gain such preponderant strength that a coalition of other nations could not in time face it with greater strength. The international scene was marked by recurring periods of violence and war, but a system of sovereign and independent states was maintained, over which no state was able to achieve hegemony.

Two complex sets of factors have now basically altered this historical distribution of power. First, the defeat of Germany and Japan and the decline of the British and French Empires have interacted with the development of the United States and the Soviet Union in such a way that power has increasingly gravitated to these two centers. Second, the Soviet Union, unlike previous aspirants to hegemony, is animated by a new fanatic faith, antithetical to our own, and seeks to impose its absolute authority over the rest of the world. Conflict has, therefore, become endemic and is waged, on the part of the Soviet Union, by violent or non-violent methods in accordance with the dictates of expediency. . . .

On the one hand, the people of the world yearn for relief from the anxiety arising from the risk of atomic war. On the other hand, any substantial further extension of the

From National Security Council, Paper Number 68, *Foreign Relations of the United States* (Washington, D.C.: U.S. Government Printing Office, 1977), 235–92.

area under the domination of the Kremlin would raise the possibility that no coalition adequate to confront the Kremlin with greater strength could be assembled. It is in this context that this Republic and its citizens in the ascendancy of their strength stand in their deepest peril.

The issues that face us are momentous, involving the fulfillment or destruction not only of this Republic but of civilization itself. They are issues which will not await our deliberations. With conscience and resolution this Government and the people it represents must now take new and fateful decisions. . . .

Our overall policy at the present time may be described as one designed to foster a world environment in which the American system can survive and flourish. It therefore rejects the concept of isolation and affirms the necessity of our positive participation in the world community.

This broad intention embraces two subsidiary policies. One is a policy which we would probably pursue even if there were no Soviet threat. It is a policy of attempting to develop a healthy international community. The other is the policy of "containing" the Soviet system. . . .

As for the policy of "containment," it is one which seeks by all means short of war to (1) block further expansion of Soviet power, (2) expose the falsities of Soviet pretensions, (3) induce a retraction of the Kremlin's control and influence and (4) in general, so foster the seeds of destruction within the Soviet system that the Kremlin is brought at least to the point of modifying its behavior to conform to generally accepted international standards.

It was and continues to be cardinal in this policy that we possess superior overall power in ourselves or in dependable combination with other like-minded nations. One of the most important ingredients of power is military strength. In the concept of "containment," the maintenance of a strong military posture is deemed to be essential for two reasons: (1) as an ultimate guarantee of our national security and (2) as an indispensable backdrop to the conduct of the policy of "containment." . . .

At the same time, it is essential to the successful conduct of a policy of "containment" that we always leave open the possibility of negotiation with the U.S.S.R. A diplomatic freeze — and we are in one now — tends to defeat the very purposes of "containment" because it raises tensions at the same time that it makes Soviet retractions and adjustments in the direction of moderated behavior more difficult. It also tends to inhibit our initiative and deprives us of opportunities for maintaining a moral ascendancy in our struggle with the Soviet system. . . .

It is quite clear from Soviet theory and practice that the Kremlin seeks to bring the free world under its dominion by the methods of the cold war. The preferred technique is to subvert by infiltration and intimidation. Every institution of our society is an instrument which it has sought to stultify and turn against our purposes. Those that touch most closely our material and moral strength are obviously the prime targets, labor unions, civil enterprises, schools, churches, and all media for influencing opinion. The effort is not so much to make them serve obvious Soviet ends as to prevent them from serving our ends, and thus to make them sources of confusion in our economy, our culture, and our body politic. The doubts and diversities that in terms of our values are part of the merit of a free system, the weaknesses and the problems that are peculiar to it, the rights and privileges that free men enjoy, and the disorganization and destruction left in the wake of the last attack in our freedoms, all are but opportunities for the Kremlin to do its evil work. Every advantage is taken of the fact that our means of prevention and retaliation are limited by those principles and scruples which are precisely the ones that give our freedom and democracy its meaning for us. None of our scruples deter those whose only code is, "morality is that which serves the revolution."

At the same time the Soviet Union is seeking to create overwhelming military force, in order to back up infiltration with intimidation. In the only terms in which it understands strength, it is seeking to demonstrate to the free world that force and the will to use it are on the side of the Kremlin, that those who lack it are decadent and doomed. In local incidents it threatens and encroaches both for the sake of local gains and to increase anxiety and defeatism in all the free world. . . .

Our position as the center of power in the free world places a heavy responsibility upon the United States for leadership. We must organize and enlist the energies and resources of the free world in a positive program for peace which will frustrate the Kremlin design for world domination by creating a situation in the free world to which the Kremlin will be compelled to adjust. Without such a cooperative effort, led by the United States, we will have to make gradual withdrawals under pressure until we discover one day that we have sacrificed positions of vital interest. . . .

In summary, we must, by means of a rapid and sustained build-up of the political, economic, and military strength of the free world, and by means of an affirmative program intended to wrest the initiative from the Soviet Union, confront it with convincing evidence of the determination and ability of the free world to frustrate the Kremlin to the new situation. Failing that, the unwillingness of the determination and ability of the free world to the Kremlin design of a world dominated by its will [sic]. Such evidence is the only means short of war which eventually may force the Kremlin to abandon its present course of action and to negotiate acceptable agreements on issues of major importance.

The whole success of the proposed program hangs ultimately on recognition by this Government, the American people, and all free peoples, that the cold war is in fact a real war in which the survival of the free world is at stake. Essential prerequisites to success are consultations with Congressional leaders designed to make the program the object of nonpartisan legislative support, and a presentation to the public of a full explanation of the facts and implications of the present international situation. The prosecution of the program will require of us all the ingenuity, sacrifice, and unity demanded by the vital importance of the issue and the tenacity to persevere until our national objectives have been attained.

DISCUSSION QUESTIONS

1. As described in the report, how did World War II transform the international distribution of power?

2. According to the report, in what ways did the Soviet Union pose a danger to Americans and all "free peoples"?

3. What solutions does the document set forth to counter this danger?

4. Why does the report describe the cold war as a "real" war?

3. Throwing Off Colonialism

Ho Chi Minh, *Declaration of Independence of the Republic of Vietnam* (1945)

The devastation wrought by World War II encompassed more than the countless bombed buildings and millions of dead. The war had also fatally weakened the European powers' grip on their empires, as colonial peoples around the globe rose up against imperialist rule. A small nationalist organization—the Viet Minh—had formed in French Indochina in 1939 and achieved new prominence in the wake of World War II when the French sought to reassert their control in the region. Less than a month after Japan's surrender, the Viet Minh declared Vietnam's independence from France, as noted in the following document. It was signed by "President Ho Chi Minh" (1890–1969)—one of the organization's original leaders—who had lived in Paris, Moscow, and China. The document explicitly draws on the language of the French Enlightenment to further the Viet Minh's cause and condemn that of France.

"All men are created equal. They are endowed by their Creator with certain unalienable rights, among these are Life, Liberty and the pursuit of happiness."

This immortal statement was made in the Declaration of Independence of the United States of America in 1776. Now if we enlarge the sphere of our thoughts, this statement conveys another meaning: All the peoples on the earth are equal from birth, all the peoples have a right to live, be happy and free.

The Declaration of the Rights of Man and of the Citizen of the French Revolution in 1791 also states: "All men are born free and with equal rights, and must always be free and have equal rights."

Before the Outbreak of War

Those are undeniable truths.

Nevertheless, for more than eighty years, the French imperialists deceitfully raising the standard of Liberty, Equality, and Fraternity, have violated our Fatherland and oppressed our fellow-citizens. They have acted contrarily to the ideals of humanity and justice.

In the province of politics, they have deprived our people of every liberty.

They have enforced inhuman laws; to ruin our unity and national consciousness, they have carried out three different policies in the North, the Center, and the South of Vietnam.

They have founded more prisons than schools. They have mercilessly slain our patriots; they have deluged our revolutionary areas with innocent blood. They have fettered public opinion; they have promoted illiteracy.

To weaken our race they have forced us to use their manufactured opium and alcohol.

From Allan B. Cole, ed., *Conflict in Indo-China and International Repercussions: A Documentary History, 1945–1955* (Ithaca, NY: Cornell University Press, 1956), 20–21.

In the province of economics, they have stripped our fellow-citizens of everything they possessed, impoverishing the individual and devastating the land.

They have robbed us of our rice fields, our mines, our forests, our raw materials. They have monopolized the printing of bank-notes, the import and export trade; they have invented numbers of unlawful taxes, reducing our people, especially our country-folk, to a state of extreme poverty.

They have stood in the way of our businessmen and stifled all their under-takings; they have extorted our working classes in a most savage way.

In the Autumn of the year 1940, when the Japanese fascists violated Indo-china's territory to get one more foothold in their fight against the Allies, the French imperialists fell on their knees and surrendered, handing over our country to the Japanese, adding Japanese fetters to the French ones. From that day on the Vietnamese people suffered hardships yet unknown in the history of mankind. The result of this double oppression was terrific: from Quangtri to the Northern border two million people were starved to death in the early months of 1945.

On the 9th of March 1945 the French troops were disarmed by the Japanese. Once more the French either fled, or surrendered unconditionally, showing thus that not only they were incapable of "protecting" us, but that they twice sold us to the Japanese.

Yet, many times before the month of March, the Vietminh had urged the French to ally with them against the Japanese. The French colonists never answered. On the contrary they intensified their terrorizing policy. Before taking their flight they even killed a great number of our patriots who had been imprisoned at Yenbay and Caobang.

Democratic Republic of Vietnam

Nevertheless, towards the French people our fellow-citizens have always manifested an attitude pervaded with toleration and humanity. Even after the Japanese putsch of March 1945 the Vietminh have helped many Frenchmen to reach the frontier, have delivered some of them from the Japanese jails, and never failed to protect their lives and properties.

The truth is that since the Autumn of 1940 our country had ceased to be a French colony and had become a Japanese outpost. After the Japanese had surrendered to the Allies our whole people rose to conquer political power and institute the Republic of Vietnam.

The truth is that we have wrested our independence from the Japanese and not from the French. The French have fled, the Japanese have capitulated, Emperor Bao Dai has abdicated, our people has broken the fetters which for over a century have tied us down; our people has at the same time overthrown the monarchic constitution that had reigned supreme for so many centuries and instead has established the present Republican Government.

For these reasons, we, members of the provisional Government, representing the whole population of Vietnam, have declared and renew here our declaration that we break off all relations with the French people and abolish all the special rights the French have unlawfully acquired on our Fatherland.

The whole population of Vietnam is united in a common allegiance to the Republican Government and is linked by a common will which is to annihilate the dark aims of the French imperialists.

We are convinced that the Allied nations which have acknowledged at Teheran and San Francisco the principles of self-determination and equality of status will not refuse to acknowledge the independence of Vietnam.

A people that has courageously opposed French domination for more than eighty years, a people that has fought by the Allies' side these last years against the fascists, such a people must be free, such a people must be independent.

For these reasons we, members of the Provisional Government of Vietnam, declare to the world that Vietnam has the right to be free and independent, and has in fact become a free and independent country. We also declare that the Vietnamese people is determined to make the heaviest sacrifices to maintain its independence and its Liberty.

DISCUSSION QUESTIONS

1. How does the document characterize the actions of the French in Vietnam? Why do you think it characterizes their actions in this way?

2. In what ways did World War II further the cause of the Viet Minh?

3. Why did the Viet Minh believe that the Vietnamese people had an undeniable right to independence? How does the document draw on Enlightenment ideals to make its case?

4. The Psychology of Colonialism

Frantz Fanon, *The Wretched of the Earth* (1961)

The Viet Minh's resistance against European efforts to return to earlier imperialist norms following the chaos of World War II was a sign of what lay ahead. In the late 1940s and 1950s, colonized peoples around the globe clamored for independence, often through violent resistance to the status quo. Frantz Fanon (1925–1961), a black psychiatrist from the French colony of Martinique, trained a critical eye on the brutal everyday and psychological realities of living under colonial rule. His ideas were rooted in both contemporary Western thought, notably existentialism's call to create one's own authentic self through action, as well as his own personal experience. After completing his education in France, in 1953 he accepted a government post as a staff psychiatrist in a hospital in Algeria that had been under French rule for more than a century. A year later, the Algerian war of liberation broke out, countered by a brutal response from the French military. Increasingly disillusioned with French colonial policies, Fanon resigned and spent the rest of his life supporting Algerians' campaign for independence as a writer, doctor, and diplomat. The Wretched of the Earth, excerpted here, was published in 1961 shortly before Fanon's death and became a seminal text of the decolonization movement. It reveals that, for Fanon, decolonization was not simply a fight to reclaim territory; it was a fight to reclaim individual human dignity.

Decolonization never goes unnoticed, for it focuses on and fundamentally alters being, and transforms the spectator crushed to a nonessential state into a privileged actor, captured in a virtually grandiose fashion by the spotlight of History. It infuses a new rhythm, specific to a new generation of men, with a new language and a new humanity. Decolonization is truly the creation of new men. But such a creation cannot be attributed to a supernatural power: The "thing" colonized becomes a man through the very process of liberation.

Decolonization, therefore, implies the urgent need to thoroughly challenge the colonial situation. Its definition can, if we want to describe it accurately, be summed up in the well-known words: "The last shall be first." Decolonization is verification of this. At a descriptive level, therefore, any decolonization is a success. . . .

You do not disorganize a society, however primitive it may be, with such an agenda if you are not determined from the very start to smash every obstacle encountered. The colonized, who have made up their mind to make such an agenda into a driving force, have been prepared for violence from time immemorial. As soon as they are born it is obvious to them that their cramped world, riddled with taboos, can only be challenged by out and out violence.

The colonial world is a compartmentalized world. It is obviously as superfluous to recall the existence of "native" towns and European towns, of schools for "natives" and schools for Europeans, as it is to recall apartheid in South Africa. Yet if we penetrate inside this compartmentalization we shall at least bring to light some of its key aspects. By penetrating its geographical configuration and classification we shall be able to delineate the backbone on which the decolonized society is reorganized.

The colonized world is a world divided in two. The dividing line, the border, is represented by the barracks and the police stations. In the colonies, the official, legitimate agent, the spokesperson for the colonizer and the regime of oppression, is the police officer or the soldier. In capitalist societies, education, whether secular or religious, the teaching of moral reflexes handed down from father to son, the exemplary integrity of workers decorated after fifty years of loyal and faithful service, the fostering of love for harmony and wisdom, those aesthetic forms of respect for the status quo, instill in the exploited a mood of submission and inhibition which considerably eases the task of the agents of law and order. In capitalist countries a multitude of sermonizers, counselors, and "confusion-mongers" intervene between the exploited and the authorities. In colonial regions, however, the proximity and frequent, direct intervention by the police and the military ensure the colonized are kept under close scrutiny, and contained by rifle butts and napalm. We have seen how the government's agent uses a language of pure violence. The agent does not alleviate oppression or mask domination. He displays and demonstrates them with the clear conscience of the law enforcer, and brings violence into the homes and minds of the colonized subject. . . .

This compartmentalized world, this world divided in two, is inhabited by different species. The singularity of the colonial context lies in the fact that economic reality, inequality, and enormous disparities in lifestyles never manage to mask the human reality. Looking at the immediacies of the colonial context, it is clear that what divides this world is first and foremost what species, what race one belongs to. In the colonies the economic infrastructure is also a superstructure. The cause is effect: You are rich because you are white, you are white because you are rich. This is why a Marxist analysis should always be slightly stretched when it comes to addressing the colonial issue. It is not just the concept of the precapitalist society, so effectively studied by Marx, which needs to be reexamined here. The serf is essentially different from the knight, but a reference to divine right is needed to justify this difference in status. In the colonies the foreigner imposed himself using his cannons and machines. Despite the success of his pacification, in spite of his appropriation, the colonist always remains a foreigner. It is not the factories, the estates, or the bank account which primarily characterize the "ruling class." The ruling species is first and foremost the outsider from elsewhere, different from the indigenous population, "the others."

The violence which governed the ordering of the colonial world, which tirelessly punctuated the destruction of the indigenous social fabric, and demolished unchecked the systems of reference of the country's economy, lifestyles, and modes of dress, this same violence will be vindicated and appropriated when, taking history into their own hands, the colonized swarm into the forbidden cities. To blow the colonial world to smithereens is henceforth a clear image within the grasp and imagination of every colonized subject. To dislocate the colonial world does not mean that once the borders have been eliminated there will be a right of way between the two sectors. To destroy the colonial world means nothing less than demolishing the colonist's sector, burying it deep within the earth or banishing it from the territory. . . .

The colonized subject thus discovers that his life, his breathing and his heartbeats are the same as the colonist's. He discovers that the skin of a colonist is not worth more than the "native's." In other words, his world receives a fundamental jolt. The colonized's revolutionary new assurance stems from this. If, in fact, my life is worth as much as the colonist's, his look can no longer strike fear into me or nail me to the spot and his voice can no longer petrify me. I am no longer uneasy in his presence. In reality, to hell with him. Not only does his presence no longer bother me, but I am already preparing to waylay him in such a way that soon he will have no other solution but to flee.

DISCUSSION QUESTIONS

1. How does Fanon describe the colonial world? What are some of its key features?

2. What impact do these features have on colonized peoples according to Fanon?

3. As Fanon describes it, what is the ultimate goal of decolonization? What role does violence play in achieving this goal, and why?

4. How does Fanon link the physical experience of colonialism to its psychological dimensions? Why are these psychological ramifications so important in his view?

5. The Condition of Modern Women

SOURCES IN CONVERSATION | Simone de Beauvoir, *The Second Sex* (1949) and Betty Friedan, *The Feminine Mystique* (1963)

Challenges to traditional assumptions extended beyond people of color in the postwar era; they also included women in Western society who questioned long-standing beliefs that female domesticity and submissiveness were the bedrock of civilization. Philosopher and novelist Simone de Beauvoir (1908–1986) was the most prominent voice in the debate on the condition of modern women, and she presented her views to the world in her book The Second Sex, *first published in French in 1949 and translated into English shortly thereafter. In the following excerpt, Beauvoir outlines the fundamental premise of her work that, throughout history, women's identities have been defined by men and thus subjugated to them. According to Beauvoir, woman as "other" could break free from her subservience only by taking charge of her own life and becoming active like man. Beauvoir's book was an international best seller and helped to galvanize the women's liberation movement in the United States and Europe during the 1960s. Inspired in part by the work of Beauvoir, during the late 1950s and early 1960s the writer Betty Friedan (1921–2006) interviewed housewives across the United States to investigate their experiences. She identified their widespread discontent as "the problem that has no name." Friedan published her findings in her book* The Feminine Mystique, *which quickly sold more than one million copies and has become a foundational text of second-wave feminism. The women's voices excerpted here come from Friedan's interviews and recount different women's experiences of daily life in the post–World War II United States.*

The Second Sex

If I wish to define myself, I must first of all say: "I am a woman"; on this truth must be based all further discussion. A man never begins by presenting himself as an individual of a certain sex; it goes without saying that he is a man . . .

Man represents both the positive and the neutral, as is indicated by the common use of *man* to designate human beings in general; whereas woman represents only the negative, defined by limiting criteria, without reciprocity. . . . A man is in the right in being a man; it is the woman who is in the wrong . . .

[Man] is the Subject, he is the Absolute — she is the Other. . . . Thus it is that no group ever sets itself up as the One without at once setting up the Other over against itself. . . . No subject will readily volunteer to become the object, the inessential; it is not the Other who, in defining himself as the Other, establishes the One. The Other is posed as such by the One in defining himself as the One. But if the Other is not to regain the status of being the One, he must be submissive enough to accept this alien point of view. Whence comes this submission in the case of woman? . . .

The reason for this is that women lack concrete means for organizing themselves into a unit. . . . They have no past, no history, no religion of their own; and they have no such solidarity of work and interest. . . . They are not even promiscuously herded together in the way that creates community feeling among the American Negroes, the ghetto Jews, . . . or the factory hands of Rennault. They live dispersed among the males, attached . . . to certain men — fathers or husbands — more firmly than they are to other women.

The Feminine Mystique

"Ye Gods, what do I do with my time? Well, I get up a six. I get my son dressed and then give him breakfast. After that I wash dishes and bathe and feed the baby. Then I get lunch

---

From Simone de Beauvoir, *The Second Sex*, trans. and ed. H. M. Parshley (New York: Knopf, 1953), xvi–xx; and Betty Friedan, *The Feminine Mystique* (New York: Norton, 1963), 21, 27–28.

and while the children nap, I sew or mend or iron and do all the other things I can't get done before noon. Then I cook supper for the family and my husband watches TV while I do the dishes. After I get the children to bed, I set my hair and then I go to bed."

. . .

"The problem is always being the children's mommy, or the minister's wife and never being myself."

. . .

"By noon I'm ready for a padded cell. Very little of what I've done has been really necessary or important. Outside pressures lash me through the day. Yet I look upon myself as one of the more relaxed housewives in the neighborhood."

. . .

"I've tried everything women are supposed to do — hobbies, gardening, pickling, canning, being very social with my neighbors, joining committees, running PTA teas. I can do it all, and I like it, but it doesn't leave you anything to think about — any feeling of who you are. I never had any career ambitions. All I wanted was to get married and have four children. I love my kids and Bob and my home. There's no problem you can even put a name to. But I'm desperate. I begin to feel I have no personality. I'm a server of food and a putter-on of pants and a bedmaker, somebody who can be called on when you want something. But who am I?"

. . .

DISCUSSION QUESTIONS

1. What does Beauvoir mean when she describes women as the "Other"?
2. According to Beauvoir, how does women's status both resemble and differ from that of other marginalized groups?
3. How do the women interviewed by Friedan describe their daily lives? What details stand out in particular, and why?
4. What connections can you draw between American women's experiences as housewives in the late 1950s and early 1960s and Beauvoir's argument in *The Second Sex*?

6. Cold War Anxieties

Life *Magazine Cover* and
Letter from President John F. Kennedy (1961)

The normalcy that people craved after two world wars proved elusive amid the pervasive climate of cold war. Tensions between the United States and the Soviet Union were especially high in the early years of John F. Kennedy's presidency. In the spring of 1961, he approved an ill-fated invasion of communist Cuba, and several months later, the Soviets began construction of what would become the Berlin Wall. The possibility that these provocations could spark nuclear war between the two superpowers was an ever-present reality. It was

From John F. Kennedy, "A Message to You from the President," *Life*, September 15, 1961, 95.

in this setting that the popular magazine Life *devoted its weekly photographic essay to the topic of how to survive a nuclear attack. The magazine's coverage included detailed, do-it-yourself-style instructions on how to build various kinds of fallout shelters both inside and outside of the home. President Kennedy introduced the essay with a letter to the American people urging them to be prepared by following the advice in the ensuing pages. With more than twenty-eight million adult readers,* Life *was a fixture in American culture at the time, thereby ensuring that Kennedy's message would circulate widely.*

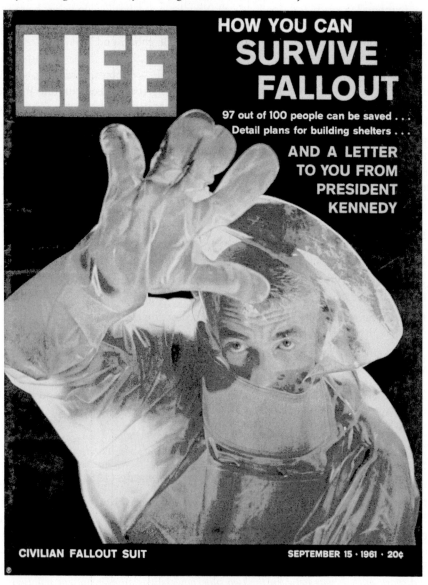

Photo by Ralph Morse / LIFE Magazine, Copyright Time Inc. / The LIFE Premium Collection / Getty Images

The White House
September 7, 1961

My Fellow Americans:

Nuclear weapons and the possibility of nuclear war are facts of life we cannot ignore today. I do not believe that war can solve any of the problems facing the world today. But the decision is not ours alone.

The government is moving to improve the protection afforded you in your communities through civil defense. We have begun, and will be continuing throughout the next year and a half, a survey of all public buildings with fallout shelter potential, and the marking of those with adequate shelter for 50 persons or more. We are providing fallout shelter in new and in some existing federal buildings. We are stocking these shelters with one week's food and medical supplies and two weeks' water supply for the shelter occupants. In addition, I have recommended to the Congress the establishment of food reserves in centers around the country where they might be needed following an attack. Finally, we are developing improved warning systems which will make it possible to sound attack warning on buzzers right in your homes and places of business.

More comprehensive measures than these lie ahead, but they cannot be brought to completion in the immediate future. In the meantime there is much that you can do to protect yourself — and in doing so strengthen your nation.

I urge you to read and consider seriously the contents of this issue of LIFE. The security of our country and the peace of the world are the objectives of our policy. But in these dangerous days when both these objectives are threatened we must prepare for all eventualities. The ability to survive coupled with the will to do so therefore are essential to our country.

John F. Kennedy

DISCUSSION QUESTIONS

1. Why do you think the editors of *Life* chose this image of a civilian fallout suit for the cover? What reactions do you think they hoped to elicit in readers, and why?

2. Based on his letter, why do you think President Kennedy chose to address the public in this way? What are the key elements of his message?

3. What do the cover image and President Kennedy's letter reveal about the impact of the cold war on U.S. politics and culture?

COMPARATIVE QUESTIONS

1. Based on the Cominform declaration and National Security Council paper, what similarities do you see between Soviet and U.S. cold war attitudes and corresponding policies?

2. What do the *Life* cover and President Kennedy's letter suggest about how these attitudes and policies helped to create a climate of cold war that pervaded everyday life?

3. How would you compare the struggles of Ho Chi Minh, Frantz Fanon, and Simone de Beauvoir against rigid traditional power structures during the postwar era?

4. How did a deep sense of anxiety permeate the period from 1945 to the 1960s? What were the sources of such anxiety, and where does it surface in the documents included here?

Postindustrial Society and the End of the Cold War Order

1960s–1989

<hr>

The 1960s and 1970s were filled with turmoil fueled by feelings of both optimism and despair. During these years, millions of people took to the streets to challenge cold war politics and society. As document 1 illustrates, for a few brief months in 1968, people in Czechoslovakia challenged Soviet communism and implemented a liberal government. A wave of public demonstrations swept across Europe and into the United States, where students protested against the war in Vietnam and for a more open political discourse. Document 2 captures some of their voices, while document 3 puts human faces on the tragedy of war. At the same time, new threats to world stability emerged, as documents 4 and 5 illustrate. In 1973, Arab countries attacked Israel and united to restrict the West's access to crude oil. The growing threat of terrorism in the major Western nations posed additional challenges. No one could have foreseen that the political landscape would dramatically shift in the late 1980s when the Soviet empire disintegrated. Document 6 pulls back the curtain on this drama, revealing how government-sponsored state reforms set the stage not for brutal repression, as they had in Prague twenty years earlier, but rather for the end of the cold war.

1. Prague Spring

Josef Smrkovský, *What Lies Ahead* (February 9, 1968)

In the immediate aftermath of World War II, the Soviet Union created a buffer of satellite states in eastern Europe, including Czechoslovakia. By 1957, when the presidency there

<hr>

From Jaromir Navrátil, ed., *The Prague Spring 1968: A National Security Archive Documents Reader* (New York: Central European Press, 1998), 45–50.

passed to Antonín Novotný (1904–1975), a politician committed to communist unity with the Soviet Union, Czechoslovakia had become an authoritarian state with collectivized property and suppressed civil liberties. However, a group led by Josef Smrkovský (1911–1974) and Alexander Dubček (1921–1992), calling for more political and social openness, secretly gathered strength in the highest ranks of the Czechoslovakian Communist Party. In January 1968, Dubček succeeded Novotný as the head of the party, and he initiated a broad range of reforms, including free speech, an independent press, the right to assemble, and religious freedom. The following newspaper article excerpt, written by Smrkovský a month after Dubček gained power, became the new government's most important manifesto. In it, Smrkovský emphasized a break with the "old" party while calling for all the people of Czechoslovakia to build a "new," liberal Communist Party. The reforms were not to last. In August 1968, Soviet dominance returned after Soviet and Warsaw Pact troops invaded Czechoslovakia, killed more than one hundred people, and arrested Dubček and his allies.

On the Conclusions of the January Plenum of the CPCz CC[1]

The questions that the Central Committee of the party considered and resolved in December and January have set the entire party in motion, and the public at large has been paying great attention to them. This is so even though we failed to ensure the prompt and sufficient release of information. We must put this right, and that is precisely what we are doing, since there must be no discrepancy between our statements of Leninist principles and democratic traditions, on the one hand, and our future practical activities, on the other.

We can already say that in general the last Central Committee session has met with a favorable response in politically active sections of society. As more information has become available, discussions have been gaining momentum, and this in turn has generated greater enthusiasm for political activity. Yet even sincere persons who in the past have often been disappointed still show signs of skepticism. Old practices are still embedded in the activities of many of our organs and in the minds of people working in them. This creates doubts and insecurity. People are demanding guarantees. . . .

A Common Republic

Still, the common interest in truly maintaining the republic's internal unity demands that we rely on proven traditions, stemming from the joint anti-fascist liberation struggle, and that we come to grips with the issue of our relations in the interest of a modern socialist community. . . . For the first time in the history of the CPCz, a Slovak communist has been placed at the helm of the party. Cde. Dubcek has become first secretary as an honest and experienced communist. At the CPCz CC session it was not at all a question of a "power seizure by the Slovaks" as we sometimes hear because of a lack of information in Czech circles.

---

[1]The Central Committee of the Czechoslovakian Communist Party.

Confidence in the Intelligentsia

By the same token, no one has threatened the working-class nature of the party. Those who spoke in the discussion could not be divided into intellectuals and workers, as is claimed erroneously in certain quarters. The open and passionate debate included intellectuals as well as workers and peasants, who were motivated by the same sincere concern for the cause of the republic, the interests of the people, and the improvement and consolidation of socialism. As a workers' official, which I consider myself to be, this is something I wish to emphasize. . . . The present era of the scientific-technical revolution — in which, unfortunately, we are badly lagging behind — demands more than ever that the creative forces of the working class, the peasantry, and the intelligentsia combine their efforts. . . .

Even further from the truth is the suggestion that what happened at the recent sessions of the CPCz CC was no more than a personal quarrel and a rotation of individuals. Of course, no one finds it easy to set aside his personal biases, not even at sessions of the party's Central Committee. Nevertheless, the personnel changes were in fact motivated by considerations that are of far greater urgency and importance to the party: the imperative to remove the obstacles that for some time have been obstructing the party's progressive efforts, and the need to remove everything . . . that inhibits the activation of all healthy forces in the party and among the people. . . . It is also essential to eliminate everything that has been distorting socialism, damaging people's spirits, causing pain, and depriving people of their faith and enthusiasm. This means we must do whatever is necessary to rehabilitate communists and other citizens who were unjustly sentenced in political trials so that we, as communists, can look ourselves in the face without shame. . . .

The CC session attempted to find the cause of the passivity and indifference in our country, things which we can no longer conceal. There is a conviction growing that everything we have achieved in transforming the structure of the society will facilitate — indeed will absolutely necessitate — a basic change of course. Such a change must be aimed at the democratization of the party and the society as a whole, and must be brought about consistently and honestly; it also must be backed by realistic guarantees that are understood by the majority to ensure that it will not be undermined by hedging and reservations. . . .

. . . What, then, lies ahead? We shall find no ready-made solutions. It is up to us, both Czechs and Slovaks, to launch out courageously into unexplored territory and search for a Czechoslovak road to socialism. . . .

The Example of the Central Committee

The first task is to inform the party, the whole party, of the content of the discussion at the CC session. . . . Scope must be given to a sincere and frank exchange of views from top to bottom, with priority to be given to the cogency of the arguments rather than to the power of the voice or the office. Priority also will be given to action instead of to indifference and passive submission. All truly progressive and responsible trends must be given a chance, and their chance must be given boldly and judiciously, sooner rather than later.

No mistake would be greater than to start carrying out these tasks on the basis of obsolete procedures, in the form of a one-off campaign that would, as usual, pay lip-service and then wither and die a few months later. . . .

The whole set of tasks and problems that are accumulating today before us can best be characterized as a steady process of democratization within both the party and the state. This process is the main precondition for a truly mature and thus voluntary form of discipline, without which the party would lose its capacity to act. Although we must cure and revive the whole party organism, we cannot do so through some "back-door" method. Nor can we compensate by relying on even the most hard-working apparatus. The entire party and each of its members must be convinced that the party as a whole is responsible not only for the implementation of tasks, but also for their conceptualization — that is, for the formulation of party policy, in which each communist must participate so that they can then regard it as their very own.

No doubt, we must "clear the table" — a phrase one often hears among comrades nowadays — but this must be done peacefully and in a businesslike manner so that we can prudently return to our former work and can reaffirm and develop whatever has been successful in the past, while rectifying shortcomings and mistakes in a just and sincere manner. Let us give to the past what it deserves — truth, purity, and justice. Let us do this without further delay and without scandals and recriminations, and let us do it consistently so we can then fully concentrate on what has always been the main interest of all communists: the future. . . .

The Position of the Party

. . . Let us not have any illusions. Nothing will happen on its own, without a struggle, or without some effort. Nothing will fall into our laps, and no one should expect charitable donations. There must be a sense of responsibility both "at the top" and "at the bottom."

People have emerged from various quarters who talk about a shake-up and turbulence; more such people will emerge, and the talk will continue. This eventful session, where people spoke frankly, openly, courageously, critically, and self-critically, may appear turbulent to some. But there are different types of turbulence. I think it will be a good thing if the December and January plenary sessions bring a real shake-up — a shake-up that is beneficial in releasing and reviving new and fresh forces that can move our society and our socialist republic forward into a new phase. All this is fully within the power of the party and within the power of our 1.5 million communists, who can count on the total help and support of broad masses of the population who want the same things that we do.

DISCUSSION QUESTIONS

1. Why do you think Smrkovský devoted so much of his newspaper article to dispelling the skepticism, doubt, and insecurity of his readers?

2. How did the practices of the Czechoslovakian Communist Party compare to the new proposals?

3. How do you think this article was received when it was first published? What aspects do you think were most controversial then, and what aspects seem most revolutionary to you today?

2. A Revolutionary Time

Student Voices of Protest (1968)

College campuses were hotbeds of social activism during the 1960s, and they exploded into action with unprecedented force in the spring of 1968. The year was beset with tragedies, from the mounting number of casualties in the Vietnam War to the assassination of American civil rights leader Martin Luther King Jr. and presidential candidate Robert F. Kennedy. Students from New York to Paris to Berlin rose up in protest, particularly over racial and antiwar issues. They demonstrated, occupied buildings, shut down classes, and went on strike. The following excerpts bring these students to life in their own words, which convey not only frustration and despair but also a desire to bring about lasting change.

My most vivid memory of May '68? The new-found ability for everyone to *speak* — to speak of anything with anyone. In that month of talking during May you learnt more than in the whole of your five years of studying. It was really another world — a dream world perhaps — but that's what I'll always remember: the need and the right for everyone to speak. — René Bourrigaud, student at the École Supérieure d'Agriculture, Angers, France

People were learning through doing things themselves, learning self-confidence. It was magic, there were all these kids from nice middle-class homes who'd never done or said anything and were now suddenly speaking. It was democracy of the public space in the market place, a discourse where nobody was privileged. If anything encapsulated what we were trying to do and why, it was that. . . . — Pete Latarche, leader of the university occupation at Hull, England, 1968

It's a moment I shall never forget. Suddenly, spontaneously, barricades were being thrown up in the streets. People were building up the cobblestones because they wanted — many of them for the first time — to throw themselves into a collective, spontaneous activity. People were releasing all their repressed feelings, expressing them in a festive spirit. Thousands felt the need to communicate with each other, to love one another. That night has forever made me optimistic about history. Having lived through it, I can't ever say, "It will never happen." . . . — Dany Cohn-Bendit, student leader at Nanterre University, on the night of the Paris barricades, 10–11 May 1968

The unthinkable happened! Everything I had ever dreamt of since childhood, knowing that it would never happen, now began to become real. People were saying, fuck hierarchy, authority, this society with its cold rational elitist logic! Fuck all the petty bosses and the mandarins at the top! Fuck this immutable society that refuses to consider the misery, poverty, inequality and injustice it creates, that divides people according to their origins and skills! Suddenly, the French were showing they understood that they had to refuse

---

From Ronald Fraser et al., *1968: A Student Generation in Revolt* (New York: Pantheon Books, 1988), 9–12.

the state's authority because it was malevolent, evil, just as I'd always thought as a child. Suddenly they realized that they had to find a new sort of solidarity. And it was happening in front of my eyes. That was what May '68 meant to me! . . . — Nelly Finkielsztejn, student at Nanterre University, Paris

My world had been very staid, very traditional, very frightened, very middle-class and respectable. And here I was doing these things that six months before I would have thought were just horrible. But I was in the midst of an enormous tide of people. There was so much constant collective reaffirmation of it. The ecstasy was stepping out of time, out of traditional personal time. The usual rules of the game in capitalist society had been set aside. It was phenomenally liberating. . . . At the same time it was a political struggle. It wasn't just Columbia. There *was* a fucking war on in Vietnam, and the civil rights movement. These were profound forces that transcend that moment. 1968 just cracked the universe open for me. And the fact of getting involved meant that never again was I going to look at something outside with the kind of reflex condemnation or fear. Yes, it was the making of me — or the unmaking. — Mike Wallace, occupation of Columbia University, New York, April 1968

We'd been brought up to believe in our hearts that America fought on the side of justice. The Second World War was very much ingrained in us, my father had volunteered. So, along with the absolute horror of the war in Vietnam, there was also a feeling of personal betrayal. I remember crying by myself late at night in my room listening to the reports of the war, the first reports of the bombing. Vietnam was the catalyst. . . . — John Levin, student leader at San Francisco State College

I was outraged, what shocked me most was that a highly developed country, the super-modern American army, should fall on these Vietnamese peasants — fall on them like the conquistadores on South America, or the white settlers on the North American Indians. In my mind's eye, I always saw those bull-necked fat pigs — like in Georg Grosz's pictures — attacking the small, child-like Vietnamese. — Michael von Engelhardt, German student

The resistance of the Vietnamese people showed that it could be done — a fight back was possible. If poor peasants could do it well why not people in Western Europe? That was the importance of Vietnam, it destroyed the myth that we just had to hold on to what we had because the whole world could be blown up if the Americans were "provoked." The Vietnamese showed that if you were attacked you fought back, and then it depended on the internal balance of power whether you won or not. . . . — Tariq Ali, a British Vietnam Solidarity Campaign leader

So we started to be political in a totally new way, making the connection between our student condition and the larger international issues. A low mark in mathematics could become the focal point of an occupation by students who linked the professor's arbitrary and authoritarian behavior to the wider issues, like Vietnam. Acting on your immediate problems made you understand better the bigger issues. If it hadn't been for that, perhaps the latter would have remained alien, you'd have said "OK, but what can *I* do?" — Agnese Gatti, student at Trento Institute of Social Sciences, Italy

Creating a confrontation with the university administration you could significantly expose the interlocking network of imperialism as it was played out on the campuses. You could prove that they were working hand-in-hand with the military and the CIA, and that ultimately, when you pushed them, they would call upon all the oppressive apparatus to defend their position from their own students. . . . — Jeff Jones, Students for a Democratic Society (SDS), New York regional organizer

Everybody was terribly young and didn't know what was going on. One had a sort of megalomaniac attitude that by sheer protest and revolt things would be changed. It was true of the music, of the hallucinogenics, of politics, it was true across the board — people threw themselves into activity without experience. The desire to do something became tremendously intense and the capacity to do it diminished by the very way one was rejecting the procedures by which things could be done. It led to all sorts of crazy ideas. — Anthony Barnett, sociology student, Leicester University, England

DISCUSSION QUESTIONS

1. What were some of the students' principal targets for criticism, and why?

2. In what ways did the events of 1968 personally transform some of these students?

3. Some historians argue that the student protests of 1968 made governments less inviolable and sacred. What evidence can you find here to support this assertion?

3. Children Fleeing
from a Napalm Attack in South Vietnam

Nick Ut, *Photograph* (June 8, 1972),
and Vanity Fair *Interview* (2015)

Although the cold war dominated the European landscape during the 1950s and 1960s, it also loomed large in Asia. Responding to years of resistance against French colonial rule led by the founder of the Indochinese Communist Party, Ho Chi Minh (1890–1969), the Geneva Convention divided Vietnam into North and South in 1954. Ho Chi Minh and his followers were ordered to retreat to the North. U.S. leaders feared that the communist presence there would spread elsewhere in the region, and gradually their commitment to a non-Communist South Vietnam escalated to all-out war. By 1966, the United States had more than half a

From Mark Edwards Harris, "Photographer Who Took Iconic Vietnam Photo Looks Back, 40 Years after the War Ended," *Vanity Fair*, April 3, 2015. https://www.vanityfair.com/news/2015/04/vietnam-war-napalm-girl-photo-today.

million soldiers in South Vietnam. One of the most compelling images of the Vietnam War is that of children running down a dusty road, screaming in terror and pain after a napalm attack on their village. The photograph was taken by Nick Ut, a native Vietnamese man who had started his career in 1966 working in the Associated Press's darkroom in Saigon and moved up the ranks to staff photographer. More than forty years later, Nick Ut shared his recollections of what proved to be a decisive moment in the conflict. Published on the front page of newspapers around the world, his photograph helped to further undermine public support for the war by exposing its violent consequences. Although South Vietnamese aircraft executed the attack, it had been ordered by the U.S. Army — a fact that shocked much of the American public. In the years following its publication, the North Vietnamese government used the photograph as evidence of American atrocities.

I left Saigon around seven A.M. by car and arrived outside of Trang Bang around 7:30 A.M. During the war, I traveled up and down Highway 1 all the time. There were no traffic lights on the highway back then. It was a very dangerous drive. The Viet Cong were hiding everywhere. After the Americans and South Vietnamese military shot the Viet Cong, they would leave dead bodies by the side of the road as a warning to not join or assist the Vietcong. Some Viet Cong were very young — 15 years old.

June 8, 1972, was the second day of heavy fighting around Trang Bang. As I drove up there, I saw thousands of refugees coming down the road. I was an Associated Press photographer and there were many other media there that day — ABC News, CBS, BBC. More than 10 cameramen were there.

Nick Ut / AP

In the morning, there was very heavy fighting and bombing in the village, so some of the media left before they dropped the napalm because they thought they had gotten enough material. They dropped the napalm around 12:30 P.M.

When I first saw the napalm explosion, I didn't think there were any civilians in the village. Four napalm bombs were dropped. In the previous two days, thousands of refugees had already fled the village. Then I started to see people come out of the fireball and smoke. I picked up my Nikon camera . . . and started shooting. As they got closer I switched to my Leica. First there was a grandmother carrying a baby who died in front of my camera. Then I saw through the viewfinder of my Leica, the naked girl running. I thought, "Oh my God. What happened? The girl has no clothes." I kept shooting with my Leica. . . .

I took almost a roll of Tri-x film of her then I saw her skin coming off and I stopped taking pictures. I didn't want her to die. I wanted to help her. I put my cameras down on the road. We poured water over this young girl. Her name was Kim Phuc. She kept yelling "nóng quá" (Too hot). We were all in shock.

Her uncle [asked if I would take all the children to the hospital]. I knew she would die soon if I didn't help. I immediately said, "Yes." . . . When we arrived at the hospital in Cu Chi, nobody wanted to help her because there were so many wounded soldiers and civilians already there. The local hospital was too small. They asked me, "Can you take all the children to the hospital in Saigon?" I said, "No. She's going to die any minute right here." I showed them my AP media pass and said, "If one of them dies you'll be in trouble." Then they brought Kim Phuc inside first because she was so badly wounded. Then I went back to develop my film at the AP office in Saigon.

Me and the best darkroom person in Southeast Asia, Ishizaki Jackson, who was also an editor, went into the darkroom and rolled the film onto the spools. I had eight rolls of film. He asked me when I got to the office, "Nicky, what do you have?" I said, "I have very important film." All the film was developed in about 10 minutes. Jackson looked at the pictures and asked, "Nicky, why is the girl naked?" I said because she was on fire from the napalm bombs. He heard that and clipped one negative and printed a five by seven of it. The editor on the desk at that time was Carl Robinson. "Oh no, sorry. I don't think we can use this picture in America."

Then Horst Faas, the AP Saigon photo editor, and Peter Arnett, the AP correspondent, came back after lunch. Horst saw my picture and asked, "Whose picture?" One of the editors said, "Nicky's." He asked me to tell the story. He then yelled at everyone, "Why's the picture still here? Move the picture right away!" . . .

We got a call from New York saying my photo was an amazing picture and was being used around the world. The news value was so important, that in this case it was O.K. The next morning around 7:30 a.m., Horst Faas, Peter Arnett, and I went to Trang Bang village. At the time, [the South Vietnamese military] didn't know who I was or that I took the picture of Kim Phuc. They got in a lot of trouble. The American military complained: "Why did you let photographers take that picture?"

DISCUSSION QUESTIONS

1. Based on the photograph and Ut's recollections, why do you think this image had such a powerful impact on the public at the time?

2. What does the image of the young girl in the center of the photograph, with her clothes having been burned off and her skin on fire, reveal about the technology of war and its human costs?

3. How might the photograph's effect on U.S. public opinion have been different had the perpetrators of the napalm attack been the North Vietnamese army rather than the South Vietnamese and the Americans?

4. Scholars during the 1970s argued that photography fostered an attitude of anti-intervention, positioning the photographer as an observer of their subject rather than an active participant. How does Ut's interview affirm and/or contradict this argument?

4. The Rising Power of OPEC

U.S. Embassy, Saudi Arabia, *Saudi Ban on Oil Shipments to the United States* (October 23, 1973)

In a show of pan-Arabian unity and nationalism, military forces from Egypt and Syria invaded Israel on October 6, 1973. The United States quickly offered extensive financial aid to Israel. As punishment for U.S. support of Israel, the Organization of the Petroleum Exporting Countries (OPEC) banned its members from exporting oil to the United States and raised the price of oil for the U.S. allies in western Europe. Overnight, the price of a barrel rose from $3 to $5.11, and by January 1974, it had risen to $11.65, resulting in widespread fuel shortages across the West. Infused with Arab nationalism, the actions of OPEC shocked citizens in Europe and the United States, who were not accustomed to being at the mercy of nations they once dominated. In this confidential cable, which was declassified only in September 2003, an unidentified writer from the U.S. embassy in Saudi Arabia offers an inside view of the Saudis' strategy in their decision to participate in the OPEC ban on exporting oil to the United States.

23 OCTOBER 1973
FROM: AMERICAN EMBASSY IN SAUDI ARABIA
TO: THE SECRETARY OF STATE, WASHINGTON D.C.
SUBJECT: SAUDI BAN ON OIL SHIPMENTS TO U.S.

SUMMARY: SAUDI DECISION TO CUT OFF OIL SHIPMENTS TO U.S. ATTRIBUTABLE TO KING'S OWN DECISION: KING ANGRY AT ANNOUNCEMENT OF LARGE U.S. MILITARY GRANT PROGRAMS TO ISRAEL AND PROBABLY FELT THAT ANY LESSER RESPONSE WOULD LEAVE SAUDI ARABIA UNCOMFORTABLY ISOLATED IN ARAB WORLD. U.S. MISSION CONTACTS WITH HIGH-LEVEL SAG [the Government of Saudi Arabia] OFFICIALS, HOWEVER, INDICATE SAG WISHES TO MINIMIZE DAMAGE THAT PRESENT CRISIS MAY DO TO U.S.-SAG

From U.S. Embassy in Saudi Arabia, Cable 4663 to U.S. State Department, "Saudi Ban on Oil Shipments to U.S.," October 23, 1973 (Washington, D.C.: National Security Archive).

RELATIONS. JOINT U.S.-USSR RESOLUTION IN SECURITY COUNCIL, POTEN-
TIALLY A RADICALLY POSITIVE STEP, BUT IF IT DOES NOT SUCCEED, SAG
MAY FEEL COMPELLED TO INCREASE PRESSURE ON U.S. INTERESTS IN MIL-
ITARY, COMMERCIAL, ENERGY AND FINANCIAL AREAS. EMBASSY IS STRESS-
ING WITH SAG NEED THAT CHANNELS OF COMMUNICATION REMAIN OPEN,
AND THAT EACH SIDE GIVE [each] OTHER MAXIMUM ADVANCE NOTICE OF
ANY MEASURES IT IS CONTEMPLATING. END SUMMARY.

1. THERE IS LITTLE DOUBT THAT SAG DECISION TO BAN PETROLEUM
   EXPORTS TO U.S. STEMMED FROM KING FAISAL HIMSELF. DISCUSSION
   BETWEEN HIGH-RANKING SAG OFFICIALS AND AMBASSADOR IN 24 HOURS
   PREVIOUS HAD NOT INDICATED SAG ON VERGE OF TAKING SUCH BIG STEP.

2. SOURCES IN ROYAL DIWAN OCT 21 HAVE CONFIRMED TO EMBASSY THAT
   DECISION [was] TAKEN BY KING, AND WAS PRINCIPALLY MOTIVATED BY
   U.S. PROPOSAL TO PROVIDE ISRAEL WITH 2.2 MILLION DOLLARS OF GRANT
   [money for] MILITARY AID. WAS TOLD BY CHIEF OF ROYAL DIWAN, AHMAD
   ABDUL WAHAB (A WELL-ADJUSTED PRO-AMERICAN FIGURE) THAT
   KING WAS AS FURIOUS AS HE HAD EVER SEEN HIM AND THAT HE TOOK
   PARTICULAR UMBRAGE AT WHAT HE CONSIDERED TO BE DIFFERENCE
   BETWEEN REASSURING TONE OF VARIOUS COMMUNICATIONS HE HAD
   RECEIVED FROM USG [the United States Government] AND U.S. ANNOUNCE-
   MENT OF "INCREDIBLE" AMOUNT OF AID TO GOI [the Government of Israel].
   KING'S SUBSEQUENT CALL FOR JIHAD CAN ALSO BE ASCRIBED TO KING'S
   DISPLEASURE. KING'S MOOD EMPHATICALLY REFLECTED ALSO BY ABLE,
   NATIONALIST MINISTER HISHAM NAZER, HEAD OF CENTRAL PLANNING
   ORGANIZATION.

3. WE SHOULD NOT, HOWEVER, OVERSTRESS THE CAUSATIVE EFFECT OF
   PURE EMOTION IN KING'S DECISION TO CUT BACK OIL SHIPMENTS TO U.S.
   A NUMBER OF ARAB COUNTRIES HAD ALREADY TAKEN STEP OF BANNING
   SUCH SHIPMENTS, AND [Sheikh Zaki] YAMANI [the official in charge of Saudi
   oil policy in 1973] HAD INFORMED AMBASSADOR THAT OTHERS WOULD
   PROBABLY FOLLOW. AS IMPACT OF U.S. AID DECISION MADE ITSELF FELT
   IN ARAB WORLD, KING MAY HAVE FELT THAT SAG WOULD OCCUPY EXPOSED
   SALIENT IF IT—ALONE AMONG ARAB OIL PRODUCERS—CONTINUED TO
   PROVIDE OIL TO U.S.

4. EMBASSY CONTACTS ELSEWHERE IN SAG, MOREOVER, TEND TO CONFIRM
   OUR ASSESSMENT THAT SAG WISHES [to] MINIMIZE DAMAGE THAT PRES-
   ENT CRISIS COULD CAUSE TO U.S.-SAUDI RELATIONS. . . . DURING MEETING
   OCT 21 BETWEEN CHIEF OF U.S. MILITARY TRAINING MISSION (USMTM),
   GENERAL HILL, DEPUTY MUDA, AND KING'S BROTHER PRINCE TURKI,
   PRINCE STATED "WE HAVE HAD TO TAKE CERTAIN POLITICAL DECISIONS
   DURING THE WAR JUST AS YOU HAVE, BUT THAT MUST BE KEPT ENTIRELY

SEPARATE FROM RELATIONSHIPS BETWEEN MUDA AND USMTM." PRINCE IN SOMBER MOOD, BUT WAS AT ALL TIMES COURTEOUS AND FRIENDLY TO GENERAL HILL AND HIS STAFF....

6. SAG ACTION COULD ALSO DELIVER A SETBACK TO IMPORTANT U.S. COMMERCIAL AND MILITARY SALES: SAG HAS GROWN TO BE ONE OF LARGEST MARKETS FOR AMERICAN PRODUCTS...WITH SALES RUNNING AT MORE THAN A THIRD OF A BILLION DOLLARS THIS YEAR. OUR MILITARY SALES PROGRAMS MOREOVER HAVE...IN THE PAST THREE YEARS EXCEEDED 500 MILLION DOLLARS, AND THERE ARE GOOD PROSPECTS FOR CASH SALES OF A SIMILAR ORDER TO BE CONCLUDED WITHIN THE NEXT TWO YEARS. WE SHOULD REMEMBER THAT EUROPE, PARTICULARLY FRENCH AND BRITISH SOURCES, ARE MORE THAN PREPARED TO PICK UP THE FALLOUT FROM THE AMERICAN DILEMMA IN THE MIDDLE EAST CONFLICT.

7. IN THE MEANTIME, AMBASSADOR HAS PASSED WORD TO CHIEF OF ROYAL DIWAN THAT IT IS ESSENTIAL FOR CHANNELS OF COMMUNICATION BETWEEN HIM AND SAG TO REMAIN OPEN AT ALL TIMES....

8. FINALLY, WITH REGARD TO SAUDI ACTIONS AGAINST U.S. OIL AND OTHER INTERESTS, WE SHOULD AVOID ACRIMONIOUS COMMENTS, SINCE THESE TEND TO KEEP AN UNHELPFUL DIALOGUE GOING.

DISCUSSION QUESTIONS

1. What do you think the writer's main concern was in sending this cable to the U.S. State Department?

2. How would you characterize the writer's attitude toward Saudi Arabian government officials?

3. How were European countries directly affected by U.S. policies toward Saudi Arabia and other OPEC countries? Where do you see direct references to this in the telegram?

5. Facing Terrorism

Jacques Chirac, *New French Antiterrorist Laws*
(September 14, 1986)

Along with the energy crisis, the rise of terrorism in the 1970s and 1980s posed a serious challenge to Western governments. Although there is disagreement as to the precise definition of "terrorism," at the most basic level it involves the premeditated use of violence for political ends. Civilian populations have often borne the brunt of terrorist attacks, as

From Bruce Maxwell, *Terrorism: A Documentary History* (Washington, D.C.: CQ Press, 2003), 85–87.

was brutally apparent in France in September 1986. In the span of eight days, a number of bombs exploded in Paris stores, restaurants, and public buildings, killing at least ten people and wounding scores more. The principal suspects were members of a group with Syrian links, the Lebanese Armed Revolutionary Faction (FARL), whose leader was imprisoned in France. It appears that the group hoped the bombings would secure his release. In response to the violence, French prime minister Jacques Chirac implemented a series of antiterrorism measures that he presented to the French people on September 14 in a televised statement, excerpted here.

Since our election and the formation of this government we have been working on a series of bills that are now ready. The laws on security and particularly on terrorism that were voted on during the last session were promulgated a few days ago according to the democratic legislative process for passing laws. We will implement their provisions immediately and with the greatest authority. What do these laws provide for? First of all, improvement of prevention by extension of police custody, general identity checks, and searches on premises.

On the question of identity checks I ask every one of our citizens to understand that, in the current situation, the constraint that these controls represent should be accepted with, so to speak, good humor. It is necessary for everyone's security.

These laws also centralize investigations and legal proceedings in Paris, in the hands of specialists, in order to be more effective in the prosecution of those who are implicated of direct or indirect involvement in terrorist acts.

The second set of decisions we have taken will naturally aggravate a certain number of our foreign friends visiting France. We have in effect decided to require a mandatory visa for all foreigners entering France, regardless of their origin, with the exception, of course, of the European Community and Switzerland.

But for all others, no matter what their origin, the North or the South, Asia or Africa, from tomorrow on visas will be required, albeit with a few days' delay, for technical reasons, before actual implementation begins. The visas will be issued by our consulates around the world and will enable us to prohibit entry into France to all sorts of people who appear at the borders and enter the territory with passports which, as everyone knows, are all too often irregularly issued, or are forgeries that we cannot verify.

I ask all our foreign friends to understand that, in the crisis situation in which we find ourselves, this measure is necessary. Unfortunately it is likely to provoke some problems when enforced, such as delays in airports or at points of entry into France, but these are inevitable incidents in the implementation of this type of measure.

My next point concerns checks and, where necessary, expulsion. Everyone knows that the police have an eye on a certain number of people whom they suspect, but cannot accuse, of belonging to what I would call the terrorist organizations' sphere of influence. We have decided to strengthen considerably checks on and surveillance of all those active in the terrorist movements' sphere of influence, hence the series of arrests which you have probably heard about in the last few days and which will result in expulsion — and which has in the last two days resulted in the expulsion of persons whose presence in France we consider a danger to the public order. That has begun, will continue and be carried out with the greatest determination and the greatest firmness.

Finally, there is the problem of security in public places. As you saw earlier, reports have just come in, and will perhaps be corrected since this occurred virtually as we were coming into the studio, of a dubious package apparently, I say apparently being discovered in the Renault Pub, a place where there are a lot of people, and being taken down into the basement, where it unfortunately exploded, wounding three policemen: that clearly illustrates the vulnerability of public places. They must have proper security. I am mayor of Paris, I see what happens in the close vicinity of my City Hall. Everyone who enters the Bazar de l'Hotel de Ville [a large department store] with a package, even a small one, has to open it. I tell you that this has not caused the slightest problem nor created the slightest incident in the last three or four years. And this has made the Bazar de l'Hotel de Ville a very safe place. Other stores, like the Galeries Lafayette and others as well, do the same thing. I want private places frequented by the public to enforce those security measures, which are a very considerable deterrent.

There you have a certain number of measures, those that can be announced. I tell you right away that there are others, but these others are the sole responsibility of the public authorities and, because of their nature, are not being publicized and I shall not answer questions or comment on them. However, they are also being taken in the context of this calm, firm fight against this veritable scourge of modern times that is terrorism.

In conclusion, I shall say that everyone must feel he or she has a part to play in these matters. Everyone's safety is at stake. Terrorism is, by definition, blind and spares no one, not you, me or anyone. . . .

I would like everyone to be certain that the day, and it will inevitably come, there's no doubt about that, when we catch a terrorist in the act, he will talk and those manipulating him must clearly realize that they will receive draconian retribution, that we shall be pitiless, regardless of the consequences. They must realize that.

DISCUSSION QUESTIONS

1. How does Chirac define terrorism and the dangers it poses to the public?

2. What specific measures did he propose to counter these dangers?

3. In these measures, what tensions do you see between maintaining security and protecting individual rights? What does this suggest about the particular threat terrorism poses to democratic societies?

6. Glasnost and the Soviet Press

SOURCES IN CONVERSATION | Nina Andreyeva, *Polemics* and *Pravda* Editorial, *Principles of Perestroika* (1988)

When Mikhail Gorbachev (b. 1931) became the general secretary of the Soviet Communist Party in 1985, the nation's economy was in ruins, and people struggled to meet even their most basic needs. Gorbachev implemented revolutionary policies of economic restructuring (perestroika) *and "openness"* (glasnost) *to confront the crisis. The two articles excerpted here illuminate the crucial role of the Soviet press in this process as a forum for public debate. Never before had Soviet citizens experienced such freedom of speech and expression. Written by Nina Andreyeva, the first article appeared as a letter to the editor on the front page of the prestigious newspaper* Sovetskaya Rossiya *in March 1988. Politically conservative, Andreyeva attacked Gorbachev's reforms as a violation of socialist ideology. Gorbachev and his supporters countered her assault in an article of their own, published three weeks later in* Pravda, *defending* glasnost *and* perestroika *as the path to a better future.*

Polemics: I Cannot Waive Principles

Nina Andreyeva

I decided to write this letter after lengthy deliberation. I am a chemist, and I lecture at Leningrad's Lensovet Technology Institute. Like many others, I also look after a student group. Students nowadays, following the period of social apathy and intellectual dependence, are gradually becoming charged with the energy of revolutionary changes. Naturally, discussions develop about the ways of restructuring and its economic and ideological aspects. *Glasnost,* openness, the disappearance of zones where criticism is taboo, and the emotional heat of mass consciousness (especially among young people) often result in the raising of problems that are, to a greater or lesser extent, "prompted" either by Western radio voices or by those of our compatriots who are shaky in their conceptions of the essence of socialism. And what a variety of topics that are being discussed! A multiparty system, freedom of religious propaganda, emigration to live abroad, the right to broad discussion of sexual problems in the press, the need to decentralize the leadership of culture, abolition of compulsory military service. There are particularly numerous arguments among students about the country's past. . . .

In the numerous discussions now taking place on literally all questions of the social sciences, as a college lecturer I am primarily interested in the questions that have a direct effect on young people's ideological and political education, their moral health, and their social optimism. Conversing with students and deliberating with them on controversial problems, I cannot help concluding that our country has accumulated quite a few anomalies and one-sided interpretations that clearly need to be corrected. I would like to dwell on some of them in particular.

Take, for example the question of Joseph Stalin's place in our country's history. The whole obsession with critical attacks is linked with his name, and in my opinion this obsession centers not so much on the historical individual himself as on the entire highly complex epoch of transition, an epoch linked with unprecedented feats by a whole generation of Soviet people who are today gradually withdrawing from active participation in political and social work. The industrialization, collectivization, and cultural revolution which brought our country to the ranks of the great world powers are being forcibly squeezed into the "personality cult" formula. All of this is being questioned. Matters have gone so far that persistent demands for "repentance" are being made of "Stalinists"

From Isaac J. Tarasulo, ed., *Gorbachev and Glasnost: Viewpoints from the Soviet Press* (Wilmington, DE: SR Books, 1989), 277–78, 281–85, 290–95, 299–302.

(and this category can be taken to include anyone you like). There is rapturous praise for novels and movies that lynch the epoch of "storms and onslaught," which is presented as a "tragedy of the peoples." . . .

I support the party's call to uphold the honor and dignity of the trailblazers of socialism. I think that these are the party-class positions from which we must assess the historical role of all leaders of the party and the country, including Stalin. In this case, matters cannot be reduced to their "court" aspect or to abstract moralizing by persons far removed both from those stormy times and from the people who had to live and work in those times, and to work in such a fashion as to still be an inspiring example for us today. . . .

I think that, no matter how controversial and complex a figure in Soviet history Stalin may be, his genuine role in the building and defense of socialism will sooner or later be given an objective and unambiguous assessment. Of course, unambiguous does not mean an assessment that is one-sided, that whitewashes, or that eclectically sums up contradictory phenomena making it possible subjectively (albeit with slight reservations) "to forgive or not forgive," "to reject or retain." Unambiguous means primarily a specific historical assessment detached from short-term considerations which would demonstrate — according to historical results! — the dialectics of the correlation between the individual's actions and the basic laws governing society's development. In our country these laws were also linked with the answer to the question "Who will defeat whom?" in its domestic as well as international aspects. If we are to adhere to the Marxist-Leninist methodology of historical analysis then, in Mikhail Gorbachev's words, we must primarily and vividly show how the millions of people lived, how they worked, and what they believed in, as well as the coupling of victories and failures, discoveries and errors, the bright and the tragic, the revolutionary enthusiasm of the masses and the violations of socialist legality and even crimes at times. . . .

It seems to me that the question of the role and position of socialist ideology is extremely acute today. The authors of timeserving articles circulating under the guise of moral and spiritual "cleansing" erode the dividing lines and criteria of scientific ideology, manipulate glasnost, and foster nonsocialist pluralism, which applies the brakes on perestroika in the public conscience. This has a particularly painful effect on young people which, I repeat, is clearly sensed by us, the college lecturers, schoolteachers, and all who have to deal with young people's problems. As Mikhail Gorbachev said at the CPSU Central Committee February plenum, "our actions in the spiritual sphere — and maybe primarily and precisely there — must be guided by our Marxist-Leninist principles. Principles comrades, must not be compromised on any pretext whatever."

This is what we stand for now, and this is what we will continue to stand for. Principles were not given to us as a gift, we have fought for them at crucial turning points in the fatherland's history.

Principles of Perestroika: The Revolutionary Nature of Thinking and Acting

Pravda Editorial

The CPSU Central Committee February plenum solidified the party's new tasks in restructuring all spheres of life at the present stage. The plenum speech of Mikhail

Gorbachev, general secretary of the CPSU Central Committee ("Revolutionary Perestroika Requires Ideology of Renewal") made a clear analysis of today's problems and set forth a program of ideological support for perestroika. People want to be better aware of the nature of the changes that have begun in society, to see the essence and significance of the proposed solutions, and to know what is meant by the new quality of society we want to achieve. The struggle for perestroika is being waged both in production and in the spiritual sphere. And even though this struggle does not take the form of class antagonisms, it is proceeding sharply. The emergence of something new always excites attitudes toward and judgments about the new thing.

The debate itself and its nature and thrust attest to the democratization of our society. The diversity of judgments, assessments, and positions is one of the most important signs of the times and attests to the socialist pluralism of opinions which really exists now.

But it is impossible not to notice one very specific dimension of this debate. It occasionally declares itself not in a desire to interpret what is happening and to investigate it nor in a wish to advance the cause but, on the contrary, in attempts to slow it down by shouting the usual incantations: "They are betraying ideals!" "Abandoning principles!" "Undermining foundations!" . . .

The long article "I Cannot Waive Principles" [pp. 548–49] that appeared in the newspaper *Sovetskaya Rossiya* on March 13 was a reflection of such feelings. . . .

Whether the author wanted it or not, primarily the article artificially sets off certain categories of Soviet people against one another. And this at precisely the moment when the unity of creative forces, despite all the shades of opinion, is more necessary than ever and when such unity is the prime requirement of perestroika and an absolute necessity simply for normal life, work, and the constructive renewal of society. Herein resides the fundamental feature of perestroika, which is designed to unite the maximum number of like-minded people in the struggle against phenomena impeding our life. Precisely and principally against all of these phenomena, not only or simply against certain incorrigible proponents of bureaucracy, corruption, abuse, and so forth.

In addition, the article is unconstructive. In an extensive, pretentiously titled article essentially no space was found to work out a single problem of perestroika. Whatever it discussed — glasnost, openness, the disappearance of areas free from criticism, youth — these processes and perestroika itself were linked only with difficulties and adverse consequences. . . .

There are, in point of fact, two basic theses running throughout the article: Why all of this perestroika, and haven't we gone too far with democratization and glasnost? The article urges us to amend and adjust perestroika; otherwise, it is alleged, "people in authority" will have to rescue socialism.

It is evident that not everyone has realized clearly yet the dramatic nature of the situation the country found itself in by April 1985, a situation which today we rightfully describe as precrisis. It is evident that not everyone is fully aware yet that administrative edict methods are totally obsolete. It is time that anyone who still places hopes in these methods or in their modification understands that all of this has already been tried, tried repeatedly, and it has failed to produce the desired results. Any ideas about the simplicity and effectiveness of these methods are nothing but illusions without any historical justification.

So, how is socialism to be "saved" today?

Should authoritarian methods, the practice of blind obedience, and the stifling of initiative be retained? Should we retain the system in which bureaucratism, lack of control, corruption, bribery, and petty bourgeois degeneration flourished lavishly?

Or should we revert to Leninist principles, whose essence is democratism, social justice, economic accountability, and respect for the individual's honor, life, and dignity? Do we have the right, in the face of the real difficulties and unsatisfied needs of the people, to adhere to the same old approaches that prevailed in the 1930s and 1940s? Has not the time come to clearly differentiate between the essence of socialism and the historically restricted forms of its implementation? Has not the time come for a scientifically critical investigation of our history, primarily in order to change the world in which we live and to learn harsh lessons for the future?

Almost half of the article is devoted to an assessment of our distant and recent history. The last few years have provided graphic proof of the growing interest in the past shown by the broadest strata of the population. The principles of scientific historicism and truth are increasingly the basis on which the people's historical awareness is taking shape. At the same time, there are instances of people playing on the idea of patriotism. Those who loudly scream about alleged "internal threats" to socialism, those who join certain political extremists and look everywhere for internal enemies, "counterrevolutionary nations," and so on, those are not patriots. The patriots are those who act in the country's interests and for the people's benefit, without fearing any difficulties. We do not need contemplative or verbal patriotism, we need creative patriotism. Not nostalgic and backward-looking patriotism, but the patriotism of socialist transformations. Patriotism based not only on love for the area of your birth, but also imbued with pride in the accomplishments of the great motherland of socialism.

Past experience is vitally necessary for the present, for solving the tasks of perestroika. Life's demand — "More socialism!" — makes it incumbent upon us to investigate what we did yesterday and how we did it, what has to be rejected and what has to be retained. Which principles and values ought to be considered really socialist? And if today we are taking a critical look at our history, we are doing so only because we want a better and more complete idea of our path into the future. . . .

The best teacher of perestroika — the one to whom we should constantly listen — is life, and life is dialectical. We should constantly remember the words of [Friedrich] Engels to the effect that nothing has been unconditionally established once and for all as sacrosanct. It is this continual motion and the constant renewal of nature, society, and our thinking that is the point of departure for and the initial, most cardinal principle in our thinking.

Let us return to the question: What has been done already? How are the party's course and the decisions of the 27th Party Congress and Central Committee plenums being implemented? What positive changes are taking place in people's lives?

We have really got down to tackling the most pressing, highest priority problems: housing, food, and the supply of goods and services to the population. A turn toward accelerated development of the social sphere has begun. Concrete decisions about restructuring education and health care have been adopted. Radical economic reform, our main lever for implementing large-scale transformations, is being put into practice.

"That is the main political result of the last three years," M. Gorbachev said at the 4th All-Union Congress of *kolkhoz* members.

The voice of the intelligentsia and of all the working people has begun to make itself heard powerfully and strongly in society's spiritual life. This is one of the first gains accomplished by perestroika. Democratism is impossible without freedom of thought and speech, without the open, broad clash of opinions, without keeping a critical eye on our life. . . .

There are no prohibited topics today. Journals, publishing houses, and studios decide for themselves what to publish. But the appearance of the article "I Cannot Waive Principles" is part of an attempt little by little to revise party decisions. It has been said repeatedly at meetings in the party Central Committee that the Soviet press is not a private concern, that Communists writing for the press and editors should have a sense of responsibility for articles and publications. In this case the newspaper *Sovetskaya Rossiya*, which, let us be frank, has done much for perestroika, departed from this principle.

Debates, discussions, and polemics are, of course, necessary. They lie in store for us in our future, too. There are also many pitfalls in store for us, traps laid by the past. We must all work together to clear these traps from our path. We need disputes that help to advance perestroika and lead to the consolidation of forces, to cohesion around perestroika, and not to disunity. . . .

More light. More initiative. More responsibility. A more rapid mastery of the full profundity of the Marxist-Leninist concept of perestroika, of the new political thinking. We can and must revive the Leninist practice of the socialist society — the most humane, the most just. We will firmly and steadily follow the revolutionary principles of perestroika: more glasnost, more democracy, more socialism.

DISCUSSION QUESTIONS

1. Why is Andreyeva so critical of Gorbachev's reforms?

2. What arguments do Gorbachev and his supporters use to counter her criticisms?

3. According to the *Pravda* article, what are the fundamental features of glasnost and perestroika?

4. In what ways do these two articles reflect different understandings of Soviet history and its role in shaping the country's future?

COMPARATIVE QUESTIONS

1. Based on the Prague Spring and student protest documents, how and why did the events of the 1960s turn Western society upside down?

2. How do documents 2 to 5 represent a broader debate concerning Western political values and global dominance?

3. How did disagreements over ideology and generational conflict drive the protests of the 1960s and 1970s?

4. What similarities do you see between the message and the medium of the Prague manifesto and those of Gorbachev two decades later? Why did Smrkovský's reforms fail and Gorbachev's succeed?

A New Globalism
1989 to the Present

After decades of superpower rivalry, the cold war came to a halt in the 1990s when the Soviet empire disintegrated, ushering in a new age of global challenges and opportunities. New countries emerged from the Soviet shadow to declare their independence, which radically changed the political map of eastern Europe. The transition from one-party rule to democracy was fraught with difficulties that sometimes had brutal consequences, as document 1 shows. Documents 2 and 3 spotlight political, economic, and demographic changes around the globe as novel forces emerged to rival those of the West and its imperial past. Documents 4 and 5 reveal that, as European governments currently move beyond the nation-state, so too do the problems they face. As we move further into the twenty-first century and the boundaries between peoples and cultures become both more fluid and more fraught, document 6 warns against forgetting the power of the past to help us grapple with the realities of the global age.

1. Ethnic Cleansing

SOURCES IN CONVERSATION | *The Diary of Zlata Filipović* (March 5, 1992–June 29, 1992) and Aida Šehović, *ŠTO TE NEMA (Why are you not here?)* (2017)

The end of communism in the multiethnic state of Yugoslavia unleashed turmoil unseen in Europe since World War II. Following the rise to power of nationalist leaders during the 1980s, the country fell into chaos when four of the six republics declared independence beginning in 1991. Serbian president Slobodan Milosevic opposed the independence movements and supported a policy of ethnic cleansing against non-Serbs to assert Serbian supremacy. Even after UN peacekeepers were put into place, the war raged on. A three-way war in Bosnia among Serb, Croat, and Muslim factions was especially deadly. Beginning in 1992, the Bosnian capital of Sarajevo was the focus of a four-year siege by Serb forces in

From Zlata Filipović, *Zlata's Diary: A Child's Life in Sarajevo*, trans. Christina Pribichevich-Zorić (New York: Penguin, 1995), 26–35, 41–43, 46–47, 54–55, 58, 65–66.

which thousands were killed. Zlata Filipović was eleven years old when fighting broke out in Sarajevo. The following entries recorded in her diary provide a child's perspective of life in a war-torn city. In 1995, one of the worst atrocities of the war, the massacre of more than eight thousand Muslim men and boys in the UN-protected safe area of Srebrenica, exposed the West's seeming indifference to the violence. Artist Aida Šehović arrived in the United States as a refugee from Bosnia and Herzegovina in 1997 and created the participatory art project ŠTO TE NEMA (Why are you not here?) as a public monument to honor those who died during the Srebrenica genocide on its anniversary, July 11. Organized with the help of local Bosnian immigrant communities, ŠTO TE NEMA consists of hundreds of small porcelain cups known as fildžani *that visitors fill with Bosnian coffee prepared on-site. The monument first was staged in 2006 in Sarajevo and has traveled annually to a different city each year since. The image below was taken in Daley Plaza in Chicago in 2017.*

Thursday, March 5, 1992

Oh, God! Things are heating up in Sarajevo. On Sunday (March 1), a small group of armed civilians (as they say on TV) killed a Serbian wedding guest and wounded the priest. On March 2 (Monday) the whole city was full of barricades. There were "1,000" barricades. We didn't even have bread. At 6:00 people got fed up and went out into the streets. The procession set out from the cathedral. It went past the parliament building and made its way through the entire city. Several people were wounded at the Marshal Tito army barracks. People sang and cried "Bosnia, Bosnia," "Sarajevo, Sarajevo," "We'll live together" and "Come outside." Zdravko Grebo[1] said on the radio that history was in the making.

At about 8:00 we heard the bell of a streetcar. The first streetcar had passed through town and life got back to normal. People poured out into the streets hoping that nothing like that would ever happen again. We joined the peace procession. When we got home we had a quiet night's sleep. The next day everything was the same as before. Classes, music school. . . . But in the evening, the news came that 3,000 Chetniks [Serbian nationalists] were coming from Pale [resort outside of Sarajevo] to attack Sarajevo, and first, Baščaršija [the old part of town]. Melica said that new barricades had been put up in front of her house and that they wouldn't be sleeping at home tonight. They went to Uncle Nedjad's place. Later there was a real fight on YUTEL TV. Radovan Karadžič [Bosnian Serb leader] and Alija Izetbegovič [president of Bosnia-Herzegovina] phoned in and started arguing. Then Goran Milič[2] got angry and made them agree to meet with some General Kukanjac.[3] Milič is great!!! Bravo!

On March 4 (Wednesday) the barricades were removed, the "kids" [a popular term for politicians] had come to some agreement. Great?!

That day our art teacher brought in a picture for our class-mistress (for March 8, Women's Day). We gave her the present, but she told us to go home. Something was wrong again! There was a panic. The girls started screaming and the boys quietly blinked

---

[1]President of the Soros Foundation in Sarajevo and editor in chief of ZID, the independent radio station.
[2]A well-known newscaster on television; one of the founders of the YUTEL television station before the war.
[3]General of the then Yugoslav army who was in Sarajevo when the war broke out.

their eyes. Daddy came home from work early that day too. But everything turned out OK. It's all too much!

Monday, March 30, 1992

Hey, Diary! You know what I think? Since Anne Frank called her diary Kitty, maybe I could give you a name too. What about:

ASFALTINA	PIDŽEAMETA
ŠEFIKA	HIKMETA
ŠEVALA	MIMMY

or something else???

    I'm thinking, thinking . . .

    I've decided! I'm going to call you

    MIMMY

    All right, then, let's start.

Dear Mimmy,

It's almost half-term. We're all studying for our tests. Tomorrow we're supposed to go to a classical music concert at the Skenderija Hall. Our teacher says we shouldn't go because there will be 10,000 people, pardon me, children, there, and somebody might take us as hostages or plant a bomb in the concert hall. Mommy says I shouldn't go. So I won't.

    Hey! You know who won the Yugovision Song Contest?! EXTRA NENA!!!???

    I'm afraid to say this next thing. Melica says she heard at the hairdresser's that on Saturday, April 4, 1992, there's going to be BOOM — BOOM, BANG — BANG, CRASH Sarajevo. Translation: they're going to bomb Sarajevo.

Love,

Zlata

Sunday, April 5, 1992

Dear Mimmy,

I'm trying to concentrate so I can do my homework (reading), but I simply can't. Something is going on in town. You can hear gunfire from the hills. Columns of people are spreading out from Dobrinja. They're trying to stop something, but they themselves don't know what. You can simply feel that something is coming, something very bad. On TV I see people in front of the B-H parliament building. The radio keeps playing the same song: "Sarajevo, My Love." That's all very nice, but my stomach is still in knots and I can't concentrate on my homework anymore.

    Mimmy, I'm afraid of WAR!!!

Zlata

Thursday, April 9, 1992

Dear Mimmy,

I'm not going to school. All the schools in Sarajevo are closed. There's danger hiding in these hills above Sarajevo. But I think things are slowly calming down. The heavy shelling and explosions have stopped. There's occasional gunfire, but it quickly falls silent. Mommy and Daddy aren't going to work. They're buying food in huge quantities. Just in case, I guess. God forbid!

Still, it's very tense. Mommy is beside herself, Daddy tries to calm her down. Mommy has long conversations on the phone. She calls, other people call, the phone is in constant use.
Zlata

Tuesday, April 14, 1992

Dear Mimmy,
People are leaving Sarajevo. The airport, train and bus stations are packed. I saw sad pictures on TV of people parting. Families, friends separating. Some are leaving, others staying. It's so sad. Why? These people and children aren't guilty of anything. Keka and Braco came early this morning. They're in the kitchen with Mommy and Daddy, whispering. Keka and Mommy are crying. I don't think they know what to do — whether to stay or to go. Neither way is good.
Zlata

Saturday, May 2, 1992

Dear Mimmy,
Today was truly, absolutely the worst day ever in Sarajevo. The shooting started around noon. Mommy and I moved into the hall. Daddy was in his office, under our apartment, at the time. We told him on the intercom to run quickly to the downstairs lobby where we'd meet him. We brought Cicko [Zlata's canary] with us. The gunfire was getting worse, and we couldn't get over the wall to the Bobars', so we ran down to our own cellar.

The cellar is ugly, dark, smelly. Mommy, who's terrified of mice, had two fears to cope with. The three of us were in the same corner as the other day. We listened to the pounding shells, the shooting, the thundering noise overhead. We even heard planes. At one moment I realized that this awful cellar was the only place that could save our lives. Suddenly, it started to look almost warm and nice. It was the only way we could defend ourselves against all this terrible shooting. We heard glass shattering in our street. Horrible. I put my fingers in my ears to block out the terrible sounds. I was worried about Cicko. We had left him behind in the lobby. Would he catch cold there? Would something hit him? I was terribly hungry and thirsty. We had left our half-cooked lunch in the kitchen.

When the shooting died down a bit, Daddy ran over to our apartment and brought us back some sandwiches. He said he could smell something burning and that the phones weren't working. He brought our TV set down to the cellar. That's when we learned that the main post office (near us) was on fire and that they had kidnapped our President. At around 8:00 we went back up to our apartment. Almost every window in our street was broken. Ours were all right, thank God. I saw the post office in flames. A terrible sight. The fire-fighters battled with the raging fire. Daddy took a few photos of the post office being devoured by the flames. He said they wouldn't come out because I had been fiddling with something on the camera. I was sorry. The whole apartment smelled of the burning fire. God, and I used to pass by there every day. It had just been done up. It was huge and beautiful, and now it was being swallowed up by the flames. It was disappearing. That's what this neighborhood of mine looks like, my Mimmy. I wonder what it's like in other parts of town? I heard on the radio that it was awful around the Eternal Flame.[4]

---

[4]**Eternal Flame**: Memorial to military and civilian victims of World War II. [Ed.]

The place is knee-deep in glass. We're worried about Grandma and Granddad. They live there. Tomorrow, if we can go out, we'll see how they are. A terrible day.

This has been the worst, most awful day in my eleven-year-old life. I hope it will be the only one. Mommy and Daddy are very edgy. I have to go to bed.
Ciao!
Zlata

Wednesday, May 13, 1992

Dear Mimmy,
Life goes on. The past is cruel, and that's exactly why we should forget it.

The present is cruel too and I can't forget it. There's no joking with war. My present reality is the cellar, fear, shells, fire.

Terrible shooting broke out the night before last. We were afraid that we might be hit by shrapnel or a bullet, so we ran over to the Bobars'. We spent all of that night, the next day and the next night in the cellar and in Nedo's apartment. (Nedo is a refugee from Grbavica. He left his parents and came here to his sister's empty apartment.) We saw terrible scenes on TV. The town in ruins, burning, people and children being killed. It's unbelievable.

The phones aren't working, we haven't been able to find out anything about Grandma and Granddad, Melica, how people in other parts of town are doing. On TV we saw the place where Mommy works, Vodoprivreda, all in flames. It's on the aggressor's side of town (Grbavica). Mommy cried. She's depressed. All her years of work and effort — up in flames. It's really horrible. All around Vodoprivreda there were cars burning, people dying, and nobody could help them. God, why is this happening?

I'M SO MAD I WANT TO SCREAM AND BREAK EVERYTHING!
Your Zlata

Sunday, May 17, 1992

Dear Mimmy,
It's now definite: there's no more school. The war has interrupted our lessons, closed down the schools, sent children to cellars instead of classrooms. They'll give us the grades we got at the end of last term. So I'll get a report card saying I've finished fifth grade.
Ciao!
Zlata

. . .

Wednesday, May 27, 1992

Dear Mimmy,
SLAUGHTER! MASSACRE! HORROR! CRIME! BLOOD! SCREAMS! TEARS! DESPAIR!

That's what Vaso Miškin Street looks like today. Two shells exploded in the street and one in the market. Mommy was nearby at the time. She ran to Grandma and Granddad's. Daddy and I were beside ourselves because she hadn't come home. I saw some of it on TV but I still can't believe what I actually saw. It's unbelievable. I've got a lump in my throat and a knot in my tummy. HORRIBLE. They're taking the wounded to the hospital. It's a madhouse. We kept going to the window hoping to see Mommy, but she wasn't back.

They released a list of the dead and wounded. Daddy and I were tearing our hair out. We didn't know what had happened to her. Was she alive? At 4:00, Daddy decided to go and check the hospital. He got dressed, and I got ready to go to the Bobars', so as not to stay at home alone. I looked out the window one more time and . . . I SAW MOMMY RUNNING ACROSS THE BRIDGE. As she came into the house she started shaking and crying. Through her tears she told us how she had seen dismembered bodies. All the neighbors came because they had been afraid for her. Thank God, Mommy is with us. Thank God.

   A HORRIBLE DAY. UNFORGETTABLE.

   HORRIBLE! HORRIBLE!

Your Zlata

. . .

Friday, June 5, 1992

Dear Mimmy,

There's been no electricity for quite some time and we keep thinking about the food in the freezer. There's not much left as it is. It would be a pity for all of it to go bad. There's meat and vegetables and fruit. How can we save it?

   Daddy found an old wood-burning stove in the attic. It's so old it looks funny. In the cellar we found some wood, put the stove outside in the yard, lit it and are trying to save the food from the refrigerator. We cooked everything, and joining forces with the Bobars, enjoyed ourselves. There was veal and chicken, squid, cherry strudel, meat and potato pies. All sorts of things. It's a pity, though, that we had to eat everything so quickly. We even overate. WE HAD A MEAT STROKE.

   We washed down our refrigerators and freezers. Who knows when we'll be able to cook like this again. Food is becoming a big problem in Sarajevo. There's nothing to buy, and even cigarettes and coffee are becoming a problem for grown-ups. The last reserves are being used up. God, are we going to go hungry to boot???

Zlata

Monday, June 29, 1992

Dear Mimmy,

BOREDOM!!! SHOOTING!!! SHELLING!!! PEOPLE BEING KILLED!!! DESPAIR!!! HUNGER!!! MISERY!!! FEAR!!!

   That's my life! The life of an innocent eleven-year-old schoolgirl!! A schoolgirl without a school, without the fun and excitement of school. A child without games, without friends, without the sun, without birds, without nature, without fruit, without chocolate or sweets, with just a little powdered milk. In short, a child without a childhood. A wartime child. I now realize that I am really living through a war, I am witnessing an ugly, disgusting war. I and thousands of other children in this town that is being destroyed, that is crying, weeping, seeking help, but getting none. God, will this ever stop, will I ever be a schoolgirl again, will I ever enjoy my childhood again? I once heard that childhood is the most wonderful time of your life. And it is. I loved it, and now an ugly war is taking it all away from me. Why? I feel sad. I feel like crying. I am crying.

Your Zlata

ŠTO TE NEMA (Why are you not here?)

Alexandra Buxbaum / Shutterstock

DISCUSSION QUESTIONS

1. How does Zlata's tone shift from the earlier entries about the war approaching her city to the later sections describing the siege of Sarajevo?

2. As described by Zlata, in what ways did the war interrupt the routines of daily life in Sarajevo? What does she suggest about the war's psychological impact?

3. Looking at the specific elements of Aida Šehović's monument captured in the photograph, what message do they convey about the Srebrenica genocide? What role does the public's participation play in shaping and conveying this message, and why do you think the artist designed her monument to travel from place to place?

4. What do both Zlata's account and Šehović's monument reveal about the nature of warfare and its remembrance in today's world?

2. An End to Apartheid

The African National Congress, *Introductory Statement to the Truth and Reconciliation Commission*
(August 19, 1996)

In 1995, Nelson Mandela, the first postapartheid president of South Africa, appointed the Truth and Reconciliation Commission (TRC) to help his country make the transition from an oppressive apartheid regime to a democratic multiracial state. The TRC was charged with establishing "as complete a picture as possible of the nature, causes, and extent of gross viola-tions of human rights" committed in South Africa between 1960 and 1994. The commission spent two and a half years evaluating more than 21,000 statements from apartheid victims and perpetrators and subpoenaed hundreds more to learn the full extent of the crimes that took place. The TRC's charge was to investigate the crimes in a way that would promote national unity and reconciliation rather than continued bitterness and hatred. The TRC offered amnesty from prosecution for perpetrators who testified about past crimes and pro-vided restitution to victims. In this excerpt, the African National Congress (ANC), a political organization that had lobbied against apartheid since 1912, introduces its statement to the TRC by outlining the need for national reconciliation and the protection of human rights.

Introduction

As part of the process of the transformation of our country, the ANC had to consider its approach to the difficult but critically important question of what the new South Africa should do with those among our citizens who were involved in gross human rights viola-tions during the struggle for our emancipation.

The choices we had to make can be stated in a simple and straightforward manner.

We could have decided to hold our own Nuremberg Trials.

We could have decided that all that should be done should be to forgive everything that has happened in the past.

We, however, reached the conclusion that neither of these would be the correct deci-sion to take.

In considering the correctness or otherwise of this conclusion, the point needs to be borne in mind that we are in transition from an apartheid to a democratic society.

This is not a single event but a protracted process.

What this speaks to is an unjust cause on one side and a just cause on the other.

Inherent to the system of white minority domination, in this and all other countries where it occurred, was the philosophy and practice of the use of force to ensure the per-petuation of the system.

Force and violence by the dominant against the dominated, the contraposition of power to powerlessness, the attribution of mystical possibilities of retribution to the gov-ernors who can visit their wrath on the third and fourth generations of those who hate them, the suspension of all social norms, to enable the state and servants of the state to resort to the unbridled use of violence — all this, and more besides, sustains the continu-ity of colonial rule.

To maintain its internal integrity, coherence and rationale, this system could not but integrate in its world vision the concept of humans with a right to govern and sub-humans privileged to be governed.

Among other things, this paradigm allows those who enjoy the right to govern the ethical framework which permits them to use maximum force against any sub-human who would dare question his or her duty to accept the sacred obligation to respect the need to be governed.

From African National Congress's Website: www.justice.gov.za/trc/hrvtrans/submit/anctruth.htm#2.

The simultaneous and interdependent legitimization of the two inherently anti-human concepts of racial superiority and the colonial state as the concentrated expression of the unlimited right to the use of force, of necessity and according to the inherent logic of the system of apartheid, produced the gross violations of human rights by the apartheid state which are the subject of part of the work of the Truth and Reconciliation Commission.

It was as a result of the correct understanding of the nature of the system of apartheid that the United Nations characterized the system itself, and not merely its logical results, as a Crime Against Humanity.

With regard to the narrower context within which the TRC is considering this matter, the theoretical foundation of the enquiry would be the matter we have referred to, the legitimization of the use of force in general but especially against those who would dare challenge the system.

This has two consequences.

One of these is the elevation of the state organs of repression above all other state structures, their exemption from all norms of common law consistent with limitations on the use of force, the conferring of powers on individuals to mete out violence as they deem fit and the consequent brutalization of such individuals so that the perpetration of violence becomes their second nature.

The second of these consequences is the demonizing by the state of those it seeks to destroy and against whom therefore, it permits the maximum use of force. . . .

National Reconciliation

The most important issue in this regard is that the grief of particular individuals, important as it is to the affected individuals and the nation, is relevant also to the extent that it contributes to the achievement of the larger goal of national reconciliation.

National reconciliation will only have meaning if it addresses the historic conflict in our country between black and white.

Through centuries of this conflict, the names of the players have changed continuously, regardless of their color and the causes they served.

What never changed was the character of the conflict, which was between the white colonizing forces and a black liberation movement, based on a social system which elevated the white at the expense of the black.

National reconciliation has to be between black and white.

Without transformation to end the disparities of privilege and deprivation which are the legacy we have inherited from our colonial and apartheid past, but which continue to define the present, national reconciliation is impossible.

Whichever way the TRC interprets its mandate, it cannot avoid the conclusion that the ghost that needs to be laid to rest is — the ending of the domination of the black by the white, in all spheres of social existence.

If our society does not achieve this, racial conflict will continue. The goal of national reconciliation will not be achieved.

Clearly, this objective cannot be achieved by the TRC alone.

It also emphasizes the obligation that rests on the Commission to make its own recommendations as to what the larger and varied society from which it is drawn might do, to contribute to the realization of the goal of national reconciliation.

Protection from Gross Violations of Human Rights

Systematic violations of human rights are a manifestation of a social system, rather than the exceptional faults of particular individuals.

To ensure that our country and people are never again exposed to such systematic violations of human rights as occurred under apartheid, it is necessary that we construct a constitutional, political, and socioeconomic order which inherently protects human rights, and has the means to defend itself against any tendency to limit or violate those rights.

The mandate for the construction of such a system of course rests with bodies other than the TRC. As a movement, we are convinced that these institutions are carrying out their mandate.

But we also believe that the TRC has an important role to play in helping to ensure that the specialized institutions established by the apartheid regime to carry out a campaign of repression are completely dismantled.

We refer here not to normal state organs, such as the police, the Defense Force, and the intelligence services, but to other clandestine structures established under the National Security Management System, some of which continue to operate as part of the "third force."

The exposure and destruction of these structures is important to ensure that they are stopped from actually or potentially engaging in any acts of destabilization.

This is particularly important in light of the fact that persons who belong to these structures have been trained and motivated as anti-democratic operatives and, in many instances, will not have changed their ideological colors.

It is also important that the nation as a whole should be familiar with this machinery as part of the process of raising the level of national vigilance so that it is difficult for any government in [the] future to create similar structures for use against the people of our country. . . .

Conclusion

The ANC is committed to doing everything in its power to help the TRC and the nation to know as much as is possible about the events of the period the TRC is mandated to investigate.

We believe that the TRC should conclude its work as quickly as possible so that we do indeed let bygones be bygones and allow the nation to forgive a past it nevertheless dare not forget.

DISCUSSION QUESTIONS

1. What do you make of the ANC's emphasis on institutions and ethics rather than individuals? Why do you suppose the ANC concerned itself mainly with these larger structures?

2. What was the ANC's main objective in making this statement to the TRC? What did they hope to achieve through the TRC?

3. What is the advantage in the TRC's granting amnesty to those who agree to tell everything they know about crimes that they or people they knew committed under apartheid? What is the disadvantage of granting amnesty to these persons?

4. At the beginning of this document, the ANC mentions that South Africans could have used a Nuremberg Trials–style system to uncover the truth about crimes committed under apartheid. Why do you think they opted for the TRC-style of investigation, which focused on reconciliation instead of punishment?

3. Changing Global Economies

World Bank, *World Development Indicators* (2010)

Changing political dynamics were not the only hallmark of the post–cold war world. Freed from cold war restraints, the global economy began a process of transformation that is still under way today. An expanding global marketplace has allowed for the spread of wealth and opportunity, particularly in Asia and Latin America. The World Bank is one of various supranational organizations designed to promote economic development as a poverty-fighting tool. The bank uses money contributed by member nations (numbering 189 in 2017) to make loans to governments and private businesses to boost local and state economies. Founded in 1944 to help fund the rebuilding of Europe after World War II, since the 1950s the World Bank's efforts have focused principally on developing nations. Since 1978, the bank has published annual reports on their development strategies, with supporting statistics on key demographic, fiscal, and other trends. The data come from a variety of sources, some more reliable than others; even so, they allow for broad comparisons over time. The following tables include data from a selection of nations that make up the G20,[1] encompassing nations from all of the world's regions. The tables excerpted here cover population, gross domestic product (GDP),[2] per capita gross national income (GNI),[3] and energy use.[4]

World Bank, World Development Indicators, 2010. Adapted from http://documents.worldbank .org/curated/en/988271468149678303/pdf/542510PUB0WDI0101Official0Use0Only1.pdf.

[1]**G20**: A group of nineteen countries plus the European Union (EU) that acts as a forum for international cooperation on economic issues. Members include the EU, Argentina, Australia, Brazil, Canada, China, France, Germany, India, Indonesia, Italy, Japan, Mexico, Russia, Saudi Arabia, South Africa, South Korea, Turkey, the United Kingdom, and the United States of America. G20 countries combined account for more than four-fifths of gross world product, three-quarters of global trade, and almost two-thirds of the world's population. [Ed.]

[2]**GDP**: Gross domestic product (GDP) is the total gross market value of goods and services produced by an economy over a specific period of time. It is often used to evaluate economic performance and to make international comparisons between economies. [Ed.]

[3]**Per capita GNI**: Per capita gross national income (GNI) represents the per resident division of the gross domestic product of a country plus net income earned by residents abroad and minus domestic income earned by nonresidents. GNI captures whether a nation's resources are being reinvested domestically or taken abroad, for example, by foreign businesses. [Ed.]

[4]Data on energy production and use are from the electronic files of the International Energy Agency (IEA) and are published in IEA's annual publications: *Energy Statistics and Balances of Non-OECD Countries, Energy Statistics of OECD Countries*, and *Energy Balances of OECD Countries*. [Ed.]

Table 1: Population Dynamics

	Population			Average annual population growth	
	millions			%	
	1990	**2008**	**2015**	**1990–2008**	**2008–15**
Argentina	32.5	39.9	42.4	1.1	0.9
Australia	17.1	21.4	23.4	1.3	1.3
Brazil	149.6	192.0	202.4	1.4	0.8
Canada	27.8	33.3	35.7	1.0	1.0
China	1,135.2	1,324.7	1,377.7	0.9	0.6
Hong Kong SAR, China	5.7	7.0	7.3	1.1	0.7
France[a]	56.7	62.3	63.9	0.5	0.4
Germany	79.4	82.1	80.6	0.2	−0.3
India	849.5	1,140.0	1,246.9	1.6	1.3
Indonesia	177.4	227.3	247.5	1.4	1.2
Italy	56.7	59.8	60.8	0.3	0.2
Japan	123.5	127.7	125.3	0.2	−0.3
Korea, Rep.	42.9	48.6	49.3	0.7	0.2
Mexico	83.2	106.4	113.1	1.4	0.9
Russian Federation	148.3	142.0	139.0	−0.2	−0.3
Saudi Arabia	16.3	24.6	28.6	2.3	2.1
South Africa	35.2	48.7	51.1	1.8	0.7
Turkey	56.1	73.9	79.9	1.5	1.1
United Kingdom	57.2	61.4	63.8	0.4	0.5
United States	249.6	304.1	323.5	1.1	0.9

[a]Excludes the French overseas departments of French Guiana, Guadeloupe, Martinique, and Réunion.

Table 2: Structure of Output

	Gross domestic product	
	$ millions	
	1995	**2008**
Argentina	258,032	328,465
Australia	361,306	1,015,217
Brazil	768,951	1,575,151
Canada	590,517	1,501,329
China	728,007	4,326,996
Hong Kong SAR, China	144,230	215,355
France	1,569,983	2,856,556
Germany	2,522,792	3,649,494
India	356,299	1,159,171
Indonesia[a]	202,132	510,730
Italy	1,126,041	2,303,079
Japan	5,247,610	4,910,840
Korea, Rep.	517,118	929,121
Mexico	286,698	1,088,128
Russian Federation	395,528	1,679,484
Saudi Arabia[a]	142,458	468,800
South Africa	151,113	276,445
Turkey	169,708	734,853
United Kingdom	1,157,119	2,674,057
United States	7,342,300	14,591,381

[a]Components are at producer prices.

Table 3: Size of the Economy

	Gross national income per capita, *Atlas* method	
	$	Rank
	2008	**2008**
Argentina	7,190	85
Australia	40,240	29
Brazil	7,300	83
Canada	43,640	22
China	2,940	127
Hong Kong SAR, China	31,420	37
France	42,000	25
Germany	42,710	23
India	1,040	162
Indonesia	1,880	145
Italy	35,460	32
Japan	38,130	31
Korea, Rep.	21,530	49
Mexico	9,990	74
Russian Federation	9,660	75
Saudi Arabia	17,870	54
South Africa	5,820	94
Turkey	9,020	78
United Kingdom	46,040	18
United States	47,930	15

[a]Components are at producer prices.

Table 4: Energy Production and Use

	Energy use								
							% of total		
	Total million metric tons of oil equivalent		Average annual % growth	Per capita kilograms of oil equivalent		Fossil fuel		Combustible renewables and waste	
	1990	2007	1990–2007	1990	2007	1990	2007	1990	2007
Argentina	46.1	73.1	2.1	1,418	1,850	88.7	89.5	3.7	3.5
Australia	86.2	124.1	2.3	5,053	5,888	93.9	94.4	4.6	4.3
Brazil	139.5	235.6	3.1	933	1,239	51.1	52.6	34.1	30.7
Canada	208.7	269.4	1.6	7,509	8,169	74.5	75.6	4.0	4.3
China	863.1	1,955.8	4.5	760	1,484	75.5	86.9	23.2	9.9
Hong Kong SAR, China	8.8	13.7	2.4	1,539	1,985	99.4	95.3	0.6	0.4
France	224.5	263.7	1.1	3,957	4,258	58.0	51.2	5.2	5.1
Germany	351.4	331.3	−0.1	4,424	4,027	86.8	80.8	1.4	6.8
India	318.2	594.9	3.5	375	529	55.6	70.0	41.9	27.2
Indonesia	102.5	190.6	3.5	575	845	54.6	68.8	43.9	27.5
Italy	146.7	178.2	1.4	2,586	3,001	93.4	90.5	0.6	2.6
Japan	438.1	513.5	0.9	3,546	4,019	84.5	83.2	1.1	1.4
Korea, Rep.	93.1	222.2	5.0	2,171	4,586	83.8	81.9	0.8	1.2
Mexico	121.2	184.3	2.3	1,456	1,750	88.1	89.3	6.1	4.5
Russian Federation	870.0	672.1	−1.3	5,867	4,730	93.3	89.3	1.4	1.0
Saudi Arabia	59.3	150.3	4.8	3,618	6,223	100.0	100.0	0.0	0.0
South Africa	90.9	134.3	2.2	2,581	2,807	86.1	87.7	11.5	10.2
Turkey	52.8	100.0	3.6	941	1,370	81.8	90.5	13.7	5.1
United Kingdom	207.2	211.3	0.2	3,619	3,464	90.7	89.6	0.3	1.9
United States	1,913.2	2,339.9	1.2	7,664	7,766	86.4	85.6	3.3	3.5

DISCUSSION QUESTIONS

1. What population trends do these tables reveal about world demographic growth? Which regions have expanded the fastest since 1990?

2. Based on the GNI information, where are the highest concentrations of wealth among G20 members? Where are the lowest?

3. What do these tables suggest about the relationship between population and economic growth and energy consumption?

4. Combating Climate Change

European Commission, *Communication from the Commission to the European Parliament and the Council: The Road from Paris* (2016) and *Reactions to the Paris Climate Agreement* (2015)

As global economic development has expanded, lifting millions of people out of poverty, so too have the challenges the world faces. European and other nations have come to recognize that with the benefits of economic growth come environmental costs, including the effects of fossil-fuel pollutants on the atmosphere. While some countries have devised their own strategies to reduce dependence on fossil fuels, in recent years there has been a push for a global approach to combat both the causes and the symptoms of climate change. Such efforts came to fruition on December 12, 2015, when 195 nations agreed to a historic agreement: the Paris Climate Accord. According to the terms of the deal, each country, rich and poor alike, commits to take action over specific increments of time to lower their contribution to planet-warming carbon emissions from the burning of fossil fuels. The European Union (EU) helped to guide the Paris Agreement to success, and in 2016, its executive arm, the European Commission, published a report, excerpted below. The report assesses the accord's implications and the EU's role as supranational entity in the increasingly global and technologically developed world of the twenty-first century. When the specifics of the Paris plan were released to the public, they received an array of responses from state leaders, business groups, and environmentalists around the globe, a selection of which are included here.

Communication from the Commission to the European Parliament and the Council: The Road from Paris

The 2015 Paris Agreement is a historically significant landmark in the global fight against climate change. The Agreement provides a lifeline, a last chance to hand over to future generations a world that is more stable, a healthier planet, fairer societies and more prosperous economies. . . . The Agreement will steer the world towards a global clean energy transition.

From European Commission, "Communication from the Commission to the European Parliament and the Council: The Road from Paris" (2016), 2–5, https://ec.europa.eu/transparency/regdoc/rep/1/2016/EN/1-2016-110-EN-F1-1.PDF, and "COP-21: Reactions to the Paris climate agreement," Carbon Pulse, updated December 12, 2015, http://carbon-pulse.com/13323/.

This transition will require changes in business and investment behaviour and incentives across the entire policy spectrum. For the EU, this provides important opportunities, notably for jobs and growth. The transition will stimulate investment and innovation in renewable energy, thereby contributing to the EU's ambition of becoming the world leader in renewable energy, and increase the growth in markets for EU produced goods and services, for instance in the field of energy efficiency.

The Paris Agreement is the first multilateral agreement on climate change covering almost all of the world's emissions. The Paris Agreement is a success for the world and a confirmation of the EU's path to low carbon economy. The EU's negotiation strategy was decisive in reaching the Agreement. The EU has pushed for ambition, bringing its experience of effective climate policy and tradition of negotiations and rules-based international co-operation. . . .

Throughout the Paris Conference, the EU maintained a high level of political coherence. All EU ministers in Paris showed willingness and determination to succeed. The EU acted as one, defending the EU position. . . . This allowed the EU to speak with a single and unified voice in all phases of the negotiations, a crucial element for the successful outcome in Paris. . . . The Paris Agreement sets out a global action plan to put the world on track to avoid dangerous climate change acknowledging that this will require a global peaking of greenhouse gas emissions as soon as possible and achieving climate neutrality in the second half of this century. . . .

The transition to a low carbon, resource-efficient economy demands a fundamental shift in technology, energy, economics, finance and ultimately society as a whole. The Paris Agreement is an opportunity for economic transformation, jobs and growth. It is a central element in achieving broader sustainable development goals, as well as the EU priorities of investment, competitiveness, circular economy, research, innovation and energy transition. Implementation of the Paris Agreement offers business opportunities for the EU to maintain and exploit its first mover advantage when fostering renewable energy, energy efficiency and competing on the development of other low carbon technology market globally. To reap those benefits, the EU will need to continue to lead by example and by action on regulatory policies to reduce emissions but also on enabling factors that accelerate public and private investment in innovation and modernisation in all key sectors, while ensuring other major economies press ahead with commitments.

Reactions to the Paris Climate Agreement

"A monumental success for the planet and its people . . . we have solid results on all key points. . . . The current level of ambition is the floor and not the ceiling. Markets now have the clear signal they need to unleash the full force of human ingenuity and scale up their investments."

— *Ban Ki-moon, UN secretary-general*

"The Agreement is fair and just, comprehensive and balanced, highly ambitious, enduring and effective . . . it sends a strong and positive signal the world is moving to a low carbon economy."

— *Xie Zhenhua, special representative on climate change, China*

"What is so special about this deal is that it puts the onus on every country to play its part."

— David Cameron, Prime Minister, United Kingdom

"Today is an historic day. We have written a new chapter of hope in the lives of 7 billion people on the planet. The path to development must be paved with equity."

— Prakash Javadekar, Environment Minister, India

"The Paris Agreement gives businesses and investors the policy certainty they crave and provides a vital foundation for a healthier, stronger and, more prosperous economy. Companies, cities and governments are realizing that can do well, by doing good. From now, on, the smart money will no longer go into fossil fuels, but into cleaner energy, smarter cities, and more sustainable land use."

— Felipe Calderón, chair of the Global Commission on the Economy and Climate and former president of Mexico

"The consequences of this agreement go far beyond the actions of governments. They will be felt in banks, stock exchanges, board rooms and research centres as the world absorbs the fact that we are embarking on an unprecedented project to decarbonise the global economy. This realisation will unlock trillions of dollars and the immense creativity and innovation of the private sector who will rise to the challenge in a way that will avert the worst effects of climate change."

— Paul Polman, CEO, Unilever

"At the moment the draft Paris agreement still puts us on track for 3 degree world. The reviews are too weak and too late. The political number mentioned for finance has no bearing on the scale of need. It's empty. The iceberg has struck, the ship is going down and the band is still playing to warm applause."

— Chee Yoke Ling, director, Third World Network

"This deal does not deliver climate justice: Justice requires accountability, responsibility, remedies and action by the perpetrators. Polluters got another unwarranted good behaviour bond and more opportunities to profit from climate change."

— Kate Lappin, Asia Pacific Forum on Women, Law and Development

DISCUSSION QUESTIONS

1. According to the European Commission, what are the global benefits of the Paris Agreement?

2. Based on the responses excerpted here, did state leaders, business groups, and environmentalists share the same views? What similarities and differences do you see?

3. How does the European Commission describe the European Union's role in negotiating the Paris climate agreement? What does the European Union specifically have to gain as both a political and an economic entity?

5. Nationalism and the EU

Paresh Nath, *European Nationalism Cartoon* (2017)

Even as the European Union (EU) flexed its muscles at the Paris climate talks, its power as a unifying force has been strained in recent years with the rise of far-right and nationalist parties in Europe. Established in the shadow of World War II, the EU embraces interconnectedness and cooperation as drivers of both economic prosperity and international security. By contrast, political parties such as the National Front in France and Party for Freedom in the Netherlands assert that national interests, often based on a specific ethnic identity, trump all else. The economic and social impacts of globalization, as well the consequences of austerity policies enacted following the 2008 recession, have helped to fuel such arguments. With jobs lost due to overseas competition and millions of refugees and migrants seeking a better life in Europe, many people believe that their national identities and economic well-being are under threat. Politicians have capitalized on such fears throughout Europe, leading to the election of right-wing populists to parliaments in Hungary, the Netherlands, and elsewhere as well as an unexpectedly successful referendum in Britain to exit the European Union in 2016. The political cartoon printed here was published in an international United Arab Emirates newspaper in 2017, and it vividly captures the uncertainty that lies ahead for the EU and, by extension, for Europe's liberal democratic institutions.

Paresh Nath, ᵗᵖ̣ᶜ Khaleej Times, UAE / www.caglecartoons.com / Cagle Cartoons, Inc.

DISCUSSION QUESTIONS

1. Why do you think the cartoonist chose a train as the setting for his cartoon? What meaning does it add to the illustration?

2. What does the cartoon suggest about the challenges facing the EU in the twenty-first century? In what ways does the vision of a united Europe clash with contemporary political realities?

3. What are the advantages and disadvantages of studying a period of time through its political cartoons?

6. Remembering European History

Tony Judt, *What Have We Learned, If Anything?* (2008)

Tony Judt (1948–2010) was a modern European historian born in London in the shadow of World War II. After receiving his PhD at Cambridge University, he launched a successful academic career as a professor and author. He expanded his audience well beyond the scholarly world, publishing widely in newspaper and journals, including many essays in the New York Review of Books. *The 2008 essay "What Have We Learned, If Anything?," excerpted here, appeared against the backdrop of the ongoing "war on terror" launched in the wake of the 9/11 terrorist attacks. Drawing on his deep knowledge of twentieth-century Europe, Judt surveyed the present with a critical eye; he deeply believed in the importance of history as an indispensable tool for contextualizing and understanding current events. Forgetting the past is dangerous, he warns, as the West enters a new era of challenges and possibilities.*

The twentieth century is hardly behind us but already its quarrels and its achievements, its ideals and its fears are slipping into the obscurity of mis-memory. In the West we have made haste to dispense whenever possible with the economic, intellectual, and institutional baggage of the twentieth century and encouraged others to do likewise. In the wake of 1989, with boundless confidence and insufficient reflection, we put the twentieth century behind us and strode boldly into its successor swaddled in self-serving half-truths: the triumph of the West, the end of History, the unipolar American moment, the ineluctable march of globalization and the free market.

The belief that that was then and this is now embraced much more than just the defunct dogmas and institutions of cold war–era communism. During the Nineties, and again in the wake of September 11, 2001, I was struck more than once by a perverse contemporary insistence on not understanding the context of our present dilemmas, at home and abroad; on not listening with greater care to some of the wiser heads of earlier decades; on seeking actively to forget rather than remember, to deny continuity and proclaim novelty on every possible occasion. We have become stridently insistent that the

From Tony Judt, "What Have We Learned, If Anything?" *The New York Review of Books*, May 1, 2008. http://www.nybooks.com/articles/2008/05/01/what-have-we-learned-if-anything/.

past has little of interest to teach us. Ours, we assert, is a new world; its risks and opportunities are without precedent.

What, then, is it that we have misplaced in our haste to put the twentieth century behind us? In the US, at least, we have forgotten the meaning of war. There is a reason for this. In much of continental Europe, Asia, and Africa the twentieth century was experienced as a cycle of wars. War in the last century signified invasion, occupation, displacement, deprivation, destruction, and mass murder. Countries that lost wars often lost population, territory, resources, security, and independence. But even those countries that emerged formally victorious had comparable experiences and usually remembered war much as the losers did.

. . .

War was not just a catastrophe in its own right; it brought other horrors in its wake. World War I led to an unprecedented militarization of society, the worship of violence, and a cult of death that long outlasted the war itself and prepared the ground for the political disasters that followed. States and societies seized during and after World War II by Hitler or Stalin (or by both, in sequence) experienced not just occupation and exploitation but degradation and corrosion of the laws and norms of civil society. The very structures of civilized life — regulations, laws, teachers, policemen, judges — disappeared or else took on sinister significance: far from guaranteeing security, the state itself became the leading source of insecurity. Reciprocity and trust, whether in neighbors, colleagues, community, or leaders, collapsed. Behavior that would be aberrant in conventional circumstances — theft, dishonesty, dissemblance, indifference to the misfortune of others, and the opportunistic exploitation of their suffering — became not just normal but sometimes the only way to save your family and yourself. Dissent or opposition was stifled by universal fear.

. . .

The United States avoided almost all of that. Americans, perhaps alone in the world, experienced the twentieth century in a far more positive light. The US was not invaded. It did not lose vast numbers of citizens, or huge swathes of territory, as a result of occupation or dismemberment. Although humiliated in distant neocolonial wars (in Vietnam and now in Iraq), the US has never suffered the full consequences of defeat. Despite their ambivalence toward its recent undertakings, most Americans still feel that the wars their country has fought were mostly "good wars." The US was greatly enriched by its role in the two world wars and by their outcome, in which respect it has nothing in common with Britain, the only other major country to emerge unambiguously victorious from those struggles but at the cost of near bankruptcy and the loss of empire. And compared with other major twentieth-century combatants, the US lost relatively few soldiers in battle and suffered hardly any civilian casualties.

. . .

As a consequence, the United States today is the only advanced democracy where public figures glorify and exalt the military, a sentiment familiar in Europe before 1945 but quite unknown today. Politicians in the US surround themselves with the symbols and trappings of armed prowess; even in 2008 American commentators excoriate allies that hesitate to engage in armed conflict. I believe it is this contrasting recollection of war and its impact, rather than any structural difference between the US and otherwise comparable countries, which accounts for their dissimilar responses to international challenges today. Indeed, the complacent neoconservative claim that war and conflict are things Americans understand — in contrast to naive Europeans with their pacifistic fantasies — seems to me exactly wrong: it is Europeans (along with Asians and Africans) who understand war all too well. Most Americans have been fortunate enough to live in blissful ignorance of its true significance.

Ignorance of twentieth-century history does not just contribute to a regrettable enthusiasm for armed conflict. It also leads to a misidentification of the enemy. We have good reason to be taken up just now with terrorism and its challenge. But before setting out on a hundred-year war to eradicate terrorists from the face of the earth, let us consider the following. Terrorists are nothing new. Even if we exclude assassinations or attempted assassinations of presidents and monarchs and confine ourselves to men and women who kill random unarmed civilians in pursuit of a political objective, terrorists have been with us for well over a century.

. . .

But what of the argument that terrorism today is different, a "clash of cultures" infused with a noxious brew of religion and authoritarian politics: "Islamofascism"? This, too, is an interpretation resting in large part on a misreading of twentieth-century history. There is a triple confusion here. The first consists of lumping together the widely varying national fascisms of interwar Europe with the very different resentments, demands, and strategies of the (equally heterogeneous) Muslim movements and insurgencies of our own time — and attaching the moral credibility of the antifascist struggles of the past to our own more dubiously motivated military adventures.

A second confusion comes from conflating a handful of religiously motivated stateless assassins with the threat posed in the twentieth century by wealthy, modern states in the hands of totalitarian political parties committed to foreign aggression and mass extermination. Nazism was a threat to our very existence and the Soviet Union occupied half of Europe. But al-Qaeda? The comparison insults the intelligence — not to speak of the memory of those who fought the dictators. Even those who assert these similarities don't appear to believe them. After all, if Osama bin Laden were truly comparable to Hitler or Stalin, would we really have responded to September 11 by invading . . . Baghdad?

But the most serious mistake consists of taking the form for the content: defining all the various terrorists and terrorisms of our time, with their contrasting and sometimes conflicting objectives, by their actions alone. . . .

This abstracting of foes and threats from their context — this ease with which we have talked ourselves into believing that we are at war with "Islamofascists," "extremists" from a strange culture, who dwell in some distant "Islamistan," who hate us for who we are and seek to destroy "our way of life" — is a sure sign that we have forgotten *the* lesson of the twentieth century: the ease with which war and fear and dogma can bring us to demonize others, deny them a common humanity or the protection of our laws, and do unspeakable things to them.

. . .

We are slipping down a slope. The sophistic distinctions we draw today in our war on terror — between the rule of law and "exceptional" circumstances, between citizens (who have rights and legal protections) and noncitizens to whom anything can be done, between normal people and "terrorists," between "us" and "them" — are not new. The twentieth century saw them all invoked. They are the selfsame distinctions that licensed the worst horrors of the recent past: internment camps, deportation, torture, and murder — those very crimes that prompt us to murmur "never again." So what exactly is it that we think we have learned from the past? . . . Far from escaping the twentieth century, we need, I think, to go back and look a bit more carefully. We need to learn again — or perhaps for the first time — how war brutalizes and degrades winners and losers alike and what happens to us when, having heedlessly waged war for no good reason, we are encouraged to inflate and demonize our enemies in order to justify that war's indefinite continuance. And perhaps, in this protracted electoral season, we could put a question to our aspirant leaders: Daddy (or, as it might be, Mommy), what did you do to prevent the war?

DISCUSSION QUESTIONS

1. What does Judt mean by "mis-memory," and what dangers does he believe it poses?

2. Why does Judt believe the twentieth century can help us navigate the twenty-first? What does he argue is its singular lesson, and why is this important to his overall argument?

3. According to Judt, what does the United States in particular have to gain from this lesson, and why?

4. Do you agree with Judt's characterization of the past as an essential guide to the present and future? Why or why not?

COMPARATIVE QUESTIONS

1. How do Zlata Filipovič's experiences and the ŠTO TE NEMA monument support Judt's argument about the important lessons we can learn from the twentieth century?

2. What are the similarities between the end of communism in eastern Europe (Chapter 28) and the end of apartheid in South Africa? What are the differences?

3. What do the economic and demographic changes in the World Bank figures suggest about current global energy usage and its possible future trends? How might the reactions to the Paris Climate Agreement have been colored by different countries' economic and demographic realities?

4. After reading the EU Commission's document on the Paris Agreement, what conclusions could you draw about the strength of the European Union as a supranational entity? How does the uncertainty posed by European nationalism as depicted in Nath's political cartoon complicate this picture?

Acknowledgments (continued from page iv)

TEXT CREDITS
Bracketed numbers indicate document numbers.

Chapter 14
[14.3] Bartolomé de Las Casas, *In Defense of the Indians* (c. 1548–1550): From *In Defense of the Indians,* translated by Stafford Poole. Copyright © 1974 by Northern Illinois University Press. Used with the permission of Northern Illinois University Press.

[14.5] *Genevan Consistory Records:* Excerpt from *Registers of the Consistory of Geneva in the Time of Calvin,* Volume 1, *1542–1544,* ed. Thomas A. Lambert and Isabella M. Watt, trans. M. Wallace McDonald, pp. 13, 155, 161–62, 252. Copyright © 2002. Reprinted by permission of the publisher.

[14.6] St. Ignatius of Loyola, *A New Kind of Catholicism* (1546, 1549, 1553): From Saint Ignatius of Loyola, *Personal Writings: Reminiscences, Spiritual Diary, Select Letters, Including the Text of The Spiritual Exercises* (New York: Penguin Classics, 1996), edited and translated by Joseph A. Munitiz and Philip Endean. Translation, introductions, and notes copyright © Joseph A. Munitiz and Philip Endean, 1996. Reproduced by permission of Penguin Books Ltd.

Chapter 15
[15.3] *Apology of the Bohemian Estates* (May 25, 1618): From *The Thirty Years War: A Documentary History,* edited and translated by Tryntje Helfferich. Copyright © 2009 by Hackett Publishing Company, Inc. Reprinted by permission of Hackett Publishing Company, Inc. All rights reserved.

[15.5] Galileo, *Letter to the Grand Duchess Christina* (1615): From *Discoveries and Opinions of Galileo* by Galileo, trans. Stillman Drake. Translation copyright © 1957 by Stillman Drake. Used by permission of Doubleday, an imprint of the Knopf Doubleday Publishing Group, a division of Penguin Random House LLC. All rights reserved. Any third-party use of this material, outside of this publication, is prohibited. Interested parties must apply directly to Penguin Random House LLC for permission.

[15.6] *The Trial of Suzanne Gaudry* (1652): From Alan C. Kors and Edward Peters, eds., *Witchcraft in Europe, 1100–1700: A Documentary History.* Copyright © 1972. Reprinted with the permission of the University of Pennsylvania Press.

Chapter 16
[16.5] Ludwig Fabritius, *The Revolt of Stenka Razin* (1670): From Anthony Glenn Cross, ed., *Russia under Western Eyes, 1517–1825* (New York: St. Martin's Press, 1971). Copyright © 1971. Reprinted by permission of Anthony Glenn Cross.

Chapter 17
[17.2] A *Brief Description of the Excellent Vertues of That Sober and Wholesome Drink, Called Coffee* (1674): From *Eighteenth-Century Coffee-House Culture,* vol. 1: *Restoration Satire,* edited by Markman Ellis. Copyright © 2006, Pickering & Chatto. Reproduced by permission of Taylor & Francis Books UK.

[17.4] Peter I, *Decrees:* From *A Source Book for Russian History from Early Times to 1917,* vol. 2, edited by George Vernadsky. Copyright © 1972 by Yale University. Reprinted by permission of Yale University Press.

Chapter 18
[18.1] Jean-Jacques Rousseau, *Discourse on the Origin and Foundations of Inequality among Men* (1753): From *Discourse on the Origin and Foundations of Inequality among Men by Jean-Jacques Rousseau, with Related Documents,* translated and edited by Helena Rosenblatt. Copyright © 2011 by Helena Rosenblatt. All rights reserved. Used by permission of the publisher Macmillan Learning.

[18.2] Jacques-Louis Ménétra, *Journal of My Life* (1764–1802): Excerpt from Jacques-Louis Ménétra, *Journal of My Life,* introduction by Daniel Roche, translated by Arthur Goldhammer. Copyright © 1986 by Columbia University Press. Reprinted with the permission of Columbia University Press.

[18.3] Cesare Beccaria, *On Crimes and Punishments* (1764): From Cesare Beccaria, *"On Crimes and Punishments" and Other Writings,* edited by Richard Bellamy and translated by Richard Davies. Copyright © 1995 in the English translation, introduction, and editorial matter by Cambridge University Press. Reprinted with the permission of Cambridge University Press.

[18.5] Frederick II, *Political Testament* (1752): From George L. Mosse, Rondo E. Cameron, Henry Bertram Hill, and Michael B. Petrovich, eds., *Europe in Review* (Rand McNally and Company, 1957). Reprinted by permission of the UW Foundation and the George Mosse Estate.

Chapter 19

[19.1] Abbé Sieyès, *What Is the Third Estate?* (1789): From *The French Revolution and Human Rights: A Brief Documentary History,* 2/e, translated and edited by Lynn Hunt. Copyright © 2016 by Bedford/St. Martin's. All rights reserved. Used by permission of the publisher Macmillan Learning.

[19.4] Olympe de Gouges, *Declaration of the Rights of Woman* (1791): From *Women in Revolutionary Paris, 1789–1795: Selected Documents Translated with Notes and Commentary,* translated with notes and commentary by Darline Gay Levy, Harriet Branson Applewhite, and Mary Durham Johnson. Copyright © 1979 by the Board of Trustees of the University of Illinois. Used with permission of the University of Illinois Press.

[19.5] Maximilien Robespierre, *Report on the Principles of Political Morality* (1794): From Richard Bienvenu, ed., *The Ninth of Thermidor: The Fall of Robespierre.* Copyright © 1968 by Oxford University Press. Reprinted by permission of Oxford University Press.

[19.6] *Decree of General Liberty* (August 29, 1793): From H. Pauléus Sannon, *Histoire de Toussaint Louverture,* in *Slave Revolution in the Caribbean, 1789–1804: A Brief History with Documents,* 2/e, by Laurent DuBois and John D. Garrigus. Copyright © 2017 by Bedford/St. Martin's. All rights reserved. Used by permission of the publisher Macmillan Learning.

[19.6b] Bramante Lazzary, *General Call to Local Insurgents* (August 30, 1793): Bramante Lazzary to Toussaint L'Ouverture, Archives Nationales, DXXV 23, 231, letter 98, in *Slave Revolution in the Caribbean, 1789–1804: A Brief History with Documents,* 2/e, by Laurent DuBois and John D. Garrigus. Copyright © 2017 by Bedford/St. Martin's. All rights reserved. Used by permission of the publisher Macmillan Learning.

Chapter 20

[20.1] *The Chronicle of Abd al-Rahman al-Jabartî* (1798): From *Napoleon in Egypt: Al-Jabartî's Chronicle of the French Occupation, 1798,* translated by Shmuel Moreh. Copyright © 1993. Reprinted by permission of Markus Wiener Publishers.

[20.2] Napoleon Bonaparte, *The Civil Code* (1804): From E. A. Arnold, ed. and trans., *A Documentary Survey of Napoleonic France.* Copyright © 1994 by University Press of America, Inc. Republished with the permission of University Press of America; permission conveyed through Copyright Clearance Center, Inc.

[20.4] Peter Kakhovsky, *The Decembrist Insurrection in Russia* (1825): From *The First Russian Revolution, 1825,* by Anatole G. Mazour. Copyright © 1937 by the Board of Trustees of the Leland Stanford Junior University, renewed 1964 by Anatole Mazour. All rights reserved. Used with the permission of Stanford University Press, www.sup.org.

Chapter 21

[21.1] *Factory Rules in Berlin* (1844): From *Documents of European Economic History,* vol. I: *The Process of Industrialization, 1750–1870,* by Sidney Pollard and C. Holmes. Copyright © 1968 by Sidney Pollard and C. Holmes. Reprinted by permission of Macmillan Publishing Group, LLC d/b/a St. Martin's Press. All rights reserved.

[21.4] Friedrich Engels, *Draft of a Communist Confession of Faith* (1847): From *Collected Works* by Karl Marx and Frederick Engels, Vol. 6. Copyright © 1975 International Publishers. Reprinted by permission of International Publishers Company, Inc.

[21.5] Gottfried Menzel, *The United States of North America, with Special Reference to German Emigration* (1853): From "What Does North America Offer to the German Emigrant?" in Edith Abbott, ed., *Historical Aspects of the Immigration Problem: Select Documents* (University of Chicago Press, 1987). Copyright © 1987 by the University of Chicago. Reprinted by permission.

[21.6] *Address by the Hungarian Parliament* (March 14, 1848): From G. A. Kertesz, ed., *Documents in the Political History of the European Continent, 1815–1939*. Copyright © 1968. Reprinted by permission of Oxford University Press.

[21.6b] *Demands of the Hungarian People* (March 15, 1848): From G. A. Kertesz, ed., *Documents in the Political History of the European Continent, 1815–1939*. Copyright © 1968. Reprinted by permission of Oxford University Press.

Chapter 22
[22.2] Camillo di Cavour, *Letter to King Victor Emmanuel* (July 24, 1858): From *The Making of Italy, 1796–1870*, edited by Denis Mack Smith. Copyright © 1968 by Harper & Row. Reproduced with the permission of SCSC.

[22.3] Rudolf von Ihering, *Two Letters* (1866): From *Germany in the Age of Bismarck* by Walter Michael Simon. Copyright © 1968 Allen and Unwin. Reproduced by permission of Taylor & Francis Books UK.

Chapter 23
[23.5] Margaret Bondfield, *A Life's Work* (1948): From *A Life's Work* by Margaret Bondfield, published by Hutchinson. Reprinted by permission of The Random House Group Ltd.

Chapter 24
[24.2] Sigmund Freud, *The Interpretation of Dreams* (1900): From *The Basic Writings of Sigmund Freud,* translated and edited by A. A. Brill. Used by permission of the Estate of A. A. Brill.

[24.3] Émile Zola, *"J'accuse!"* (January 13, 1898): From *The Dreyfus Affair, "J'Accuse" and Other Writings,* edited by Alain Pagès, translated by Eleanor Levieux. Copyright © 1996 by Yale University. English language translation copyright © Eleanor Levieux, 1996. Reprinted by permission of Yale University Press.

[24.6] Henri Massis and Alfred de Tarde, *"The Young People of Today"* (1912): From John W. Boyer and Jan Goldstein, eds., *University of Chicago Readings in Western Civilization,* Volume 9: *Twentieth-Century Europe* (University of Chicago Press, 1987). Copyright © 1987 by the University of Chicago. Reprinted by permission.

Chapter 25
[25.2] L. Doriat, *Women on the Home Front* (1917): From *Lines of Fire: Women Writers of World War I,* edited by Margaret R. Higonnet. Copyright © 1999 by Margaret R. Higonnet. Reprinted by permission of Sanford J. Greenburger Associates.

[25.3] Vladimir Ilyich Lenin, *The State and Revolution* (1917): From *V. I. Lenin: Collected Works,* Volume 25: *June–September 1917,* edited and translated by Stepan Apresyan and Jim Riordan. Copyright © 1970. Reprinted by permission of Lawrence & Wishart.

[25.4] Benito Mussolini, *The Doctrine of Fascism* (1932): From *The Social and Political Doctrines of Contemporary Europe,* edited and translated by Michael Oakeshott. Copyright 1947 by Cambridge University Press. Reprinted by permission of Cambridge University Press.

[25.5] Excerpts from *Mein Kampf* by Adolf Hitler, translated by Ralph Manheim. Copyright © 1943, renewed 1971 by Houghton Mifflin Harcourt Publishing Company. Reprinted by permission of Houghton Mifflin Harcourt Publishing Company. All rights reserved.

Chapter 29

[29.1] *The Diary of Zlata Filipović* (March 5, 1992–June 29, 1992): Excerpts from Zlata Filipović, *Zlata's Diary: A Child's Life in Sarajevo,* translated by Christina Pribichevich-Zorić. Copyright © 1993 by Fixot et Éditions Robert Laffont; translation copyright © 1994 by Fixot et Éditions Robert Laffont. Used by permission of Viking Books, an imprint of Penguin Publishing Group, a division of Penguin Random House LLC, and by permission of Les Éditions Robert Laffont. All rights reserved. Any third-party use of this material, outside of this publication, is prohibited. Interested parties must apply directly to Penguin Random House LLC for permission.

[29.4] *Reactions to the Paris Climate Agreement*: From "COP-21: Reactions to the Paris Climate Agreement," *Carbon Pulse,* December 12, 2015, http://carbon-pulse.com/13323. Copyright © 2015. Reprinted by permission of Carbon Pulse.

[29.6] Tony Judt, *What Have We Learned, If Anything?* (2008): Excerpt from Tony Judt, "What Have We Learned, If Anything?," from *When the Facts Change: Essays, 1995–2010* by Tony Judt, edited by Jennifer Homans. Originally published in the *New York Review of Books,* May 1, 2008. Copyright © 2015 by Jennifer Homans. Used by permission of Penguin Books, an imprint of Penguin Publishing Group, a division of Penguin Random House LLC. All rights reserved. Any third-party use of this material, outside of this publication, is prohibited. Interested parties must apply directly to Penguin Random House LLC for permission.